MW01132203

One Story
House Plans
Bible

CREATIVE HOMEOWNER®, Upper Saddle River, New Jersey

President: Brian H. Toolan
VP/Editorial Director: Timothy O. Bakke
Production Manager: Kimberly H. Vivas

Home Plans Editor: Kenneth D. Stuts
Home Plans Designer Liaison: Timothy Mulligan

Design and Layout: Arrowhead Direct (David Kroha,
    Cindy DiPierdomenico, Judith Kroha)

Cover Design: 3R1 Group

Printed In China

Current Printing (last digit)
10 9 8 7 6 5 4 3 2 1

One-Story House Plans Bible
Library of Congress Control Number: 2006902940
ISBN-10: 1-58011-325-7
ISBN-13: 978-1-58011-325-0

CREATIVE HOMEOWNER®
A Division of Federal Marketing Corp.
24 Park Way
Upper Saddle River, NJ 07458
www.creativehomeowner.com

Note: The homes as shown in the photographs and renderings in this book may differ from the actual blueprints. When studying the house of your choice, please check the floor plans carefully.

Photo Credits
All landscape illustrations by Steve Buchanan

Front Cover: *plan* 121051, page 169 **page 3:** *top plan* 121010, page 180; *center plan* 271063, page 305; *bottom plan* 121011, page 111 **page 4:** *plan* 121059, page 142 **page 5:** *plan* 111004, page 310 **page 6:** *top plan* 161037, page 312; *bottom plan* 151055, page 370 **page 7:** *plan* 161098, page 265 **pages 74-81:** *illustrations* Warren Cutler **page 152:** courtesy of Kraftmaid Cabinetry, Inc. **page 153:** *top* Brian Vanden Brink, design: Custom Electronics; *center* courtesy of IKEA; *center* Ken Hayden/Redcover.com **page 154:** courtesy of Kraftmaid Cabinetry, Inc. **page 155:** Phillip H. Ennis, design: Greenbaum Interiors/Lynn Cone, architect: Moisan Architects **pages 156–157:** *left* courtesy of La-Z-Boy; *center* Mark York/Redcover.com; *top right* courtesy of Stickley Furniture; *bottom right* courtesy of Kraftmaid Cabinetry, Inc. **page 206:** Alan Shortall Photography **page 207:** *top* Mark Lohman; *center* Leonard Lammi, design: Cheryl Casey Ross; *bottom* Philip Clayton-Thompson, design: Nancy Setterquist **page 208:** *top and top inset* Jessie Walker, design: Claire Golan; *bottom* courtesy of York Wallcoverings **page 209:** Leonard Lammi; design Cheryl Casey Ross **page 210:** *top* Tria Giovan; *bottom* Mark Lohman **page 212:** *top left* Mark Samu; *top right & bottom left* Brian Vanden Brink, design: Atlantic Kitchens; *bottom right* Mark Lohman **page 213:** *top right* Mark Samu; *bottom right* Philip Clayton-Thompson, design: Nancy Setterquist; *bottom left* courtesy of American Olean; *top left* Brian Vanden Brink, design: Atlantic Kitchens **pages 256–257:** *both* courtesy of Kraftmaid Cabinetry, Inc. **page 258:** *both* courtesy of Wellborn Cabinets **page 259:** courtesy of Kraftmaid Cabinetry, Inc. **page 260:** courtesy of Wellborn Cabinets **page 261:** *top left & bottom left* courtesy of Merillat Industries; *top right* courtesy of Wellborn Cabinets **page 350:** Nancy Hill, design Gillian Drummond **page 351:** *top* Jessie Walker, artist & sculptor: Diana McNich; *center* davidduncanlivingston.com; *bottom* Jessie Walker, design: Donna Aylesworth **page 352:** Elizabethwhiting.com **page 353:** davidduncanlivingston.com **page 354:** *left* davidduncanlivingston.com; *right* Nancy Hill, design: Deborah T. Lipner, LTD **page 355:** *both* davidduncanlivingston.com **page 356:** *top* Nancy Hill, design: Diana Sawicki Interiors; *bottom* Anne Gummerson **page 373:** *plan* 151001, page 371 **page 377:** *top plan* 131036, page 301; *center plan* 161026, pages 274–275; *bottom plan* 151002, page 296 **page 384:** *top plan* 151063, page 295; *center plan* 161037, page 312; *bottom plan* 121006, page 86

Contents

Getting Started

Maybe you can't wait to bang the first nail. Or you may be just as happy leaving town until the windows are cleaned. The extent of your involvement with the construction phase is up to you. Your time, interests, and abilities can help you decide how to get the project from lines on paper to reality. But building a house requires more than putting pieces together. Whoever is in charge of the process must competently manage people as well as supplies, materials, and construction. He or she will have to

- Make a project schedule to plan the orderly progress of the work. This can be a bar chart that shows the time period of activity by each trade.
- Establish a budget for each category of work, such as foundation, framing, and finish carpentry.
- Arrange for a source of construction financing.
- Get a building permit and post it conspicuously at the construction site.
- Line up supply sources and order materials.
- Find subcontractors and negotiate their contracts.
- Coordinate the work so that it progresses smoothly with the fewest conflicts.
- Notify inspectors at the appropriate milestones.
- Make payments to suppliers and subcontractors.

You as the Builder

You'll have to take care of every logistical detail yourself if you decide to act as your own builder or general contractor. But along with the responsibilities of managing the project, you gain the flexibility to do as much of your own work as you want and subcontract out the rest. Before taking this path, however, be sure you have the time and capabilities. Do you also have the

time and ability to schedule the work, hire and coordinate subs, order materials, and keep ahead of the accounting required to manage the project successfully? If you do, you stand to save the amount that a general contractor would charge to take on these responsibilities, normally 15 to 30 percent of the construction cost. If you take this responsibility on but mismanage the project, the potential savings will erode and may even cost you more than if you had hired a builder in the first place. A subcontractor might charge extra for hav-

Acting as the builder, above, requires the ability to hire and manage subcontractors.

Building a home, opposite, includes the need to schedule building inspections at the appropriate milestones.

ing to return to the site to complete work that was originally scheduled for an earlier date. Or perhaps because you didn't order the windows at the beginning, you now have to pay for a recent cost increase. (If you had hired a builder in the first place he or she would absorb the increase.)

Hiring a Builder to Handle Construction

A builder or general contractor will manage every aspect of the construction process. Your role after signing the construction contract will be to make regular progress payments and ensure that the work for which you are paying has been completed. You will also consult with the builder and agree to any changes that may have to be made along the way.

Leads for finding builders might come from friends or neighbors who have had contractors build, remodel, or add to their homes. Real-estate agents and bankers may have some names handy but are more likely familiar with the builder's ability to complete projects on time and budget than the quality of the work itself.

The next step is to narrow your list of candidates to three or four who you think can do a quality job and work harmoniously with you. Phone each builder to see whether he or she is interested in being considered for your project. If so, invite the builder to an interview at your home. The meeting will serve two purposes. You'll be able to ask the candidate about his or her experience, and you'll be able to see whether or not your personalities are compatible. Go over the plans with the builder to make certain that he or she understands the scope of the project. Ask if they have constructed similar houses. Get references, and check the builder's standing with the Better Business Bureau. Develop a short list of builders, say three, and ask them to submit bids for the project.

Contracts

Lump-Sum Contracts

A lump-sum, or fixed-fee, contract lets you know from the beginning just what the project will cost, barring any changes made because of your requests or unforeseen conditions. This form works well for projects that promise few surprises and are well defined from the outset by a complete set of contract documents. You can enter into a fixed-price contract by negotiating with a single builder on your short list or by obtaining bids from three or four builders. If you go the latter route, give each bidder a set of documents and allow at least two weeks for them to submit their bids. When you get the bids, decide who you want and call the others to thank them for their efforts. You don't have to accept the lowest bid, but it probably makes sense to do so since you have already honed the list to builders you trust. Inform this builder of your intentions to finalize a contract.

Cost-Plus-Fee Contracts

Under a cost-plus-fee contract, you agree to pay the builder for the costs of labor and materials, as verified by receipts, plus a fee that represents the builder's overhead and profit. This arrangement is sometimes referred to as "time and materials." The fee can range between 15 and 30 percent of the incurred costs. Because you ultimately pick up the tab—whatever the costs—the contractor is never at risk, as he is with a lump-sum contract. You won't know the final total cost of a cost-plus-fee contract until the project is built and paid for. If you can live with that uncertainty, there are offsetting advantages. First, this form allows you to accommodate unknown conditions much more easily than does a lump-sum contract. And rather than being tied down by the project documents, you will be free to make changes at any point along the way. This can be a trap, though. Watching the project take shape will spark the desire to add something or do something differently. Each change costs more, and the accumulation can easily exceed your budget. Because of the uncertainty of the final tab and the built-in advantage to the contractor, you should think twice before entering into this form of contract.

Contract Content

The conditions of your agreement should be spelled out thoroughly in writing and signed by both parties, whatever contractual arrangement you make with your builder. Your contract should include provisions for the following:

- The names and addresses of the owner and builder.
- A description of the work to be included ("As described in the plans and specifications dated . . .").
- The date that the work will be completed if time is of the essence.
- The contract price for lump-sum contracts and the builder's allowed profit and overhead costs for changes.
- The builder's fee for cost-plus-fee contracts and the method of accounting and requesting payment.
- The criteria for progress payments (monthly, by project milestones) and the conditions of final payment.
- A list of each drawing and specification section that is to be included as part of the contract.
- Requirements for guarantees. (One year is the standard period for which contractors guarantee the entire project, but you may require specific guarantees on

When submitting bids, all of the builders should base their estimates on the same specifications. Once the work begins, communicate with your builder to keep the work proceeding smoothly.

Inspect your newly built home, if possible, before the builder closes it up and finishes it.

certain parts of the project, such as a 20-year guarantee on the roofing.)
- Provisions for insurance.
- A description of how changes in the work orders will be handled.

The builder may have a standard contract that you can tailor to the specifics of your project. These contain complete specific conditions with blanks that you can fill in to fit your project and a set of "general conditions" that cover a host of issues from insurance to termination provisions. It's always a good idea to have an attorney review the draft of your completed contract before signing it.

Working with Your Builder

The construction phase officially begins when you have a signed copy of the contract and copies of any insurance required from the builder. It's not unheard of for a builder to request an initial payment of 10 to 20 percent of the total cost to cover mobilization costs, those costs associated with obtaining permits and getting set up to begin the actual construction. If you agree to this, keep a careful eye on the progress of the work to ensure that the total paid out at any one time doesn't get too far out of sync with the actual work completed.

What about changes? From here on, it's up to you and your builder to proceed in good faith and to keep the channels of communication open. Even so, changes of one sort or another beset every project, and they usually add to its cost.

Light at the End of the Tunnel.

The builder's request for a final inspection marks the end of the construction phase—almost. At the final inspection meeting, you and the builder will inspect the work, noting any defects or incomplete items on a "punch list." When the builder tidies up the punch list items, you should reinspect. Sometimes, builders go on to another job and take forever to clean up the last few details, so only after all items on the list have been completed satisfactorily should you release the final payment, which often accounts for the builder's profit.

Some Final Words

Having a positive attitude is important when undertaking a project as large as building a home. A positive attitude can help you ride out the rigors and stress of the construction process.

Stay Flexible. Expect problems, because they certainly will occur. Weather can upset the schedule you have established for subcontractors. A supplier may get behind on deliveries, which also affects the schedule. An unexpected pipe may surprise you during excavation. Just as certain, every problem that comes along has a solution if you are open to it.

Be Patient. The extra days it may take to resolve a construction problem will be forgotten once the project is completed.

Express Yourself. If what you see isn't exactly what you thought you were getting, don't be afraid to look into changing it. Or you may spot an unforeseen opportunity for an improvement. Changes usually cost more money, though, so don't make frivolous decisions.

Finally, watching your home go up is exciting, so stay upbeat. Get away from your project from time to time. Dine out. Take time to relax. A positive attitude will make for smoother relations with your builder. An optimistic outlook will yield better-quality work if you are doing your own construction. And though the project might seem endless while it is under way, keep in mind that all the planning and construction will fade to a faint memory at some time in the future, and you will be getting a lifetime of pleasure from a home that is just right for you.

Plan #131014

Dimensions: 48' W x 43'4" D
Levels: 1
Square Footage: 1,380
Bedrooms: 3
Bathrooms: 2
Foundation: Crawl space, slab, or basement
Materials List Available: Yes
Price Category: C

Images provided by designer/architect.

The exterior of this home looks formal, thanks to its twin dormers, gables, and the bay windows that flank the columned porch, but the inside is contemporary in both design and features.

Features:

- **Great Room:** Centrally located, this great room has a 10-ft. ceiling. A fireplace, built-in cabinets, and windows that overlook the rear covered porch make it as practical as it is attractive.

- **Dining Room:** A bay window adds to the charm of this versatile room.

- **Kitchen:** This U-shaped room is designed to make cooking and cleaning jobs efficient.

- **Master Suite:** With a bay window, a walk-in closet, and a private bath with an oval tub, the master suite may be your favorite area.

- **Additional Bedrooms:** Located on the opposite side of the house from the master suite, these rooms share a full bath in the hall.

Living Room

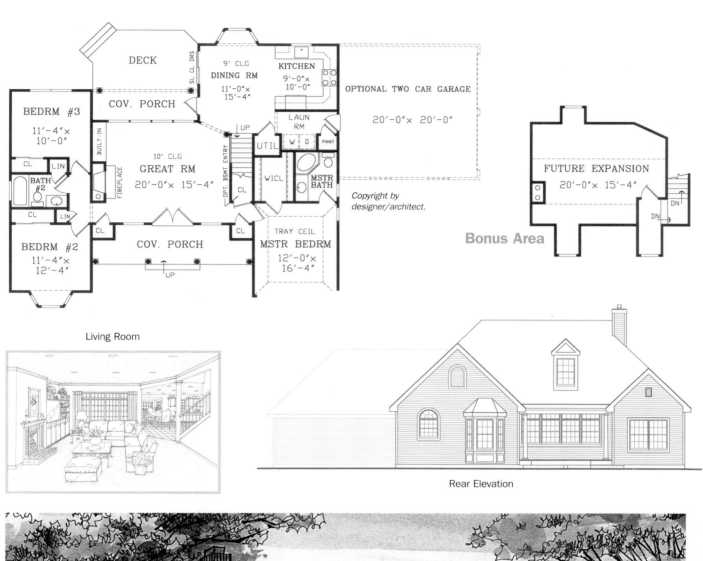

DECK

9' CLG
DINING RM
11'-0"×
15'-4"

KITCHEN
9'-0"×
10'-0"

SL. GL. DRS

COV. PORCH

OPTIONAL TWO CAR GARAGE

20'-0"× 20'-0"

BEDRM #3
11'-4"×
10'-0"

CL   LIN

BATH
#2

CL   LIN

BUILT-IN

FIREPLACE

10' CLG
GREAT RM
20'-0"× 15'-4"

OPT. BSMT. ENTRY

UP

LAUN
RM

UTIL

W   D

PANT

WICL

CL

MSTR
BATH

CL

BEDRM #2
11'-4"×
12'-4"

CL

COV. PORCH

UP

CL

TRAY CEIL
MSTR BEDRM
12'-0"×
16'-4"

Copyright by
designer/architect.

FUTURE EXPANSION
20'-0"× 15'-4"

DN

DN

Bonus Area

Living Room

Rear Elevation

Plan #131003

Dimensions: 60' W x 39'10" D
Levels: 1
Square Footage: 1,466
Bedrooms: 3
Bathrooms: 2
Foundation: Crawl space, slab, or basement
Materials List Available: Yes
Price Category: C

Images provided by designer/architect.

Victorian styling adds elegance to this compact and easy-to-maintain ranch design.

Features:

- Ceiling Height: 8 ft.

- Foyer: Bridging between the front door and the great room, this foyer is a surprise feature.

- Great Room: A 10-ft. ceiling adds to the spacious feeling of this room, while the corner fireplace gives it an intimate feeling. Sliding glass doors at the rear of the room open to the backyard.

- Dining Room: This formal room adjoins the great room, allowing guests and family to flow between the rooms.

- Breakfast Room: Turrets add a Victorian feeling to this room that's just off the kitchen and overlooks the front porch.

- Master Suite: Privacy is assured in this suite, which is separated from the main part of the house. A compartmented bath and large walk-in closet add convenience to its beauty.

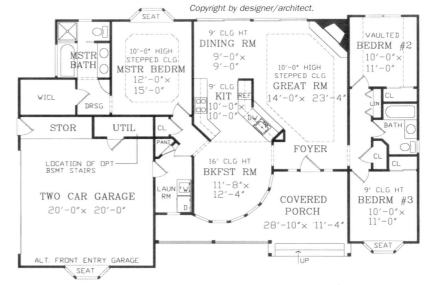

Copyright by designer/architect.

Breakfast Room

Plan #121105

Dimensions: 44' W x 26' D
Levels: 1
Square Footage: 1,125
Bedrooms: 3
Bathrooms: 2
Foundation: Basement; crawl space for fee
Material List Available: Yes
Price Category: B

Images provided by designer/architect.

This traditional, economical split-level ranch home is the ideal beginning for the growing family.

Features:

- Entry: Through the covered stoop is this small entryway, which gives you two options for entertaining. A few short steps lead to the great room, providing a charming introduction to the home, while the basement, finished to your taste, awaits beneath the descending stairs.

- Great Room: Cathedral ceilings and their connection to both kitchen and dining room make this space open and inviting for family and guests alike.

- Kitchen: This efficiently designed L-shaped kitchen features a snack bar and flows into the dining room, providing an easy transition between preparing and serving.

- Master Suite: A cozy, romantic area, this master suite includes a walk-in closet and private master bath. The area is self-contained for privacy but close enough to the other bedrooms to comfort young families.

- Basement: This spacious area is yours for the designing. A small space is reserved for the laundry, while the remaining area is full of possibility. Finish the basement for an extra bedroom or even a fun entertainment and game room.

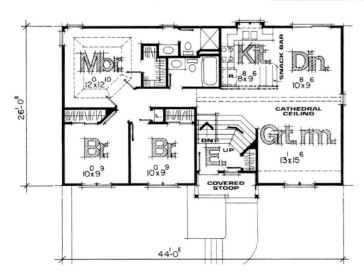

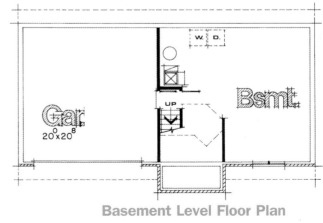

Basement Level Floor Plan

Copyright by designer/architect.

Plan #401041

Dimensions: 38' W x 31' D
Levels: 1
Square Footage: 1,108
Bedrooms: 3
Bathrooms: 2
Foundation: Basement
Materials List Available: Yes
Price Category: B

Craftsman styling and a welcoming porch create marvelous curb appeal for this design. A compact footprint allows economy in construction.

Features:

- **High Ceiling:** This volume ceiling in the living and dining rooms and the kitchen make the home live larger than its modest square footage suggests.

- **Kitchen:** This area features generous cabinet space and flows directly into the dining room to create a casual country feeling. (Note the optional buffet.)

- **Master Bedroom:** This room offers a walk-in closet, a full bath, and a bumped-out window overlooking the rear yard.

- **Expansion:** The lower level provides room for an additional bedroom, den, family room, and full bath.

Copyright by designer/architect.

Images provided by designer/architect.

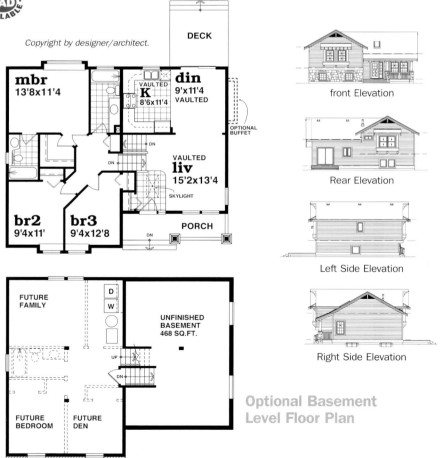

front Elevation

Rear Elevation

Left Side Elevation

Right Side Elevation

Optional Basement Level Floor Plan

Plan #271002

Dimensions: 44'8" W x 50'8" D
Levels: 1
Square Footage: 1,252
Bedrooms: 3
Bathrooms: 2
Foundation: Basement
Materials List Available: Yes
Price Category: B

This traditional home combines a modest square footage with stylish extras.

Features:

• Living Room: Spacious and inviting, this gathering spot is brightened by a Palladian window arrangement, warmed by a fireplace, and topped by a vaulted ceiling.

• Dining Room: The vaulted ceiling also crowns this room, which shares the living room's fireplace. Sliding doors lead to a backyard deck.

• Kitchen: Smart design ensures a place for everything.

• Master Suite: The master bedroom boasts a vaulted ceiling, cheery windows, and a private bath.

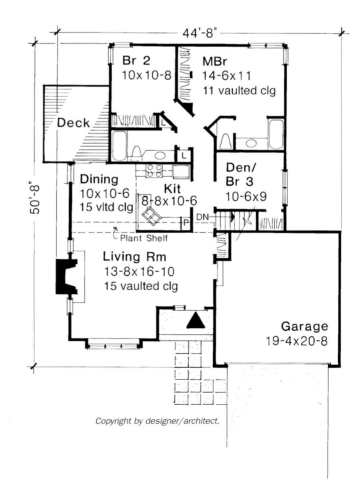

Plan #401020

Dimensions: 55'6" W x 30' D
Levels: 1
Square Footage: 1,230
Bedrooms: 3
Bathrooms: 2
Foundation: Basement
Materials List Available: Yes
Price Category: B

This is a grand vacation or retirement home, designed for views and the outdoor lifestyle. The full-width deck complements the abundant windows in the rooms that face it.

Features:

• Living Room: This area, with a vaulted ceiling, a fireplace, and full-height windows overlooking the deck, is made for gathering.

• Dining Room: This room is open to the living room; it has sliding glass doors that lead to the outdoors.

• Kitchen: This room has a pass-through counter to the dining room and is U-shaped in design.

• Bedrooms: Two family bedrooms in the middle of the plan share a full bath.

• Master Suite: This area has a private bath and deck views.

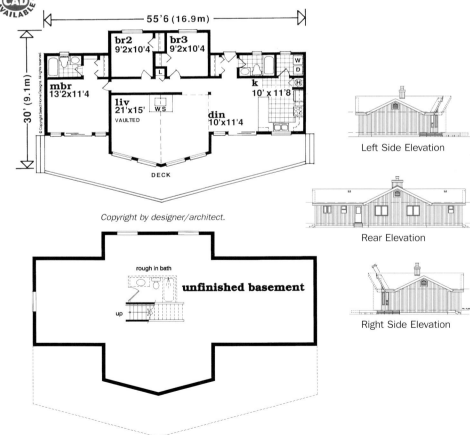

Optional Basement Level Floor Plan

Left Side Elevation

Rear Elevation

Right Side Elevation

Plan #391060

Dimensions: 58' W x 34'4" D
Levels: 1
Square Footage: 1,359
Bedrooms: 3
Bathrooms: 2
Foundation: Crawl space, slab or basement
Materials List Available: Yes
Price Category: B

Images provided by designer/architect.

Big bay windows and one-story styling make this home irresistible.

Features:

- **Living Room:** This great-sized living room winds its way to a formal dining room and kitchen.

- **Master Suite:** This area (with luxury bath room) shows off a tray ceiling and a window seat with a front-yard view.

- **Bedroom 2:** This room has a spacious closet and a personal view of the backyard, plus a full bath.

- **Den:** This room with double doors can become bedroom 3 if necessary.

Copyright by designer/architect.

Rear View

Plan #161116

Dimensions: 52'8" W x 45' D
Levels: 1
Square Footage: 1,442
Bedrooms: 3
Bathrooms: 2
Foundation: Basement
Material List Available: Yes
Price Category: B

This delightful home offers space-saving convenience and functional living space.

Images provided by designer/architect.

Features:

• Great Room: This gathering area features an over-11-foot-tall ceiling and a corner gas fireplace. A few steps out the back door, and you are on the rear deck.

• Kitchen: This fully equipped kitchen offers a counter with seating, dishwasher, and built-in microwave. The garage and laundry areas are conveniently a few steps away.

• Master Suite: Split bedrooms offer privacy to this elegant area, which enjoys a 9-ft. ceiling height and large walk-in closet. The master bath boasts a double-bowl vanity and compartmented lavatory and shower area.

• Bedrooms: Two secondary bedrooms are located just off the great room and share the second bathroom.

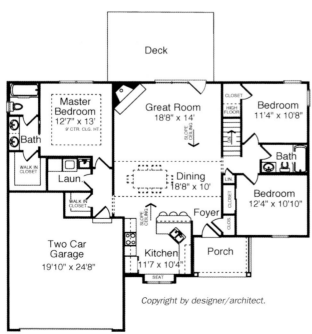

Copyright by designer/architect.

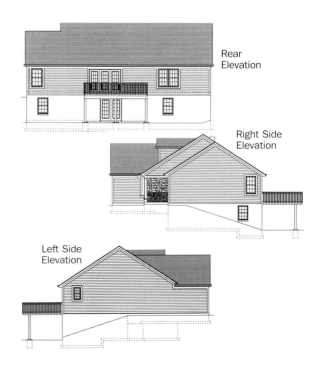

Plan #131034

Dimensions: 40' W x 32' D
Levels: 2 (upper unfinished)
Square Footage: 1,040
Bedrooms: 5
Bathrooms: 2½
Foundation: Crawl space, slab, or basement
Materials List Available: Yes
Price Category: C

Images provided by designer/architect.

You'll love the versatility this expandable ranch-style home gives, with its unfinished, second story that you can transform into two bedrooms and a bath if you need the space.

Features:

- **Porch:** Decorate this country-style porch to accentuate the charm of this warm home.

- **Living Room:** This formal room features a wide, dramatic archway that opens to the kitchen and the dining room.

- **Kitchen:** The angled shape of this kitchen gives it character, while the convenient island and well-designed floor plan make cooking and cleaning tasks unusually efficient.

- **Bedrooms:** Use the design option in the blueprints of this home to substitute one of the bedrooms into an expansion of the master bedroom, which features an amenity-laden, private bathroom for total luxury.

Optional Main Level Floor Plan

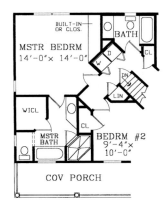

Main Level Floor Plan

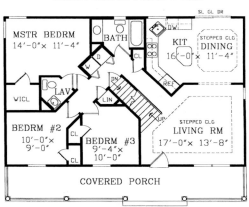

Kitchen

Upper Level Floor Plan

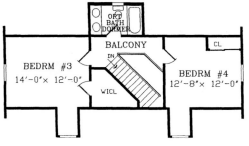

Copyright by designer/architect.

Plan #271006

Dimensions: 50' W x 55' D
Levels: 1
Square Footage: 1,444
Bedrooms: 3
Bathrooms: 2
Foundation: Basement
Material List Available: Yes
Price Category: B

With vaulted ceilings and transom windows bringing in an abundance of natural light, this cozy home seems to expand from the inside out.

Features:

- Family Room: This spacious area feeds into the open kitchen. Vaulted ceilings and the fireplace provide a whimsical atmosphere with practical possibilities.

- Kitchen: This area is truly the heart of the home. The L-shaped workspace facing the family room, combined with the stovetop island, adds to the airy feel of the home. Place a table between the kitchen and family room, and you have a flowing family or entertainment space.

- Master Suite: Vaulted ceilings, a walk-in closet, and a private bath with a skylight combine to make a romantic getaway indoors.

- Bedrooms: If two bedrooms are not enough, the den can easily be transformed into a third bedroom. Both the second bedroom and the den have easy access to the second full bathroom.

Images provided by designer/architect.

This home, as shown in the photograph, may differ from the actual blueprints. For more detailed information, please check the floor plans carefully.

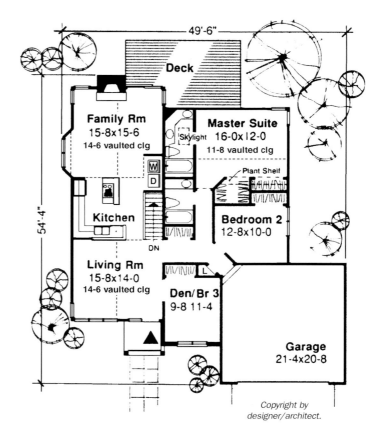

Copyright by designer/architect.

Plan #251002

Dimensions: 55'6" W x 64'3" D
Levels: 1
Square Footage: 1,333
Bedrooms: 3
Bathrooms: 2
Foundation: Crawl space, slab
Materials List Available: Yes
Price Category: B

Although compact, this farmhouse has all the amenities for comfortable modern living.

Features:

• Ceiling Height: 8 ft. unless otherwise noted.

• Foyer: This gracious and welcoming foyer opens to the family room.

• Family Room: This inviting family room is designed to accommodate all kinds of family activities. It features a 9-ft. ceiling and a handsome, warming fireplace.

• Kitchen: Cooking in this kitchen is a real pleasure. It includes a center island, so you'll never run out of counter space for food preparation.

• Master Bedroom: This master bedroom features a large walk-in closet and an elegant 9-ft. recessed ceiling.

• Master Bath: This master bath offers a double vanity, a tub, and a walk-in shower.

• Garage: This attached garage provides plenty of extra storage space, as well as parking for two cars.

Images provided by designer/architect.

SMARTtip

Arts and Crafts Style

The heart of this style rests in its earthy connection. The more you can bring nature into it, the more authentic it will be. An easy way to do this is with plants. A bonus is that plants naturally thrive in the bathroom, where they enjoy the humid environment.

Copyright by designer/architect.

Plan #121009

Dimensions: 50' W x 58' D
Levels: 1
Square Footage: 1,422
Bedrooms: 3
Bathrooms: 2
Foundation: Basement
Materials List Available: Yes
Price Category: B

Images provided by designer/architect.

This amenity-filled home is perfect for the growing family or as a retirement retreat.

Features:

- Ceiling Height: 8 ft. unless otherwise noted.

- Great Room: This inviting space is the perfect place for gatherings of all sizes. It shares 12-ft. ceilings with the dining room and kitchen.

- Dining Room: In addition to the 12-ft. ceiling, arched openings, and built-in book cases make this an elegant place to dine.

- Private Porch: After dinner, step through a door in the dining room to enjoy a summer breeze in this inviting porch.

- Master Suite: The boxed ceiling lends drama to this suite and a walk-in closet adds convenience. Luxury comes from the whirlpool bath.

- Garage: You won't be short of parking and storage space in this two-bay garage. As a bonus there is space for a workbench.

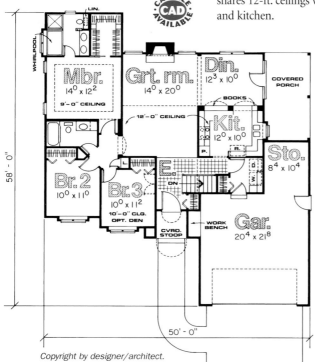

Copyright by designer/architect.

SMARTtip
Window Cornices

You can transform plain rooms by making jogs in cornice molding that will hold shades, blinds, and other window treatments. You can create individual pockets over each window or continue the molding past narrow wall sections between windows to form a more expansive detail. Housings below the cornice can be painted or papered.

Plan #321025

Dimensions: 28' W x 28' D

Levels: 1

Square Footage: 914

Bedrooms: 2

Bathrooms: 1

Foundation: Basement, walkout

Materials List Available: Yes

Price Category: A

This cute little home's great layout packs in an abundance of features.

Features:

- Living Room: The cozy fireplace in this open, welcoming room invites you to relax awhile.

- Dining Room: This area has a bay window and is open to the kitchen and the living room.

- Kitchen: This compact kitchen has everything you'll need, including a built-in pantry.

- Master Bedroom: Generously sized, with a large closet, this room has a private door into the common bathroom.

- Bedroom: This secondary bedroom can also be used as a home office.

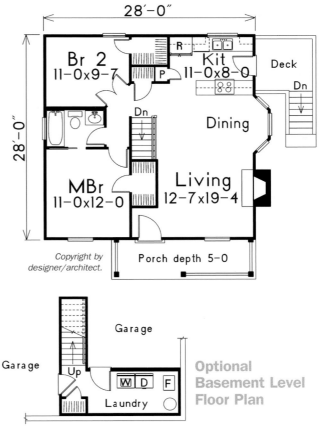

Copyright by designer/architect.

Optional Basement Level Floor Plan

Plan #471002

Dimensions: 38' W x 26' D

Levels: 1

Square Footage: 835

Bedrooms: 2

Bathrooms: 2

Foundation: Crawl space or slab

Material List Available: No

Price Category: A

Images provided by designer/architect.

Copyright by designer/architect.

Plan #381048

Dimensions: 32' W x 40' D

Levels: 1

Square Footage: 895

Bedrooms: 2

Bathrooms: 1

Foundation: Crawl space or basement

Material List Available: Yes

Price Category: A

Images provided by designer/architect.

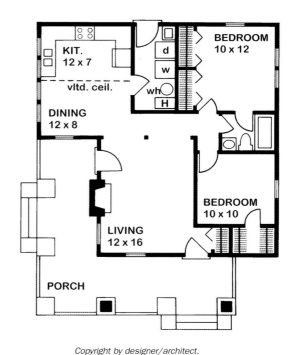

Copyright by designer/architect.

Plan #121012

Dimensions: 40' W x 48'8" D
Levels: 1
Square Footage: 1,195
Bedrooms: 3
Bathrooms: 2
Foundation: Basement
Materials List Available: Yes
Price Category: B

This home, as shown in the photograph, may differ from the actual blueprints. For more detailed information, please check the floor plans carefully.

CAD FILE AVAILABLE

This compact one-level home uses an open plan to make the most of its square footage.

Features:

• Ceiling Height: 8 ft.

• Covered Porch: This delightful area, located off the kitchen, provides a private spot to enjoy some fresh air.

• Open Plan: The family room, dining area and kitchen share a big open space to provide a sense of spaciousness. Moving so easily between these interrelated areas provides the convenience demanded by a busy lifestyle.

• Master Suite: An open plan is convenient, but it is still important for everyone to have their private space. The master suite enjoys its own bath and walk-in closet. The secondary bedrooms share a nearby bath.

• Garage: Here you will find parking for two cars and plenty of extra storage space as well.

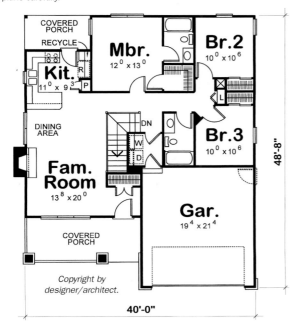

COVERED PORCH
RECYCLE
Kit. 11⁰ x 9³
Mbr. 12⁰ x 13⁰
Br.2 10⁰ x 10⁶
DINING AREA
DN
Br.3 10⁰ x 10⁶
Fam. Room 13⁸ x 20⁰
Gar. 19⁴ x 21⁴
COVERED PORCH
48'-8"
40'-0"

Copyright by designer/architect.

Rendering reflects floor plan

Plan #401024

Dimensions: 70' W x 36' D
Levels: 1
Square Footage: 1,298
Bedrooms: 3
Bathrooms: 2
Foundation: Basement
Materials List Available: Yes
Price Category: B

Images provided by designer/architect.

A front veranda, cedar lattice, and a solid-stone chimney enhance the appeal of this one-story country-style home.

CAD FILE AVAILABLE

Features:

- **Great Room:** The open plan begins with this great room, which includes a fireplace and a plant ledge over the wall separating the living space from the country kitchen.

- **Kitchen:** This U-shaped kitchen provides an island work counter and sliding glass doors to the rear deck and screened porch.

- **Master Suite:** This area has a wall closet and a private bath with window seat.

Copyright by designer/architect.

Left Side Elevation

Right Side Elevation

Optional Floor Plan

Rear Elevation

Plan #391008

Dimensions: 50' W x 40' D
Levels: 1
Square Footage: 1,312
Bedrooms: 3
Bathrooms: 2
Foundation: Crawl space, slab, or basement
Materials List Available: Yes
Price Category: B

Here's the sum of brains and beauty, which will please all types of families, from starters and nearly empty nesters to those going golden.

Features:

- **Entry:** This restful fresh-air porch and formal foyer bring you graciously toward the great room, with its fireplace and vaulted ceiling.

- **Dining Room:** This adjacent dining room features sliding doors to the deck and smooth open access to the U-shaped kitchen.

- **Laundry Room:** The laundry area has its own separate landing from the garage, so it's conveniently out of the way.

- **Master Suite:** This master suite with tray ceilings features nearly "limitless" closet space, a private bath, and large hall linen closet.

- **Bedrooms:** The two secondary bedrooms, also with roomy closets, share a full bath. Bedroom 3 easily becomes a home office with direct foyer access and a window overlooking the porch.

Images provided by designer/architect.

Copyright by designer/architect.

Crawl Space Option

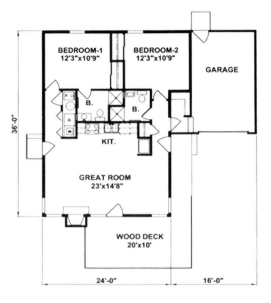

Images provided by designer/architect.

Plan #471003

Dimensions: 40' W x 36' D

Levels: 1

Square Footage: 920

Bedrooms: 2

Bathrooms: 2

Foundation: Crawl space

Material List Available: Yes

Price Category: A

Copyright by designer/architect.

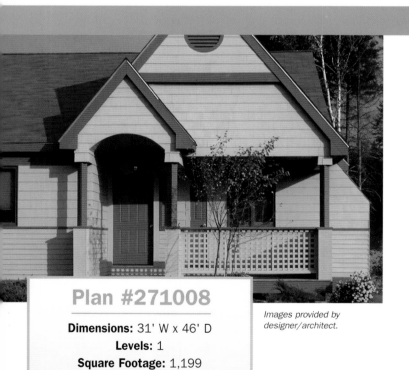

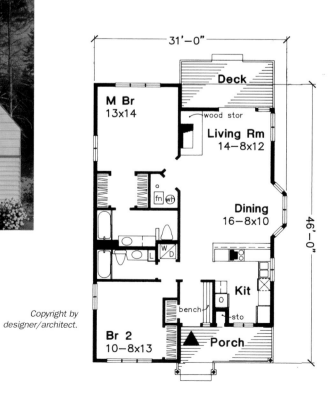

Images provided by designer/architect.

Plan #271008

Dimensions: 31' W x 46' D

Levels: 1

Square Footage: 1,199

Bedrooms: 2

Bathrooms: 2

Foundation: Slab

Materials List Available: No

Price Category: B

Copyright by designer/architect.

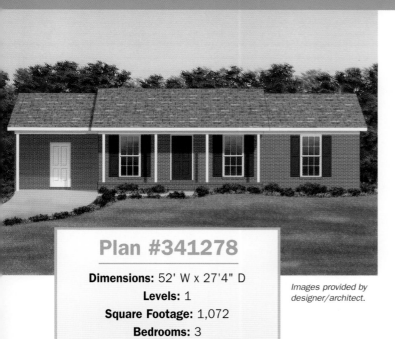

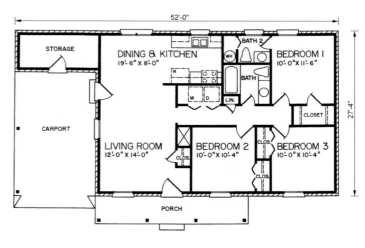

Images provided by designer/architect.

Copyright by designer/architect.

Plan #341278

Dimensions: 52' W x 27'4" D

Levels: 1

Square Footage: 1,072

Bedrooms: 3

Bathrooms: 1½

Foundation: Crawl space, slab, basement, or walkout

Material List Available: Yes

Price Category: B

Images provided by designer/architect.

Copyright by designer/architect.

Plan #471014

Dimensions: 40' W x 26' D

Levels: 1

Square Footage: 950

Bedrooms: 2

Bathrooms: 2

Foundation: Crawl space

Material List Available: No

Price Category: A

Plan #401043

Dimensions: 38' W x 32' D
Levels: 1
Square Footage: 988
Bedrooms: 3
Bathrooms: 1
Foundation: Basement
Materials List Available: Yes
Price Category: A

This economical, compact home is the ultimate in efficient use of space.

Features:

- Porch: The front entry is sheltered by this casual country porch, which also protects the living room windows.

- Living Room: This central living room features a cozy fireplace and outdoor access to the front porch.

- Kitchen: This U-shaped kitchen serves both a dining area and a breakfast bar. Sliding glass doors lead from here to the rear yard.

- Master Bedroom: This room has a walk-in closet and shares a full bathroom with the secondary bedrooms.

- A single or double garage may be built to the side or to the rear of the home.

Images provided by designer/architect.

Copyright by designer/architect.

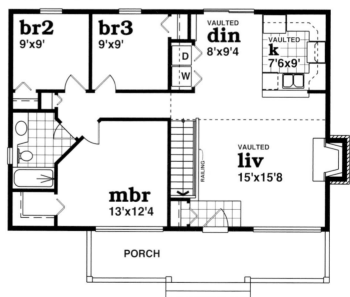

Right Side Elevation   Rear Elevation   Left Side Elevation

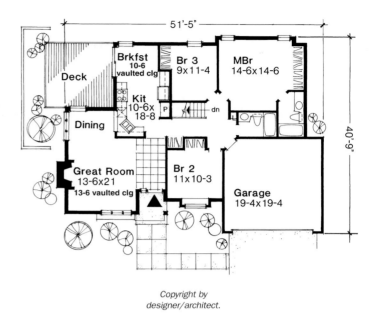

Images provided by designer/architect.

Copyright by designer/architect.

Deck

Brkfst
10-6
vaulted clg

Br 3
9x11-4

MBr
14-6x14-6

Kit
10-6x
18-8

Dining

Great Room
13-6x21
13-6 vaulted clg

Br 2
11x10-3

Garage
19-4x19-4

51'-5"

40'-9"

Plan #271007

Dimensions: 52' W x 41' D
Levels: 1
Square Footage: 1,283
Bedrooms: 3
Bathrooms: 2
Foundation: Basement
Materials List Available: Yes
Price Category: B

Copyright by designer/architect.

Images provided by designer/architect.

CAD FILE AVAILABLE

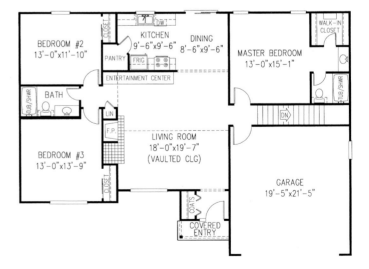

BEDROOM #2
13'-0"x11'-10"

KITCHEN
9'-6"x9'-6"

DINING
8'-6"x9'-6"

WALK-IN CLOSET

PANTRY

FRIG

MASTER BEDROOM
13'-0"x15'-1"

ENTERTAINMENT CENTER

BATH

LIN

BEDROOM #3
13'-0"x13'-9"

F.P.

LIVING ROOM
18'-0"x19'-7"
(VAULTED CLG)

DN

GARAGE
19'-5"x21'-5"

COATS

COVERED ENTRY

Plan #421001

Dimensions: 54' W x 41' D
Levels: 1
Square Footage: 1,433
Bedrooms: 3
Bathrooms: 2
Foundation: Crawl space, slab, or basement
Material List Available: Yes
Price Category: B

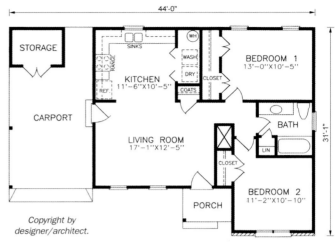

44'-0"

STORAGE

CARPORT

KITCHEN
11'-6"X10'-5"

RANGE

SINKS

REF.

WH

WASH

DRY

COATS

CLOSET

BEDROOM 1
13'-0"X10'-5"

BATH

LIN

LIVING ROOM
17'-1"X12'-5"

CLOSET

BEDROOM 2
11'-2"X10'-10"

PORCH

31'-1"

Plan #341208

Dimensions: 44' W x 31'1" D

Levels: 1

Square Footage: 853

Bedrooms: 2

Bathrooms: 1

Foundation: Crawl space, slab, basement, or walkout

Materials List Available: Yes

Price Category: A

Images provided by designer/architect.

CAD FILE AVAILABLE CAD

Copyright by designer/architect.

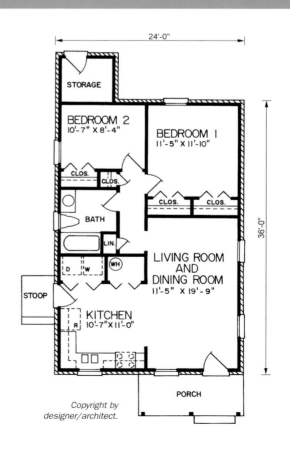

24'-0"

STORAGE

BEDROOM 2
10'-7" X 8'-4"

BEDROOM 1
11'-5" X 11'-10"

CLOS.

CLOS.

CLOS.

CLOS.

BATH

LIN.

D   W

WH

LIVING ROOM
AND
DINING ROOM
11'-5" X 19'-9"

STOOP

KITCHEN
10'-7"X 11'-0"

R

36'-0"

PORCH

Plan #341157

Dimensions: 24' W x 36' D

Levels: 1

Square Footage: 861

Bedrooms: 2

Bathrooms: 1

Foundation: Crawl space, slab, basement, or walkout

Materials List Available: Yes

Price Category: A

Images provided by designer/architect.

CAD FILE AVAILABLE CAD

Copyright by designer/architect.

Plan #321040

Dimensions: 35' W x 40'8" D

Levels: 1

Square Footage: 1,084

Bedrooms: 2

Bathrooms: 2

Foundation: Basement

Materials List Available: Yes

Price Category: B

Images provided by designer/architect.

This cute cottage, with its front porch, would make a great starter home or a weekend getaway home.

Features:

- Living Room: This room features an entry closet and a cozy fireplace.

- Kitchen: This well-designed kitchen opens into the breakfast area.

- Master Suite: This retreat has a walk-in closet and a private bath.

- Bedroom: This second bedroom features a walk-in closet and has access to the hall bathroom.

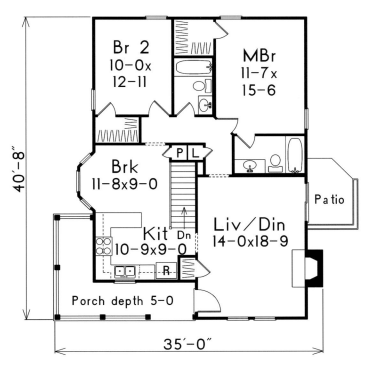

Copyright by designer/architect.

Plan #351018

Dimensions: 40'8" W x 38'6" D
Levels: 1
Square Footage: 1,251
Bedrooms: 3
Bathrooms: 2
Foundation: Crawl space or slab
Materials List Available: Yes
Price Category: C

This traditional home has great curb appeal and a great floor plan.

Features:

- Ceilings: All ceilings are a minimum of 9-ft. high.

- Great Room: This entertainment area, with a 12-ft.-high ceiling, features a gas fireplace and has views of the front yard through round-top windows and doors.

- Kitchen: This kitchen fulfills all the needs of the active family, plus it has a raised bar.

- Dining Room: Being adjacent to the kitchen allows this room to be practical as well as beautiful by means of the numerous windows overlooking the porch and backyard.

- Bedrooms: Vaulted ceilings in two of the three bedrooms provide a feeling of spaciousness. One bedroom has its own bathroom.

Images provided by designer/architect.

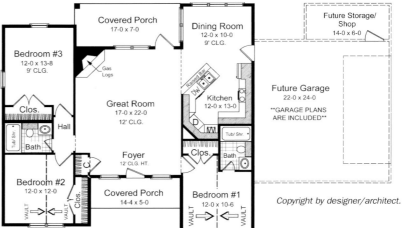

Copyright by designer/architect.

Front View

Plan #341300

Dimensions: 44' W x 38' D

Levels: 1

Square Footage: 1,334

Bedrooms: 3

Bathrooms: 2

Foundation: Crawl space, slab, basement, or walkout

Material List Available: Yes

Price Category: B

Images provided by designer/architect.

CAD FILE AVAILABLE

Copyright by designer/architect.

Plan #361490

Dimensions: 67' W x 37' D

Levels: 1

Square Footage: 1,356

Bedrooms: 3

Bathrooms: 2

Foundation: Crawl space

Material List Available: No

Price Category: B

Images provided by designer/architect.

CAD FILE AVAILABLE

Copyright by designer/architect.

Plan #381016

Dimensions: 32' W x 39'8" D

Levels: 1

Square Footage: 910

Bedrooms: 2

Bathrooms: 1

Foundation: Basement

Materials List Available: Yes

Price Category: A

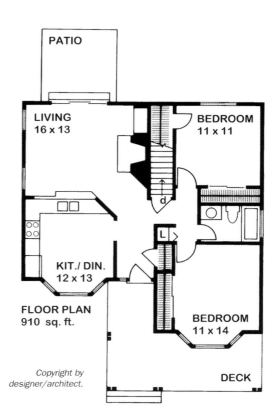

Images provided by designer/architect.

PATIO

LIVING
16 x 13

BEDROOM
11 x 11

KIT./ DIN.
12 x 13

FLOOR PLAN
910 sq. ft.

BEDROOM
11 x 14

DECK

Copyright by designer/architect.

Plan #321023

Dimensions: 39'8" W x 41' D

Levels: 1

Square Footage: 1,092

Bedrooms: 3

Bathrooms: 1½

Foundation: Basement

Materials List Available: Yes

Price Category: B

Images provided by designer/architect.

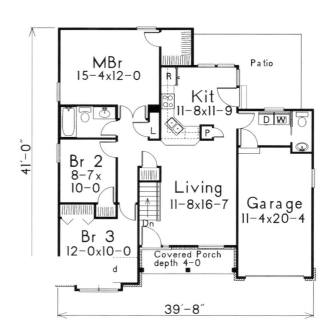

MBr
15-4x12-0

Patio

Kit
11-8x11-9

Br 2
8-7x
10-0

Living
11-8x16-7

Garage
11-4x20-4

Br 3
12-0x10-0

Covered Porch
depth 4-0

41'-0"

39'-8"

Copyright by designer/architect.

Plan #131004

Dimensions: 59'4" W x 35'8" D

Levels: 1

Square Footage: 1,097

Bedrooms: 3

Bathrooms: 2

Foundation: Crawl space, slab, or basement

Materials List Available: Yes

Price Category: B

You'll love the extra features you'll find in this charming but easy-to-build ranch home.

Features:

- Porch: This full-width porch is graced with impressive round columns, decorative railings, and ornamental moldings.

- Living Room: Just beyond the front door, the living room entrance has a railing that creates the illusion of a hallway. The 10-ft. tray ceiling makes this room feel spacious.

- Dining Room: Flowing from the living room, this room has a 9-ft.-high stepped ceiling and leads to sliding glass doors that open to the large rear patio.

- Kitchen: This kitchen is adjacent to the dining room for convenience and has a large island for efficient work patterns.

- Master Suite: Enjoy the privacy in this bedroom with its private bathroom.

This home, as shown in the photograph, may differ from the actual blueprints. For more detailed information, please check the floor plans carefully.

Images provided by designer/architect.

Alternate Basement Floor Plan

Copyright by designer/architect.

Plan #401047

Dimensions: 38' W x 34' D
Levels: 1
Square Footage: 1,064
Bedrooms: 2
Bathrooms: 1
Foundation: Basement
Materials List Available: Yes
Price Category: B

This farmhouse squeezes space-efficient features into its compact plan. Twin dormer windows flood the vaulted interior with natural light and accentuate the high ceilings.

Images provided by designer/architect.

Features:

- Porch: This cozy front porch opens into a vaulted great room and its adjoining dining room.

- Great Room: A warm hearth in this gathering place for the family adds to its coziness.

- Kitchen: This U-shaped kitchen has a breakfast bar open to the dining room and a sink overlooking a flower box. Nearby side-door access is found in the handy laundry room.

- Bedrooms: Vaulted bedrooms are positioned along the back of the plan. They contain wall closets and share a full bathroom with a soaking tub.

- Future Expansion: An open-rail staircase leads to the basement, which can be developed into living or sleeping space at a later time, if needed.

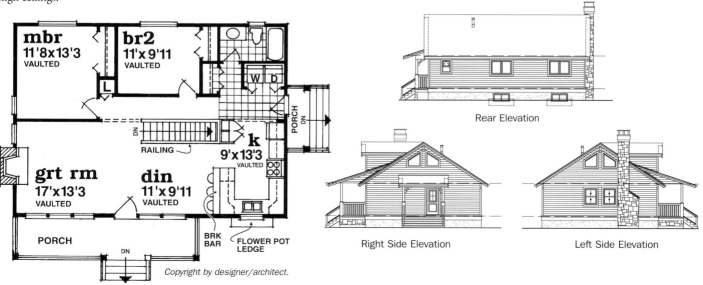

Rear Elevation

Right Side Elevation

Left Side Elevation

Copyright by designer/architect.

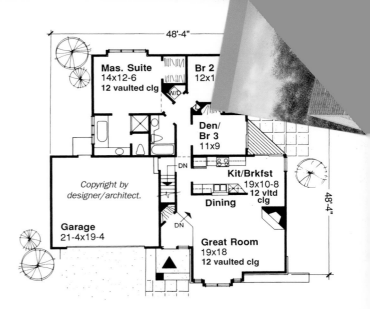

Copyright by designer/architect.

Plan #271005

Dimensions: 48'4" W x 48'4" D

Levels: 1

Square Footage: 1,368

Bedrooms: 3

Bathrooms: 2

Foundation: Basement

Materials List Available: Yes

Price Category: B

Images provided by designer/architect.

Plan #341229

Dimensions: 50' W x 38'2" D

Levels: 1

Square Footage: 1,445

Bedrooms: 3

Bathrooms: 2

Foundation: Crawl space, slab, basement, or walkout

Materials List Available: Yes

Price Category: B

Images provided by designer/architect.

Copyright by designer/architect.

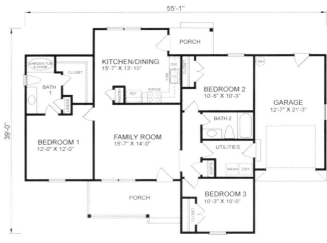

Images provided by designer/architect.

Copyright by designer/architect.

Plan #341287

Dimensions: 55'1" W x 39' D

Levels: 1

Square Footage: 1,217

Bedrooms: 3

Bathrooms: 2

Foundation: Crawl space, slab, basement, or walkout

Material List Available: Yes

Price Category: B

Images provided by designer/architect.

Copyright by designer/architect.

Optional Basement Level Floor Plan

Plan #371093

Dimensions: 50' W x 45' D

Levels: 1

Square Footage: 1,300

Bedrooms: 3

Bathrooms: 2

Foundation: Crawl space, slab, or basement

Material List Available: No

Price Category: B

Plan #391042

Dimensions: 50' W x 40' D
Levels: 1
Square Footage: 1,307
Bedrooms: 3
Bathrooms: 2
Foundation: Crawl space, slab, or basement
Materials List Available: Yes
Price Category: B

This home, as shown in the photograph, may differ from the actual blueprints. For more detailed information, please check the floor plans carefully.

Images provided by designer/architect.

This comfortable home has an air of cozy seclusion in an economical design.

Features:

• Living Room: Open ceiling beams lend height and space to this roomy living room. It is an area that's ideal for gathering and entertainment.

• Kitchen: This efficiently designed L-shape kitchen opens directly into the dining room, making transitions simple. The laundry room is just a few footsteps away, the perfect distance for cleaning up table linens and other kitchen messes.

• Master Suite: Imagine a relaxing breakfast in bed in a room with a vaulted ceiling, a large closet. and a full master bath. Close enough to the other bedrooms without sacrificing privacy, you can be near your loved ones.

• Bedrooms: Both secondary bedrooms have easy access to the nearby full bathroom. If a third bedroom is unnecessary, the space could be used equally well as a den.

Copyright by designer/architect.

Rear View

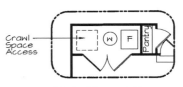

Slab/Crawl Space Option Floor Plan

Plan #251003

Dimensions: 42' W x 42' D
Levels: 1
Square Footage: 1,393
Bedrooms: 3
Bathrooms: 2
Foundation: Crawl space or slab
Materials List Available: Yes
Price Category: B

Come home to this three-bedroom home with front porch and unattached garage.

Features:

- Family Room: This room feels large and warm, with its high ceiling and cozy fireplace.

- Kitchen: This island kitchen with dining area has plenty of cabinet space.

- Master Bedroom: This large master bedroom features a walk-in closet and a view of the backyard.

- Master Bath: Located in the rear of the home, this master bath features a soaking tub and a separate shower.

Images provided by designer/architect.

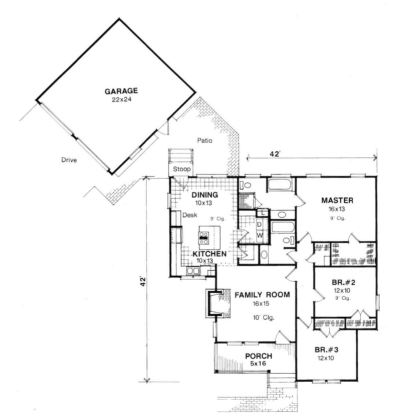

Copyright by designer/architect.

Plan #271001

Dimensions: 52'8" W x 35'4" D
Levels: 1
Square Footage: 1,400
Bedrooms: 3
Bathrooms: 2
Foundation: Basement
Materials List Available: Yes
Price Category: B

This contemporary design builds on the basics, creating a comfortable home that offers possibilities for entertaining or quiet downtime.

Features:

• Great room: The heart of the home, this massive gathering room features a handsome fireplace and a handy wet bar, and flows into the dining space. Sliding glass doors between the two spaces lead to a deck.

• Kitchen/Breakfast: This combination space uses available space efficiently and comfortably.

• Master Suite: The inviting master bedroom includes a private bath.

Images provided by designer/architect.

Copyright by designer/architect.

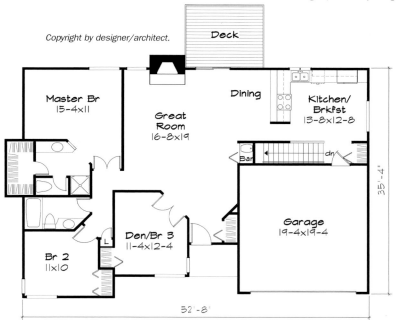

SMARTtip

Candid Camera for Your Landscaping

To see your home and yard as others see them, take some camera shots. Seeing your house and landscaping on film will create an opportunity for objectivity. Problems will become more obvious, and you will then be better able to prioritize your home improvements, as well as your landscaping plan.

Plan #391069

Dimensions: 56' W x 48' D

Levels: 1

Square Footage: 1,492

Bedrooms: 3

Bathrooms: 2

Foundation: Crawl space, slab, or basement

Materials List Available: Yes

Price Category: B

This design opens wide from the living room to the kitchen and dining room. All on one level, even the bedrooms are easy to reach.

Features:

- Living Room: This special room features a fireplace and entry to the deck.

- Dining Room: This formal room shows off special ceiling effects.

- Bedrooms: Bedroom 3 is inspired by a decorative ceiling, and bedroom 2 has double closet doors. There's a nearby bath for convenience.

- Master Suite: This private area features a roomy walk-in closet and private bath.

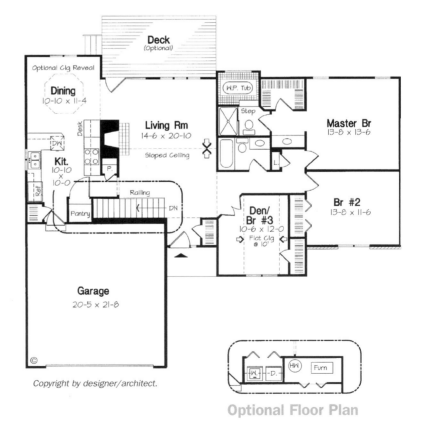

Copyright by designer/architect.

Optional Floor Plan

Plan #151336

Dimensions: 39'4" W x 63'2" D

Levels: 1

Square Footage: 1,480

Bedrooms: 3

Bathrooms: 2

Foundation: Crawl space or slab

CompleteCost List Available: Yes

Price Category: B

Images provided by designer/architect.

CAD FILE AVAILABLE

Copyright by designer/architect.

Front View

Plan #341285

Dimensions: 74'6" W x 37'5" D

Levels: 1

Square Footage: 1,481

Bedrooms: 3

Bathrooms: 2

Foundation: Crawl space, slab, basement, or walkout

Material List Available: Yes

Price Category: B

Images provided by designer/architect.

CAD FILE AVAILABLE

Copyright by designer/architect.

Plan #121137

Dimensions: 42' W x 54' D
Levels: 1
Square Footage: 1,392
Bedrooms: 3
Bathrooms: 2
Foundation: Basement; crawl space for fee
Material List Available: Yes
Price Category: B

Siding and brick make a charming combination on this contemporary home, which makes a great start for young families.

Features:

• Great Room: Just through the entryway, this great room welcomes guests and provides an area that's ideal for family gatherings and entertaining.

• Kitchen: An efficient space, this kitchen features a snack bar and stands near the laundry room, the great room, and the breakfast room. The trio of windows in the breakfast room functions to extend and open the kitchen area.

• Master Suite: Privately tucked away, this bedroom suite features a walk-in closet and a full master bath with dual sinks, shower stall, and large tub.

• Secondary Bedrooms: These bright bedrooms are also slightly isolated and share the second full bathroom.

Images provided by designer/architect.

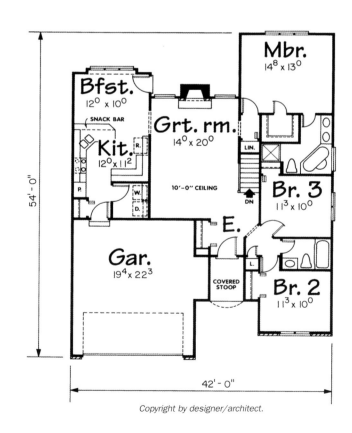

Copyright by designer/architect.

Plan #121002

Dimensions: 42' W x 54' D

Levels: 1

Square Footage: 1,347

Bedrooms: 3

Bathrooms: 2

Foundation: Basement

Materials List Available: Yes

Price Category: B

This home's convenient single level and luxury amenities are a recipe for gracious living.

Features:

- Ceiling Height: 8 ft. except as noted.

- Great Room: The entry enjoys a long view into this great room where a pair of transom-topped windows flanks the fireplace and a 10-ft. ceiling visually expands the space.

- Snack Bar: This special feature adjoins the great room, making it a real plus for informal entertaining, as well as the perfect spot for family get-togethers.

- Kitchen: An island is the centerpiece of this well-designed convenient kitchen that features a door to the backyard, a pantry, and convenient access to the laundry room.

- Master Suite: Located at the back of the home for extra privacy, the master suite feels like its own world. It features a tiered ceiling and sunlit corner whirlpool.

Images provided by designer/architect.

This home, as shown in the photograph, may differ from the actual blueprints. For more detailed information, please check the floor plans carefully.

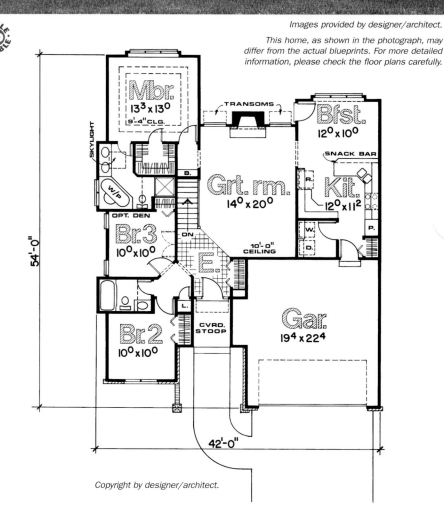

Copyright by designer/architect.

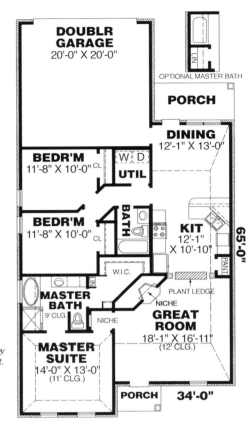

Plan #241040

Dimensions: 34' W x 65' D

Levels: 1

Square Footage: 1,468

Bedrooms: 3

Bathrooms: 2

Foundation: Slab

Material List Available: No

Price Category: B

Images provided by designer/architect.

Copyright by designer/architect.

DOUBLR GARAGE 20'-0" X 20'-0"

OPTIONAL MASTER BATH

PORCH

DINING 12'-1" X 13'-0"

BEDR'M 11'-8" X 10'-0" CL

W D

UTIL

BEDR'M 11'-8" X 10'-0" CL

BATH

KIT 12'-1" X 10'-10"

W.I.C.

PANT

65'-0"

LIN

MASTER BATH 9' CLG.

NICHE

PLANT LEDGE

NICHE

GREAT ROOM 18'-1" X 16'-11" (12' CLG.)

MASTER SUITE 14'-0" X 13'-0" (11' CLG.)

PORCH

34'-0"

Plan #341290

Dimensions: 50'8" W x 49' D

Levels: 1

Square Footage: 1,472

Bedrooms: 3

Bathrooms: 2

Foundation: Crawl space, slab, basement, or walkout

Material List Available: Yes

Price Category: B

Images provided by designer/architect.

CAD FILE **CAD** AVAILABLE

50'-8"

PORCH

DINING 10'-10" X 11'-0"

SHWR

GARDEN TUB

BATH 1

MASTER SUITE 15'-0" X 11'-2"

FAMILY ROOM 13'-8" X 21'-2"

RANGE

KITCH. 10'-10" X 9'-9"

DW

REF

BATH 2

CLOSET

49'-0"

STOR

CLOSET

CLOSET

WH

FOYER

COATS

GARAGE 20'-5" X 20'-7"

BEDROOM 3 11'-1" X 10'-0"

BEDROOM 2 12'-2" X 10'-0"

PORCH

Copyright by designer/architect.

Plan #251001

Dimensions: 61'3" W x 40'6" D
Levels: 1
Square Footage: 1,253
Bedrooms: 3
Bathrooms: 2
Foundation: Crawl space, slab
Materials List Available: No
Price Category: B

This charming country home has a classic full front porch for enjoying summertime breezes.

Features:

- Ceiling Height: 8 ft.

- Foyer: Guests will walk through the front porch into this foyer, which opens to the family room.

- Screened Porch: A second porch is screened and is located at the rear of the home off the dining room, so your guests can step out for a bit of fresh air after dinner.

- Family Room: Family and friends will be drawn to this large open space, with its handsome fireplace and sloped ceiling.

- Kitchen: This open and airy kitchen is a pleasure in which to work. It has ample counter space and a pantry.

- Master Bedroom: This master bedroom features a large walk-in closet. It has its own master bath with a single vanity, a tub, and a walk-in shower.

- Garage: This attached garage provides plenty of extra storage space, as well as parking for two cars.

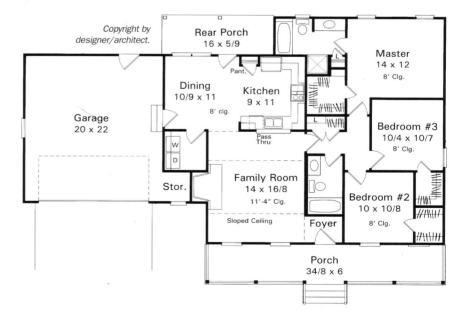

Plan #151529

Dimensions: 43' W x 66'6" D
Levels: 1
Square Footage: 1,474
Bedrooms: 2
Bathrooms: 2
Foundation: Crawl space or slab
CompleteCost List Available: Yes
Price Category: B

Images provided by designer/architect.

This elegant design is reflective of the Arts and Crafts era. Copper roofing and carriage style garage doors warmly welcome guests into this split-bedroom plan.

Features:

- Great Room: With access to the grilling porch as a bonus, this large gathering area features a 10-ft.-high ceiling and a beautiful fireplace.

- Kitchen: This fully equipped island kitchen has a raised bar and a built-in pantry. The area is open to the great room and dining room, giving an open and airy feeling to the home.

- Master Suite: Located on the opposite side of the home from the secondary bedroom, this retreat offers a large sleeping area and two large closets. The master bath features a spa tub, a separate shower, and dual vanities.

- Bedroom: This secondary bedroom has a large closet and access to the full bathroom in the hallway.

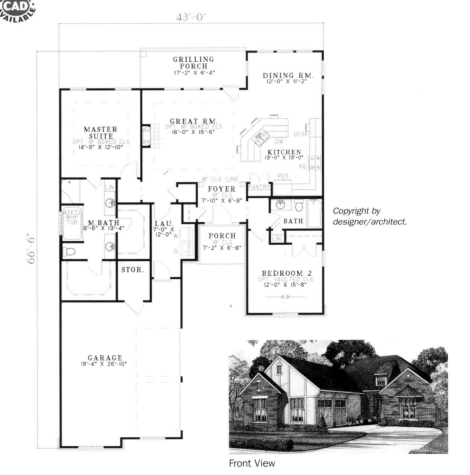

Copyright by designer/architect.

Front View

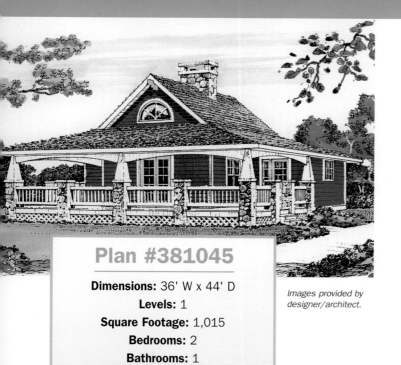

Plan #381045

Dimensions: 36' W x 44' D

Levels: 1

Square Footage: 1,015

Bedrooms: 2

Bathrooms: 1

Foundation: Crawl space

Material List Available: Yes

Price Category: B

Images provided by designer/architect.

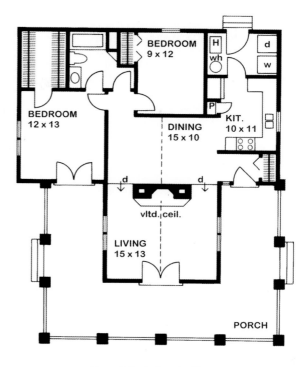

Copyright by designer/architect.

Plan #241019

Dimensions: 46'6" W x 34'2" D

Levels: 1

Square Footage: 1,397

Bedrooms: 3

Bathrooms: 2

Foundation: Slab

Materials List Available: No

Price Category: B

Images provided by designer/architect.

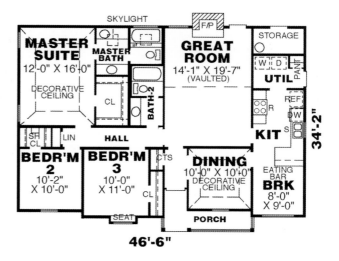

Copyright by designer/architect.

Plan #141005

Dimensions: 38' W x 66' D

Levels: 1

Square Footage: 1,532

Bedrooms: 3

Bathrooms: 2

Foundation: Slab, basement

Materials List Available: Yes

Price Category: C

Images provided by designer/architect.

Living Room

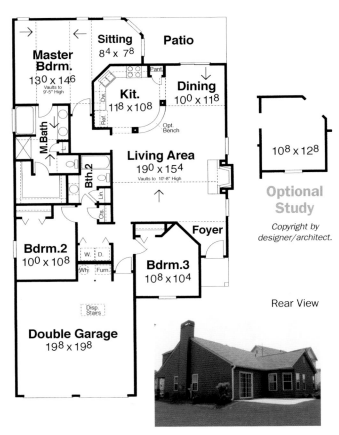

Master Bdrm. 13⁰ x 14⁶
Vaults to 9'-5" High

Sitting 8⁴ x 7⁸

Patio

M.Bath

Kit. 11⁸ x 10⁸

Dining 10⁰ x 11⁸

Opt. Bench

Living Area 19⁰ x 15⁴
Vaults to 10'-8" High

Bth.2

Bdrm.2 10⁰ x 10⁸

Bdrm.3 10⁸ x 10⁴

Foyer

Double Garage 19⁸ x 19⁸

Disp. Stairs

Optional Study 10⁸ x 12⁸

Copyright by designer/architect.

Rear View

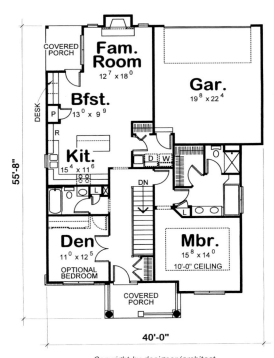

Plan #121013

Dimensions: 40' W x 55'8" D

Levels: 1

Square Footage: 1,375

Bedrooms: 1

Bathrooms: 2

Foundation: Basement

Materials List Available: Yes

Price Category: B

Images provided by designer/architect.

CAD FILE AVAILABLE

COVERED PORCH

Fam. Room 12⁷ x 18⁰

Gar. 19⁸ x 22⁴

Bfst. 13⁰ x 9⁹

DESK

Kit. 15⁴ x 11⁶

Den 11⁰ x 12⁵
OPTIONAL BEDROOM

Mbr. 15⁸ x 14⁰
10'-0" CEILING

DN

55'-8"

40'-0"

COVERED PORCH

Copyright by designer/architect.

Plan #151010

Dimensions: 38'4" W x 68'6" D
Levels: 1
Square Footage: 1,379
Bedrooms: 3
Bathrooms: 2
Foundation: Crawl space, slab
CompleteCost List Available: Yes
Price Category: B

CAD FILE AVAILABLE

This French Country home has a spacious great room for friends and family to gather, but you can sneak away to the covered rear porch or patio off the master suite for cozy tête-à-têtes.

Features:

- Entry: Take advantage of the marvelous 10-ft. ceilings to hang groups of potted flowering plants.

- Great Room: This spacious room, with an optional 10-ft. boxed ceiling, is the place to curl up by the gas fireplace on a cold winter night.

- Kitchen: The kitchen includes a bar for casual meals, and is open to the breakfast room.

- Rear Porch: Enjoy leisurely meals on the covered rear porch that you can access from both the master suite and the breakfast room.

- Master Suite: The 10-ft. boxed ceiling in the bedroom and the master bath with a whirlpool tub and separate shower make this suite a luxurious place to end a long day.

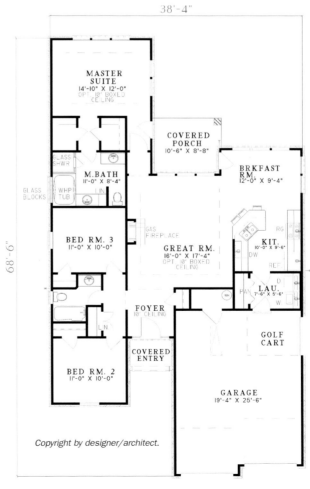

Copyright by designer/architect.

Plan #351013

Dimensions: 30' W x 36' D
Levels: 1
Square Footage: 800
Bedrooms: 2
Bathrooms: 1
Foundation: Crawl space or basement
Materials List Available: Yes
Price Category: B

The design and layout of this home bring back the memories of days gone by and places in which we feel comfortable.

Features:

- Living Room: When you enter this room from the front porch, you can feel the warmth from its fireplace.

- Kitchen: This kitchen features a raised bar and is open to the living room.

- Bedrooms: Two equally sized bedrooms share a common bathroom located in the hall.

- Screened Porch: Located in the rear of the home and accessible from bedroom 1 and the kitchen, this area is for relaxing.

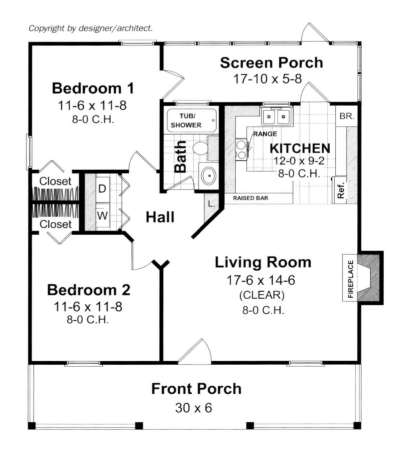

Screen Porch 17-10 x 5-8

Bedroom 1 11-6 x 11-8 8-0 C.H.

TUB/SHOWER

RANGE

BR.

KITCHEN 12-0 x 9-2 8-0 C.H.

Bath

Ref.

Closet

D

RAISED BAR

L.

Closet

W

Hall

Bedroom 2 11-6 x 11-8 8-0 C.H.

Living Room 17-6 x 14-6 (CLEAR) 8-0 C.H.

FIREPLACE

Front Porch 30 x 6

Plan #391006

Dimensions: 50' W x 45'4" D
Levels: 1
Square Footage: 1,456
Bedrooms: 3
Bathrooms: 2
Foundation: Crawl space, slab, or basement
Materials List Available: Yes
Price Category: B

Celebrating the union of beauty and function, this single-level layout makes a large appearance, with its peaked rooflines, elongated windowing, and sloping ceilings in the living room and bedroom #3 (or home office).

Features:

• Foyer: Soft angles define the space in the house, beginning with this foyer entry that curves to all the important rooms.

• Master Suite: Private rooms gather on the opposite side of the plan, with this master suite owning special windowing, an enormous walk-in closet, and a highly specialized bathroom with compartments that maintain privacy as two people use the various facilities at once.

• Bedroom: This other secondary bedroom enjoys a full bath and plenty of closet space.

• Utility Areas: Laundry facilities are easy to access, and a two-car garage has convenient front entry.

Images provided by designer/architect.

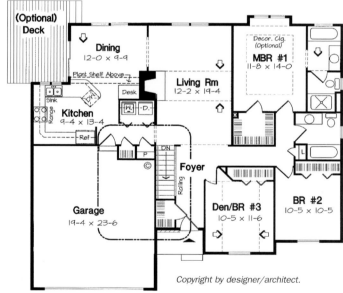

Copyright by designer/architect.

Crawl Space/ Slab Option

Rear View

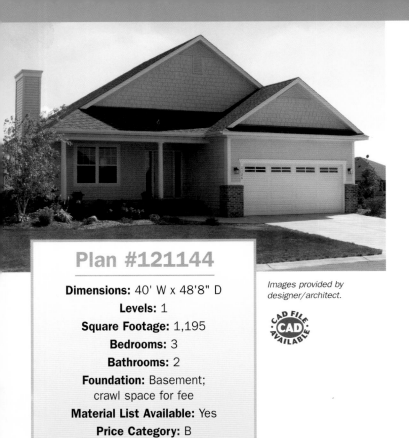

Plan #121144

Dimensions: 40' W x 48'8" D

Levels: 1

Square Footage: 1,195

Bedrooms: 3

Bathrooms: 2

Foundation: Basement; crawl space for fee

Material List Available: Yes

Price Category: B

Images provided by designer/architect.

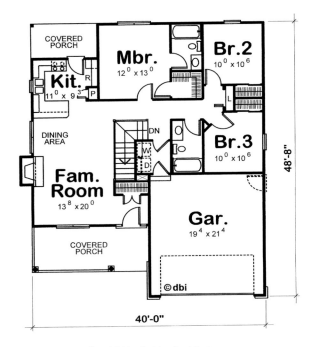

Copyright by designer/architect.

Plan #241036

Dimensions: 33' W x 57'4" D

Levels: 1

Square Footage: 1,166

Bedrooms: 2

Bathrooms: 2

Foundation: Slab

Material List Available: No

Price Category: B

Images provided by designer/architect.

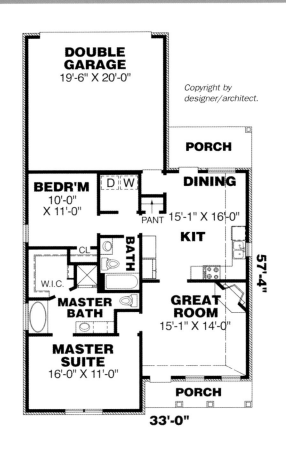

Copyright by designer/architect.

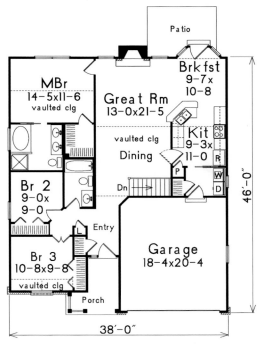

Plan #321033

Dimensions: 38' W x 46' D

Levels: 1

Square Footage: 1,268

Bedrooms: 3

Bathrooms: 2

Foundation: Basement

Materials List Available: Yes

Price Category: B

Images provided by designer/architect.

Copyright by designer/architect.

MBr
14-5x11-6
vaulted clg

Br 2
9-0x
9-0

Br 3
10-8x9-8
vaulted clg

Entry

Great Rm
13-0x21-5

vaulted clg
Dining

Dn

Patio

Brk fst
9-7 x
10-8

Kit
9-3x
11-0

P

W D

Garage
18-4x20-4

Porch

46'-0"

38'-0"

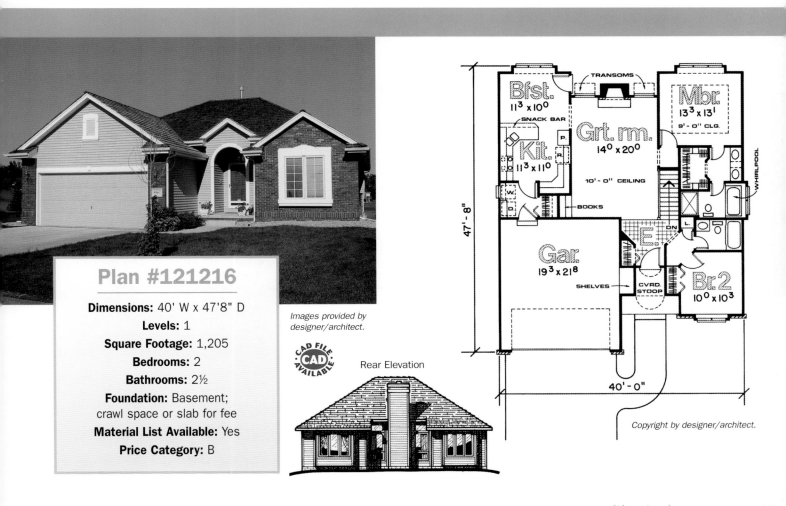

Plan #121216

Dimensions: 40' W x 47'8" D

Levels: 1

Square Footage: 1,205

Bedrooms: 2

Bathrooms: 2½

Foundation: Basement; crawl space or slab for fee

Material List Available: Yes

Price Category: B

Images provided by designer/architect.

CAD FILE AVAILABLE

Rear Elevation

Bfst.
11³ x10⁰

SNACK BAR

Kit.
11³ x11⁰

Grt. rm.
14⁰ x20⁰

10'-0" CEILING

BOOKS

TRANSOMS

Mbr.
13³ x13¹
9'-0" CLG.

WHIRLPOOL

Gar.
19³ x21⁸

SHELVES

CVRD. STOOP

Br 2
10⁰ x10³

47'-8"

40'-0"

Copyright by designer/architect.

Plan #191030

Dimensions: 33' W x 36' D
Levels: 1
Square Footage: 864
Bedrooms: 2
Bathrooms: 1
Foundation: Crawl space or slab
Materials List Available: No
Price Category: A

Images provided by designer/architect.

Enjoy the view from the spacious front porch of this cozy cottage, which is ideal for a retirement home, vacation retreat, or starter home.

Features:

• **Porch:** This 6-ft.-wide porch, which runs the length of the home, gives you plenty of space to set up a couple of rockers next to a potted herb garden.

• **Living/Dining Room:** This huge living and dining area gives you many options for design. The snack bar that it shares with the kitchen is a practical touch.

• **Kitchen:** The first thing you'll notice in this well-planned kitchen is how much counter and storage space it offers.

• **Laundry Room:** Opening to the backyard, this room also features ample storage space.

• **Bedrooms:** Both rooms have good closet space and easy access to the large, luxurious bath.

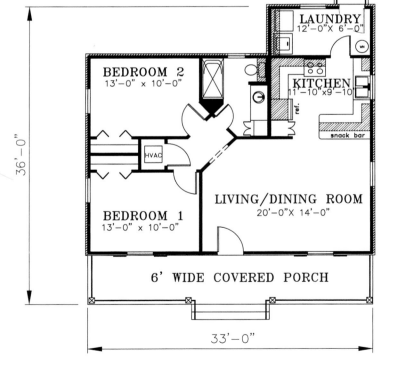

Copyright by designer/architect.

Plan #321035

Dimensions: 55'8" W x 46' D
Levels: 1
Square Footage: 1,384
Bedrooms: 2
Bathrooms: 2
Foundation: Walkout
Materials List Available: Yes
Price Category: B

Images provided by designer/architect.

You'll love the way the two-story atrium windows meld this home with your sloped site.

Features:

- **Great Room:** A masonry fireplace, vaulted ceiling, huge bayed area, and stairs to the atrium below make this room a natural gathering spot.

- **Dining Area:** You'll love sitting here and admiring the view by sunlight or starlight.

- **Kitchen:** An angled bar is both a snack bar and work space in this well-designed kitchen with an attached laundry room.

- **Master Suite:** Double doors open into the spacious bedroom with a huge walk-in closet. The bath has a garden tub, separate shower, and double vanity.

- **Optional Basement Plan:** Take advantage of this space to build a family room, media room, or home studio that's lit by the huge atrium windows and opens to the patio.

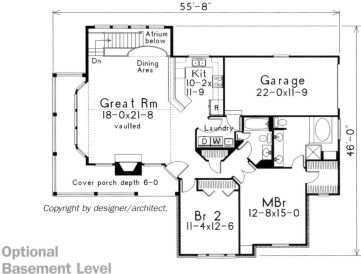

Copyright by designer/architect.

**Optional
Basement Level
Floor Plan**

Rear View

Plan #131013

Dimensions: 50' W x 41'8" D
Levels: 1
Square Footage: 1,489
Bedrooms: 3
Bathrooms: 2
Foundation: Crawl space, slab or basement
Materials List Available: Yes
Price Category: C

Images provided by designer/architect.

You'll love the Victorian details on the exterior of this charming ranch-style home.

Features:

- Front Porch: This porch is large enough so that you can sit out on warm summer nights to catch a breeze or create a garden of potted ornamentals.

- Great Room: Running from the front of the house to the rear, this great room is bathed in natural light from both directions. The volume ceiling adds a luxurious feeling to it, and the fireplace creates a cozy place on chilly afternoons.

- Kitchen: Cooking will be a pleasure in this kitchen, thanks to the thoughtful layout and well-designed work areas.

- Master Suite: Enjoy the quiet in this room, where it will be easy to relax and unwind, no matter what the time of day. The walk-in closet gives you plenty of storage space, and you're sure to appreciate both the privacy and large size of the master bath.

WICL

TRAY CEIL
MSTR BEDRM
12'-4"x
15'-2"

MSTR BATH

BATH

CL

VAULTED
BEDRM #2
11'-2"x
10'-0"

VAULTED
BEDRM #3
10'-4"x
12'-0"

SEAT

10'-0" CLG STEPPED CLG
GREAT RM
15'-4"x
20'-6"

CL CL

LIN

BKFST RM
8'-2"/ 10'-4"
x 15'-8"

KIT

STEPPED CLG
DINING RM
10'-0"x
11'-0"

CL

COV. PORCH

LAUN RM

REF

W D

OPTIONAL
TWO CAR GARAGE
20'-4"x 19'-6"

Copyright by designer/architect.

Rear Elevation

Plan #351077

Dimensions: 54' W x 47' D

Levels: 1

Square Footage: 1,426

Bedrooms: 3

Bathrooms: 2

Foundation: Crawl space, slab, or basement

Material List Available: Yes

Price Category: C

This home features many of the most-requested features in a space efficient design.

Features:

- **Great Room:** When you enter the lovely home from the covered porch, this large gathering area greets you. The open floor plan allows you to look through the dining room and out to the backyard.

- **Kitchen:** This peninsula kitchen has an abundance of cabinets and counter space. The open counter, which reaches into the dining room, will be a great place to sit and be involved in conversations in the kitchen or great room.

- **Master Suite:** Located on the opposite side of the home from the secondary bedrooms, this retreat offers its large sleeping area a view of the backyard. His and her bathrooms each feature walk in closets; one bathroom boasts a garden tub.

- **Garage:** This front-loading two-car garage has ample room for cars and a storage area.

Rear Elevation

Copyright by designer/architect.

Optional Basement Level Floor Plan

Plan #511016

Dimensions: 50' W x 49'6" D

Levels: 1

Square Footage: 1,294

Bedrooms: 3

Bathrooms: 2

Foundation: Crawl space or slab

Material List Available: No

Price Category: B

Images provided by designer/architect.

Copyright by designer/architect.

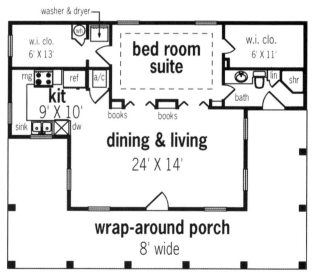

Plan #211153

Dimensions: 40' W x 34' D

Levels: 1

Square Footage: 848

Bedrooms: 1

Bathrooms: 1

Foundation: Crawl space

Material List Available: No

Price Category: A

Images provided by designer/architect.

Copyright by designer/architect.

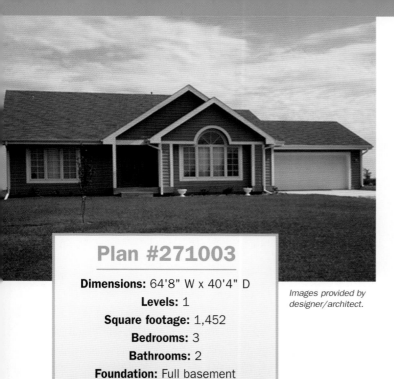

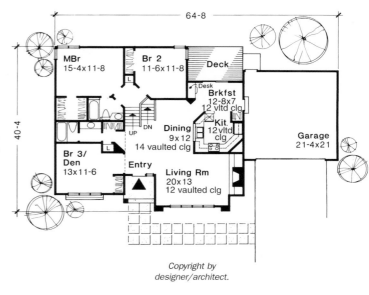

Images provided by designer/architect.

Plan #271003

Dimensions: 64'8" W x 40'4" D

Levels: 1

Square footage: 1,452

Bedrooms: 3

Bathrooms: 2

Foundation: Full basement

Materials List Available: Yes

Price Category: B

Copyright by designer/architect.

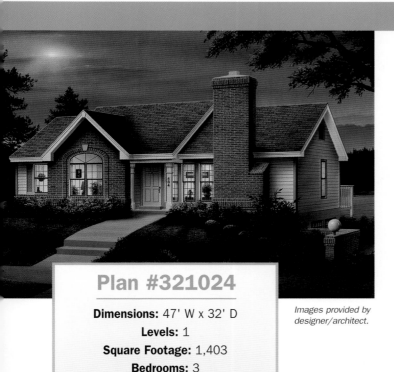

Images provided by designer/architect.

Plan #321024

Dimensions: 47' W x 32' D

Levels: 1

Square Footage: 1,403

Bedrooms: 3

Bathrooms: 1-2

Foundation: Daylight basement

Materials List Available: Yes

Price Category: B

Copyright by designer/architect.

Optional Basement Level Floor Plan

Plan #321002

Dimensions: 72' W x 28' D
Levels: 1
Square Footage: 1,400
Bedrooms: 3
Bathrooms: 2
Foundation: Crawl space, basement
Materials List Available: Yes
Price Category: B

If you're looking for a well-designed compact home with contemporary amenities, this could be the home of your dreams.

Features:

- **Porch:** Just the right size for some rockers and a swing, this porch could become your outdoor living area when the weather is fine.

- **Living Room:** A vaulted ceiling adds to the spacious feeling in this room, where friends and family are sure to gather.

- **Kitchen:** This space-saving design, in combination with the ample counter and cabinet space, makes cooking a pleasure.

- **Utility Room:** This large room is fitted with cabinets for extra storage space. You'll find storage space in the large garage, too.

- **Master Bedroom:** This room is somewhat secluded for privacy, making it an ideal place for some quiet time at the end of the day.

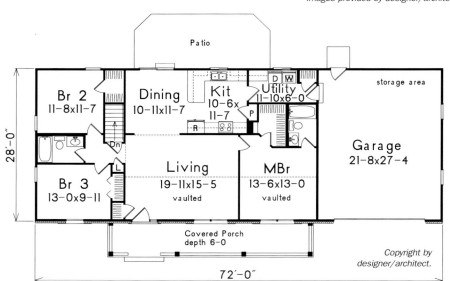

Copyright by designer/architect.

SMARTtip
Fabric Draping Ability

Test a fabric's draping ability by looking at a large piece in a fabric store. Gather at least two to three yards of material, holding one end in your hand. Check how it drapes. Does it fall into folds easily? Also look at the pattern when it is gathered. Does the design become lost in the folds? Ask a salesclerk or a friend to hold the fabric, and look at it from a few feet away.

Plan #121005

Dimensions: 48' W x 52' D
Levels: 1
Square Footage: 1,496
Bedrooms: 3
Bathrooms: 2
Foundation: Basement
Materials List Available: Yes
Price Category: B

CAD FILE AVAILABLE

A beautiful starter or retirement home with all the amenities you'd expect in a much bigger house.

Features:

• Ceiling Height: 8 ft.

• Great Room: A cathedral ceiling visually expands the great room making it the perfect place for family gatherings or formal entertaining.

• Formal Dining Room: This elegant room is ideal for entertaining dinner guests. It conveniently shares a wet bar and service counter with a bayed breakfast area next door.

• Breakfast Area: In addition to the service area shared with the dining room, this cozy area features a snack bar, pantry, and desk that's perfect for household paperwork.

• Master Suite: The master bedroom features special ceiling details. It's joined by a private bath with a whirlpool, shower, and spacious walk-in closet.

• Garage: The two-bay garage offers plenty of storage space.

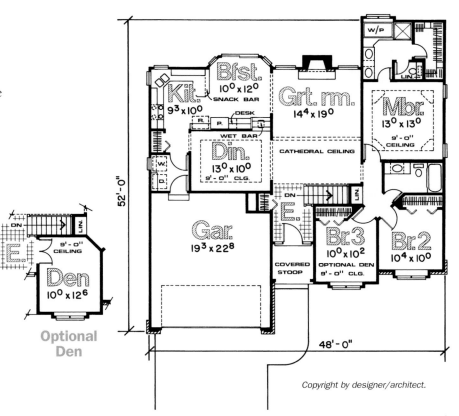

Optional Den

Copyright by designer/architect.

Plan #281031

Dimensions: 48' W x 58' D

Levels: 1

Square Footage: 1,493

Bedrooms: 3

Bathrooms: 2

Foundation: Basement or walkout

Material List Available: Yes

Price Category: B

Images provided by designer/architect.

Copyright by designer/architect.

Rear Elevation

Plan #211134

Dimensions: 48' W x 30' D

Levels: 1

Square Footage: 998

Bedrooms: 3

Bathrooms: 1

Foundation: Slab

Material List Available: Yes

Price Category: A

Images provided by designer/architect.

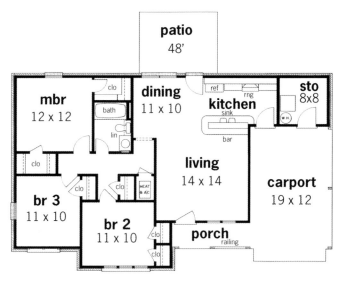

Copyright by designer/architect.

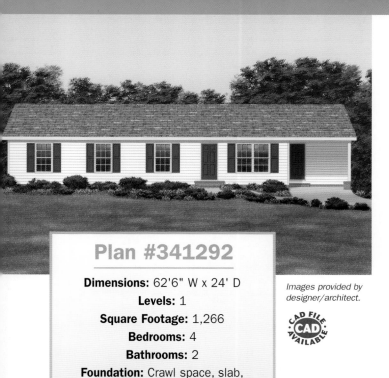

Plan #341292

Dimensions: 62'6" W x 24' D

Levels: 1

Square Footage: 1,266

Bedrooms: 4

Bathrooms: 2

Foundation: Crawl space, slab, basement, or walkout

Material List Available: Yes

Price Category: B

Images provided by designer/architect.

CAD FILE AVAILABLE

Copyright by designer/architect.

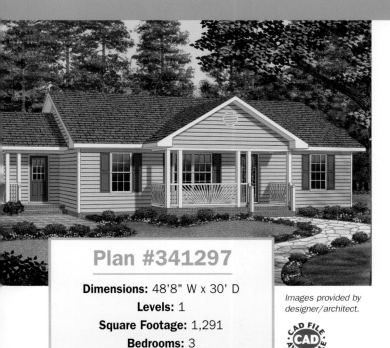

Plan #341297

Dimensions: 48'8" W x 30' D

Levels: 1

Square Footage: 1,291

Bedrooms: 3

Bathrooms: 2

Foundation: Crawl space, slab, basement, or walkout

Material List Available: Yes

Price Category: B

Images provided by designer/architect.

CAD FILE AVAILABLE

Copyright by designer/architect.

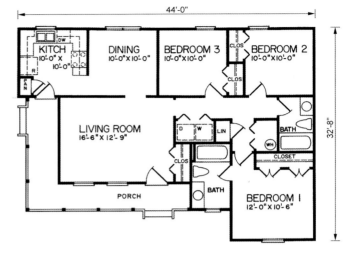

Plan #341299

Dimensions: 44' W x 32'8" D

Levels: 1

Square Footage: 1,115

Bedrooms: 3

Bathrooms: 2

Foundation: Crawl space, slab, basement, or walkout

Material List Available: Yes

Price Category: B

Images provided by designer/architect.

Copyright by designer/architect.

Plan #341302

Dimensions: 52'1" W x 39'11" D

Levels: 1

Square Footage: 1,317

Bedrooms: 3

Bathrooms: 2

Foundation: Crawl space, slab, basement, or walkout

Material List Available: Yes

Price Category: B

Images provided by designer/architect.

Copyright by designer/architect.

Plan #391064

Dimensions: 54' W x 28' D
Levels: 1
Square Footage: 988
Bedrooms: 3
Bathrooms: 2
Foundation: Crawl space, basement
Materials List Available: Yes
Price Category: A

Images provided by designer/architect.

Wishing for a sweet place of your own? Here's one that generates more comfort and style than many of its larger relatives.

Features:

• Facade: Gabled roofs, arched windows, and a covered patio charm the exterior.

• Dining Room: This curvaceous room is open to both the kitchen and living room for a big, bright feeling.

• Master Bedroom: This sanctuary features a bedroom and private bath.

• Bedrooms: Two secondary bedrooms share a full bath.

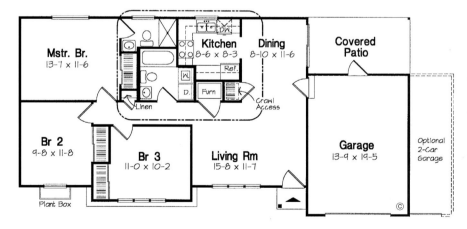

Copyright by designer/architect.

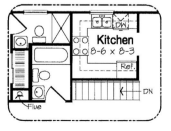

**Optional
Basement Level
Floor Plan**

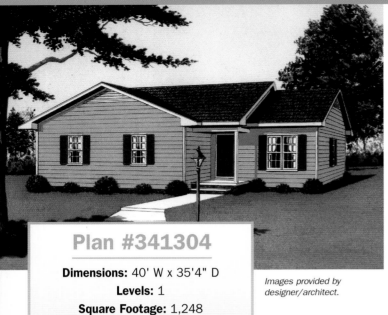

Plan #341304

Dimensions: 40' W x 35'4" D
Levels: 1
Square Footage: 1,248
Bedrooms: 3
Bathrooms: 2
Foundation: Crawl space, slab, basement, or walkout
Material List Available: Yes
Price Category: B

Images provided by designer/architect.

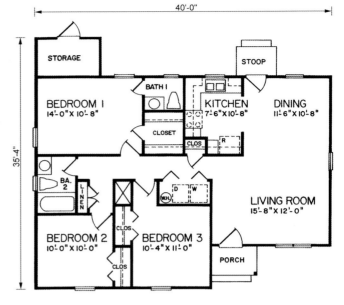

Copyright by designer/architect.

Plan #341307

Dimensions: 65'6" W x 38' D
Levels: 1
Square Footage: 1,358
Bedrooms: 3
Bathrooms: 2
Foundation: Crawl space, slab, basement, or walkout
Material List Available: Yes
Price Category: B

Images provided by designer/architect.

Copyright by designer/architect.

Plan #361517

Dimensions: 48' W x 60' D
Levels: 1
Square Footage: 1,321
Bedrooms: 2
Bathrooms: 2
Foundation: Crawl space
Material List Available: No
Price Category: B

Images provided by designer/architect.

This charismatic vacation home is full of amenities in an economical and proficient design.

CAD FILE AVAILABLE

Features:

- **Porch:** One rocking chair away from cool breezes and relaxing summer nights, this wraparound porch is perfect for stargazing or getting to know your neighbors.

- **Living Room:** An area full of possibilities, this spacious area has a vaulted ceiling and flows into the dining room. Together or separately, these areas are ready to accommodate everything and everyone.

- **Kitchen:** With a utility room through one walkway and the living room through another, both the one-time cook and the gourmet chef will appreciate the convenience and efficiency of this design. A vaulted ceiling lends space to the area.

- **Utility Area:** Next to the busiest room of the house-the kitchen-this utility room has an abundance of cabinets and work-space, as well as a laundry area, to simplify your life at home. Even more convenient: this area opens to the garage, serving several purposes.

- **Bedrooms:** Both the master suite and the second bedroom have everything you need, with plenty of room, large full bathrooms and lots of closet space for everyone.

Copyright by designer/architect.

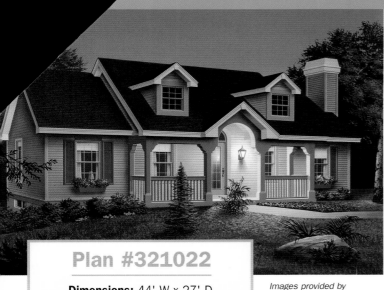

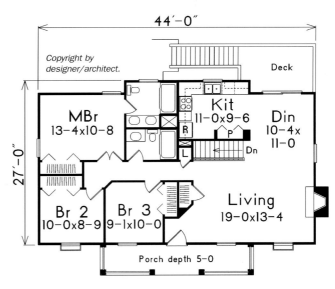

Deck

MBr
13-4x10-8

Kit
11-0x9-6

Din
10-4x
11-0

Br 2
10-0x8-9

Br 3
9-1x10-0

Living
19-0x13-4

Porch depth 5-0

44'-0"

27'-0"

Images provided by designer/architect.

Plan #321022

Dimensions: 44' W x 27' D
Levels: 1
Square Footage: 1,140
Bedrooms: 3
Bathrooms: 2
Foundation: Basement
Materials List Available: Yes
Price Category: B

SMARTtip
Basement Moldings

Keep moldings simple in a basement with lower ceilings. Elaborate moldings around the ceiling or floor can shorten the height of the room.

MASTER BEDROOM
11-6 X 15

BRK'FST

FAMILY ROOM
13-6 X 19-6

KIT

BEDROOM 3
11 X 10

BEDROOM 2
11 X 11

ENTRY

DINING ROOM
12-9 X 11

STOOP

Images provided by designer/architect.

UNFINISHED SPACE

GARAGE
22-3 X 30

Basement Level Floor Plan

Plan #461093

Dimensions: 42'10" W x 30'6" D
Levels: 1
Square Footage: 1,371
Bedrooms: 3
Bathrooms: 2
Foundation: Slab or basement
Material List Available: No
Price Category: B

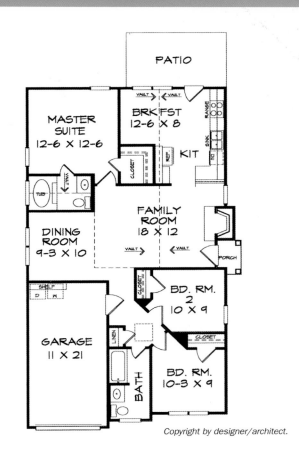

Plan #461097

Dimensions: 30' W x 50' D

Levels: 1

Square Footage: 1,123

Bedrooms: 3

Bathrooms: 2

Foundation: Slab; crawl space or basement for fee

Material List Available: No

Price Category: B

Images provided by designer/architect.

Copyright by designer/architect.

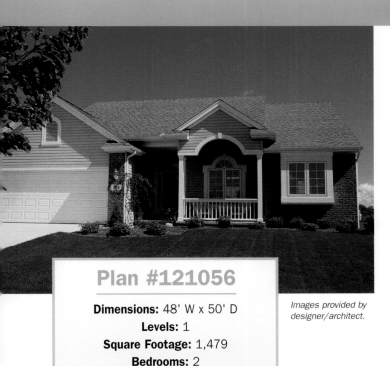

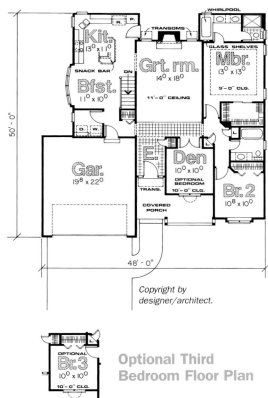

Plan #121056

Dimensions: 48' W x 50' D

Levels: 1

Square Footage: 1,479

Bedrooms: 2

Bathrooms: 2

Foundation: Basement

Materials List Available: Yes

Price Category: B

Images provided by designer/architect.

Copyright by designer/architect.

Optional Third Bedroom Floor Plan

Plan #361516

Dimensions: 30' W x 64' D
Levels: 1
Square Footage: 1,237
Bedrooms: 3
Bathrooms: 2
Foundation: Crawl space
Material List Available: No
Price Category: B

Modest and charming, this comfortable ranch-style home will put your mind at ease.

Features:

- Kitchen: This welcoming and efficient space is open to the dining area, lending itself to warm gatherings and easy transitions between preparing and serving.

- Master Suite: A walk-in closet and private full bath provide you with respite from the outside world. This spacious, inviting area is everything you need to comfortably unwind.

- Bedrooms: The secondary bedrooms make this home ideal for families. Their size and proximity to both the second full bathroom and the master suite allow everyone to rest easier.

- Garage: A spacious two-car garage is attached to the front of the home, providing necessary space in an economical design.

Images provided by designer/architect.

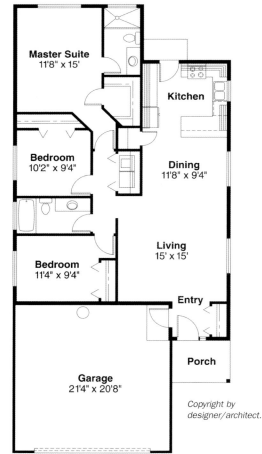

Copyright by designer/architect.

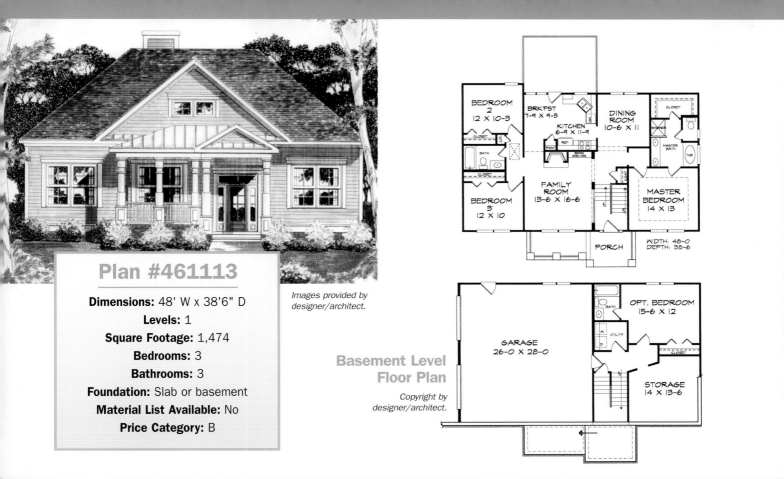

Plan #461113

Dimensions: 48' W x 38'6" D

Levels: 1

Square Footage: 1,474

Bedrooms: 3

Bathrooms: 3

Foundation: Slab or basement

Material List Available: No

Price Category: B

Images provided by designer/architect.

Basement Level Floor Plan

Copyright by designer/architect.

BEDROOM 2 12 X 10-3 · BRK'FST 7-9 X 9-3 · KITCHEN 6-9 X 11-9 · DINING ROOM 10-6 X 11 · CLOSET · SHOWER · MASTER BATH · TUB · BATH · CLOSET · FAMILY ROOM 13-6 X 16-6 · BEDROOM 3 12 X 10 · MASTER BEDROOM 14 X 13 · PORCH

WIDTH: 48-0
DEPTH: 38-6

GARAGE 26-0 X 28-0 · BATH · OPT. BEDROOM 15-6 X 12 · UTILITY · CLOSET · STORAGE 14 X 13-6

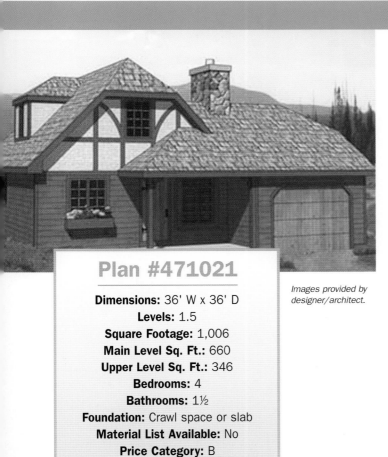

Plan #471021

Dimensions: 36' W x 36' D

Levels: 1.5

Square Footage: 1,006

Main Level Sq. Ft.: 660

Upper Level Sq. Ft.: 346

Bedrooms: 4

Bathrooms: 1½

Foundation: Crawl space or slab

Material List Available: No

Price Category: B

Images provided by designer/architect.

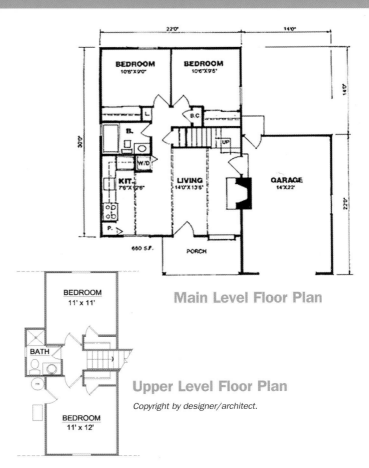

BEDROOM 10'8"X9'0" · BEDROOM 10'6"X9'6" · B.C. · UP · B. · W/D · KIT. 7'6"X12'6" · LIVING 14'0"X13'6" · GARAGE 14'X22' · P. · PORCH

660 S.F.

Main Level Floor Plan

BEDROOM 11' x 11' · BATH · BEDROOM 11' x 12'

Upper Level Floor Plan

Copyright by designer/architect.

This article was reprinted from *The New Smart Approach to Kids' Rooms* (Creative Homeowner 2005).

Bathrooms Designed for Kids

Bathing is a key part in everyone's life, and children are no exception. The bathroom, therefore, is an important environment that deserves particular attention. One that is designed around a child's smaller size enables him to move most effortlessly into taking charge of his own personal hygiene. Special safety concerns should always take precedence over other design elements. If you share a bathroom with your child, take prudent steps to accommodate his size and needs in addition to your own.

Most newer homes contain a second bath, which is often designated for the children in the family. What should be included in it depends on the ages and number of children who will use it. If your child is lucky enough to have the room all to herself, plan it for her growing and changing needs. Anticipate the storage and lighting requirements of a teenage girl's grooming habits, for example. If more than one child will share the bath, consider their genders, and whether they will use the room at the same time. How many lavatories do they need? At least two. The best designs for shared bathrooms include compartmentalized spaces—one for the toilet, one for bathing (with a separate shower, if space permits), and one for grooming. A double-bowl vanity would be most practical. At least try to set the toilet apart from the bathing area—even a half wall will help.

There are fixtures on the market that are tailored for a child's use, but you may not want to make the investment in something that will have to be replaced once your child matures or leaves home. As always, it's a matter of choice. If you want to make the room appealing to the younger set but your funds are limited, look into wallpaper

Top left: A rubber mat will prevent slipping.

Above: Avoid accidents by installing antiscalding devices on faucets.

Below: Make the room accessible for children.

patterns that have a juvenile theme and use lively, kid-friendly colors and accessories.

Sensible and Basic

There are lots of things you can do to make any bathroom practical, comfortable, and safe for family members of all ages. When you're planning to build a bath that will be used by a child, careful consideration should be given to both of you, but pay particular attention to the age-specific needs of the youngster.

Caring for Baby

The baby's bathroom should be a warm, draft-free environment. You should organize this space around your needs for bathing the baby. You'll want everything right at hand so you can keep a constant vigil. Remember: a child can drown in less than 2 inches of water in a baby tub or toilet, or even in a bucket filled with water.

Appropriate furnishings include a comfortable seating area where you can dry the baby or towel a toddler, a convenient place to house the baby bath, perhaps a changing table, and ample storage for the baby's bath toiletries and linens, diapers, bath toys, a hamper, and a diaper pail.

Consider your own comfort when positioning the baby bath. Counter height will probably be most comfortable, or you may consider a freestanding bathing unit. Install an anti-scald faucet, which contains a device that keeps water temperate. Because a child's skin is thinner and more tender than an adult's, it can be burned within 3 seconds after coming into contact with water that's over 120 degrees Fahrenheit. Fixtures equipped with a pressure-balancing feature will maintain the same degree of hotness even when cold-

water flow is reduced (when you flush the toilet, for example). Style-wise, a single-lever faucet, as opposed to two separate valves, is much easier for a child to use when regulating water flow and temperature. You can present some of them, as well.

A hand-held shower device that allows you to position the showerhead at a convenient level can be retrofitted onto a con-

Above: Special hand-painted tile looks charming in this one-of-a-kind boys' bathroom.

ventional showerhead or installed separately. Look for one that's been designed for children to handle.

Once you start to bathe the baby in the tub, you'll want to make it slip-resistant. A textured surface helps. You can easily add this with antislip decals and mats. Install soft covers over the faucet and spout so that a little one can't be bruised. Parents can protect themselves by using a mat that extends over the side of the tub to cushion their arms while holding up and bathing the baby. Part of the mat also rests on the floor to pad adult knees.

It's a good idea to install easy-care wallcovering and flooring. From the first moment a toddler learns to splash, all claims to toughness are tested. Classic selections include tiles, water-proof wallcovering that has a built-in

mildewcide, solid-surfacing material or a fiberglass tub surround, and gloss or semi-gloss paint, with a mildewcide.

A one-piece toilet hugs closer to the wall and has an elongated bowl that makes toilet training a little easier. Because it sits lower than a two-piece model, this type is better-scaled for a child yet comfortable for an adult.

Helping Preschoolers

Toilet training and the beginning of self-grooming mark this stage, necessitating a few changes in the way your child will use the bathroom. Tubs and toys seem to go together here. You'll need more room for toy storage; gear it to something your child can access himself, such as a plastic basket that can be kept inside a vanity cabinet or on the floor of the linen closet. You'll also need a place to keep a small step stool when it's not in use as a booster in front of the lav. If you're renovating or building a new bathroom for a child, consider installing a lav into a vanity or countertop that is built at a lower height.

Because the standard rule of thumb is to install a mirror 8 inches above a standard-height vanity countertop (to avoid splatters), you may want to include a standing mirror or one that extends from the wall at a proper height to suit your child. To encourage neatness, a towel rack that is within a child's reach is another good idea. A low freestanding rack works well, too.

Accommodating School-Age Kids

Socializing skills in school reinforce the needs for individual identity at home, including specific grooming styles as a child gets older. Storage niches once devoted to bathtub toys can be used for hair ribbons, special soaps and shampoos, or other toiletries. Keep electrical appliances, such as hair dryers and steam rollers, or electric shavers out of the room until your child is old enough to handle them responsibly and understand the hazards posed by electricity and water.

More About Shared Spaces. The crunch starts when kids begin toilet training and continues through the school years when everybody has to get bathed, dressed, and out of the house at the same time. To cope with the increased demands, create private areas within the room, such as the separate bathing, grooming, and toilet areas suggested earlier. Color-code towels and accessories so that everyone can clearly see what belongs to each person who uses the room.into a vanity or countertop that is built at a lower height.

Above: Hang a deep basket from a peg, and tuck bath toys or small laundry items into it.

Left: Here's a stylish way to make sure everyone has his or her own bath towel.

Bathroom Safety

Here's a list of things that you should have on hand at all times to make sure any bathroom
that is intended for a child's use is safe and comfortable.

Tub & Shower Areas

· Safety glazing on glass doors

· Doors that are hinged to swing out into the room

· Grab bars at adult and child heights

· A shower seat

Toilets & Water Closets

· No lock on the water-closet door

· Locked toilet lid

· Tip-resistant training step stool

· Toilet-paper holder installed within the child's reach

Plumbing

· Water valves within easy reach

· Single-lever controls

· Anti-scald and pressure-balanced faucets

· Adjustable child-size hand shower

Electric

· Ground-fault circuit interrupters (GFCIs) on all outlets

· Covered receptacles

· Vapor-proof light fixtures installed out of the child's reach

· Low-voltage task lighting

· Night light

Cabinet & Counter Surfaces

· Small doors that can be easily opened

· Childproof locks

· Locked medicine cabinet

· No more than 8-inch-deep cabinets installed over the toilet

· Rounded corners and edges

· Seating for drying off and dressing

Flooring

· Nonslip surface

· Water-resistant surface

· Anchors for area rugs and mats

Windows & Doors

· Doors that swing into the room

· Door locks that can be opened from the outside

· Safety bars on all windows

Finally, move certain activities to other rooms. Dressing and grooming can be done in the bedroom, for example. Whether your home has one small bathroom that is shared by all or a separate bathroom for each member of the family, there are steps you can take to make space more efficient.

Step One: Plan storage. If you don't have a linen closet or large cabinet in the room, add shelving to hold extra towels, bars of soap, and other necessities. Small storage niches created between the wall studs make handy spots for shampoo and toiletries. Mount hooks or pegged racks to the wall or behind the door for hanging extra towels or robes. New medicine cabinets come with extra deep shelves that are large enough to hold rolls of toilet paper or bulky hair dryers.

Step Two: Consider a better way to use space. Cramped floor space? Replace the bathroom door with a pocket door to free up floor space that might allow you to create a separate shower stall or a double vanity.

Step Three: Light it properly. Besides general lighting, plan adequate task lighting at the sink and mirror for grooming. Avoid locating lights above the mirror where they create glare and shadows. Side lights are better.

Step Four: Keep the air clear. Invest in a good exhaust fan to make the room's air quality healthier and surfaces less slick. It will also deter water build up and mildew, which can damage surfaces and materials.

1. Rounded edges are gentle on kids.
2. Here's one way to keep towels neat.
3. A spacious vanity and lots of storage are important when kids share a bathroom.
4. Kids can help pick out cute accessories for their bathroom.
5. A shower seat is a safety feature that should be included in every bathroom.
6. Secure all rugs with a nonskid backing.
7. A handheld sprayer in the bath makes it easy to rinse shampoo out of hair.
8. Kids can personalize the space by painting their own designs in the room.

Design Ideas for Kids' Baths

7

5

6

8

Plan #101004

Dimensions: 55'8" W x 56'6" D
Levels: 1
Square Footage: 1,787
Bedrooms: 3
Bathrooms: 2
Foundation: Crawl space, slab, or basement
Materials List Available: Yes
Price Category: C

Images provided by designer/architect.

This carefully designed ranch provides the feel and features of a much larger home.

Features:

- Ceiling Height: 9 ft. unless otherwise noted.

- Foyer: Guests will step up onto the inviting front porch and into this foyer, with its impressive 11-ft. ceiling.

- Dining Room: Open to the entry and to its left is this elegant dining room, perfect for entertaining or informal family gatherings.

- Family Room: This family gathering place features an 11-ft. ceiling to enhance its sense of spaciousness.

- Kitchen: This intelligently designed kitchen has an open plan. A breakfast bar and a serving bar are features that add to its convenience.

- Master Suite: This suite is loaded with amenities, including a double-step tray ceiling, direct access to the screened porch, a sitting room, deluxe bath, and his and her walk-in closets.

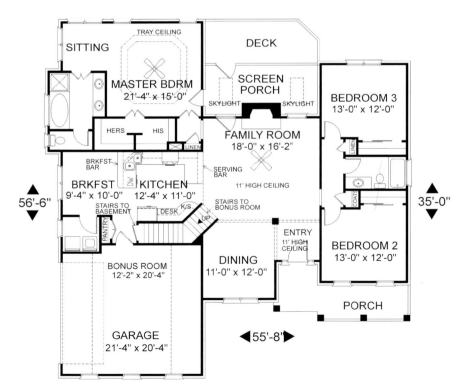

Copyright by designer/architect.

Kitchen

Family Room

Dining Room

Master Bath

Bedroom

Master Bedroom

Images provided by designer/architect.

Plan #251004

Dimensions: 50'9" W x 42'1" D
Levels: 1
Square Footage: 1,550
Bedrooms: 3
Bathrooms: 2
Foundation: Crawl space, slab
Materials List Available: Yes
Price Category: C

Combine the old-fashioned appeal of a country farmhouse with all the comforts of modern living.

Features:

- Ceiling Height: 9 ft.

- Foyer: When guests enter this inviting foyer, they will be greeted by a view of the lovely family room.

- Family Room: Usher family and friends into this welcoming family room, where they can warm up in front of the fireplace. The room's 12-ft. ceiling enhances its sense of spaciousness.

- Kitchen: Gather around and keep the cook company at the snack bar in this roomy kitchen. There's still plenty of counter space for food preparation, thanks to the kitchen island.

- Master Bedroom: This elegant master bedroom features a large walk-in closet and a 9-ft. recessed ceiling.

- Master Bath. This master bath includes a double vanity, a tub, and a walk-in shower.

- Garage: This attached garage provides plenty of extra storage space, as well as parking for two cars.

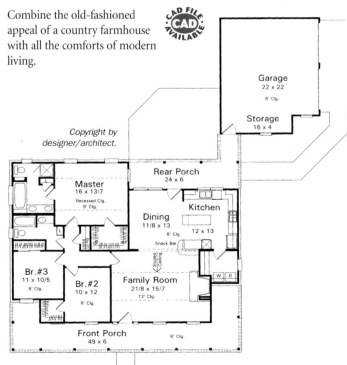

Copyright by designer/architect.

SMARTtip

Shaker Style in Your Bathroom

This warm, likable style fits in perfectly with a country home because of its old-fashioned values. But it blends in well with contemporary interiors, too, because of its clean lines and plain geometric shapes. In fact, adding a few Shaker elements can warm up the sometimes cold look of a thoroughly modern room.

Plan #121121

Dimensions: 47'4" W x 45'8"D
Levels: 1
Square Footage: 1,341
Bedrooms: 3
Bathrooms: 2
Foundation: Basement;
crawl space for fee
Material List Available: Yes
Price Category: C

Images provided by designer/architect.

This traditional home is charming and bound to make your life simpler with all its amenities.

Features:

- Great Room: Already equipped with an entertainment center, bookcase and a fireplace by which you can enjoy those books, this room has endless possibilities. This is a room that will bring the whole family together.

- Kitchen: This design includes everything you need and everything you want: a pantry waiting to be filled with your favorite foods, plenty of workspace, and a snack bar that acts as a useful transition between kitchen and breakfast room.

- Breakfast Room: An extension of the kitchen, this room will fill with the aroma of coffee and a simmering breakfast, so you'll be immersed in your relaxing morning. With peaceful daylight streaming in through a window-lined wall, this will easily become the best part of your day.

- Master Suite: Plenty of breathing room for both of you, there will be no fighting for sink or closet space in this bedroom. The full master bath includes dual sinks, and the walk-in closet will hold everything you both need. Another perk of this bathroom is the whirlpool bathtub.

- Garage: This two-car garage opens directly into the home, so there is no reason to get out of your warm, dry car and into unpleasant weather.

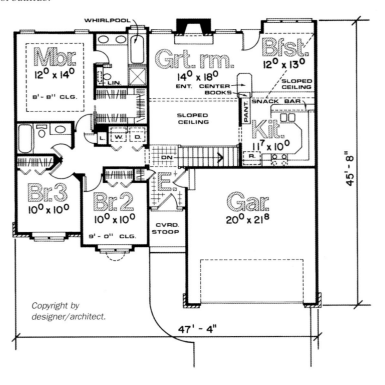

Plan #121006

Dimensions: 46' W x 58' D
Levels: 1
Square Footage: 1,762
Bedrooms: 3
Bathrooms: 2
Foundation: Slab
Materials List Available: Yes
Price Category: C

The entry has a trio of arched openings that leads you to other areas of this amenity-packed home.

Features:

• Ceiling Height: 8 ft. except as noted.

• Eating Bar: Conveniently located between the kitchen and family room, this is sure to be a favorite spot for informal entertaining and family gatherings.

• Family room: A wall of windows, a fireplace, and a vaulted ceiling stretching to 11 ft. work together to make this a bright and warm room.

• Kitchen: There's no shortage of counter space in this well-planned kitchen that features a center island in addition to the eating bar.

• Master Suite: Luxuriate at the end of the day in this large bedroom with its decorative tray ceiling and walk-in closet. Enjoy the pampering bath with its sunlit corner whirlpool flanked by vanities.

• Garage: Two bays provide room for cars and plenty of storage as well.

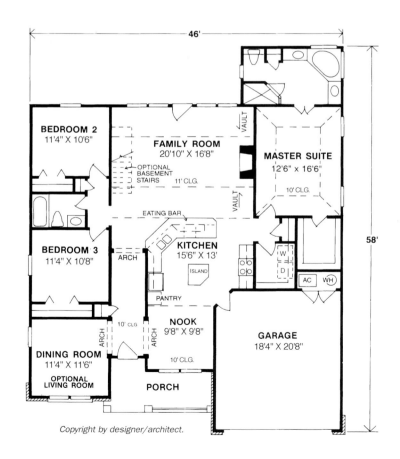

Copyright by designer/architect.

Plan #391028

Dimensions: 54' W x 50' D
Levels: 1
Square Footage: 1,771
Bedrooms: 2
Bathrooms: 2
Foundation: Crawl space, slab
Materials List Available: Yes
Price Category: C

Images provided by designer/architect.

Here's a "real-life" rancher, where there's plenty of room for stretching out and growing your family in contemporary comfort.

Features:

- Dining Area: This dining area, a demure space for formal affairs, owns an entrance to the back deck and flows easily into the great room.

- Kitchen: This creative U-shaped kitchen serves up a snack bar that reaches into the enormous sunken great room with fireplace.

- Master Suite: This expansive suite with dual walk-in closets and private entrance to the deck lives luxuriously on the other side of this home. The master bath flaunts a platform tub set beneath a grand geometric window.

- Bedroom: A stylish secondary bedroom, with nearby full bathroom, and cheerful den with a window seat are arranged on one side of the house.

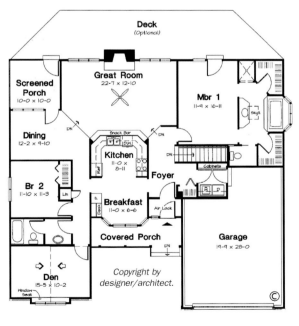

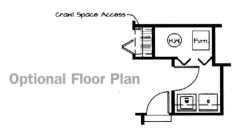

Optional Floor Plan

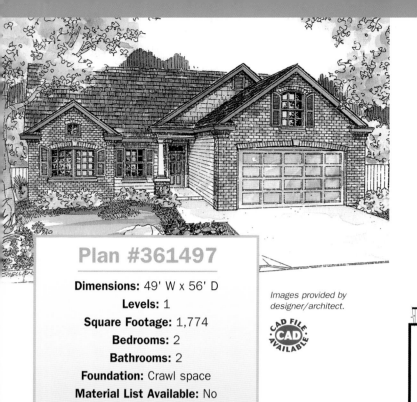

Patio
30' x 10'

Master Suite
11' x 15'10"

Dining
13' x 10'6"

Living
16'6" x 20'6"

Kitchen
12'8" x 11'8"

Foyer
Up

Vaulted Bedroom
10'8" x 13'6"

Den
10' x 14'10"

Utility

Porch

Garage
21'4" x 20'

Plan #361497

Dimensions: 49' W x 56' D

Levels: 1

Square Footage: 1,774

Bedrooms: 2

Bathrooms: 2

Foundation: Crawl space

Material List Available: No

Price Category: C

Images provided by designer/architect.

CAD FILE AVAILABLE — CAD

Dn

Storage
12' x 26'10"

Bonus Area Floor Plan

Copyright by designer/architect.

Rear View

Plan #391034

Dimensions: 72'4" W x 43' D

Levels: 1

Square Footage: 1,737

Bedrooms: 3

Bathrooms: 2

Foundation: Crawl space, slab, or basement

Material List Available: Yes

Price Category: C

Images provided by designer/architect.

This home, as shown in the photograph, may differ from the actual blueprints. For more detailed information, please check the floor plans carefully.

DECK

MASTER BEDROOM
13'-4" x 14'-8"
VAULT CLG. TO 10'-0"

LIVING ROOM
16'-0" x 19'-4"

BRKFST
7'-6" x 10'-0"

GARAGE
21'-8" x 21'-4"

KITCHEN
13'-6" x 9'-6"

BEDROOM
11'-2" x 11'-4"

BEDROOM
14'-10" x 11'-4"

FOYER
VAULT CLG. TO 10'-0"

DINING
11'-4" x 11'-4"

PORCH

43'-0"

72'-4"

Copyright by designer/architect.

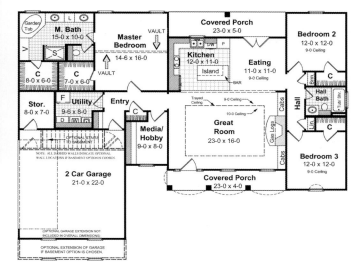

Images provided by designer/architect.

CAD FILE AVAILABLE

Plan #351002

Dimensions: 64' W x 45'10" D

Levels: 1

Square Footage: 1,751

Bedrooms: 3

Bathrooms: 2

Foundation: Crawl space, slab, or basement

Materials List Available: Yes

Price Category: D

Copyright by designer/architect.

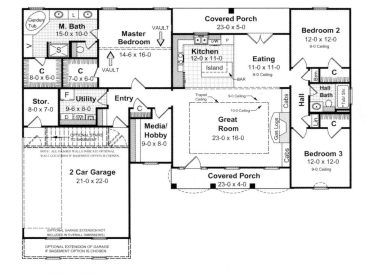

Images provided by designer/architect.

CAD FILE AVAILABLE

Plan #351003

Dimensions: 64' W x 45'10" D

Levels: 1

Square Footage: 1,751

Bedrooms: 3

Bathrooms: 2

Foundation: Crawl space, slab, or basement

Materials List Available: Yes

Price Category: D

Copyright by designer/architect.

Plan #341276

Dimensions: 52' W x 32' D

Levels: 1

Square Footage: 1,520

Bedrooms: 3

Bathrooms: 2

Foundation: Crawl space, slab, basement, or walkout

Material List Available: Yes

Price Category: C

Images provided by designer/architect.

Copyright by designer/architect.

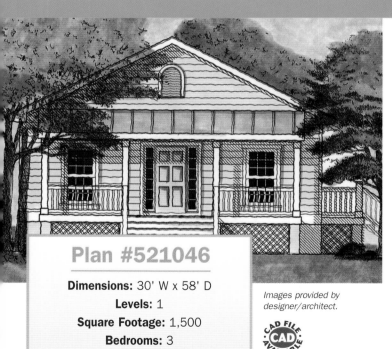

Plan #521046

Dimensions: 30' W x 58' D

Levels: 1

Square Footage: 1,500

Bedrooms: 3

Bathrooms: 2

Foundation: Crawl space

Material List Available: No

Price Category: C

Images provided by designer/architect.

CAD FILE AVAILABLE

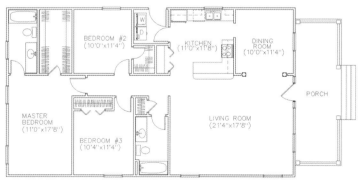

Copyright by designer/architect.

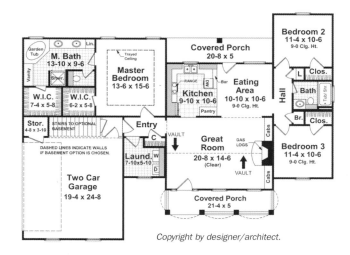

Copyright by designer/architect.

Plan #351078

Dimensions: 61' W x 47' D

Levels: 1

Square Footage: 1,508

Bedrooms: 3

Bathrooms: 2

Foundation: Crawl space, slab, or basement

Material List Available: Yes

Price Category: D

Images provided by designer/architect.

CAD FILE AVAILABLE — CAD

Rear Elevation

Plan #321015

Dimensions: 48' W x 64' D

Levels: 1

Square Footage: 1,501

Bedrooms: 3

Bathrooms: 2

Foundation: Crawl space, slab, or basement

Materials List Available: Yes

Price Category: C

Images provided by designer/architect.

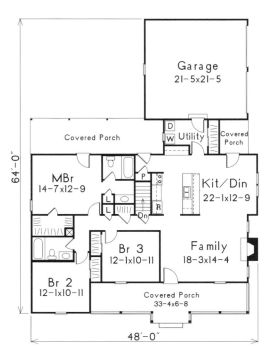

Copyright by designer/architect.

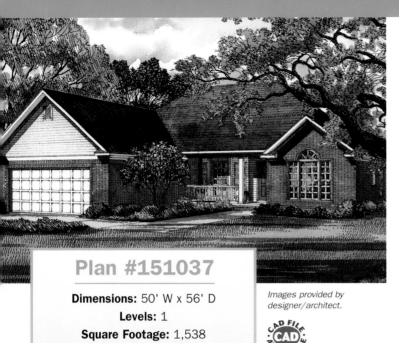

Plan #151037

Dimensions: 50' W x 56' D

Levels: 1

Square Footage: 1,538

Bedrooms: 3

Bathrooms: 2

Foundation: Crawl space, slab, or basement

CompleteCost List Available: Yes

Price Category: C

Images provided by designer/architect.

CAD FILE AVAILABLE

Copyright by designer/architect.

Plan #311052

Dimensions: 51'5" W x 66'6" D

Levels: 1

Square Footage: 1,539

Bedrooms: 3

Bathrooms: 2

Foundation: Crawl space or slab

Material List Available: Yes

Price Category: C

Images provided by designer/architect.

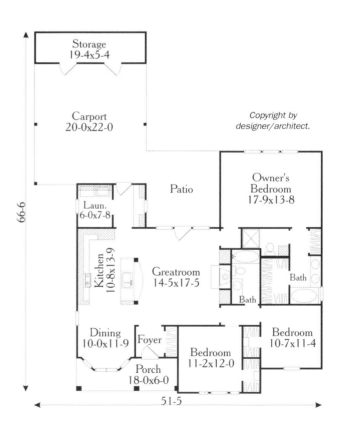

Copyright by designer/architect.

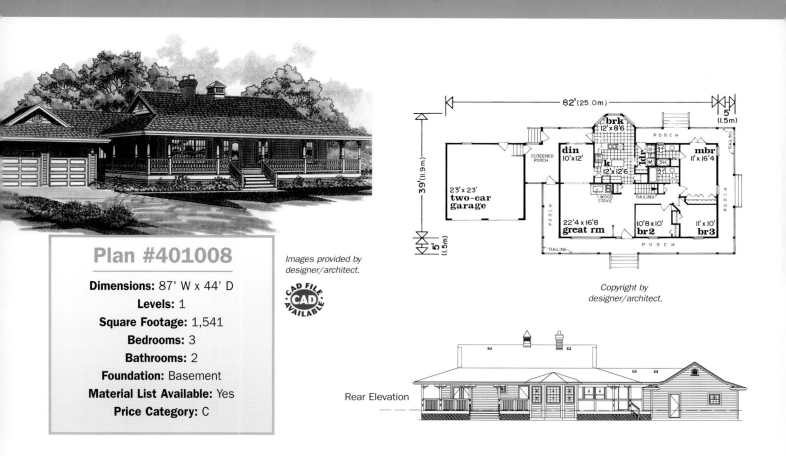

Plan #401008

Dimensions: 87' W x 44' D
Levels: 1
Square Footage: 1,541
Bedrooms: 3
Bathrooms: 2
Foundation: Basement
Material List Available: Yes
Price Category: C

Images provided by designer/architect.

CAD FILE AVAILABLE

Copyright by designer/architect.

Rear Elevation

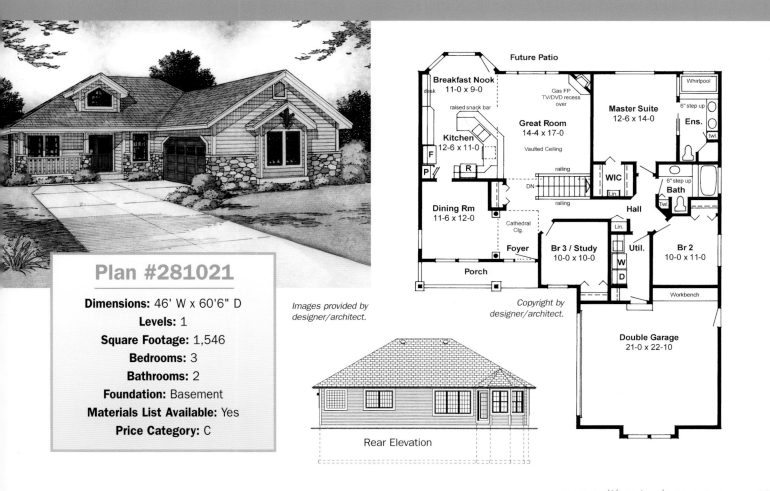

Plan #281021

Dimensions: 46' W x 60'6" D
Levels: 1
Square Footage: 1,546
Bedrooms: 3
Bathrooms: 2
Foundation: Basement
Materials List Available: Yes
Price Category: C

Images provided by designer/architect.

Copyright by designer/architect.

Rear Elevation

Plan #121058

Dimensions: 50' W x 52'8" D

Levels: 1

Square Footage: 1,554

Bedrooms: 3

Bathrooms: 2

Foundation: Basement

Materials List Available: Yes

Price Category: C

Images provided by designer/architect.

The high ceilings and well-placed windows make this home bright and airy.

Features:

- Great Room: A soaring cathedral ceiling sets the tone for this gracious room. Enjoy the fireplace that's framed by views to the outside.

- Dining Room: A 10-ft. ceiling highlights formality, while a built-in display cabinet and picturesque window give it even more character.

- Kitchen: This well-designed kitchen shares a snack bar with the breakfast area.

- Breakfast Area: Natural light streams into this room, and the door to the backyard lets everyone move outside for a meal or drink in fine weather.

- Master Suite: A tray ceiling gives elegance to the bedroom, with its practical walk-in closet. The bath features a sunlit whirlpool tub, double vanity, and separate shower.

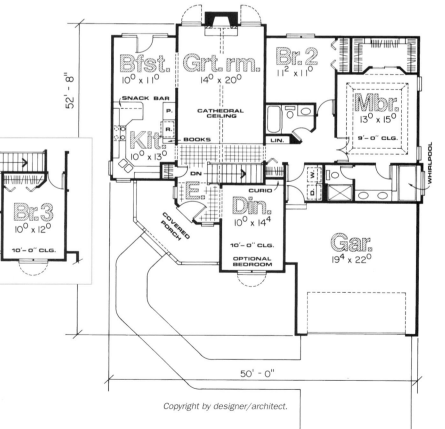

Copyright by designer/architect.

Plan #131068

Dimensions: 64'2" W x 40'8" D

Levels: 1

Square Footage: 1,554

Bedrooms: 3

Bathrooms: 2

Foundation: Crawl space, slab, or basement

Material List Available: Yes

Price Category: D

This smart looking postmodern style ranch boasts a great floor plan.

Features:

- Living Room: Family and friends will love to gather in this area, with its high ceiling and large windows with a view of the backyard. The cozy fireplace can provide a relaxing atmosphere.

- Kitchen: This peninsula kitchen overlooks the informal dinette space. The formal dining room is found at the other end of the area.

- Master Suite: Located on the opposite side of the home from the secondary bedrooms for privacy, this oasis has it all. The large walk-in closet and luxurious master bath are the highlights of this area.

- Bedrooms: The two large secondary bedrooms with large closets share the common hallway bathroom.

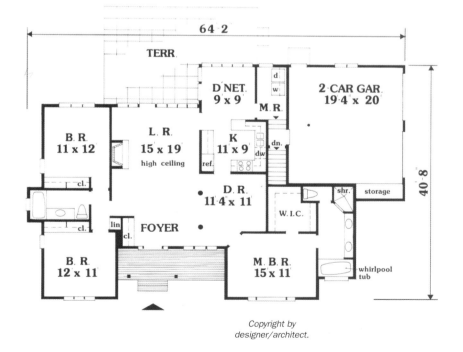

Copyright by designer/architect.

Plan #521040

Dimensions: 42'2" W x 57' D
Levels: 1
Square Footage: 1,555
Bedrooms: 3
Bathrooms: 2½
Foundation: Slab
Material List Available: No
Price Category: C

Beautifully and intelligently designed, this house has everything you want and everything you need.

Features:

- **Porches:** The front porch provides a covered entry while still being open to the sights and sounds of the outdoors, ideal for sitting outside on a lovely evening. On the opposite end of the house is a screened-in porch that opens into the master suite, the living room, and the deck. It is perfect for keeping out unwanted pests and bringing in the breeze. Next to that is the deck, great for soaking up the sun and barbecuing.

- **Living Room:** With light from the dining-area windows and the deck and warmth from the fireplace, this room can become anything you want it to be: warm and cozy or light and airy.

- **Kitchen:** This working area has a walk-in pantry and plenty of workspace and storage, and it opens freely into the dining room. As the busiest part of any home, the kitchen is perfect for gatherings or simple family dinners, making the transition between preparing and serving simple.

- **Master Suite:** A spacious full bath, a large walk-in closet, and a direct entrance to the screened porch make this the ideal place to rest and relax. It is truly a master's bedroom.

- **Bedrooms:** The secondary bedrooms each have their highlights. Bedroom No. 2 has a wide closet and lots of light from its three extended windows while being a short distance from the second full bathroom. Bedroom No. 3 has a direct connection with the bathroom and a small walk-in closet. Both are also a short distance from the large laundry room.

Copyright by designer/architect.

Front View

This home, as shown in the photographs, may differ from the actual blueprints. For more detailed information, please check the floor plans carefully.

Rear View

Plan #401026

Dimensions: 83' W x 40'6" D

Levels: 1

Square Footage: 1,578

Bedrooms: 3

Bathrooms: 2

Foundation: Basement

Materials List Available: Yes

Price Category: C

With a graceful pediment above and a sturdy, colonnaded veranda below, this quaint home was made for country living.

Features:

- Foyer: The veranda wraps slightly around on two sides of the facade and permits access to this central foyer with a den (or third bedroom) on the right and the country kitchen on the left.

- Kitchen: This functional kitchen features an island workspace and a plant ledge over the entry to the great room.

- Great Room: A fireplace warms this room and is flanked by windows overlooking the rear deck.

- Dining Area: This casually defined dining space has double-door access to the same deck as that off the great room.

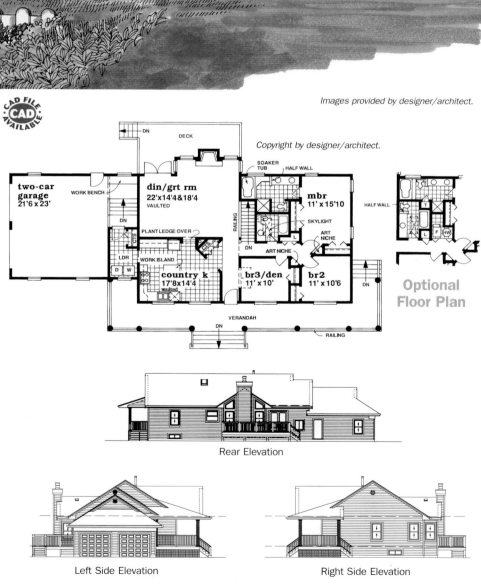

Images provided by designer/architect.

Copyright by designer/architect.

Optional Floor Plan

Rear Elevation

Left Side Elevation

Right Side Elevation

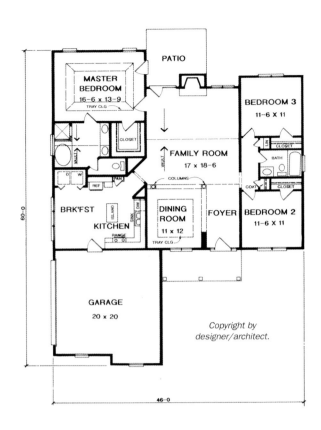

Images provided by designer/architect.

Plan #461063

Dimensions: 60' W x 46' D
Levels: 1
Square Footage: 1,569
Bedrooms: 3
Bathrooms: 2
Foundation: Slab
Material List Available: No
Price Category: C

Copyright by designer/architect.

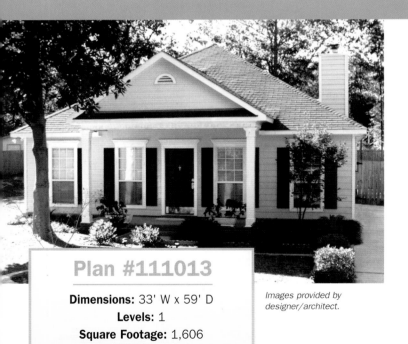

Images provided by designer/architect.

Plan #111013

Dimensions: 33' W x 59' D
Levels: 1
Square Footage: 1,606
Bedrooms: 3
Bathrooms: 2
Foundation: Slab
Materials List Available: No
Price Category: C

Copyright by designer/architect.

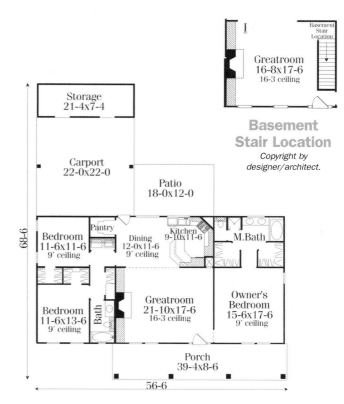

Plan #311051

Dimensions: 56'6" W x 68'6" D

Levels: 1

Square Footage: 1,680

Bedrooms: 3

Bathrooms: 2

Foundation: Crawl space, slab, or basement

Material List Available: Yes

Price Category: C

Images provided by designer/architect.

Storage 21-4x7-4

Carport 22-0x22-0

Patio 18-0x12-0

Bedroom 11-6x11-6 9' ceiling

Pantry

Dining 12-0x11-6 9' ceiling

Kitchen 9-10x11-6

M.Bath

Bedroom 11-6x13-6 9' ceiling

Bath

Greatroom 21-10x17-6 16-3 ceiling

Owner's Bedroom 15-6x17-6 9' ceiling

Porch 39-4x8-6

68-6

56-6

Greatroom 16-8x17-6 16-3 ceiling

Basement Stair Location

Basement Stair Location

Copyright by designer/architect.

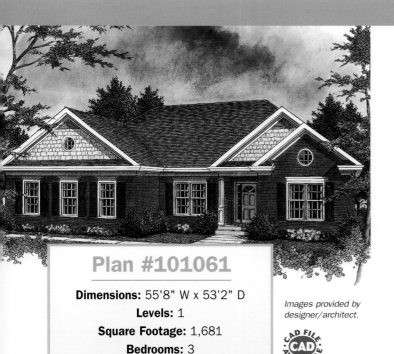

Plan #101061

Dimensions: 55'8" W x 53'2" D

Levels: 1

Square Footage: 1,681

Bedrooms: 3

Bathrooms: 2

Foundation: Crawl space or slab

Materials List Available: No

Price Category: C

Images provided by designer/architect.

CAD FILE AVAILABLE

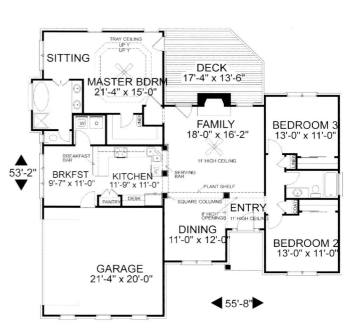

SITTING

MASTER BDRM 21'-4" x 15'-0"

TRAY CEILING UP 1'

DECK 17'-4" x 13'-6"

FAMILY 18'-0" x 16'-2" 11' HIGH CEILING

BEDROOM 3 13'-0" x 11'-0"

53'-2"

BREAKFAST BAR

BRKFST 9'-7" x 11'-0"

KITCHEN 11'-9" x 11'-0"

PANTRY   DESK

SERVING BAR

PLANT SHELF

SQUARE COLUMNS

8' HIGH OPENINGS

ENTRY 11' HIGH CEILING

DINING 11'-0" x 12'-0"

GARAGE 21'-4" x 20'-0"

BEDROOM 2 13'-0" x 11'-0"

55'-8"

Copyright by designer/architect.

Plan #441003

Dimensions: 50' W x 48' D
Levels: 1
Square Footage: 1,580
Bedrooms: 3
Bathrooms: 2½
Foundation: Crawl space; slab or basement available for fee
Materials List Available: No
Price Category: C

Craftsman styling with modern floor planning—that's the advantage of this cozy design. Covered porches at front and back enhance both the look and the livability of the plan.

Features:

• Great Room: This vaulted entertaining area boasts a corner fireplace and a built-in media center. The area is open to the kitchen and the dining area.

• Kitchen: This large, open island kitchen will please the chef in the family. The raised bar is open to the dining area and the great room.

• Master Suite: Look for luxurious amenities such as double sinks and a separate tub and shower in the master bath. The master bedroom has a vaulted ceiling and a walk-in closet with built-in shelves.

• Bedrooms: Two secondary bedrooms are located away from the master suite. Each has a large closet and access to a common bathroom.

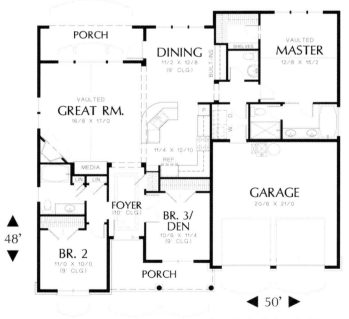

Copyright by designer/architect.

Rear Elevation

Plan #131002

Dimensions: 70'1" W x 60'7" D
Levels: 1
Square Footage: 1,709
Bedrooms: 3
Bathrooms: 2½
Foundation: Crawl space, slab, or basement
Materials List Available: Yes
Price Category: D

Images provided by designer/architect.

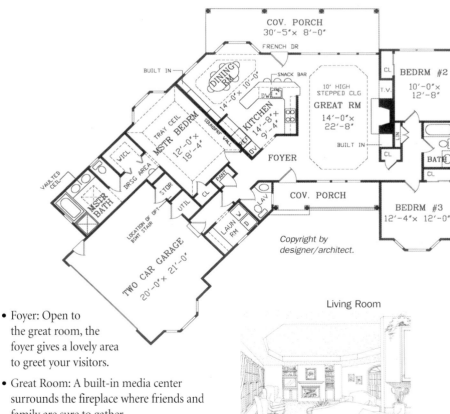

Rear View

You'll love the way this angled ranch brings out the best in a corner lot or on a slope.

Features:

• Ceiling Height: 8 ft.

• Front Porch: Hang baskets of plants from the roof of this porch, which is just the right size for a couple of rockers and a side table.

• Dining Room: Well-placed windows flood this room with sunlight during the day and a built-in cabinet gives ample storage space for all your china, linens, and collectables.

• Foyer: Open to the great room, the foyer gives a lovely area to greet your visitors.

• Great Room: A built-in media center surrounds the fireplace where friends and family are sure to gather.

• Master Suite: You'll love the privacy of this somewhat isolated but easily accessed room. Decorate to show off the large bay window and tray ceiling, and enjoy the luxury of a compartmented bathroom.

Living Room

Copyright by designer/architect.

Plan #191023

Dimensions: 56' W x 42' D
Levels: 1
Square Footage: 1,785
Bedrooms: 3
Bathrooms: 2
Foundation: Basement
Materials List Available: No
Price Category: C

Two large porches and a spacious family room make this lovely home ideal for a busy family with an active social life.

Features:

- Ceiling Height: 9-ft. ceilings add to the airy feeling inside this cheery home.

- Great Room: Highlights here include a built-in entertainment center and French doors with overhead transoms that open onto the rear covered porch.

- Dining Room: An arched opening to this room emphasizes its lovely dimensions.

- Kitchen: This well-planned kitchen includes a central island with downdraft range, a snack bar, and lots of counter and cabinet space.

- Breakfast Area: You'll find the family using this convenient and sunny room at all times of day.

- Master Suite: With its walk-in closet and deluxe bath, this suite will live up to your fondest dreams.

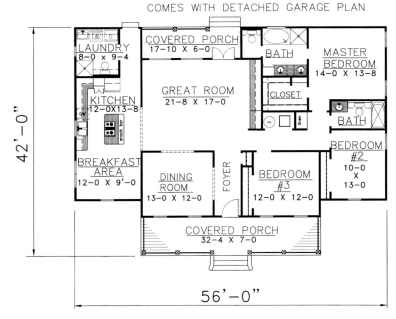

COMES WITH DETACHED GARAGE PLAN

Copyright by designer/architect.

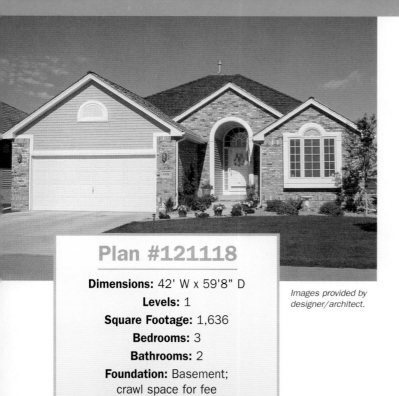

Plan #121118

Dimensions: 42' W x 59'8" D

Levels: 1

Square Footage: 1,636

Bedrooms: 3

Bathrooms: 2

Foundation: Basement; crawl space for fee

Material List Available: Yes

Price Category: C

Images provided by designer/architect.

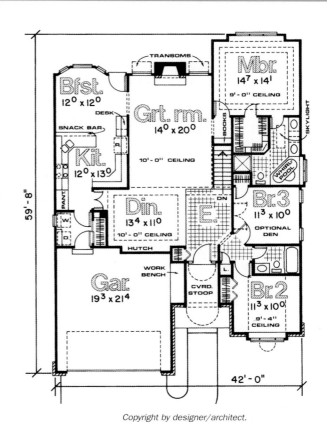

Copyright by designer/architect.

Plan #241041

Dimensions: 65' W x 45' D

Levels: 1

Square Footage: 1,612

Bedrooms: 3

Bathrooms: 2

Foundation: Slab

Material List Available: No

Price Category: C

Images provided by designer/architect.

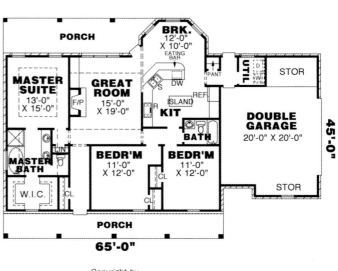

Copyright by designer/architect.

Plan #131005

Dimensions: 70' W x 37'4" D
Levels: 1
Square Footage: 1,595
Bedrooms: 3
Bathrooms: 2
Foundation: Crawl space, slab, or basement
Materials List Available: Yes
Price Category: C

SMARTtip
Create a Courtyard

Create a private walled-garden retreat with fences covered by climbing vines. Add height with trellises, and divide spaces with clipped boxwood hedges. Include an (almost) instant patio by digging away an area of sod and then covering it with a layer of sand and landscaping mesh to discourage weeds. Then cover it with pea gravel, and add a garden bench, statuary, and perhaps an antique or two. The result? European ambiance for even the most nondescript suburban yard.

With the finest features of an open design in the main living areas, this home gives privacy where you need it. Best of all, it's wheelchair accessible.

Features:

• Foyer: A high ceiling gives this area real presence and serves to blend it seamlessly with the great room and the dining room.

• Great Room: The open design allows you to use this room as an extension of the dining room or, if you wish, furnish it to create a private reading nook or visually separate media center.

• Breakfast Room: Both this room and the adjacent well-appointed kitchen flow into the rest of the living area. However, access to the rear porch, where you can sit out and enjoy the weather while you eat, distinguishes this room.

• Master Suite: Located in the same wing as the other bedrooms, this suite has a separate entrance and features a vaulted ceiling, three closets, and a compartmented bath.

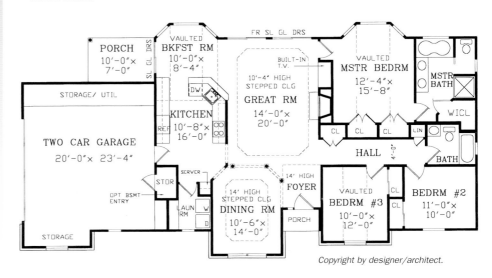

Copyright by designer/architect.

Foyer

Dining Room

Great Room

Living Room

SMARTtip

Natural Trellis

Create a natural rustic trellis that might even, if growing conditions are right, produce its own pretty blooms. Cut and place saplings in the ground as uprights. Then weave old grapevines with smaller saplings for the lattice.

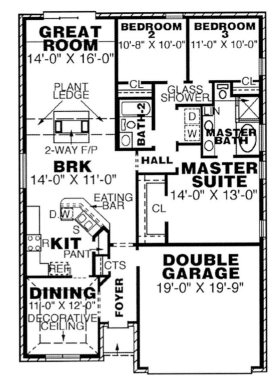

Images provided by designer/architect.

Plan #241042

Dimensions: 38' W x 55'10" D

Levels: 1

Square Footage: 1,675

Bedrooms: 3

Bathrooms: 2

Foundation: Slab

Material List Available: No

Price Category: C

GREAT ROOM 14'-0" X 16'-0"

BEDROOM 2 10'-8" X 10'-0"

BEDROOM 3 11'-0" X 10'-0"

PLANT LEDGE

2-WAY F/P

CL

GLASS SHOWER

CL

BATH-2

D
W

LIN

MASTER BATH

BRK 14'-0" X 11'-0"

HALL

MASTER SUITE 14'-0" X 13'-0"

EATING BAR

CL

D.W.

S

R

KIT PANT

REF

CTS

FOYER

DOUBLE GARAGE 19'-0" X 19'-9"

DINING 11'-0" X 12'-0"

DECORATIVE CEILING

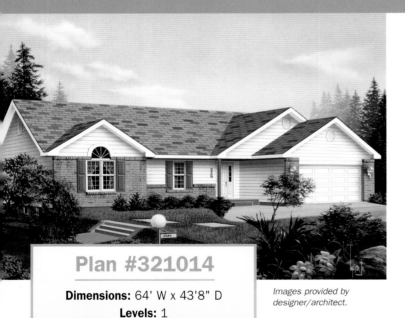

Images provided by designer/architect.

Plan #321014

Dimensions: 64' W x 43'8" D

Levels: 1

Square Footage: 1,676

Bedrooms: 3

Bathrooms: 2

Foundation: Basement

Materials List Available: Yes

Price Category: C

Deck

MBr 15-1x14-4

sky lts

Living 18-10x19-1 vaulted

Dining 10-0x12-9

Kit/Brk 11-10x13-2

R

Dn

P

W D

plant sh.

Foyer

Garage 21-5x24-0

Br 3 15-1x10-7 vaulted

Br 2 13-8x11-8

Porch

43'-8"

64'-0"

SMARTtip

Blending Architecture

An easy way to blend the new deck with the architecture of a house is with railings. Precut railings and caps come in many styles and sizes.

Plan #151528

Dimensions: 41'4" W x 84'2" D
Levels: 1
Square Footage: 1,747
Bedrooms: 2
Bathrooms: 2
Foundation: Crawl space or slab
CompleteCost List Available: Yes
Price Category: C

Images provided by designer/architect.

This Craftsman-inspired design combines a rustic exterior with an elegant interior. The 10-ft.-high ceilings and abundance of windows enhance the family areas with plenty of natural lighting.

CAD FILE AVAILABLE

Features:

- **Great Room:** Featuring a fireplace and built-in computer center, this central gathering area is open to the breakfast room and has access to the rear covered porch.

- **Kitchen:** This combination kitchen and breakfast room enjoys a bar counter for additional seating. Note the large laundry room with pantry, which is located between the kitchen and the garage.

- **Master Suite:** You'll spend many luxurious hours in this beautiful suite, with its 10-ft.-high boxed ceiling, his and her walk-in closets, and large bath with glass shower, whirlpool tub, and double vanity.

- **Bedrooms:** On the same side of the home as the master suite are these two other bedrooms, which have large closets and an adjoining bathroom between them.

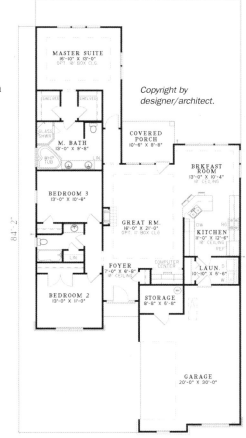

Copyright by designer/architect.

Front View

Plan #271061

Dimensions: 68' W x 52' D
Levels: 1
Square Footage: 1,750
Bedrooms: 1
Bathrooms: 1½
Foundation: Walkout basement
Material List Available: No
Price Category: C

Stucco and a contemporary design give this home a simplistically elegant look.

Images provided by designer/architect.

Features:

- Entry: A small porch area welcomes guests out of the weather and into the warmth. Inside, this entryway provides an inviting introduction to the rest of the home.

- Kitchen: Opening to both the full dining room and a bayed dinette, this kitchen is both beautifully and efficiently designed. The space includes a walk-in pantry and plenty of work-space for the budding gourmet.

- Master Suite: This space is fit for the king (or queen) of the castle. Separated from the rest

of the house by a small entry, the suite includes its own full bath with dual sinks, bathtub, shower stall, and water closet.

- Basement: This area can be finished to include two bedrooms with wide closets, a full bathroom, a family room, and storage space.

- Garage: Whether you actually have three cars you need kept from the climate, you are a collector of things, or you prefer a hobby area, this three-bay garage has plenty of space to fit your needs.

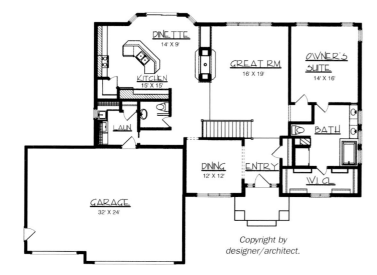

Copyright by designer/architect.

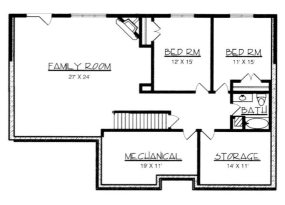

Optional Basement Level Floor Plan

Plan #351080

Dimensions: 50' W x 62'2"D
Levels: 1
Square Footage: 1,625
Bedrooms: 3
Bathrooms: 2
Foundation: Basement
Material List Available: Yes
Price Category: D

Brick and siding give a traditional feeling to this sweet country home.

Features:

- **Kitchen:** This efficient L-shaped kitchen, with its island with raised bar, opens directly into the living room and the eating area. It also opens out onto the patio, ideal for barbecues with family and friends.

- **Master Suite:** This substantial space includes its own full bath with shower, bathtub, and dual sinks; a linen closet; and two full walk-in closets. Sectioned off from the rest of the home, the suite ensures luxury and privacy.

- **Secondary Bedrooms:** The foyer opens into a separate hallway containing both secondary bedrooms and their shared full bathroom, providing both privacy and convenience.

- **Utility:** A large utility room has space for the washer and dryer, with plenty of room to spare for the care of your home.

- **Garage:** This two-car garage includes a storage area and entry directly into the home.

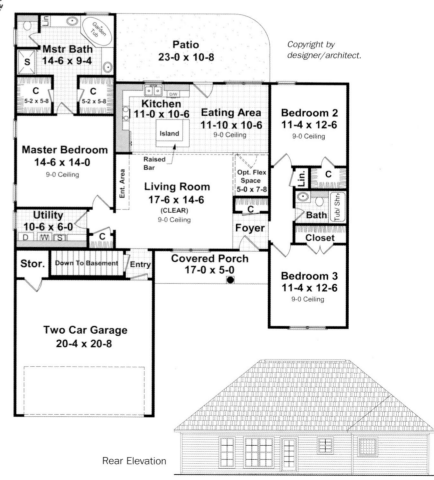

Rear Elevation

Plan #121109

Dimensions: 60' W x 50' D
Levels: 1
Square Footage: 1,735
Bedrooms: 3
Bathrooms: 2
Foundation: Basement;
crawl space for fee
Material List Available: Yes
Price Category: C

Images provided by designer/architect.

A handsome brick facade and welcoming covered entry with arched trim give this home an elegant modernity. The compact design is misleading, as this home contains the amenities of a larger space.

Features:

• Great Room: With large windows, light from the dining room windows, and a door that opens to the backyard, you are never too removed from cool breezes and singing birds in warm weather. The fireplace and the smell of a holiday meal from the dining room combine to make this space a cozy retreat in winter.

• Kitchen: This efficiently designed L-shaped kitchen includes an island and a desk for organizing grocery lists, the family calendar, and mail. Opening into the bright and cheerful breakfast room, the kitchen gleans light from the trio of windows and free space in this adjoining room.

• Master Suite: This area features bay windows and a uniquely efficient design. The walk-in closet is placed just within the master bath, and a door separates the toilet and shower from the whirlpool tub and dual sinks.

• Garage: An entry to the house from this two-car garage feeds into the laundry room, a clean transition from adventuring outdoors to coming home.

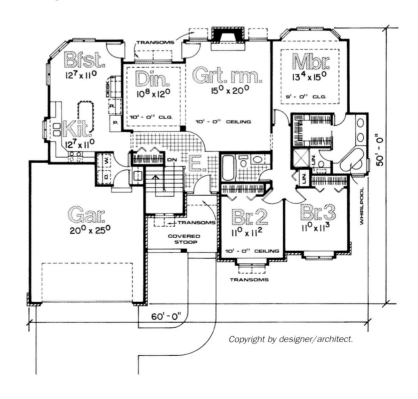

Copyright by designer/architect.

Plan #121011

Dimensions: 50' W x 50' D
Levels: 1
Square Footage: 1,724
Bedrooms: 3
Bathrooms: 2
Foundation: Slab, basement
Materials List Available: Yes
Price Category: C

This home, as shown in the photograph, may differ from the actual blueprints. For more detailed information, please check the floor plans carefully.

CAD FILE AVAILABLE

This one-level home is perfect for retirement or for convenient living for the growing family.

Features:

• Ceiling Height: 8 ft.

• Master Suite: For privacy and quiet, the master suite is segregated from the other bedrooms.

• Family Room: Sit by the fire and read as light streams through the windows flanking the fireplace. Or enjoy the built-in entertainment center.

• Breakfast Area: Located just off the family room, the sunny breakfast area will lure you to linger over impromptu family meals. Here you will find a built-in desk for compiling shopping lists and menus.

• Private Porch: Step out of the breakfast area to enjoy a breeze on this porch.

• Kitchen: Efficient and attractive, this kitchen offers an angled pantry and an island that doubles as a snack bar.

SMARTtip

Measuring for Kitchen Countertops

Custom cabinetmakers will sometimes come to your house to measure for a countertop, but home centers and kitchen stores may require that you come to them with the dimensions already in hand. Be sure to double-check measurements carefully. Being off by only ½ in. can be quite upsetting.

To ensure accuracy, sketch out the countertop on a sheet of graph paper. Include all the essential dimensions. To be on the safe side, have someone else double-check your numbers.

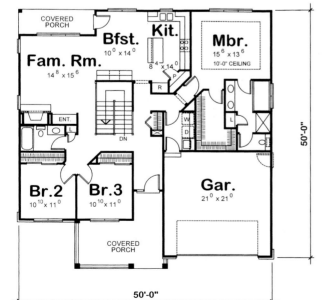

Copyright by designer/architect.

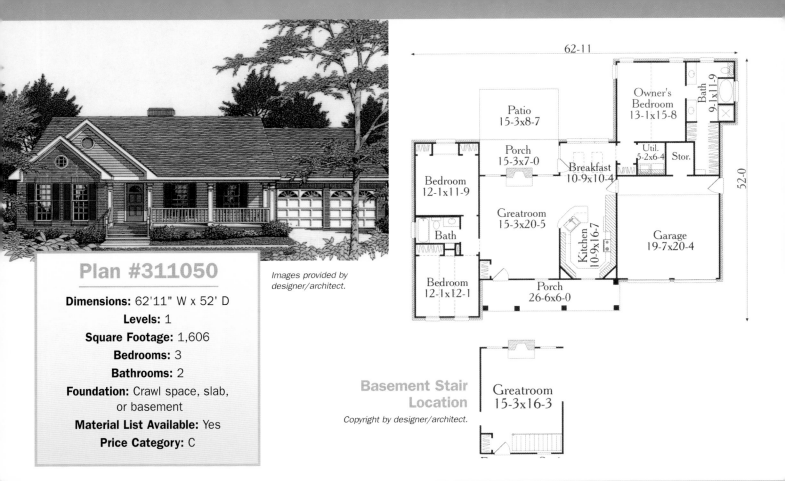

Plan #311050

Dimensions: 62'11" W x 52' D

Levels: 1

Square Footage: 1,606

Bedrooms: 3

Bathrooms: 2

Foundation: Crawl space, slab, or basement

Material List Available: Yes

Price Category: C

Images provided by designer/architect.

62-11

Patio 15-3x8-7

Porch 15-3x7-0

Owner's Bedroom 13-1x15-8

Bath 9-1x11-9

Bedroom 12-1x11-9

Breakfast 10-9x10-4

Util. 5-2x6-4

Stor.

Bath

Greatroom 15-3x20-5

Kitchen 10-9x16-7

Garage 19-7x20-4

52-0

Bedroom 12-1x12-1

Porch 26-6x6-0

Basement Stair Location

Greatroom 15-3x16-3

Copyright by designer/architect.

Plan #421003

Dimensions: 59' W x 61' D

Levels: 1

Square Footage: 1,698

Bedrooms: 3

Bathrooms: 2½

Foundation: Crawl space, slab, or basement

Materials List Available: Yes

Price Category: C

Images provided by designer/architect.

CAD FILE AVAILABLE

GARAGE 21'-0"x22'-0" (CARPORT OR NO GARAGE OPTIONAL)

WORK BENCH/STORAGE

16' OVERHEAD DOOR

PATIO 20'-0"x12'-0"

WALK-IN CLOSET

MSTR BATH

PWDR

HALL

PANTRY

KITCHEN 13'-0"x10'-0"

DINING 11'-0"x10'-0"

BEDROOM #3 13'-0"x11'-10"

BATH

COLUMNS

OPTIONAL PRIVACY DOOR (POCKET)

SITTING AREA

RIDGE OF VAULT

GREAT ROOM 24'-0"x20'-0" (10' CLG)

BEDROOM #2 13'-0"x11'-10"

MASTER BEDROOM 15'-5"x16'-0" (VAULTED CLG)

OPTIONAL ROOM DIVIDER

COVERED PORCH 25'-0"x8'-0" (10' CLG)

Copyright by designer/architect.

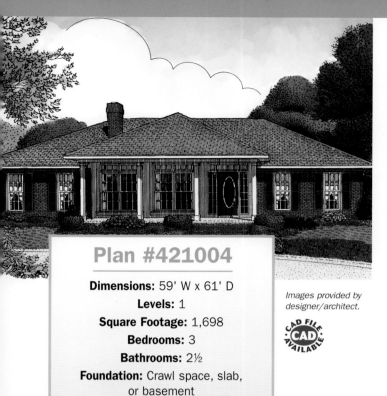

Images provided by designer/architect.

Copyright by designer/architect.

Plan #421004

Dimensions: 59' W x 61' D

Levels: 1

Square Footage: 1,698

Bedrooms: 3

Bathrooms: 2½

Foundation: Crawl space, slab, or basement

Material List Available: Yes

Price Category: C

Images provided by designer/architect.

Copyright by designer/architect.

Plan #131001

Dimensions: 72'4" W x 32'4" D

Levels: 1

Square Footage: 1,615

Bedrooms: 3

Bathrooms: 2

Foundation: Crawl space, slab, basement, or walkout

Materials List Available: Yes

Price Category: D

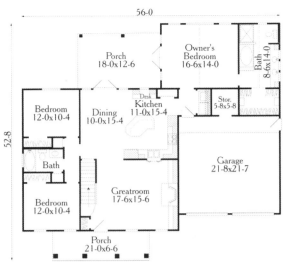

Plan #311048

Dimensions: 56' W x 52'8" D

Levels: 1

Square Footage: 1,551

Bedrooms: 3

Bathrooms: 2

Foundation: Crawl space, slab, or basement

Material List Available: Yes

Price Category: C

Images provided by designer/architect.

Bonus Area Floor Plan

Copyright by designer/architect.

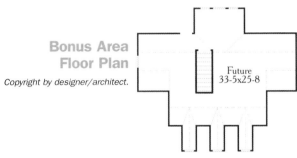

Plan #281018

Dimensions: 50' W x 52'6" D

Levels: 1

Square Footage: 1,565

Bedrooms: 3

Bathrooms: 2

Foundation: Basement

Materials List Available: Yes

Price Category: C

Images provided by designer/architect.

Copyright by designer/architect.

Rear Elevation

Plan #151006

Dimensions: 54'2" W x 52'10" D

Levels: 1

Square Footage: 1,758

Bedrooms: 3

Bathrooms: 2

Foundation: Crawl space, slab, basement, or walkout

CompleteCost List Available: Yes

Price Category: C

Images provided by designer/architect.

This home, as shown in the photograph, may differ from the actual blueprints. For more detailed information, please check the floor plans carefully.

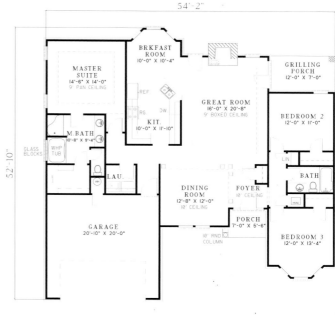

Copyright by designer/architect.

Plan #121165

Dimensions: 46' W x 55' D

Levels: 1

Square Footage: 1,678

Bedrooms: 3

Bathrooms: 2

Foundation: Basement; crawl space for fee

Material List Available: Yes

Price Category: C

Images provided by designer/architect.

This home, as shown in the photograph, may differ from the actual blueprints. For more detailed information, please check the floor plans carefully.

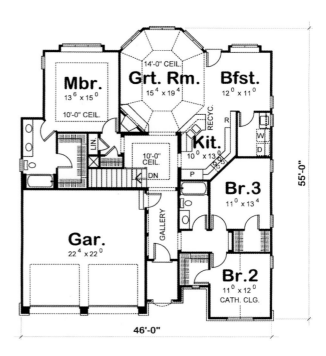

Copyright by designer/architect.

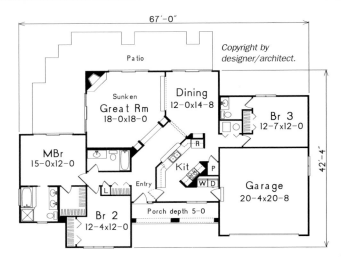

67'-0"

Patio

Dining
12-0x14-8

Sunken
Great Rm
18-0x18-0

Br 3
12-7x12-0

MBr
15-0x12-0

Kit

R

P

Garage
20-4x20-8

W D

Entry

L

42'-4"

Porch depth 5-0

Br 2
12-4x12-0

Copyright by
designer/architect.

Plan #321026

Dimensions: 67' W x 42'4" D

Levels: 1

Square Footage: 1,712

Bedrooms: 3

Bathrooms: 2½

Foundation: Crawl space

Materials List Available: Yes

Price Category: C

*Images provided by
designer/architect.*

Deck Design with Computers

Consider using a computer-aided design (CAD)
program to plan your deck. Some programs let you
see three-dimensional views of your design
complete with railings, stairs, planters, hot tubs,
and the surrounding landscaping.

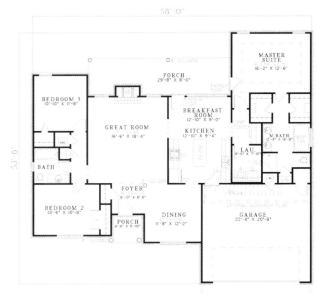

58'-0"

MASTER
SUITE
16'-2" X 12'-6"

BEDROOM 3
10'-10" X 11'-8"

PORCH
29'-8" X 8'-0"

53'-6"

GREAT ROOM
16'-6" X 18'-4"

BREAKFAST
ROOM
12'-10" X 9'-0"

KITCHEN
12'-10" X 9'-4"

M. BATH
12'-4" X 16'-8"

BATH

LAU
6'-0" X 7'-10"

FOYER
6'-10" X 6'-6"

BEDROOM 2
13'-6" X 10'-8"

DINING
11'-8" X 12'-2"

GARAGE
22'-4" X 20'-8"

PORCH
6'-6" X 5'-10"

Plan #151173

Dimensions: 58' W x 53'6" D

Levels: 1

Square Footage: 1,739

Bedrooms: 3

Bathrooms: 2

Foundation: Crawl space, slab,
basement, or walkout

CompleteCost List Available: Yes

Price Category: C

*Images provided by
designer/architect.*

CAD FILE
AVAILABLE
CAD

*Copyright by
designer/architect.*

Plan #321008

Dimensions: 57' W x 52'2" D
Levels: 1
Square Footage: 1,761
Bedrooms: 4
Bathrooms: 2
Foundation: Basement
Materials List Available: Yes
Price Category: C

One look at the roof dormers and planter boxes that grace the outside of this ranch, and you'll know that the interior is planned for comfortable family living.

Features:

- Great Room: A vaulted ceiling in this room points up its generous dimensions. Put a grouping of chairs near the fireplace to take advantage of the cozy spot it creates in chilly weather.

- Kitchen: Open to the great room, this kitchen has been planned for convenience. It features a pass-through to the dining area for easy serving when you've got a crowd to feed.

- Master Bedroom: A vaulted ceiling here makes you feel especially pampered, and the walk-in closet and amenity-filled bath add to that feeling.

- Additional Bedrooms: Great closet space characterizes all the rooms in this home, making it easy for children of any age to keep it organized and tidy.

Images provided by designer/architect.

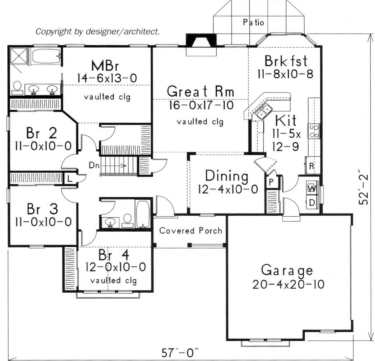

Copyright by designer/architect.

SMARTtip

Hanging Wallpaper

Use liner paper to smooth out a damaged wall and to provide uniform support for expensive paper.

Plan #131047

Dimensions: 69'10" W x 51'8" D
Levels: 1
Square Footage: 1,793
Bedrooms: 3
Bathrooms: 2
Foundation: Crawl space, slab, or basement
Materials List Available: Yes
Price Category: D

The country charm of this well-designed home is mixed with the convenience and luxury normally reserved for more contemporary plans.

Features:

- Great Room: The spaciousness of this great room is enhanced by the 11-ft. stepped ceiling. A fireplace makes it cozy on cool evenings or on chilly winter days, and two sets of French sliding glass doors open to the back porch.

- Kitchen: In addition to the convenient layout of this design, you'll also love its bright, airy position. It includes an old-fashioned pantry,

a sink under a window, and a sunny breakfast area that opens to the wraparound porch.

- Master Suite: You'll find 11-ft. ceilings in both the master bedroom and the bayed sitting area that the suite includes. In the bath, the circular spa tub is surrounded by a glass-block wall.

- Bonus Space: A permanent staircase leads to an unfinished bonus space on the upper level.

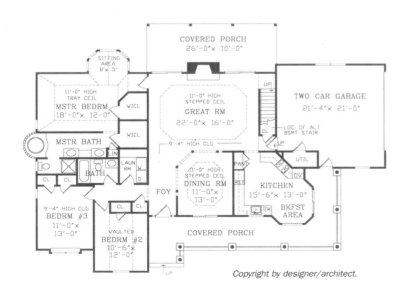

Copyright by designer/architect.

Rear Elevation

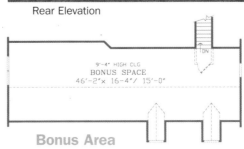

Bonus Area

Plan #391004

Dimensions: 66' W x 52' D

Levels: 1

Square Footage: 1,750

Bedrooms: 2

Bathrooms: 2

Foundation: Crawl space, slab, or basement

Materials List Available: Yes

Price Category: C

This creatively compact ranch is made especially for effortless everyday living.

Features:

- Kitchen: This centralized U-shaped kitchen and look-alike breakfast nook with professional pantry have a wonderful view of the porch.

- Laundry Room: Laundry facilities are cleverly placed within reach while neatly out of the way.

- Great Room: Step into this lavish-looking sunken great room for fireside gatherings, and move easily into the nearby formal dining area where a screened porch allows you to entertain guests after dinner.

- Master Suite: Flanking one side of the house, this master suite is serenely private and amenity-filled. Its features include full bath, a wall of walk-in closets and a dressing area.

- Bedroom: This second spacious bedroom enjoys great closeting (with double-doors), a full bath, and a close-at-hand den (or bedroom #3).

- Garage: This three-car garage goes beyond vehicle protection, providing plenty of storage and work space.

Images provided by designer/architect.

Crawl Space/Slab Option

Copyright by designer/architect.

Rear View

Plan #371104

Dimensions: 57' W x 52'6" D

Levels: 1

Square Footage: 1,795

Bedrooms: 3

Bathrooms: 2

Foundation: Crawl space or slab

Material List Available: No

Price Category: C

Images provided by designer/architect.

CAD FILE AVAILABLE

Copyright by designer/architect.

Plan #281020

Dimensions: 60' W x 48' D

Levels: 1

Square Footage: 1,734

Bedrooms: 3

Bathrooms: 2½

Foundation: Basement

Materials List Available: Yes

Price Category: C

Images provided by designer/architect.

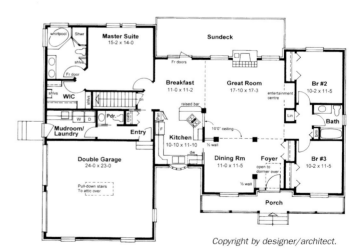

Copyright by designer/architect.

Plan #161001

Dimensions: 67'2" W x 47' D
Levels: 1
Square Footage: 1,782
Bedrooms: 3
Bathrooms: 2
Foundation: Basement
Materials List Available: Yes
Price Category: C

Images provided by designer/architect.

An all-brick exterior displays the solid strength that characterizes this gracious home.

CAD FILE AVAILABLE

Features:

- **Great Room:** A feeling of spaciousness permeates the gathering area created by the foyer, great room, and dining room. Multiple windows provide natural light that dances along a sloped ceiling, spilling onto decorative columns and a fireplace.

- **Breakfast Area:** A continuation of the sloped ceiling leads to the breakfast area where French doors open to a screened porch.

- **Kitchen:** An abundance of cabinets and counter space are the hallmarks of this large kitchen with its easy access to a spacious laundry room and storage area.

- **Master Suite:** A tray ceiling and spacious walk-in closet in the master bedroom, along with a whirlpool tub and double-bowl vanity in the bathroom, enable you to pamper yourself.

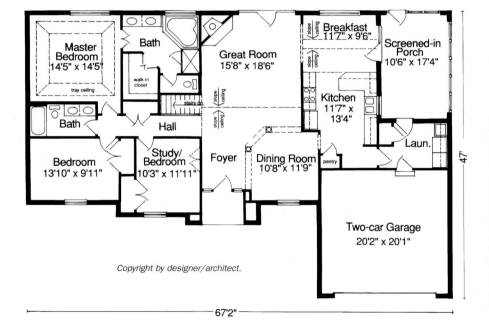

Copyright by designer/architect.

Great Room/Foyer

Rear Elevation

www.ultimateplans.com   121

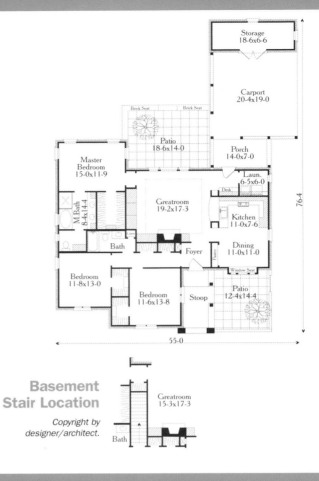

Plan #311058

Dimensions: 55' W x 76'4" D

Levels: 1

Square Footage: 1,702

Bedrooms: 3

Bathrooms: 2

Foundation: Crawl space, slab, or basement

Material List Available: Yes

Price Category: C

Images provided by designer/architect.

Storage 18-6x6-6

Carport 20-4x19-0

Brick Seat   Brick Seat

Patio 18-6x14-0

Porch 14-0x7-0

Master Bedroom 15-0x11-9

Laun. 6-5x6-0

Greatroom 19-2x17-3

M.Bath 8-4x14-4

Kitchen 11-0x7-6

Bath

Foyer

Dining 11-0x11-0

Window Seat

Bedroom 11-8x13-0

Bedroom 11-6x13-8

Stoop

Patio 12-4x14-4

55-0

76-4

Basement Stair Location

Copyright by designer/architect.

Greatroom 15-3x17-3

Bath

Plan #321021

Dimensions: 80' W x 42' D

Levels: 1

Square Footage: 1,708

Bedrooms: 3

Bathrooms: 2

Foundation: Crawl space or basement

Materials List Available: Yes

Price Category: C

Images provided by designer/architect.

SMARTtip

Planning a Safe Children's Room

Keep safety in mind when planning a child's room. Make sure that there are covers on electrical outlets, guard rails on high windows, sturdy screens in front of radiators, and gates blocking any steps. Other suggestions include safety hinges for chests and nonskid backing for rugs.

Porch

Family 15-5x20-3

Garage 23-8x23-5

Br 3 10-4x12-4

Dn   P

MBr 13-7x15-11

W D

R

Kit 9-8x 10-0

Foyer

Dining 10-0x11-6

Brk 9-8x 8-0

Br 2 11-5x12-11

Porch depth 4-0

42'-0"

80'-0"

Copyright by designer/architect.

Plan #151007

Dimensions: 54'2" W x 56'2" D

Levels: 1

Square Footage: 1,787

Bedrooms: 3

Bathrooms: 2

Foundation: Crawl space, slab, basement, or walkout

CompleteCost List Available: Yes

Price Category: C

Images provided by designer/architect.

CAD FILE AVAILABLE

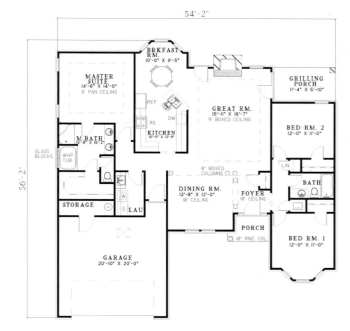

Plan #171009

Dimensions: 68' W x 50' D

Levels: 1

Square Footage: 1,771

Bedrooms: 3

Bathrooms: 2

Foundation: Crawl space, slab

Materials List Available: Yes

Price Category: C

Images provided by designer/architect.

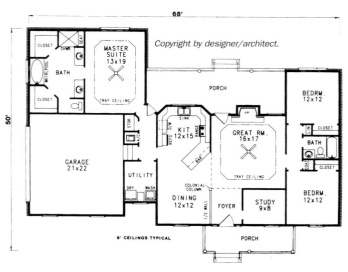

SMARTtip

Deck Awnings

Awnings come in bright colors. As light filters through, it will cast a hue to anything under the deck. Warm colors, such as red or pink, will create a rosy glow; cool colors, such blues or greens, will enhance the shade.

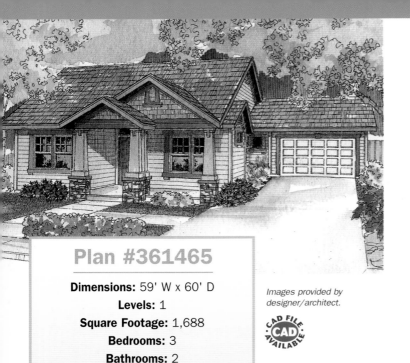

Plan #361465

Dimensions: 59' W x 60' D

Levels: 1

Square Footage: 1,688

Bedrooms: 3

Bathrooms: 2

Foundation: Crawl space

Material List Available: No

Price Category: C

Images provided by designer/architect.

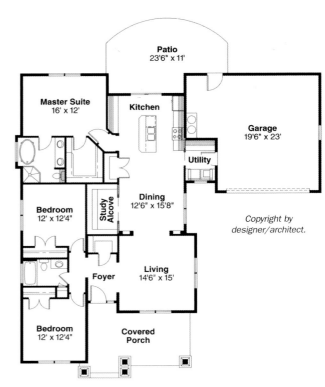

Copyright by designer/architect.

Plan #461147

Dimensions: 45' W x 65'6" D

Levels: 1

Square Footage: 1,693

Bedrooms: 3

Bathrooms: 2½

Foundation: Slab or basement

Material List Available: No

Price Category: C

Images provided by designer/architect.

Copyright by designer/architect.

Plan #321001

Dimensions: 83' W x 42' D

Levels: 1

Square Footage: 1,721

Bedrooms: 3

Bathrooms: 2

Foundation: Crawl space, slab, or basement

Materials List Available: Yes

Price Category: C

You'll love the atrium which creates a warm, naturally lit space inside this gracious home, as well as the roof dormers that give the house wonderful curb appeal from the outside.

Features:

- Great Room: Bathed in light from the atrium window wall, this room, with its vaulted ceiling, will be the hub of your family life.

- Dining Room: This room also has a vaulted ceiling and is lit by the atrium, but you can draw drapes at night to create a cozy, warm feeling.

- Kitchen: Designed for functionality, this step-saving kitchen is easy to organize and makes cooking a pleasure.

- Breakfast Room: For convenience, this room is located between the kitchen and the rear covered porch.

- Master Suite: Retire with pleasure to this lovely retreat, with its luxurious bath.

Images provided by designer/architect.

Rear View

Copyright by designer/architect.

Plan #131007

Dimensions: 59'10" W x 47'8" D

Levels: 1

Square Footage: 1,595

Bedrooms: 3

Bathrooms: 2

Foundation: Crawl space, slab, basement, or walkout

Materials List Available: Yes

Price Category: D

Imagine living in this home, with its traditional country comfort and individual brand of charm.

Features:

• Exterior elements: The mixture of a front porch with a cameo front door, decorative posts, bay windows, and dormers will delight you.

• Great Room: A tray ceiling gives distinction to this large room, and a wet bar eases entertaining.

• Screened Porch: At dusk and dawn, this porch is sure to be your favorite outdoor spot.

• Kitchen: Eat any meal in this large kitchen for a touch of homey charm.

• Dining Room: Perfect for hosting a formal dinner, this bayed dining room can increase your enjoyment of simple family meals.

• Master Bedroom: For the sake of privacy, this room is somewhat secluded. Decorate to emphasize the elegant tray ceiling.

Images provided by designer/architect.

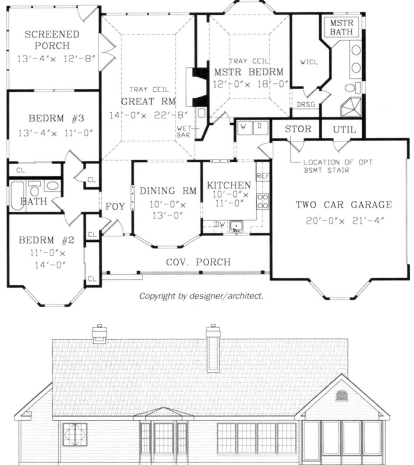

Copyright by designer/architect.

Rear Elevation

Alternate Front View

Foyer / Dining Room

Great Room

Add the Extras

Simple or plain, it's the little conveniences and miscellaneous touches that push the dining experience to perfection. Here are some extra things to think about.

- You can never have too many serving trays when you entertain outside. For carrying food or drinks from the kitchen or the grill, trays are indispensable.

- A serving cart on wheels makes a perfect movable outdoor bar and provides an additional serving surface. Look for one at yard sales or buy one new.

- Chances are you won't have a sideboard, but a few small tables to hold excess items are great substitutes for one. They're also easier to position in the different places where you need them.

- For cooler weather or even a summer's evening with a bit of nip in the air, nothing beats an outdoor fireplace for comfort. You could build one into the house, but various types of stand-alone units are sold in home centers. To add a Southwest ambiance, consider a chiminea, a clay fireplace. Try burning some piñon pine, and you'll feel as if you're in Santa Fe. Be sure to follow manufacturers' instructions when using these fireplaces. You might also have to store them during the winter.

- Pots of fragrant plants—lavender, scented geraniums, flowering tobacco, or jasmine—provide a sensual aroma. Flowers such as roses climbing up an arbor or trellis are beautiful, evoke a romantic feeling, and lend a delicate scent to the atmosphere as well.

Nothing adds romance and intrigue to an evening soiree as candlelight does. Include just a few candles for an intimate dinner. Use more for a larger gathering, placing one or more on each table. Scatter luminaries around the yard. As the beautiful evening dusk begins, light candles, a few at a time, so your eyes can adjust to the dimming light. Not only do the candles illuminate the night in a magical way but they can also keep bugs at bay.

Plan #391025

Dimensions: 54' W x 48'4" D
Levels: 1
Square Footage: 1,625
Bedrooms: 3
Bathrooms: 2
Foundation: Crawl space, slab, or basement
Materials List Available: Yes
Price Category: C

This lovely home, ideal for starters or empty nesters, conveys rustic charm while maintaining clean contemporary lines.

Features:

• Kitchen: This functional U-shaped kitchen features an adjacent utility area that can serve as a pantry and direct access to the garage for unloading groceries after a shopping trip.

• Fireplace: This cozy two-sided fireplace joins the living room and dining room, which is open to the adjacent kitchen.

• Den: The roomy den (or guest bedroom) features a beautiful Palladian window.

• Master Suite: With plenty of elbowroom, this master suite has a large walk-in closet and bathroom with double sinks, a whirlpool tub, and separate shower.

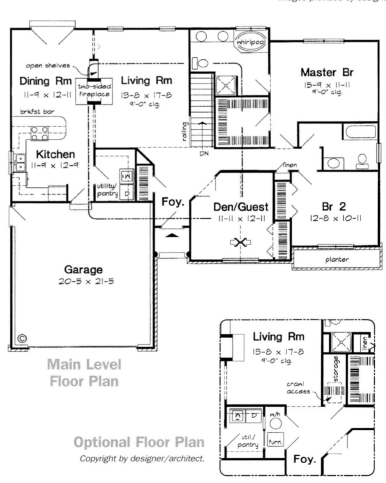

Main Level Floor Plan

Optional Floor Plan

Plan #211002

Dimensions: 68' W x 62' D
Levels: 1
Square Footage: 1,792
Bedrooms: 3
Bathrooms: 2
Foundation: Crawl space
Materials List Available: Yes
Price Category: C

Arched windows on the front of this home give it a European style that you're sure to love.

SMARTtip

Water Features

Water features create the ambiance of a soothing oasis on a deck. A water-filled urn becomes a mirror that reflects the sky—making a small deck look larger. Fish flashing in an ornamental pool add color and act as a focal point for a deck with no view.

A water fountain introduces a pleasant rhythmical sound that helps drown out the background noises of traffic and nearby neighbors.

Features:

- Living Room: The 12-ft. ceiling in this large, open room enhances its spacious feeling. A fireplace adds warmth on chilly days and cool evenings.

- Dining Room: Decorate to accentuate the 12-ft. ceiling and formal feeling of this room.

- Kitchen: Designed for comfort and efficiency, this room also has a 12-ft. ceiling. The cozy breakfast bar is a natural gathering spot for friends and family.

- Master Suite: A split design guarantees privacy here. A sloped cathedral ceiling adds elegance, and a walk-in closet makes it practical. The bath has two vanities, a tub, and a walk-in shower.

- Garage: Park two cars here, and use the balance of this 520 sq. ft. area as a handy storage area.

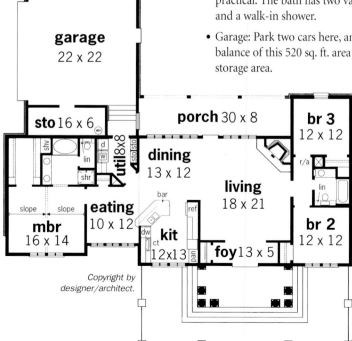

Copyright by designer/architect.

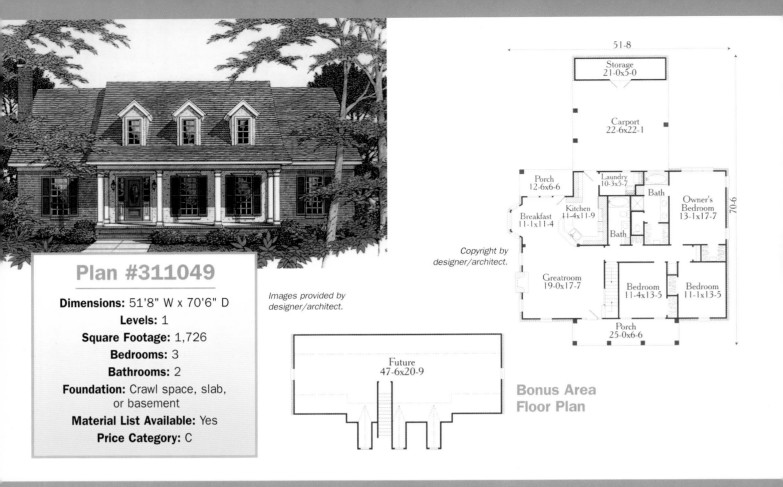

Plan #311049

Dimensions: 51'8" W x 70'6" D
Levels: 1
Square Footage: 1,726
Bedrooms: 3
Bathrooms: 2
Foundation: Crawl space, slab, or basement
Material List Available: Yes
Price Category: C

Images provided by designer/architect.

Copyright by designer/architect.

Bonus Area Floor Plan

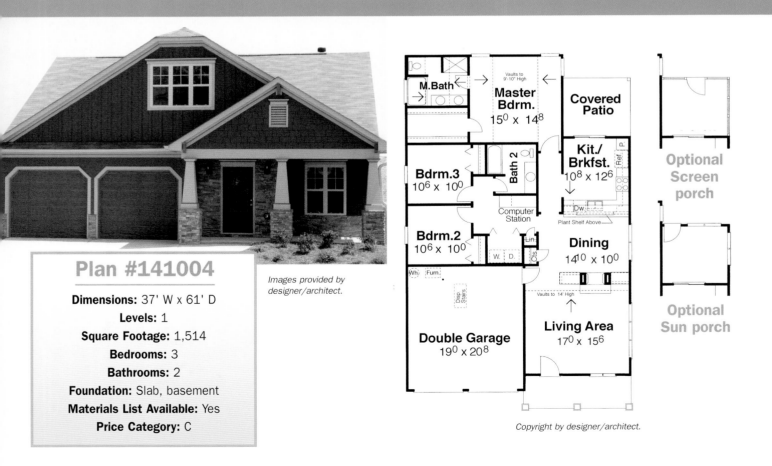

Plan #141004

Dimensions: 37' W x 61' D
Levels: 1
Square Footage: 1,514
Bedrooms: 3
Bathrooms: 2
Foundation: Slab, basement
Materials List Available: Yes
Price Category: C

Images provided by designer/architect.

Copyright by designer/architect.

Plan #271077

Dimensions: 69'6" W x 53' D
Levels: 1
Square Footage: 1,786
Bedrooms: 1
Bathrooms: 1½
Foundation: Basement or daylight basement
Materials List Available: No
Price Category: C

Images provided by designer/architect.

CAD FILE AVAILABLE

Optional Basement Level Floor Plan

Copyright by designer/architect.

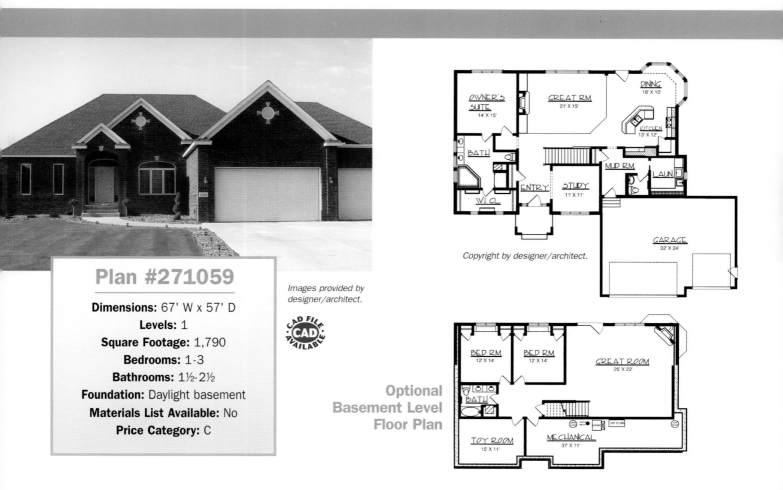

Plan #271059

Dimensions: 67' W x 57' D
Levels: 1
Square Footage: 1,790
Bedrooms: 1-3
Bathrooms: 1½-2½
Foundation: Daylight basement
Materials List Available: No
Price Category: C

Images provided by designer/architect.

CAD FILE AVAILABLE

Copyright by designer/architect.

Optional Basement Level Floor Plan

Plan #371124

Dimensions: 77'6" W x 39'9" D

Levels: 1

Square Footage: 1,746

Bedrooms: 3

Bathrooms: 2

Foundation: Crawl space or slab

Material List Available: No

Price Category: C

Images provided by designer/architect.

Copyright by designer/architect.

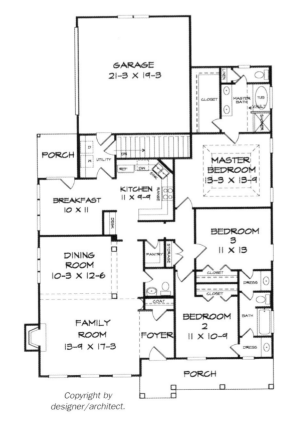

Plan #461009

Dimensions: 67'6" W x 43'6" D

Levels: 1

Square Footage: 1,758

Bedrooms: 3

Bathrooms: 2½

Foundation: Slab or basement; crawl space available for fee

Material List Available: No

Price Category: C

Images provided by designer/architect.

Copyright by designer/architect.

Plan #151009

Dimensions: 44' W x 86'2" D
Levels: 1
Square Footage: 1,601
Bedrooms: 3
Bathrooms: 2
Foundation: Crawl space, slab
CompleteCost List Available: Yes
Price Category: C

CAD FILE AVAILABLE

This can be the perfect home for a site with views you can enjoy in all seasons and at all times.

Features:

- **Porches:** Enjoy the front porch with its 10-ft. ceiling and the more private back porch where you can set up a grill or just get away from it all.

- **Foyer:** With a 10-ft. ceiling, this foyer opens to the great room for a warm welcome.

- **Great Room:** Your family will love the media center and the easy access to the rear porch.

- **Kitchen:** This well-designed kitchen is open to the dining room and the breakfast nook, which also opens to the rear porch.

- **Master Suite:** The bedroom has a 10-ft. boxed ceiling and a door to the rear. The bath includes a corner whirlpool tub with glass block windows.

- **Bedrooms:** Bedroom 2 has a vaulted ceiling, while bedroom 3 features a built-in desk.

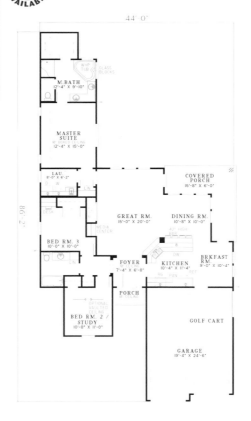

Copyright by designer/architect.

Plan #241005

Dimensions: 53' W x 55'9" D
Levels: 1
Square Footage: 1,670
Bedrooms: 3
Bathrooms: 2
Foundation: Crawl space or slab; basement option for fee
Materials List Available: No
Price Category: C

This charming starter home, in split-bedroom format, combines big-house features in a compact design.

Features:

- **Great Room:** With easy access to the formal dining room, kitchen, and breakfast area, this great room features a cozy fireplace.

- **Kitchen:** This big kitchen, with easy access to a walk-in pantry, features an island for added work space and a lovely plant shelf that separates it from the great room.

- **Master Suite:** Separated for privacy, this master suite offers a roomy bath with whirlpool tub, dual vanities, a separate shower, and a large walk-in closet.

- **Additional Rooms:** Additional rooms include a laundry/utility room—with space for a washer, dryer, and freezer—a large area above the garage, well-suited for a media or game room, and two secondary bedrooms.

Images provided by designer/architect.

Copyright by designer/architect.

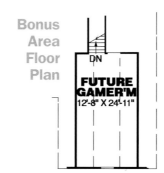

Bonus Area Floor Plan

Plan #151003

Dimensions: 51'6" W x 52'4" D

Levels: 1

Square Footage: 1,680

Bedrooms: 3

Bathrooms: 2

Foundation: Crawl space, slab, or basement

CompleteCost List Available: Yes

Price Category: C

Images provided by designer/architect.

This home, as shown in the photograph, may differ from the actual blueprints. For more detailed information, please check the floor plans carefully.

Copyright by designer/architect.

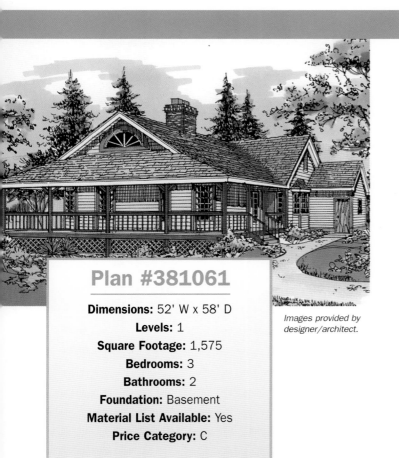

Plan #381061

Dimensions: 52' W x 58' D

Levels: 1

Square Footage: 1,575

Bedrooms: 3

Bathrooms: 2

Foundation: Basement

Material List Available: Yes

Price Category: C

Images provided by designer/architect.

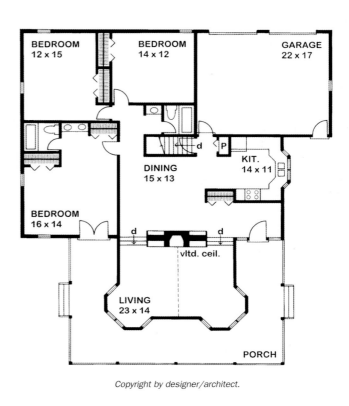

Copyright by designer/architect.

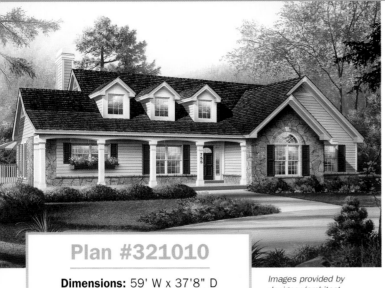

Plan #321010

Dimensions: 59' W x 37'8" D
Levels: 1
Square Footage: 1,787
Bedrooms: 3
Bathrooms: 2
Foundation: Basement
Materials List Available: Yes
Price Category: C

Images provided by designer/architect.

Copyright by designer/architect.

59'-0"

Deck

skylights

Great Rm
23-8x15-4
vaulted

MBr
15-6x14-6
vaulted

W D

37'-8"

Brk

P

Kitchen
14-7x15-8

Dining
11-1x13-8

Entry

Dn

L

R

Porch depth 5-0

Br 3
12-0x12-0

Br 2
12-0x12-0

vaulted

Plan #321003

Dimensions: 67'4" W x 48' D
Levels: 1
Square Footage: 1,791
Bedrooms: 4
Bathrooms: 2
Foundation: Basement
Materials List Available: Yes
Price Category: C

Images provided by designer/architect.

Copyright by designer/architect.

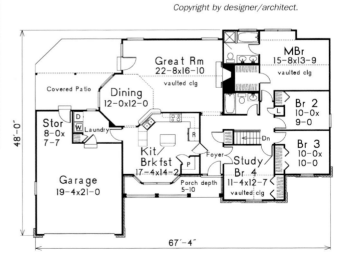

Covered Patio

Great Rm
22-8x16-10
vaulted clg

MBr
15-8x13-9
vaulted clg

Dining
12-0x12-0

Br 2
10-0x
9-0

48'-0"

Stor
8-0x
7-7

D
W
Laundry

Kit
Brkfst
17-4x14-2

Foyer

Dn

Study
Br 4
11-4x12-7
vaulted clg

Br 3
10-0x
10-0

L

R

P

Garage
19-4x21-0

Porch depth
5-10

67'-4"

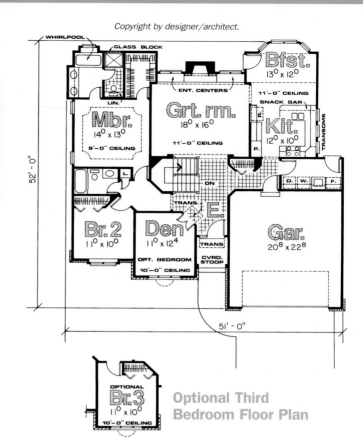

Plan #121055

Dimensions: 51' W x 52' D

Levels: 1

Square Footage: 1,622

Bedrooms: 3

Bathrooms: 2

Foundation: Basement

Materials List Available: Yes

Price Category: C

Images provided by designer/architect.

Optional Third Bedroom Floor Plan

Plan #401045

Dimensions: 78'6" W x 48' D

Levels: 1

Square Footage: 1,652

Bedrooms: 3

Bathrooms: 2

Foundation: Basement

Material List Available: Yes

Price Category: C

Images provided by designer/architect.

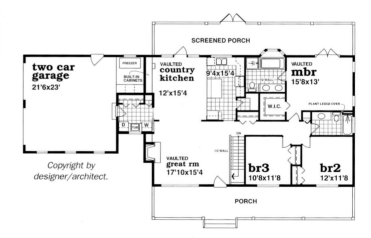

Rear Elevation

Plan #131064

Dimensions: 74' W x 47' D
Levels: 1
Square Footage: 1,783
Bedrooms: 3
Bathrooms: 2
Foundation: Crawl space, slab, or basement
Material List Available: Yes
Price Category: D

Images provided by designer/architect.

- Kitchen: This island kitchen boasts an abundance of cabinet and counter space. The adjoining breakfast room's large windows flood the space with natural light.
- Master Suite: This private retreat boasts a large sleeping area with a tray ceiling. The

master bath features his and her vanities, a second walk-in closet, and a compartmentalized toilet area.

- Bedrooms: Two secondary bedrooms with walk-in closets share a common full bathroom.

High ceilings and a flowing, open, interior distinguish this charming, country-style ranch.

Features:

- Great Room: This large gathering area boasts a stepped ceiling and a beautiful fireplace. There are built-in cabinets on either side of the fireplace, which would be a perfect entertainment center.

- Dining Room: Accented with columns and a stepped ceiling, this dining room is able to handle all formal gatherings. Open to the foyer and the great room, the area allows friends and family to have easy access to the rest of the house.

Rear Elevation

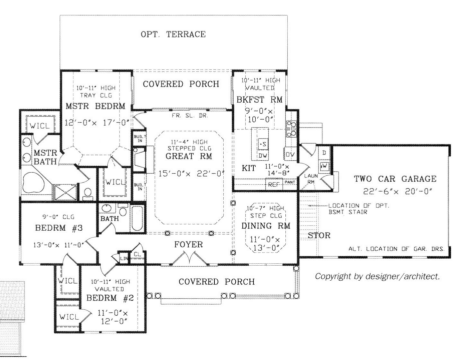

Copyright by designer/architect.

Plan #371073

Dimensions: 54'6" W x 52' D
Levels: 1
Square Footage: 1,783
Bedrooms: 3
Bathrooms: 2
Foundation: Slab
Materials List Available: No
Price Category: C

CAD FILE AVAILABLE

Images provided by designer/architect.

The tall arched windows make this home stand out.

Features:

- Living Room: This large gathering area has a lovely fireplace, a built-in media center, and a view onto the rear porch.

- Dining Room: A sloped ceiling makes this formal eating area feel much larger than it is.

- Kitchen: This efficient U-shaped kitchen looks into the adjoining breakfast nook, which has a bay window.

- Master Suite: Secluded and luxurious, this area features a sloped ceiling and a huge master bathroom with his and her walk-in closets.

- Bedrooms: The two secondary bedrooms have large closets and share a common bathroom.

Copyright by designer/architect.

Plan #121008

Dimensions: 62' W x 56' D
Levels: 1
Square Footage: 1,651
Bedrooms: 2
Bathrooms: 2
Foundation: Basement
Materials List Available: Yes
Price Category: C

Images provided by designer/architect.

This elegant home is packed with amenities that belie its compact size.

Features:

• Ceiling Height: 8 ft.

• Dining Room: The foyer opens into a view of the dining room, with its distinctive boxed ceiling.

• Great Room: The whole family will want to gather around the fireplace and enjoy the views and sunlight streaming through the transom-topped window.

• Breakfast Area: Next to the great room and sharing the transom-topped windows, this cozy area invites you to linger over morning coffee.

• Covered Porch: When the weather is nice, take your coffee through the door in the breakfast area and enjoy this large covered porch.

• Master Suite: French doors lead to this comfortable suite featuring a walk-in. Enjoy long, luxurious soaks in the corner whirlpool accented with boxed windows.

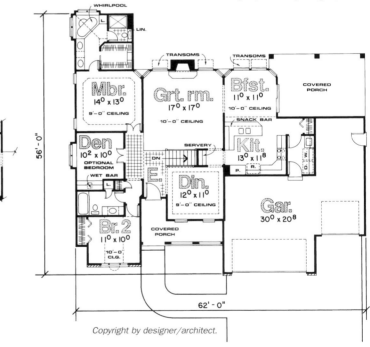

Optional
Bedroom

Copyright by designer/architect.

SMARTtip
Finishing Your Fireplace with Tile

An excellent finishing material for a fireplace is tile. Luckily, there are reproductions of art tiles today. Most showrooms carry examples of Arts and Crafts, Art Nouveau, California, Delft, and other European tiles. Granite, limestone, and marble tiles are affordable alternatives to custom stone slabs.

Plan #461064

Dimensions: 62'6" W x 54'6" D
Levels: 1
Square Footage: 1,677
Bedrooms: 3
Bathrooms: 2
Foundation: Crawl space or slab; basement for fee
Material List Available: No
Price Category: C

Images provided by designer/architect.

Copyright by designer/architect.

Plan #461032

Dimensions: 67'6" W x 36' D
Levels: 1
Square Footage: 1,799
Bedrooms: 3
Bathrooms: 2
Foundation: Slab; crawl space or basement for fee
Material List Available: No
Price Category: C

Images provided by designer/architect.

Copyright by designer/architect.

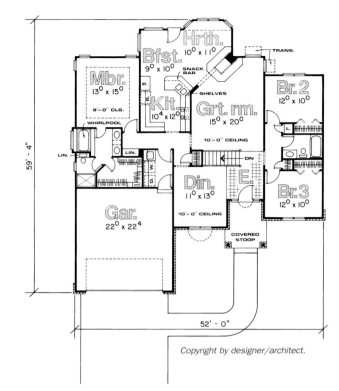

Plan #121059

Dimensions: 52' W x 59'4" D

Levels: 1

Square Footage: 1,782

Bedrooms: 3

Bathrooms: 2

Foundation: Basement

Materials List Available: Yes

Price Category: C

Images provided by designer/architect.

Copyright by designer/architect.

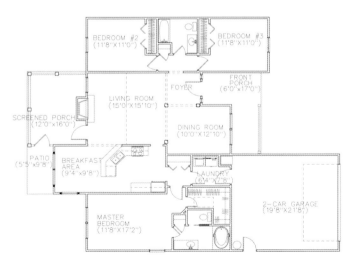

Plan #521038

Dimensions: 49' W x 63'8" D

Levels: 1

Square Footage: 1,567

Bedrooms: 3

Bathrooms: 2

Foundation: Slab

Material List Available: No

Price Category: C

Images provided by designer/architect.

Copyright by designer/architect.

Plan #251005

Dimensions: 50' W x 44'2" D
Levels: 1
Square Footage: 1,631
Bedrooms: 3
Bathrooms: 2
Foundation: Basement
Materials List Available: Yes
Price Category: C

Images provided by designer/architect.

This elegant home features hip roof lines that will add appeal in any neighborhood.

Features:

- Ceiling Height: 9 ft.

- Front Porch: The porch stretches across the entire front of the home, offering plenty of space to sit and enjoy evening breezes.

- Family Room: This family room features a handsome fireplace and has plenty of room for all kinds of family activities.

- Dining Room: This dining room has plenty of room for dinner parties. After dinner, guests can step through French doors onto the rear deck.

- Kitchen: This kitchen is a pleasure in which to work. It features an angled snack bar with plenty of room for informal family meals.

- Master Bedroom: You'll enjoy retiring at day's end to this master bedroom, with its large walk-in closet.

- Master Bath. This master bath features a double vanity, a deluxe tub, and a walk-in shower.

Copyright by designer/architect.

SMARTtip

Victorian Style

Victorian, today, is a very romantic look. To underscore this, add the scent of lavender or some other dried flower to the room or use potpourri, which you can keep in a bowl on the vanity. Hang a fragrant pomander on a hook, display lavender soaps on a wall shelf, or tuck sachets between towels on a shelf. For an authentic touch, display a Victorian favorite, the spider plant.

Plan #161007

Dimensions: 66'4" W x 43'10" D
Levels: 1
Square Footage: 1,611
Bedrooms: 3
Bathrooms: 2
Foundation: Basement;
crawl space option for fee
Materials List Available: Yes
Price Category: C

A lovely front porch and an entry with side-lights invite you to experience the impressive amenities offered in this exceptional ranch home.

Features:

• **Great Room:** Grand openings, featuring columns from the foyer to this great room and continuing to the bayed dining area, convey an open, spacious feel. The fireplace and matching windows on the rear wall of the great room enhance this effect.

• **Kitchen:** This well-designed kitchen offers convenient access to the laundry and garage. It also features an angled counter with ample space and an abundance of cabinets.

• **Master Suite:** This deluxe master suite contains many exciting amenities, including a lavishly appointed dressing room and a large walk-in closet.

• **Porch:** Sliding doors lead to this delightful screened porch for relaxing summer interludes.

Images provided by designer/architect.

Copyright by designer/architect.

Rear Elevation

Plan #271060

Dimensions: 72' W x 64'8" D

Levels: 1

Square Footage: 1,726

Bedrooms: 2

Bathrooms: 2½

Foundation: Walkout basement

Materials List Available: No

Price Category: C

Images provided by designer/architect.

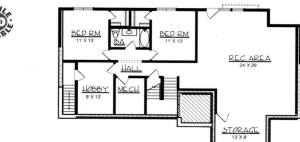

Copyright by designer/architect.

Optional Basement Level Floor Plan

Plan #521041

Dimensions: 69'8" W x 50'6" D

Levels: 1

Square Footage: 1,553

Bedrooms: 3

Bathrooms: 2

Foundation: Crawl space

Material List Available: No

Price Category: C

Images provided by designer/architect.

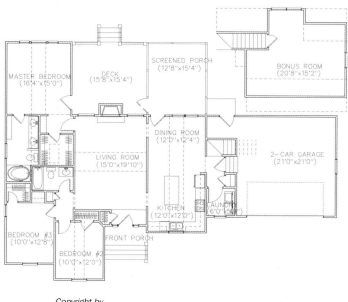

Copyright by designer/architect.

Plan #161005

Dimensions: 60' W x 48'10" D
Levels: 1
Square Footage: 1,593
Bedrooms: 3
Bathrooms: 2
Foundation: Basement
Materials List Available: Yes
Price Category: C

CAD FILE AVAILABLE

Images provided by designer/architect.

This delightful ranch home includes many thoughtful conveniences and a full basement to expand your living enjoyment.

Features:

- **Great Room:** Take pleasure in welcoming guests through a spacious foyer into the warm and friendly confines of this great room with corner fireplace, sloped ceiling, and view to the rear yard.

- **Kitchen:** Experience the convenience of enjoying meals while seated at the large island that separates the dining area from this well-designed kitchen. Also included is an over-sized pantry with an abundance of storage.

- **Master Suite:** This master suite features a compartmented bath, large walk-in closet, and master bedroom that has a tray ceiling with 9-ft. center height.

- **Porch:** Retreat to this delightful rear porch to enjoy a relaxing evening.

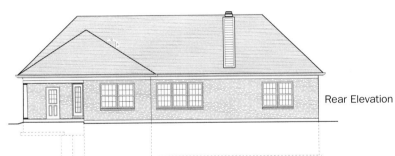

Rear Elevation

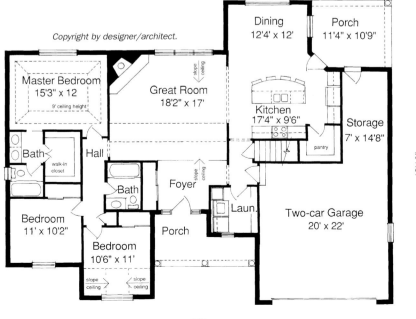

Copyright by designer/architect.

Plan #121107

Dimensions: 48'8" W x 48' D
Levels: 1
Square Footage: 1,604
Bedrooms: 3
Bathrooms: 2
Foundation: Basement;
crawl space for fee
Material List Available: Yes
Price Category: C

This sweet traditional home is beautifully designed with practicality in mind.

Features:

- **Great Room:** With plenty of room for entertaining, this space creates an inviting atmosphere and features a cathedral ceiling and a fireplace.

- **Breakfast Room:** Transitioning between the kitchen and the great room, this room brings an abundance of light into the home through an entire boundary of bay windows. Equipped with a wet bar, a desk, and the pantry, the space keeps convenience in mind.

- **Dining Room:** The great room opens into this elegant dining room, complete with a built-in hutch, for stylish dinner parties. The space also shares the wet bar with the breakfast room.

- **Master Suite:** Privacy, romance, relaxation, and comfort are a few things that come to mind in this bedroom. A skylight lends natural light to the master bath, which features dual vanities, a shower, and a whirlpool bathtub. The walk-in closet acts as one vast storage space or, with a bit of separation, can be shared by two.

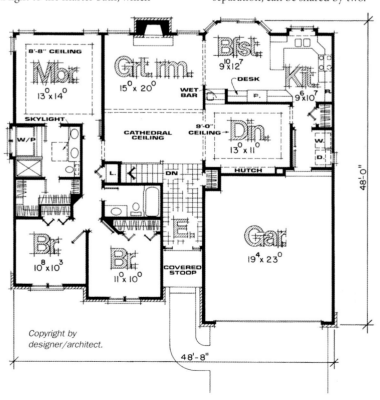

Copyright by designer/architect.

Plan #521045

Dimensions: 68'8" W x 50'6" D

Levels: 1

Square Footage: 1,507

Bedrooms: 3

Bathrooms: 2

Foundation: Slab

Material List Available: No

Price Category: C

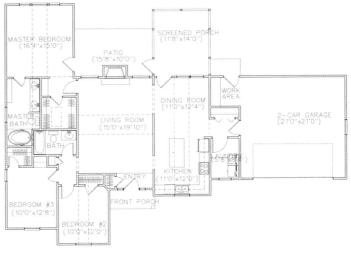

Plan #241006

Dimensions: 51' W x 63' D

Levels: 1

Square Footage: 1,744

Bedrooms: 3

Bathrooms: 2

Foundation: Crawl space, slab

Materials List Available: No

Price Category: C

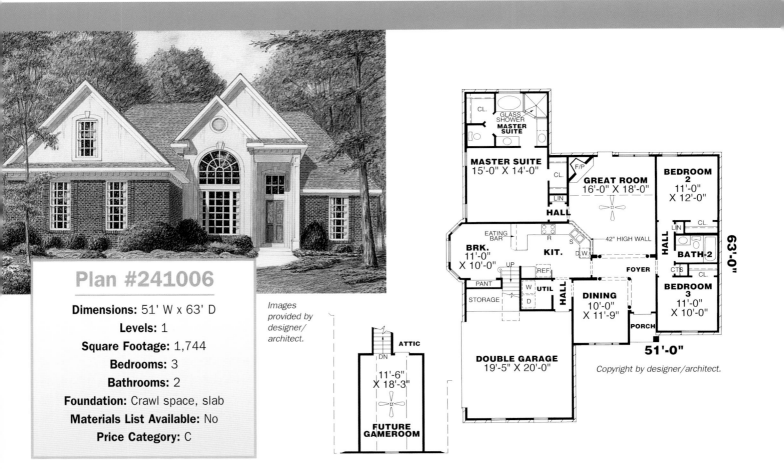

Plan #281027

Dimensions: 52' W x 52' D
Levels: 1
Square Footage: 1,626
Bedrooms: 3
Bathrooms: 2
Foundation: Basement
Material List Available: Yes
Price Category: C

Images provided by designer/architect.

Beautiful on the outside, lovely and functional on the inside, best describes this home.

Features:

• Great Room: This large gathering area boasts a vaulted ceiling and cozy fireplace. Decorative columns frame the entry to the magnificent space.

• Kitchen: This central kitchen is close to the formal dining room and just a few convenient steps away from the laundry and garage. The raised bar adds additional seating and is open to the breakfast room.

• Master Suite: This luxurious suite is off by itself, well separated from the other two bedrooms, with its own well-appointed master bath. It also has access to the private rear patio.

• Bedrooms: The two additional bedrooms are tucked away on the far end of the house and share the hall bathroom.

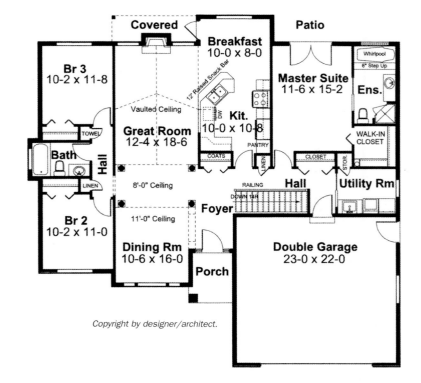

Copyright by designer/architect.

Rear Elevation   Left Side Elevation   Right Side Elevation

Plan #391038

Dimensions: 59' W x 44' D
Levels: 1
Square Footage: 1,642
Bedrooms: 3
Bathrooms: 2
Foundation: Crawl space, slab, or basement
Materials List Available: Yes
Price Category: C

This home features triple arches trimming a restful exterior front porch, great arched windows with shutters, and a complex classic roofline that steals the eye.

Features:

• Dining Room: A formal parlor sits across the hall from this spectacular room with decorative tray ceiling and built-in cabinetry.

• Kitchen: This kitchen is the heart of the home, with an island and peninsula counter/snack bar that opens into the great room.

• Great Room: This expansive room boasts a big, open layout with a corner fireplace.

• Master Suite: This super-private suite has a large walk-in closet and a sunny bath with a tub beneath a window.

Images provided by designer/architect.

• Bedrooms: These two additional bedrooms flank a full bathroom.

• Garage: This two-car garage makes all the difference for families with more than one automobile.

Copyright by designer/architect.

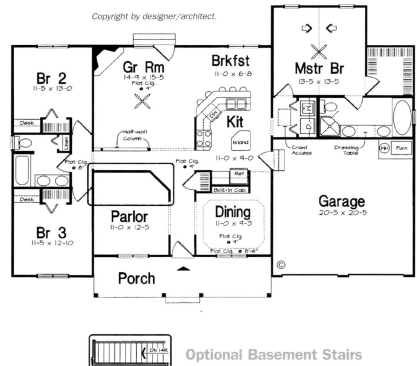

Optional Basement Stairs

Plan #121004

Dimensions: 55'4" W x 48' D
Levels: 1
Square Footage: 1,666
Bedrooms: 3
Bathrooms: 2
Foundation: Basement
Materials List Available: Yes
Price Category: C

An efficient floor plan and plenty of amenities create a luxurious lifestyle.

Features:

- Ceiling Height: 8 ft. except as noted.

- Entry: Enjoy summer breezes on the porch; then step inside the entry where sidelights and an arched transom create a bright, cheery welcome.

- Great Room: The 10-ft. ceiling and the transom-topped windows flooding the room with light provide a sense of spaciousness. The fireplace adds warmth and style.

- Dining Room: You'll usher your guests into this room located just off the great room.

- Breakfast Area: Also located off the great room, the breakfast area offers another dining option.

- Master Suite: The master bedroom is highlighted by a tray ceiling and a large walk-in closet. Luxuriate in the private bath with its sunlit whirlpool, separate shower, and double vanity.

Images provided by designer/architect.

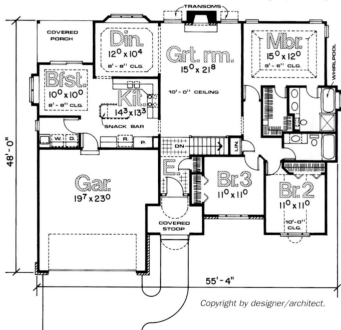

Copyright by designer/architect.

SMARTtip
Carpeting

Install the best underlayment padding available, as well as the highest grade of carpeting you can afford. This will guarantee a feeling of softness beneath your feet and protect your investment for years to come by reducing wear and tear on the carpet.

Organizing the Media Room

You and your significant other have finally carved out the time and staked out prime seats in your home theater for a private screening of Casablanca or the latest must-see DVD release. The kids' bedtime rituals are over, the stories are read, and the little ones are finally off in dreamland, so the house is quiet. Your favorite brand of popcorn is ready to make, the cabernet is ripe, and the lights are low... "Honey, have you seen the remote?"

If the hunt for the remote, or worse yet, for the movie you planned to watch, is part of the spare time routine at your house, it may be time to hit the rewind button on your media room's organization. It makes no difference whether your personal Paramount is the domain of a serious movie buff or someone more interested in a PG-rated space epic where Baby Einstein and The Wiggles rule, you'll need to plan suitable storage to hold it all.

On other days your idea of leisure bliss may be an hour or two cozied up in a plush armchair or the hammock out back with the latest biography or bestseller. And perhaps your kids are avid readers, too, with a collection that ranges from tiny cardboard picture books for the baby to the latest Harry Potter adventure. Many of the ideas presented here can help you keep your library organized as well. Your surroundings play a role in your ability to relax and be entertained, whatever your pleasure—reading, watching TV, or listening to music. That makes clearing out distracting clutter essential. This chapter will discuss furnishing a room that is designated specifically for movie and TV lovers, as well as audio- and bibliophiles. Plus, you'll find

special tips for making space for all of the related accoutrements.

The Media Room

In the media room or home theater, there are two major categories of items to be organized: the equipment, which, while basically boxy, can vary in size; and the media—discs, tapes, and cassettes—items that, due to their often standardized dimensions, can be tucked away tidily without too much trouble.

There are two ways to go in the media room: show off all your hi-tech equipment or house it in a built-in or free-standing cabinet.

Built-In Media Storage

Built-in cabinets and shelves are the most sophisticated way of housing elaborate media systems. You can design them to either blend into your decor or become a high-tech focal point. Amplifiers and mixing boards, disc players, recorders, and video-game modules—every component from sub-woofers to turntables—can be nestled into its own tailor-made niche in an arrangement that is based on your viewing and listening habits.

Stock Cabinets

When it comes to integral storage for media, the options boil down to drawers and cabinets. In most cases, the aesthetic appearance of the installation will play a determining role in this decision; simply put, drawers bring a horizontal element to the design, and cabinets introduce a vertical element. Fitting them into a composition that is both functional and attractive is the objective.

In terms of design, the cabinetry should accommodate components at eye level for easy operation. The topmost and lowest shelves can be reserved for less frequently used items. If you are designing a custom built unit, be sure to include plenty of drawers to hold your library of discs and tapes.

Opposite: Semi-custom cabinets can do it all in a TV room. Besides housing the TV and related equipment, this cabinetry houses a beverage center.

Above: Owning a front projection system is a lot like having your own movie theater. Note the projector on the ceiling in this media room. It requires a separate screen that either drops down from the ceiling or remains fixed on a wall.

SMARTtip

Media Stats

When you're shopping for storage racks or other types of containment for your audio and video recordings, keep these standard measurements handy:

Audio cassette case	2¾" x 4¼"
Video cassette case	4⅛" x 7½"
CD case	5⅝" x 5"
LP-record sleeve	12⅜" x 12⅜"
DVD case	5⅝" x 7½"

Right: Is it hip wall art or a TV? This thin-profile, wide-screen model is a sleek alternative to the big black box.

Below: Some manufacturers make furniture designed specifically for a home theater.

Drawers. Easiest for children to use, drawers should be shallow and just deep enough for one layer of storage. The idea is to discourage piling up discs and tapes because too many of them can block visual access to the drawer's contents—a fatal blow to any storage situation.

Pullouts. In a home theater, standard-depth cupboards also pose an invitation to overcrowding. Pullout pantry cabinets, which are available in a wide range of heights and widths, can be sized to fit collections to a T. To be sure, it's not practical—or even possible—for everyone to deed over significant amounts of cabinet space for a home theater. If you think your system will change somewhere down the line, hold off on committing to a built-in design unless you anticipate those changes and allow for them in the design.

Safe Shelves

When using shelf units or freestanding bookcases to house media components, there are a couple of special considerations to bear in mind. When storing elec-

tronics that are both fragile and heavy above waist height, it's vital that the shelving be stable and strong. Many manufacturers provide information on the maximum load a shelf can safely support, so know how much each piece of your equipment weighs (and bring along component dimensions) when you are shopping for storage. And it's always a good idea to attach a tall bookcase to the wall, so it won't topple over.

SMARTtip

Avoid disc organizers that have preformed slots because boxed sets won't fit into them. Also, if your collection is alphabetized, you'll have to move every disc to accommodate each new addition.

Above: Freestanding entertainment furniture can accommodate numerous components.

Now is not the time to cut corners on installation: locate a stud and anchor the bookcase to it.

Regardless of whether you've opted for built-in or standalone storage for your electronic gear, make sure there is adequate ventilation for all the modules. If there's not at least one inch of open space on all sides, they may overheat, which hastens the demise of the circuitry.

Right: These divided bins roll out to the user for easy retrieval of the contents.

to good use. While the major house-hold-goods charities are certainly worthy, try to think beyond them: a local college-radio station might be interested in your golden oldies, or the staff at a seniors' home could be looking to expand their residents' listening or viewing list. This advice can be effectively applied to your electronic equipment, too; at this point in the twenty-first century, you can be reasonably

Above and right: The doors and pullout drawers completely conceal the media center. When open, they reveal a large format TV and floor-to-ceiling racks for videos and discs.

Conceal The TV

When not in use, large TV monitors can look like big ugly black boxes. It is possible to hide smaller televisions behind the doors of a TV cabinet. Very large screens should probably be housed behind pocket, tambour, or concealed doors. Large cabinet doors that swing into the room can obstruct traffic or the view of the TV screen from portions of the room.

Flat-panel TV monitors are only a few inches thick. Their sleek design allows you to enjoy a big-screen theater without sacrificing a lot of floor space.

When disorganization disrupts the intended experience of the home theater, media room—or your library for that matter— be it a single shelf or a single room, start to reclaim a sense of order by taking three simple steps.

Step One: Sift. Gather all the duplicate recordings and titles and donate them to an organization that can put them

SMARTtip

If you don't make allowances for expansion of your collection when forecasting your storage space, you could be caught short by the time the next video of the month club selection arrives. Once you've calculated how much space your current media consume, tack on an additional 20 percent for future acquisitions.

Top left: A wall of custom cabinetry integrates the large-screen TV into this room.

Above: Plan plenty of seating and include dimmable lights to ensure comfortable use of the media room.

confident that eight-track tapes will not be making a comeback, and it's all right to pull the plug on the Betamax.

Step Two: Sort. Once your collection has been whittled down, take the opportunity to give some thought about how you want to organize it. There's no hard and fast rule about the best way to do this; just select a system that everyone in the home can use and understand. According to general categories—all jazz, all horror films, all cartoons—is a flexible, broad-based method that has virtually no limitations. The more disciplined and detail-oriented among us can go a little further in their filing; within these topical groupings, items can be ordered alphabetically by artist.

Step Three: Measure. Take stock of the dozens—possibly hundreds—of discs and tapes and volumes that are to be stored. Stack them up and measure how many linear feet of space will be needed to accommodate all of them. When measuring equipment, don't forget to take into account the wiring run-outs; otherwise, you run the risk of not having enough room between the wall and the electronic unit for the cords and cables.

Bonus Area Floor Plan

Copyright by designer/architect.

Plan #511012

Dimensions: 50' W x 57'8" D

Levels: 1

Square Footage: 1,573

Bedrooms: 3

Bathrooms: 2

Foundation: Crawl space or slab

Material List Available: No

Price Category: C

Images provided by designer/architect.

Basement Level Floor Plan

Copyright by designer/architect.

Plan #521033

Dimensions: 47'4" W x 48' D

Levels: 1

Square Footage: 1,603

Bedrooms: 3

Bathrooms: 2

Foundation: Pier

Material List Available: No

Price Category: C

Images provided by designer/architect.

Plan #521039

Dimensions: 49' W x 63'8" D
Levels: 1
Square Footage: 1,567
Bedrooms: 3
Bathrooms: 2
Foundation: Slab
Material List Available: No
Price Category: C

Images provided by designer/architect.

CAD FILE AVAILABLE

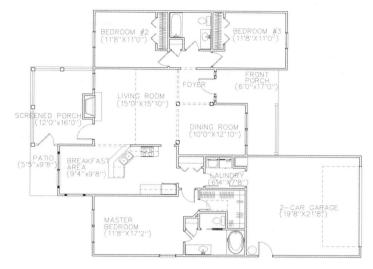

Copyright by designer/architect.

Plan #511018

Dimensions: 50'10" W x 58'6" D
Levels: 1
Square Footage: 1,643
Bedrooms: 3
Bathrooms: 2
Foundation: Crawl space or slab
Material List Available: No
Price Category: C

Images provided by designer/architect.

Copyright by designer/architect.

Plan #211001

Dimensions: 52' W x 66' D
Levels: 1
Square Footage: 1,655
Bedrooms: 3
Bathrooms: 2
Foundation: Slab
Materials List Available: Yes
Price Category: C

You'll love this elegant one-story home, both practical and gorgeous, with its many amenities.

Features:

• Entry: A covered porch and three glass doors with transoms announce this home.

• Living Room: At the center of the house, this living room has a 15-ft. ceiling and a fireplace. A glass door flanked by windows opens to a skylighted porch at the rear of the home.

• Dining Room: This elegant octagonal room, which is shaped by columns and cased openings, overlooks both backyard porches.

• Kitchen: A 14-ft. sloped ceiling with a skylight adds drama.

• Master Suite: Enjoy the seclusion of this area at the rear of the home, as well as its private access to a rear porch. The bath features an oval spa tub, separate shower, dual vanities, and huge walk-in closet.

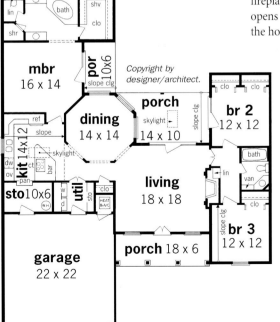

Copyright by designer/architect.

SMARTtip

Plotting a Potting Space

Whether you opt for a simple corner potting bench or a multipurpose shed or greenhouse, organization is key. You'll need a work surface —a counter or table that's a convenient height for standing while at work — plus storage accommodations for hand tools, long-handled tools, watering cans, extra lengths of hose, hose nozzles, flowerpots, bags of fertilizer and potting soil, gardening books, and notebooks. Plastic garbage cans (with lids) are good for soil and seeds. Most of these spaces are small, so use hooks and stacking bins, which keep items neat and at hand's reach. High shelves free up floor space while holding least-used things.

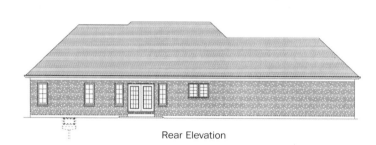

Images provided by designer/architect.

Plan #161110

Dimensions: 75' W x 39'1" D
Levels: 1
Square Footage: 1,623
Bedrooms: 3
Bathrooms: 2
Foundation: Crawl space, slab, or basement; walkout for fee
Materials List Available: Yes
Price Category: C

CAD FILE AVAILABLE

Rear Elevation

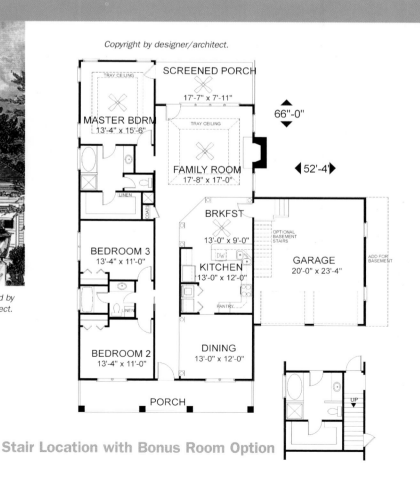

Images provided by designer/architect.

CAD FILE AVAILABLE

Plan #101067

Dimensions: 52'4" W x 66' D
Levels: 1
Square Footage: 1,770
Bedrooms: 3
Bathrooms: 2
Foundation: Crawl space
Materials List Available: No
Price Category: C

Stair Location with Bonus Room Option

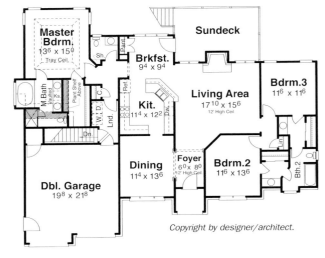

Copyright by designer/architect.

Images provided by designer/architect.

Plan #141006

Dimensions: 64' W x 52' D

Levels: 1

Square Footage: 1,787

Bedrooms: 3

Bathrooms: 2½

Foundation: Basement

Materials List Available: No

Price Category: C

SMARTtip

Arts and Crafts Style in Your Kitchen

The heart of this style lies in its earthy connection. The more you can bring nature into it, the more authentic it will appear. An easy way to do this is with plants. Open the space up to nature with glass doors that provide a view to a green garden.

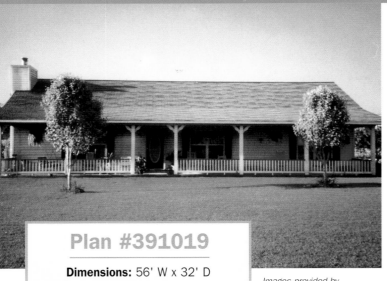

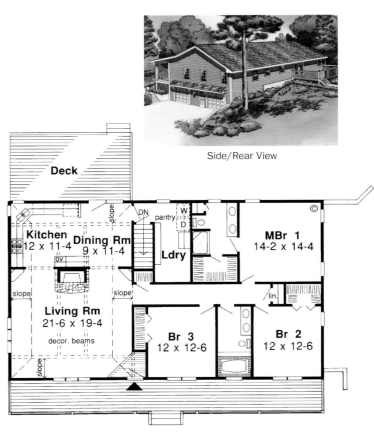

Side/Rear View

Copyright by designer/architect.

Images provided by designer/architect.

Plan #391019

Dimensions: 56' W x 32' D

Levels: 1

Square Footage: 1,792

Bedrooms: 3

Bathrooms: 2

Foundation: Basement

Materials List Available: Yes

Price Category: C

Plan #521044

Dimensions: 55'8" W x 57' D

Levels: 1

Square Footage: 1,515

Bedrooms: 3

Bathrooms: 2

Foundation: Slab

Material List Available: No

Price Category: C

Images provided by designer/architect.

Copyright by designer/architect.

Plan #511019

Dimensions: 57'8" W x 53'10" D

Levels: 1

Square Footage: 1,712

Bedrooms: 3

Bathrooms: 2

Foundation: Crawl space or slab

Material List Available: No

Price Category: C

Images provided by designer/architect.

Bonus Area Floor Plan

Copyright by designer/architect.

Plan #341063

Dimensions: 50' W x 43'4" D
Levels: 1
Square Footage: 1,566
Bedrooms: 3
Bathrooms: 2
Foundation: Crawl space, slab, basement or walkout basement
Material List Available: Yes
Price Category: C

Images provided by designer/architect.

This traditional ranch home, with its charmingly simple design, is ideal for raising a family.

Features:

- Porches: The covered front porch welcomes guests into your home or onto your stoop as twilight spills over the house. The screened porch, which opens into the kitchen, allows for enjoying breakfast with the morning sun and a warm summer breeze.

- Living Room: One thing the budding family needs is space for toys and playpens or entertainment centers and leather recliners. This living room has plenty of space, a blank canvas waiting for your touch.

- Kitchen: The L-shaped design in this large space makes room for a convenient dining area. Though the kitchen usually is the "brightest" place in a home, the light streaming in through a wall of windows makes this particularly true with this design. Also attached is the spacious utility room,

ready to hold a washer and dryer, as well as anything else you need to maintain the home.

- Master Suite: This suite gives you space to make it your own while providing you with what you need: a walk-in closet and sectioned full master bath.

- Secondary Bedrooms: Often, the secondary bedrooms are dwarfed by the master suite, but not in this design. The bedrooms give you room to grow. They are both equipped with large closets and share the second full bathroom.

Copyright by designer/architect.

Plan #341226

Dimensions: 54'6" W x 53' D
Levels: 1
Square Footage: 1,633
Bedrooms: 3
Bathrooms: 2
Foundation: Crawl space, slab, basement, or walkout
Material List Available: No
Price Category: C

CAD FILE AVAILABLE

This home captures a bit of yesteryear in a vacation-styled three-bedroom design.

Features:

- Dining Room: Beyond the fireplace lies this dining room, which enjoys plenty of natural light, easy pass-through service from the kitchen, and access to the back porch.

- Master Suite: This suite is located for privacy and has its own luxurious bathroom outfitted with a two vanities, a garden tub, a separate shower, a linen closet, and a walk-in closet.

- Family Room: This large gathering area features a cozy fireplace. The kitchen and the dinning room are just a few steps away.

- Bedrooms: The two secondary bedrooms, each with a walk-in closets, share the common hallway bathroom.

Plan #121124

Dimensions: 55'4" W x 56' D
Levels: 1
Square Footage: 1,806
Bedrooms: 3
Bathrooms: 2
Foundation: Basement; crawl space for fee
Material List Available: Yes
Price Category: D

Images provided by designer/architect.

This brick ranch will be the best-looking home in the neighborhood.

Features:

• Great Room: This area is a great place to gather with family and friends. The 10-ft.-high ceiling and arched windows make this room bright and airy. On cold nights, gather by the warmth of the fireplace.

• Dining Room: A column off the entry defines this formal dining area. Arched windows and a 10-ft.-high ceiling add to the elegance of the space.

• Kitchen: This island kitchen will inspire the chef in the family to create a symphony at every meal. The triple window in the adjoining breakfast area floods this area with natural light.

• Master Suite: Located on the opposite side of the home from the secondary bedrooms, this private area features a 10-ft.-high ceiling in the sleeping area. The master bath boasts a compartmentalized lavatory and shower area in addition to dual vanities and a walk-in closet.

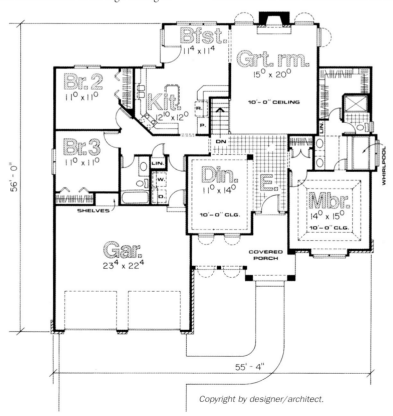

Copyright by designer/architect.

Plan #121051

Dimensions: 64' W x 44' D
Levels: 1
Square Footage: 1,808
Bedrooms: 3
Bathrooms: 2½
Foundation: Basement
Materials List Available: Yes
Price Category: D

Images provided by designer/architect.

You'll love the way that natural light pours into this home from the gorgeous windows you'll find in room after room.

Features:

• Great Room: You'll notice the bayed, transom-topped window in this lovely great room as soon as you step into the home. A wet-bar makes the room a natural place for entertaining, and the see-through fireplace makes it cozy on chilly days and winter evenings.

• Kitchen: This well-designed kitchen will be a delight for everyone who cooks here, not only because of the ample counter and cabinet space but also because of its location in the home.

• Master Suite: Angled ceilings in both the bedroom and the bathroom of this suite make it feel luxurious, and the picturesque window in the bedroom gives it character. The bath includes a corner whirlpool tub where you'll love to relax at the end of the day.

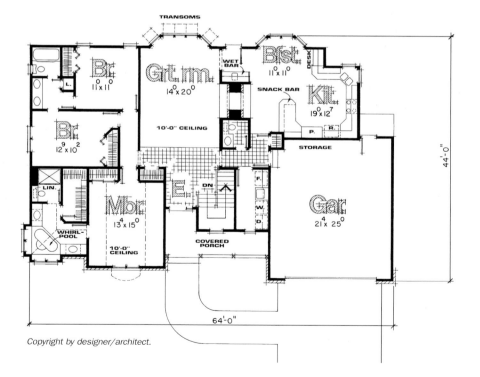

Copyright by designer/architect.

Plan #161121

Dimensions: 66' W x 74' D
Levels: 1
Square Footage: 1,824
Bedrooms: 3
Bathrooms: 2
Foundation: Basement
Material List Available: Yes
Price Category: D

This wonderfully designed three-bedroom brick ranch is the perfect place to call home.

Features:

- **Great Room:** This large gathering area features a high ceiling and a corner fireplace. The open floor plan allows flow between the breakfast room and the dining room, enabling all three areas to act as one.

- **Kitchen:** This peninsula kitchen boasts a built-in pantry and is open to the breakfast area. The laundry facilities and garage are just a few steps away.

- **Master Suite:** This private oasis boasts an oversized sleeping area and large windows with a view of the backyard. The master bath features dual vanities, a large shower, and a separate lavatory area.

- **Screened in Porch:** Located in the rear of the home, this area is reached through sliding glass doors from the breakfast area.

Copyright by designer/architect.

Rear Elevation

Right Side Elevation

Left Side Elevation

Plan #121119

Dimensions: 62' W x 48' D
Levels: 1
Square Footage: 1,850
Bedrooms: 3
Bathrooms: 2
Foundation: Basement; crawl space for fee
Material List Available: Yes
Price Category: D

With beautiful architectural details and abundant amenities, this home will steal your heart.

Features:

- Kitchen: Keeping this kitchen cheerful are walls surrounded by transom windows, bringing the morning sun into your home. The kitchen has everything you want, including an island, a pantry, counter space to spare, and a desk area, and it opens directly into the breakfast room.

- Dining Room: Separated from the kitchen and breakfast room by a hallway, this dining room can adopt an air of elegance and decorum. It has a built-in hutch and, with the right furniture, can be used for family dinners and small dinner parties alike.

- Master Suite: This bedroom, sectioned in two, is simply a dream. Through double doors is a walk-in closet to the left, dual vanities to the front, a skylight above, and a full master bath to the right, equipped with a whirlpool tub, shower stall, and window seat. Here, "staying in" sounds romantic.

- Secondary Bedrooms: If three bedrooms are more than you need, Bedroom 2 will work wonderfully as a den. With transom windows bringing in the sunlight and double doors opening to the entryway, this room would be a welcoming place to entertain guests who have just arrived.

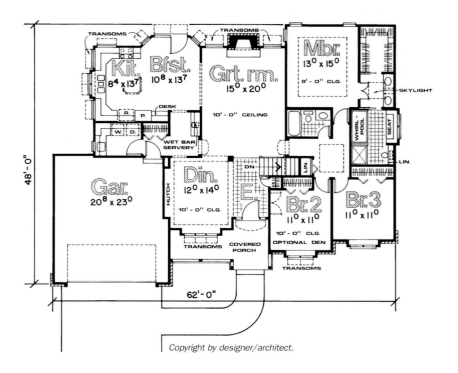

Copyright by designer/architect.

Plan #441005

Dimensions: 50' W x 59' D
Levels: 1
Square Footage: 1,800
Bedrooms: 3
Bathrooms: 2
Foundation: Crawl space
Materials List Available: No
Price Category: D

This home looks as if it's a quaint little abode—with its board-and-batten siding, cedar shingle detailing, and column-covered porch—but even a quick peek inside will prove that there is much more to this plan than meets the eye.

CAD FILE AVAILABLE

Features:

• Foyer: This entry area rises to a 9-ft.-high ceiling. On one side is a washer-dryer alcove with a closet across the way; on the other is another large storage area. Just down the hallway is a third closet.

• Kitchen: This kitchen features a center island, built-in desk/work center, and pantry. This area and the dining area also boast 9-ft.-high ceilings and are open to a vaulted great room with corner fireplace.

• Dining Room: Sliding doors in this area lead to a covered side porch, so you can enjoy outside dining.

• Master Suite: This suite has a vaulted ceiling. The master bath is wonderfully appointed with a separate shower, spa tub, and dual sinks.

• Bedrooms: Three bedrooms (or two plus an office) are found on the right side of the plan.

Rear Elevation

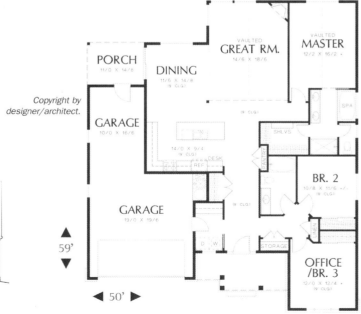

Copyright by designer/architect.

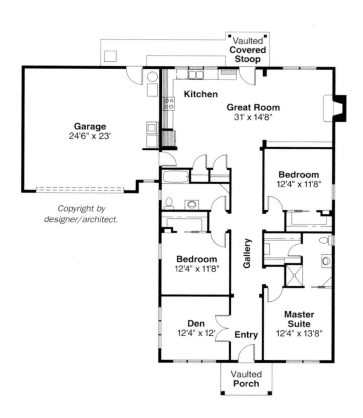

Plan #361512

Dimensions: 59' W x 68' D

Levels: 1

Square Footage: 1,802

Bedrooms: 3

Bathrooms: 2

Foundation: Crawl space

Material List Available: No

Price Category: D

Images provided by designer/architect.

CAD FILE AVAILABLE

Copyright by designer/architect.

Vaulted Covered Stoop

Kitchen

Great Room
31' x 14'8"

Garage
24'6" x 23'

Bedroom
12'4" x 11'8"

Bedroom
12'4" x 11'8"

Gallery

Den
12'4" x 12'

Entry

Master Suite
12'4" x 13'8"

Vaulted Porch

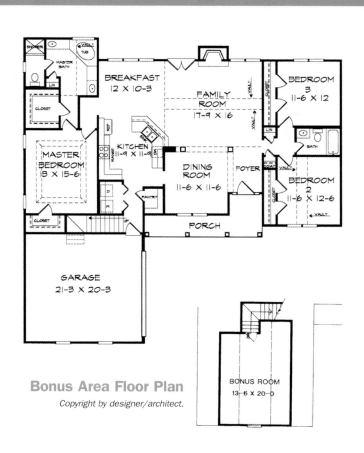

Plan #461037

Dimensions: 58' W x 57' D

Levels: 1

Square Footage: 1,819

Bedrooms: 3

Bathrooms: 2

Foundation: Crawl space or slab; basement for fee

Material List Available: No

Price Category: D

Images provided by designer/architect.

MASTER BATH

CLOSET

BREAKFAST
12 X 10-3

FAMILY ROOM
17-9 X 16

BEDROOM
11-6 X 12

MASTER BEDROOM
13 X 15-6

KITCHEN
11-9 X 11-9

DINING ROOM
11-6 X 11-6

FOYER

BEDROOM 2
11-6 X 12-6

CLOSET

PANTRY

PORCH

BATH

BEDROOM 3

GARAGE
21-3 X 20-3

Bonus Area Floor Plan

Copyright by designer/architect.

BONUS ROOM
13-6 X 20-0

Plan #271078

Dimensions: 83' W x 52' D

Levels: 1

Square Footage: 1,855

Bedrooms: 2

Bathrooms: 1½

Foundation: Daylight basement

Materials List Available: No

Price Category: D

Images provided by designer/architect.

Optional Basement Level Floor Plan

Copyright by designer/architect.

Plan #421008

Dimensions: 74'6" W x 43' D

Levels: 1

Square Footage: 1,954

Bedrooms: 3

Bathrooms: 2½

Foundation: Crawl space, slab, or basement

Material List Available: Yes

Price Category: D

Images provided by designer/architect.

Copyright by designer/architect.

Optional Basement Level Floor Plan

Plan #111014

Dimensions: 78' W x 47' D

Levels: 1

Square Footage: 1,865

Bedrooms: 4

Bathrooms: 2

Foundation: Slab

Materials List Available: No

Price Category: D

Images provided by designer/architect.

Copyright by designer/architect.

Floor plan labels: Master Bedroom 14'8"x 14', Porch, Breakfast, Bedroom 11'x 10', Living 19'4"x 15'6", Bedroom 10'6"x 11'6", Dining 10'6"x 11'6", Bedroom 11'x 10'6", Porch, Two Car Garage 19'6"x 22'8"

Plan #371111

Dimensions: 61'2" W x 65'6" D

Levels: 1

Square Footage: 1,901

Bedrooms: 3

Bathrooms: 2½

Foundation: Crawl space or slab

Material List Available: No

Price Category: D

Images provided by designer/architect.

CAD FILE AVAILABLE

Copyright by designer/architect.

Floor plan labels: 61'-2", 65'-6", MASTER SUITE 15'-0" x 12'-0", NOOK 9'-6" x 9'-8", PORCH, BED RM.2 11'-0" x 11'-0", LIVING RM. 18'-1" x 14'-11", B.1, KIT. 10'-10" x 12'-0", B.2, BED RM.3 11'-1" x 10'-0", DINING RM. 11'-0" x 12'-0", ENT., STUDY 10'-0" x 10'-0", B.3, UT., GARAGE 20'-6" x 23'-0", STORAGE

Plan #371107

Dimensions: 60' W x 52'10" D
Levels: 1
Square Footage: 1,825
Bedrooms: 4
Bathrooms: 2
Foundation: Crawl space or slab
Material List Available: No
Price Category: D

Handsome architectural details and combinations of siding materials make the exterior of this country house almost as striking as the interior.

CAD FILE AVAILABLE

Features:

• Kitchen: Surrounded by functional space, this kitchen is both attractive and practical. The space is open to the family room, dining room, and breakfast nook, gleaning natural light from all three.

• Breakfast Nook: Filled with light from the surrounding windows, the nook also opens onto the back porch. Imagine summer mornings with your family sitting at the patio table eating fresh bacon and eggs in the morning or barbecue in the afternoon.

• Master Suite: Privacy and luxury combine in this room. Separated by double doors are two walk-in closets, a stall shower, and dual

vanities divided by the bathtub. A window next to the tub allows you to soak up the moonlight with the bathwater for a relaxing evening. And if you want breakfast in bed, the kitchen is just a doorway away.

• Secondary Bedrooms: The third and fourth bedrooms both have large closets and are close to the family room and a full bathroom. If four bedrooms are one too many, you can use Bedroom 2 as a study.

Copyright by designer/architect.

Images provided by designer/architect.

Plan #211004

Dimensions: 64' W x 62' D

Levels: 1

Square Footage: 1,828

Bedrooms: 4

Bathrooms: 2

Foundation: Crawl space, slab, or basement

Materials List Available: Yes

Price Category: D

This super-energy-efficient home has the curb appeal of a much larger house.

Features:

• Ceiling Height: 9 ft.

• Kitchen: You will love cooking in this bright, airy, and efficient kitchen. It features an angled layout that allows a great view to the outside through a window wall in the breakfast area.

• Breakfast Area: With morning sunlight streaming through the wall of windows in this area, you won't be able to resist lingering over a cup of coffee.

• Rear Porch: This breezy rear porch is designed to accommodate the pleasure of old-fashioned rockers or swings.

• Master Bedroom: Retreat at the end of a long day to this bedroom, which is isolated for privacy yet conveniently located a few steps from the kitchen and utility area.

• Attic Storage: No need to fuss with creaky pull-down stairs. This attic has a permanent stairwell to provide easy access to its abundant storage.

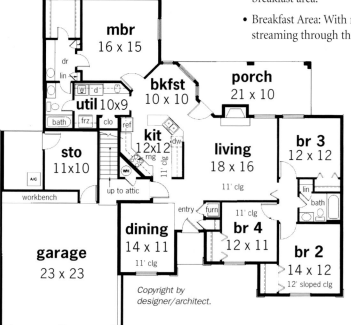

Copyright by designer/architect.

SMARTtip

Resin Furniture

Resin furniture is made of molded plastic. Most resin pieces are quite affordable, but lacquered resin with brass fittings is a high-end item. Resin doesn't corrode and cleans easily, but a scratched finish cannot be repaired. However, lacquered resin can be touched up.

www.ultimateplans.com   177

Plan #101005

Dimensions: 63' W x 57'2" D

Levels: 1

Square Footage: 1,992

Bedrooms: 3

Bathrooms: 2½

Foundation: Crawl space, slab, or basement

Materials List Available: Yes

Price Category: D

CAD FILE AVAILABLE

Images provided by designer/architect.

Rear View

This midsized ranch is accented with Palladian windows and inviting front porch.

Features:

- Ceiling Height: 9 ft. unless otherwise noted.

- Special Ceilings: Tray or vaulted ceilings adorn the living room, family room, dining room, and master suite.

- Kitchen: This bright and airy kitchen is designed to be a pleasure in which to work. It shares a big bay window with the contiguous breakfast room.

- Breakfast Room: The light streaming in from the bay window makes this the perfect place to linger with coffee and the Sunday paper.

- Master Suite: This lovely suite is exceptional, with its sitting area and direct access to the deck, as well as a full-featured bath, and spacious walk-in closet.

- Secondary Bedrooms: The other bedrooms each measure about 13 ft. x 11 ft. They have walk-in closets and share a "Jack-and-Jill" bath.

Copyright by designer/architect.

Kitchen

Living Room

Dining Room

Family Room

Master Bedroom

Master Bath

Plan #121010

Dimensions: 50' W x 62' D
Levels: 1
Square Footage: 1,902
Bedrooms: 2
Bathrooms: 2
Foundation: Basement
Materials List Available: Yes
Price Category: D

CAD FILE AVAILABLE

SMARTtip

Accentuating Your Fireplace with Faux Effects

Experiment with faux effects to add an aged look or a specific style to a fireplace mantel and surround. Craft stores sell inexpensive kits with directions for adding the appearance of antiqued or paneled wood or plaster, rusticated stone, marble, terra cotta, and other effects that make any style achievable.

Plan #461132

Dimensions: 68' W x 56' D
Levels: 1
Square Footage: 1,958
Bedrooms: 3
Bathrooms: 2
Foundation: Slab or basement; crawl space for fee
Material List Available: No
Price Category: D

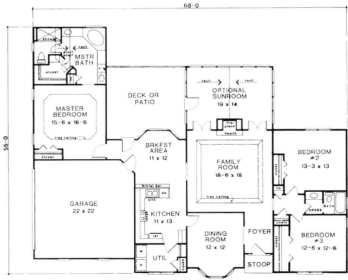

Plan #371108

Dimensions: 52' W x 51'6" D
Levels: 1
Square Footage: 1,829
Bedrooms: 3
Bathrooms: 2
Foundation: Crawl space or slab
Material List Available: No
Price Category: D

There is more than meets the eye in this quaint, traditional brick home. Large rooms, high ceilings, and lots of natural light give this house an expansive feel.

Features:

- **Family Room:** Accessible straight from the entryway, this is the perfect place to relax after a hard day or to welcome guests. A triplet of windows cools you down in warm weather, and a fireplace heats you up in cold.

- **Dining Room:** This formal dining room has the same light and airy feel as the rest of the house due to its two walls filled with windows and access to the porch. The arrangement simplifies grilled meals and large summer barbecues, as well as providing plenty of peaceful scenery at routine dinners.

- **Kitchen:** An L-shaped design with an island gives this kitchen plenty of workspace and leaves it open to the breakfast nook. Storage units also surround the kitchen, providing functional and attractive organization.

- **Master Suite:** You could easily get lost in the spacious and elegantly designed master bath, especially since it is as large as the bedroom. Dual vanities, an isolated toilet, and a walk-in closet speak practicality. A shower with a glass-block wall separating it and a bathtub beneath a window, letting in moonlight, shout romance.

- **Utility Room:** Adding to the abundance of storage options in the home is this utility room, with space planned for a washer, dryer, and even an ironing board. The design has you covered.

Copyright by designer/architect.

Plan #461035

Dimensions: 58' W x 57' D
Levels: 1
Square Footage: 1,831
Bedrooms: 3
Bathrooms: 2
Foundation: Crawl space or slab; basement for fee
Material List Available: No
Price Category: D

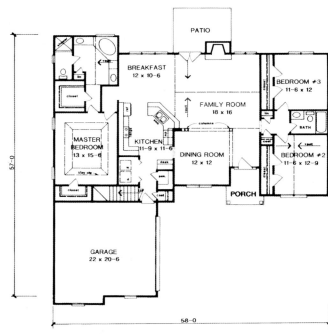

Images provided by designer/architect.

Plan #151536

Dimensions: 37' W x 74'4" D
Levels: 1
Square Footage: 1,933
Bedrooms: 3
Bathrooms: 2
Foundation: Crawl space or slab
CompleteCost List Available: Yes
Price Category: D

Images provided by designer/architect.

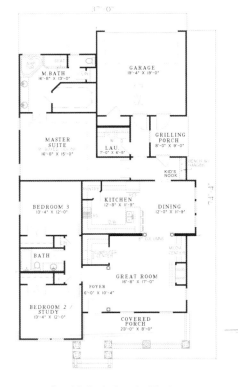

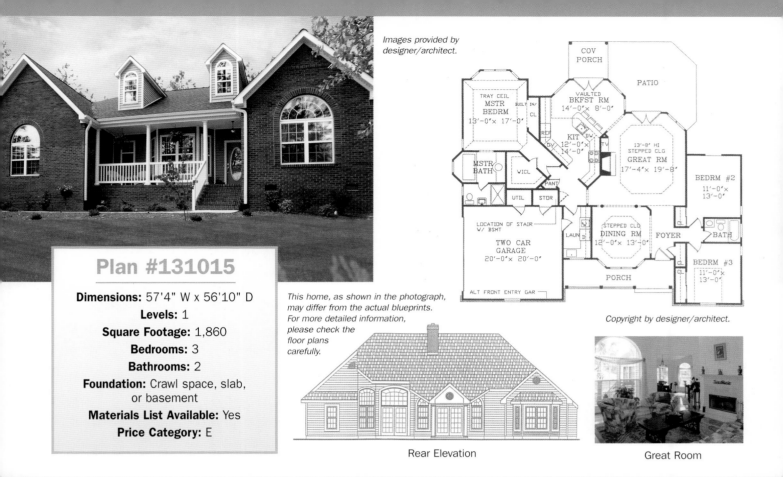

COV PORCH

PATIO

TRAY CEIL MSTR BEDRM 13'-0" x 17'-0"

BUILT IN

CL

VAULTED BKFST RM 14'-0" x 8'-0"

REF

KIT 12'-0" x 14'-0"

DW

TV

13'-8" HI STEPPED CLG GREAT RM 17'-4" x 19'-8"

BEDRM #2 11'-0" x 13'-0"

MSTR BATH

WICL

PANT

UTIL

STOR

LOCATION OF STAIR W/ BSMT

TWO CAR GARAGE 20'-0" x 20'-0"

LAUN

STEPPED CLG DINING RM 12'-0" x 13'-0"

FOYER

BATH

BEDRM #3 11'-0" x 13'-0"

PORCH

ALT FRONT ENTRY GAR

Copyright by designer/architect.

Plan #131015

Dimensions: 57'4" W x 56'10" D

Levels: 1

Square Footage: 1,860

Bedrooms: 3

Bathrooms: 2

Foundation: Crawl space, slab, or basement

Materials List Available: Yes

Price Category: E

This home, as shown in the photograph, may differ from the actual blueprints. For more detailed information, please check the floor plans carefully.

Rear Elevation

Great Room

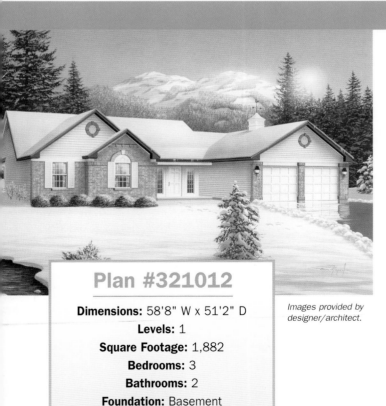

Plan #321012

Dimensions: 58'8" W x 51'2" D

Levels: 1

Square Footage: 1,882

Bedrooms: 3

Bathrooms: 2

Foundation: Basement

Materials List Available: Yes

Price Category: D

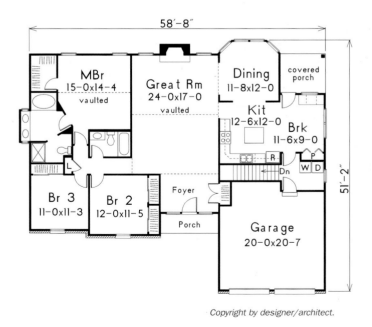

58'-8"

MBr 15-0x14-4

Great Rm 24-0x17-0 vaulted

Dining 11-8x12-0

covered porch

Kit 12-6x12-0

Brk 11-6x9-0

R

W D

Dn

51'-2"

Br 3 11-0x11-3

Br 2 12-0x11-5

Foyer

Porch

Garage 20-0x20-7

Copyright by designer/architect.

Plan #321020

Dimensions: 58' W x 47'6" D
Levels: 1
Square Footage: 1,882
Bedrooms: 4
Bathrooms: 2
Foundation: Basement
Materials List Available: Yes
Price Category: D

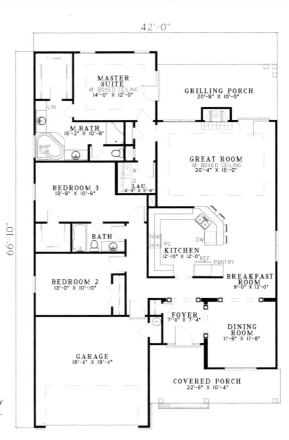

Images provided by designer/architect.

Dining 13-0x12-0
Kitchen 14-0x14-7
MBr 14-8x13-2
Patio
Br 4 15-0x10-6
Great Rm 14-11x15-0
Br 3 11-8x11-5
Br 2 13-0x12-0
vaulted
Porch
Garage 21-4x20-10
Dn
58'-0"
47'-6"

Copyright by designer/architect.

Plan #151008

Dimensions: 42' W x 66'10" D
Levels: 1
Square Footage: 1,892
Bedrooms: 3
Bathrooms: 2
Foundation: Crawl space, slab, basement, or daylight basement
CompleteCost List Available: Yes
Price Category: D

Images provided by designer/architect.

This home, as shown in the photograph, may differ from the actual blueprints. For more detailed information, please check the floor plans carefully.

MASTER SUITE 10' BOXED CEILING 14'-0" X 12'-0"
GRILLING PORCH 20'-8" X 10'-0"
M.BATH 15'-2" X 10'-8"
WHP TUB
LIN
GREAT ROOM 10' BOXED CEILING 20'-4" X 15'-0"
BEDROOM 3 13'-8" X 10'-6"
LAU. 6'-8" X 5'-6"
BATH
KITCHEN 12'-10" X 12'-0"
PANTRY
BEDROOM 2 13'-0" X 10'-10"
BREAKFAST ROOM 9'-8" X 12'-0"
FOYER 7'-0" X 7'-4"
DINING ROOM 11'-8" X 11'-8"
GARAGE 19'-4" X 19'-4"
COVERED PORCH 22'-6" X 10'-4"
42'-0"
66'-10"

Copyright by designer/architect.

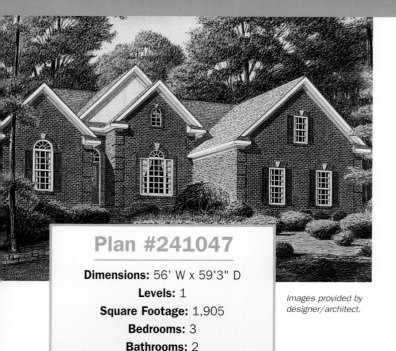

Plan #241047

Dimensions: 56' W x 59'3" D

Levels: 1

Square Footage: 1,905

Bedrooms: 3

Bathrooms: 2

Foundation: Crawl space or slab

Material List Available: No

Price Category: D

Images provided by designer/architect.

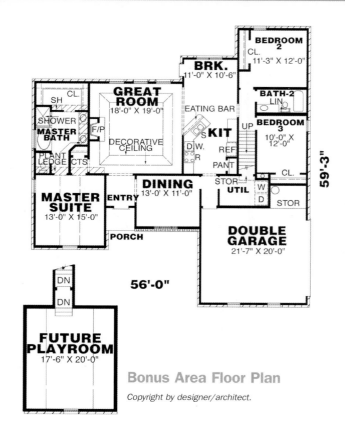

Bonus Area Floor Plan

Copyright by designer/architect.

Plan #511022

Dimensions: 68'6" W x 49' D

Levels: 1

Square Footage: 1,880

Bedrooms: 3

Bathrooms: 2

Foundation: Crawl space or slab

Material List Available: No

Price Category: D

Images provided by designer/architect.

Bonus Area Floor Plan

Copyright by designer/architect.

Plan #121001

Dimensions: 56' W x 58' D
Levels: 1
Square Footage: 1,911
Bedrooms: 3
Bathrooms: 2
Foundation: Basement
Materials List Available: Yes
Price Category: D

CAD FILE AVAILABLE

Detailed, soaring ceilings and top-notch amenities set this distinctive home apart.

Features:

- Ceiling Height: 8 ft. except as noted.

- Great Room: A soaring ceiling and six tall transom-topped windows make this a light and airy spot for entertaining.

- Formal Dining Room: The entry enjoys a pleasing view of this dining room's detailed 12-ft. ceiling and picture window.

- Great Room: At the back of the home, a see-through fireplace in this great room is joined by a built-in entertainment center.

- Hearth Room: This bayed room shares the see-through fireplace with the great room.

- Master Suite: Enjoy the stars and the sun in the private bath's whirlpool and separate shower. The bath features the same decorative ceiling as the dining room.

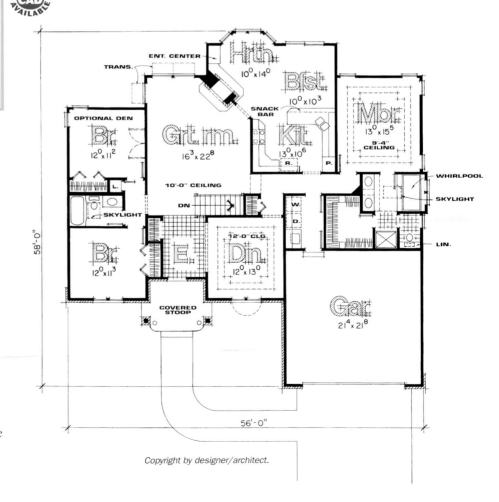

Copyright by designer/architect.

Plan #441006

Dimensions: 48' W x 64' D
Levels: 1
Square Footage: 1,891
Bedrooms: 3
Bathrooms: 2
Foundation: Crawl space
Materials List Available: No
Price Category: D

If you prefer the look of Craftsman homes, you'll love the details this plan includes. Wide-based columns across the front porch, Mission-style windows, and a balanced mixture of exterior materials add up to true good looks.

Features:

- Great Room: A built-in media center and a fireplace in this room make it distinctive.

- Kitchen: A huge skylight over an island eating counter brightens this kitchen. A private office space opens through double doors nearby.

- Dining Room: This room has sliding glass doors opening to the rear patio.

- Bedrooms: Two bedrooms with two bathrooms are located on the right side of the plan. One of the bedrooms is a master suite with a vaulted salon and a bath with a spa tub.

- Garage: You'll be able to reach this two-car garage via a service hallway that contains a laundry room, a walk-in pantry, and a closet.

Images provided by designer/architect.

Copyright by designer/architect.

Rear Elevation

Plan #221015

Dimensions: 69'8" W x 46' D

Levels: 1

Square Footage: 1,926

Bedrooms: 3

Bathrooms: 2½

Foundation: Basement; optional walk-out basement available for extra fee

Materials List Available: No

Price Category: D

Images provided by designer/architect.

You'll love the open plan in this lovely ranch and admire its many features, which are usually reserved for much larger homes.

Features:

- Ceiling Height: 8 ft.

- Great Room: A vaulted ceiling and tall windows surrounding the centrally located fireplace give distinction to this handsome room.

- Dining Room: Positioned just off the entry, this formal room makes a lovely spot for quiet dinner parties.

- Dining Nook: This nook sits between the kitchen and the great room. Central doors in the bayed area open to the backyard.

- Kitchen: An island will invite visitors while you cook in this well-planned kitchen, with its corner pantry and ample counter space.

- Master Suite: A tray ceiling, bay window, walk-in closet, and bath with whirlpool tub, dual-sink vanity, and standing shower pamper you here.

Rear Elevation

Copyright by designer/architect.

Plan #351083

Dimensions: 78' W x 51' D
Levels: 1
Square Footage: 1,896
Bedrooms: 3
Bathrooms: 2½
Foundation: Crawl space or slab
Material List Available: Yes
Price Category: D

Images provided by designer/architect.

A beautifully classic exterior and an interior designed with modern life in mind combine to make this the ideal home for a growing family.

CAD FILE AVAILABLE

Features:

- **Great Room:** The foyer opens into this large space, welcoming guests into your home. Vaulted ceilings and a cozy fireplace make the room an ideal place for family get-togethers.

- **Dining Room:** This room has a door to the covered back porch. Imagine relaxing family meals or small gatherings outside on warm evenings.

- **Kitchen:** A smartly designed workspace, this kitchen has the use of a nearby walk-in pantry and utility area and opens into the dining room for smooth transitions between preparing and serving.

- **Master Suite:** There will be no more fights over closet space or sink room. This area features his and her walk-in closets and a

compartmentalized master bath with a large shower stall, dual vanities and an oversized tub.

- **Secondary Bedrooms:** Two equally sized bedrooms, both with walk-in closets and two nearby bathrooms, keep peace between the younger members of the family.

Rear Elevation

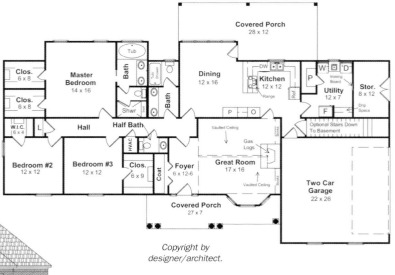

Copyright by designer/architect.

Plan #441002

Dimensions: 70' W x 51' D
Levels: 1
Square Footage: 1,873
Bedrooms: 3
Bathrooms: 2
Foundation: Crawl space
Materials List Available: No
Price Category: D

Shutters flank tall windows to adorn the front of this charming home. A high roofline gives presence to the façade and allows vaulted ceilings in all the right places inside.

Features:

• Great Room: The entry hall overlooks this room, where a fireplace warms gatherings on chilly evenings and built-in shelves, to the right of the fireplace, add space that might be used as an entertainment center. A large three-panel window wall allows for a rear-yard view.

• Dining Room: This area is connected directly to the great room and features double doors to a covered porch.

• Kitchen: This open work area contains ample counter space with an island cooktop and large pantry.

• Bedrooms: The bedrooms are split, with the master suite in the back and additional bedrooms at the front.

Images provided by designer/architect.

• Master Suite: This suite boasts a 9-ft.-high ceiling and is graced by a luxurious bathroom and a walk-in closet.

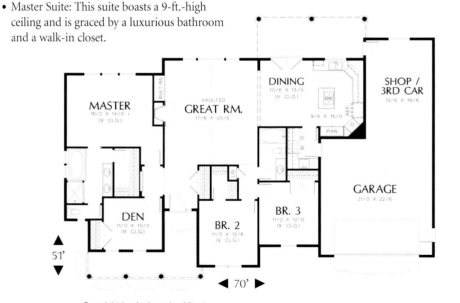

Copyright by designer/architect.

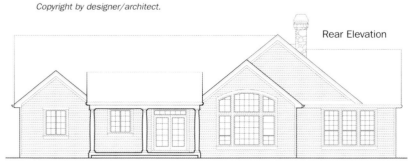

Rear Elevation

Plan #151490

Dimensions: 52' W x 69'6" D
Levels: 1
Square Footage: 1,869
Bedrooms: 3
Bathrooms: 2
Foundation: Crawl space or slab
CompleteCost List Available: Yes
Price Category: D

Images provided by designer/architect.

Bonus Area Floor Plan

Plan #461090

Dimensions: 67' W x 51' D
Levels: 1
Square Footage: 1,922
Bedrooms: 3
Bathrooms: 2
Foundation: Crawl space or slab; basement for fee
Material List Available: No
Price Category: D

Images provided by designer/architect.

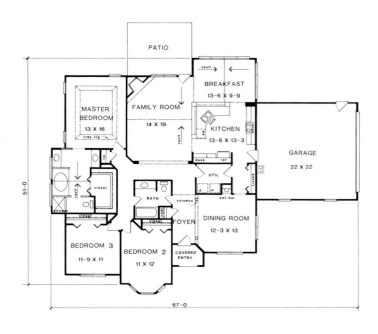

Plan #101006

Dimensions: 63' W x 58' D
Levels: 1
Square Footage: 1,982
Bedrooms: 3
Bathrooms: 2½
Foundation: Crawl space, slab basement, or walkout
Materials List Available: Yes
Price Category: D

Radius-top windows and siding accented with wood shingles give this home a distinctive look.

Features:

- Ceiling Height: 9 ft. unless otherwise noted.

- Family Room: This room is perfect for all kinds of informal family activities. A vaulted ceiling adds to its sense of spaciousness.

- Dining Room: This room, with its tray ceiling, is designed for elegant dining.

- Porch: When the weather gets warm, you'll enjoy stepping out onto this large screened porch to catch a breeze.

- Master Suite: You'll love ending your day and getting up in the morning to this exquisite master suite, with its vaulted ceiling, sitting area, and large walk-in closet.

- Bonus Room: Just off the kitchen are stairs leading to this enormous bonus room, offering more than 330 sq. ft. of future expansion space.

Images provided by designer/architect.

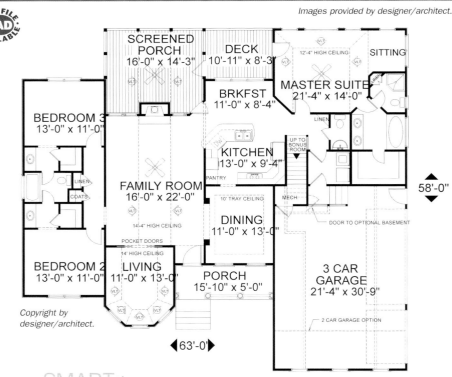

CAD FILE AVAILABLE

SCREENED PORCH 16'-0" x 14'-3"
DECK 10'-11" x 8'-3"
12'-4" HIGH CEILING   SITTING
BRKFST 11'-0" x 8'-4"
MASTER SUITE 21'-4" x 14'-0"
BEDROOM 3 13'-0" x 11'-0"
LINEN
KITCHEN 13'-0" x 9'-4"
UP TO BONUS ROOM
LINEN
COATS
PANTRY
FAMILY ROOM 16'-0" x 22'-0"
10' TRAY CEILING
MECH
14'-4" HIGH CEILING
DINING 11'-0" x 13'-0"
DOOR TO OPTIONAL BASEMENT
POCKET DOORS
58'-0"
14' HIGH CEILING
BEDROOM 2 13'-0" x 11'-0"
LIVING 11'-0" x 13'-0"
PORCH 15'-10" x 5'-0"
3 CAR GARAGE 21'-4" x 30'-9"
2 CAR GARAGE OPTION

Copyright by designer/architect.

◄ 63'-0" ►

SMARTtip
Art in Pools

The tiled walls and floor of a pool make great canvases for art, so incorporate a serious or whimsical design. Also, make the stairs wide and shallow to form a wading area for kids.

Plan #211003

Dimensions: 62' W x 64' D
Levels: 1
Square Footage: 1,865
Bedrooms: 3
Bathrooms: 2
Foundation: Crawl space or slab
Materials List Available: Yes
Price Category: D

Images provided by designer/architect.

SMARTtip
Fire Extinguishers

The word PASS is an easy way to remember the proper way to use a fire extinguisher.

Pull the pin at the top of the extinguisher that keeps the handle from being accidentally pressed.

Aim the nozzle of the extinguisher toward the base of the fire.

Squeeze the handle to discharge the extinguisher. Stand approximately 8 feet away from the fire.

Sweep the nozzle back and forth at the base of the fire. After the fire appears to be out, watch it carefully because it may reignite!

The traditional style of this home is blended with all the amenities required for today's lifestyle.

Features:

• Ceiling Height: 8 ft. unless otherwise noted.

• Front Porch: Guests will feel welcome arriving at the front door under this sheltering front porch.

• Dining Room: This large room will accommodate dinner parties of all sizes, from large formal gatherings to more intimate family get-togethers.

• Living Room: Guests and family alike will feel right at home in this inviting room. Sunlight streaming through the skylights in the 12-ft. ceiling, combined with the handsome fireplace, makes the space both airy and warm.

• Back Patio: When warm weather comes around, step out the sliding glass doors in the living room to enjoy entertaining or just relaxing on this patio.

• Kitchen: A cathedral ceiling soars over this efficient modern kitchen. It includes an eating area that is perfect for informal family meals.

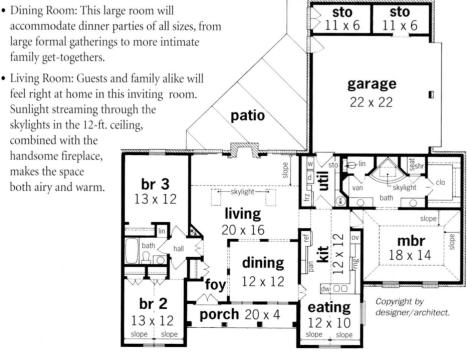

Copyright by designer/architect.

Plan #461046

Dimensions: 67'6" W x 48' D

Levels: 1

Square Footage: 1,839

Bedrooms: 3

Bathrooms: 2½

Foundation: Slab or basement;
crawl space for fee

Material List Available: No

Price Category: D

*Images provided by
designer/architect.*

Copyright by designer/architect.

Plan #461048

*Images provided by
designer/architect.*

Dimensions: 45' W x 67'6" D

Levels: 1

Square Footage: 1,846

Bedrooms: 3

Bathrooms: 2½

Foundation: Slab or basement;
crawl space for fee

Material List Available: No

Price Category: D

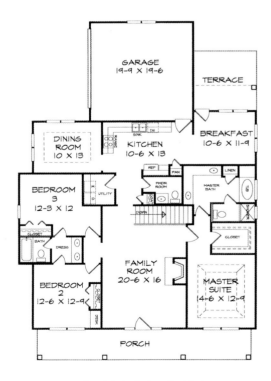

Copyright by designer/architect.

Plan #441001

Dimensions: 44' W x 68' D

Levels: 1

Square Footage: 1,850

Bedrooms: 3

Bathrooms: 2

Foundation: Crawl space

Materials List Available: No

Price Category: D

Images provided by designer/architect.

With all the tantalizing elements of a cottage and the comfortable space of a family-sized home, this Arts and Crafts-style one-story design is the best of both worlds. Exterior accents such as stone wainscot, cedar shingles under the gable ends, and mission-style windows just add to the effect.

CAD FILE AVAILABLE

Features:

- **Great Room:** A warm hearth lights this room—right next to a built-in media center.

- **Dining Room:** This area features a sliding glass door to the rear patio for a breath of fresh air.

- **Den:** This quiet area has a window seat and a vaulted ceiling, giving the feeling of openness and letting your mind wander.

- **Kitchen:** This open corner kitchen features a 42-in. snack bar and a giant walk-in pantry.

- **Master Suite:** This suite boasts a tray ceiling and a large walk-in closet.

Rear Elevation

Copyright by designer/architect.

Plan #101022

Dimensions: 66'2" W x 62' D
Levels: 1
Square Footage: 1,992
Bedrooms: 3
Bathrooms: 3
Foundation: Crawl space, slab, or basement
Materials List Available: Yes
Price Category: D

The exterior of this lovely home is traditional, but the unusually shaped rooms and amenities are contemporary.

Features:

- Foyer: This two-story foyer is open to the family room, but columns divide it from the dining room.

- Family Room: A gas fireplace and TV niche, flanked by doors to the covered porch, sit at the rear of this seven-sided, spacious room.

- Breakfast Room: Set off from the family room by columns, this area shares a snack bar with the kitchen and has windows looking over the porch.

- Bedroom 3: Use this room as a living room if you wish, and transform the guestroom to a media room or a family bedroom.

- Master Suite: The bedroom features a tray ceiling, has his and her dressing areas, and opens to the porch. The bath has a large corner tub, separate shower, linen closet, and two vanities.

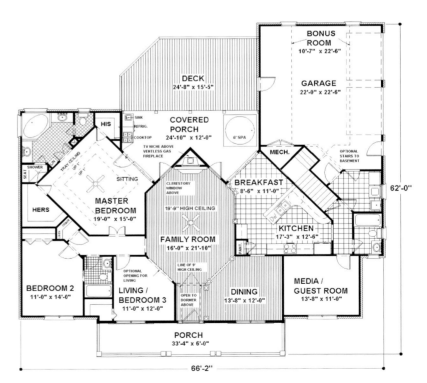

Kitchen

Living Room

Dining Room

Family Room

Master Bedroom

Master Bath

Plan #321006

Dimensions: 76' W x 45' D

Levels: 1, optional lower

Square Footage: 1,977

Optional Basement Level Sq. Ft.: 1,416

Bedrooms: 4

Bathrooms: 2½

Foundation: Basement

Materials List Available: Yes

Price Category: D

Images provided by designer/architect.

This design is ideal if you're looking for a home with space to finish as your family and your budget grow.

Features:

- Great Room: A vaulted ceiling in this room sets an elegant tone that the gorgeous atrium windows pick up and amplify.

- Atrium: Elegance marks the staircase here that leads to the optional lower level.

- Kitchen: Both experienced cooks and beginners will appreciate the care that went into the design of this step-saving kitchen, with its ample counter space and generous cabinets.

- Master Suite: Enjoy the luxuries you'll find in this suite, and revel in the quiet that the bedroom can provide.

- Lower Level: Finish the 1,416 sq. ft. here to create a family room, two bedrooms, two bathrooms, and a study.

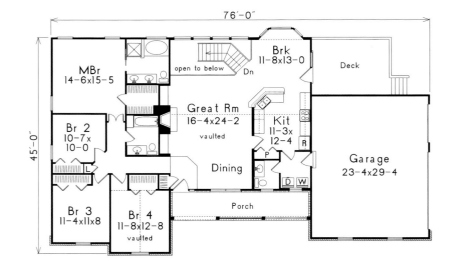

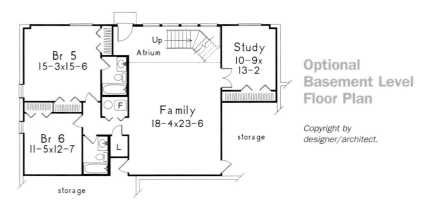

Optional Basement Level Floor Plan

Copyright by designer/architect.

Plan #131011

Dimensions: 75'2" W x 60'9" D
Levels: 1
Square Footage: 1,897
Bedrooms: 4
Bathrooms: 2
Foundation: Crawl space, slab, or basement
Materials List Available: Yes
Price Category: E

Images provided by designer/architect.

You'll love this home if you're looking for a plan for a sloping lot or flat one or if you want to orient the rear porch to face into or away from the sun.

Features:

• Ceiling Height: 8 ft.

• Living Area: The whole family will find it easy to congregate in this lovely room.

• Kitchen: The angle of this home makes the kitchen especially convenient while also giving it an unusual amount of character.

• Study: Located near the front door, this room can serve as a home office or fourth bedroom as easily as it does a private study.

• Master Suite: Located at the opposite end of the home from the other two bedrooms, this master suite offers privacy and quiet.

• Additional Bedrooms: These two bedrooms share a distinctive hall bathroom.

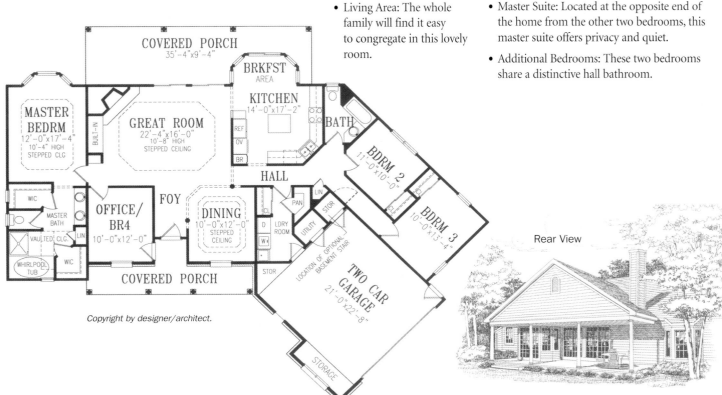

Copyright by designer/architect.

Rear View

Plan #151005

Dimensions: 58' W x 54'10" D
Levels: 1
Square Footage: 1,940
Bedrooms: 4
Bathrooms: 2
Foundation: Crawl space, slab, or basement
CompleteCost List Available: Yes
Price Category: D

A covered front porch with stately 10-in. round columns and a classically-styled foyer invite family and guests into this well-designed, traditional 4-bedroom home.

Features:

- Great Room: The 9-ft. boxed-ceiling, radiant fireplace, and built-in shelving add up to create a cozy and practical room where friends and family will love to gather.

- Dining Room: Open access from this dining room to the kitchen, and from there to the breakfast room, makes this room an ideal place for entertaining.

- Master Suite: This luxuriously appointed suite, with a 9-ft. pan ceiling in the bedroom, is located just of the breakfast room. The spectacular bath is fitted with a whirlpool tub, separate shower, and double vanities.

- Bedrooms 2 and 3: Large walk-in closets make these rooms easy to organize and keep tidy.

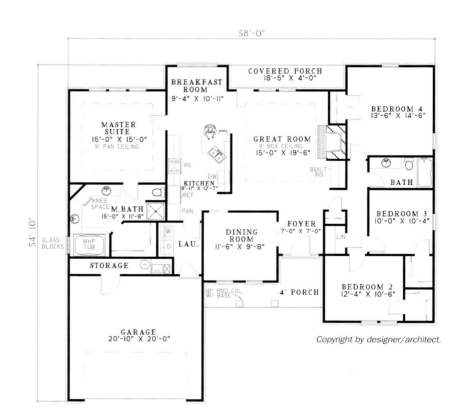

Plan #151089

Dimensions: 84' W x 55'6" D
Levels: 1
Square Footage: 1,921
Bedrooms: 3
Bathrooms: 3
Foundation: Crawl space, slab, or basement
CompleteCost List Available: Yes
Price Category: D

Images provided by designer/architect.

If your family loves to combine indoor and out-door living, this home's fabulous porches and deck space make it perfect.

Features:

- Porches: A huge wraparound front porch, sizable rear porch, and deck that joins them give you space for entertaining or simply lounging.

- Living Room: A fireplace and built-in media center could be the focal points in this large room.

- Hearth Room: Open to both the living room and kitchen, this hearth room also features a fireplace.

- Kitchen: This step-saving kitchen includes ample storage and work space, as well as an angled bar it shares with the hearth room. Atrium doors lead to the rear porch.

- Bonus Upper Level: A large game room and a full bath make this area a favorite with the children.

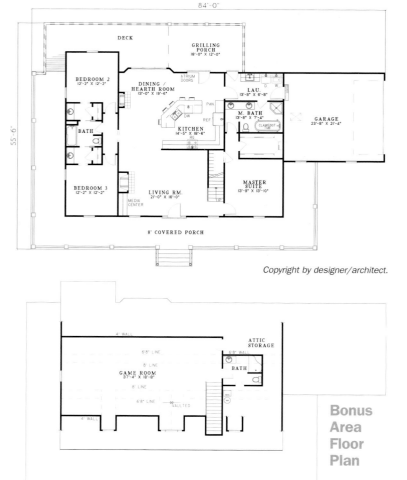

Copyright by designer/architect.

Bonus Area Floor Plan

Images provided by designer/architect.

Plan #371110

Dimensions: 57' W x 57' D
Levels: 1
Square Footage: 1,844
Bedrooms: 3
Bathrooms: 2
Foundation: Crawl space or slab
Material List Available: No
Price Category: D

This beautiful traditional brick home is all charm and grace. The home is sure to show off your good taste.

Features:

• Living Room: This massive gathering area, with its step-up ceiling and fireplace flanked by built-in cabinets, is sure to be the favorite place in your home. The large windows flood the space with natural light.

• Dining Room: This formal eating area is conveniently located just off the entry. The area features a built-in hutch.

• Kitchen: This U-shaped kitchen has a raised bar that's open to the breakfast nook. The butler's pantry will help serve in the dining room. The utility room, with the washer and dryer, is just off the kitchen.

• Master Suite: Split from the secondary bed rooms for privacy, this retreat boasts a ceiling sloping up to 10 ft. high and access to the rear porch. The master bath boasts a marble tub, shower, dual vanities, and a separate lavatory.

Copyright by
designer/architect.

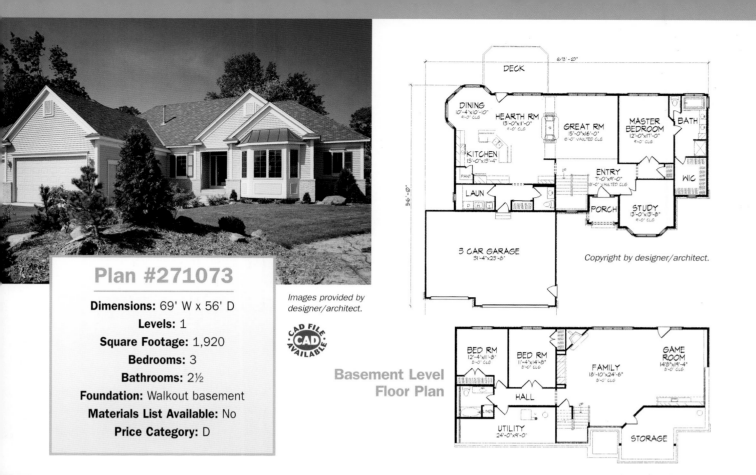

Images provided by designer/architect.

Copyright by designer/architect.

Plan #271073

Dimensions: 69' W x 56' D

Levels: 1

Square Footage: 1,920

Bedrooms: 3

Bathrooms: 2½

Foundation: Walkout basement

Materials List Available: No

Price Category: D

CAD FILE AVAILABLE

Basement Level Floor Plan

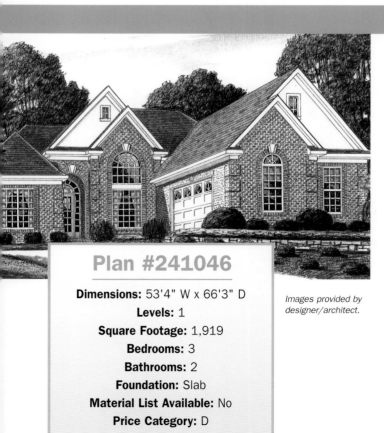

Plan #241046

Dimensions: 53'4" W x 66'3" D

Levels: 1

Square Footage: 1,919

Bedrooms: 3

Bathrooms: 2

Foundation: Slab

Material List Available: No

Price Category: D

Images provided by designer/architect.

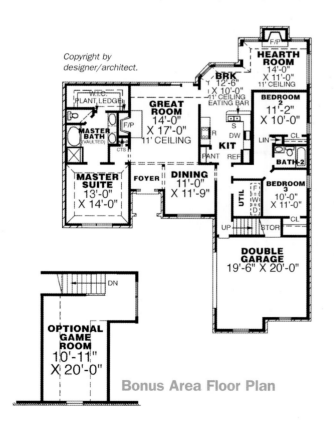

Copyright by designer/architect.

Bonus Area Floor Plan

Images provided by designer/architect.

Copyright by designer/architect.

Plan #251006

Dimensions: 65'5" W x 59'11" D

Levels: 1

Square Footage: 1,849

Bedrooms: 3

Bathrooms: 2

Foundation: Crawl space

Materials List Available: Yes

Price Category: D

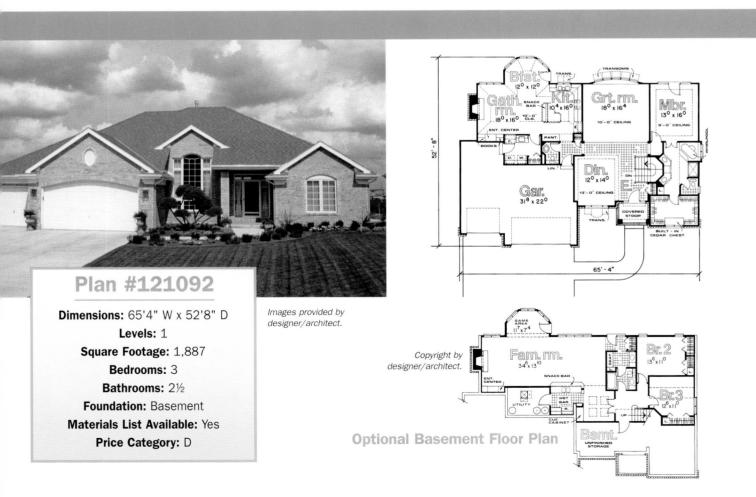

Images provided by designer/architect.

Copyright by designer/architect.

Optional Basement Floor Plan

Plan #121092

Dimensions: 65'4" W x 52'8" D

Levels: 1

Square Footage: 1,887

Bedrooms: 3

Bathrooms: 2½

Foundation: Basement

Materials List Available: Yes

Price Category: D

Plan #151117

Dimensions: 66' W x 55' D

Levels: 1

Square Footage: 1,957

Bedrooms: 3

Bathrooms: 3

Foundation: Crawl space, slab, or basement

CompleteCost List Available: Yes

Price Category: D

Images provided by designer/architect.

You'll love this home if you have a family-centered lifestyle and enjoy an active social life.

Features:

- **Foyer:** A 10-ft. ceiling sets the tone for this home.

- **Great Room:** A 10-ft. boxed ceiling and fireplace are the highlights of this room, which also has a door leading to the rear covered porch.

- **Dining Room:** Columns mark the entry from the foyer to this lovely formal dining room.

- **Study:** Add the French doors from the foyer to transform bedroom 3, with its vaulted ceiling, into a quiet study.

- **Kitchen:** This large kitchen includes a pantry and shares an eating bar with the adjoining, bayed breakfast room.

- **Master Suite:** You'll love the access to the rear porch, as well as the bath with every amenity, in this suite.

Copyright by designer/architect.

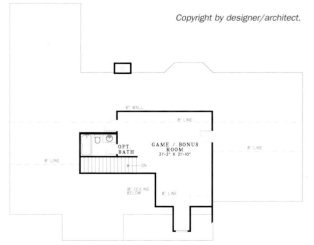

Bonus Area Floor Plan

Plans For Your Landscape

Landscapes change over the years. As plants grow, the overall look evolves from sparse to lush. Trees cast cool shade where the sun used to shine. Shrubs and hedges grow tall and dense enough to provide privacy. Perennials and ground covers spread to form colorful patches of foliage and flowers. Meanwhile, paths, arbors, fences, and other structures gain the patina of age.

Constant change over the years—sometimes rapid and dramatic, sometimes slow and subtle—is one of the joys of landscaping. It is also one of the challenges. Anticipating how fast plants will grow and how big they will eventually get is difficult, even for professional designers.

To illustrate the kinds of changes to expect in a planting, these pages show a landscape design at three different "ages." Even though a new planting may look sparse at first, it will soon fill in. And because of careful spacing, the planting will look as good in 10 to 15 years as it does after 3 to 5. It will, of course, look different, but that's part of the fun.

At Planting

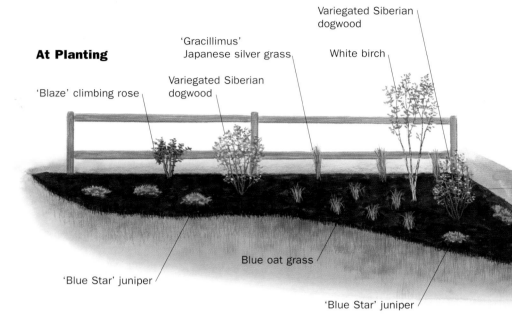

'Blaze' climbing rose

Variegated Siberian dogwood

'Gracillimus' Japanese silver grass

Variegated Siberian dogwood

White birch

'Blue Star' juniper

Blue oat grass

'Blue Star' juniper

Three to Five Years

At Planting—Here's how the corner might appear in early summer immediately after planting. The white birch tree is only 5 to 6 ft. tall, with trunks no thicker than broomsticks. The variegated Siberian dogwoods each have a few main stems about 3 to 4 ft. tall. The 'Blaze' rose has just short stubs where the nursery cut back the old stems, but it will grow fast and may bloom the first year. The 'Blue Star' junipers are low mounds about 6 to 10 in. wide. The blue oat grass forms small, thin clumps of sparse foliage. The 'Gracillimus' Japanese silver grass may still be dormant, or it may have a short tuft of new foliage. Both grasses will grow vigorously the first year.

Three to Five Years—The birch tree has grown 1 to 2 ft. taller every year but is still quite slender. Near the base, it's starting to show the white bark typical of maturity. The variegated Siberian dogwoods are well established now. If you cut them to the ground every year or two in spring, they grow back 4 to 6 ft. tall by midsummer, with strong, straight stems. The 'Blaze' rose covers the fence, and you need to prune out a few of its older stems every spring. The slow-growing 'Blue Star' junipers make a series of low mounds; you still see them as individuals, not a continuous patch. The grasses have reached maturity and form lush, robust clumps. It would be a good idea to divide and replant them now, to keep them vigorous.

Ten to Fifteen Years—The birch tree is becoming a fine specimen, 20 to 30 ft. tall, with gleaming white bark on its trunks. Prune away the lower limbs up to 6 to 8 ft. above ground to expose its trunks and to keep it from crowding and shading the other plants. The variegated dogwoods and 'Blaze' rose continue to thrive and respond well to regular pruning. The 'Blue Star' junipers have finally merged into a continuous mass of glossy foliage. The blue oat grass and Japanese silver grass will still look good if they have been divided and replanted over the years. If you get tired of the grasses, you could replace them with cinnamon fern and astilbe, as shown here, or other perennials or shrubs.

Ten to Fifteen Years

Cinnamon fern

Astilbe

First Impressions

Make a Pleasant Passage to Your Front Door

Here's a way to welcome visitors to your home with landscaping. Well-chosen plants and a revamped walkway not only make the short journey a pleasant one, they can also enhance your home's most public face and help settle it comfortably in its surroundings.

The curved walk in this design offers visitors a friendly welcome and a helpful "Please come this way." The first stage of the journey passes between two clipped shrub roses into a handsome garden "room" with larger shrubs near the house and smaller, colorful perennials by the walk. An opening in a hedge of long-blooming shrub roses then leads to a wider paved area that functions as an outdoor foyer. There you can greet guests or relax on the bench and enjoy the plantings that open out onto the lawn. A double course of pavers intersects the walk and an adjacent planting bed, and the circle it describes contrasts nicely with the rectilinear lines of the house and hedge.

Site: Sunny

Season: Summer

Concept: A distinctive walkway and colorful plantings make an enticing entry to your home.

C 'Frau Dagmar Hartop' rose

J Walk

'Frau Dagmar Hartop' rose C

Plants & Projects

Mixing shrubs and perennials, this planting offers colorful flowers and attractive foliage from spring through fall. The shrubs provide structure through the winter and are handsome when covered with new snow. The perennials are dormant in winter; cut them to the ground to make room for snow shoveled off the walk. Maintenance involves pruning the shrubs and clipping spent flowers to keep everything tidy.

A **'Sea Green'** *Juniperus chinensis* (use 3 plants)
This rugged evergreen shrub anchors a corner of the first garden "room" with arching branches that provide year-round pale green color.

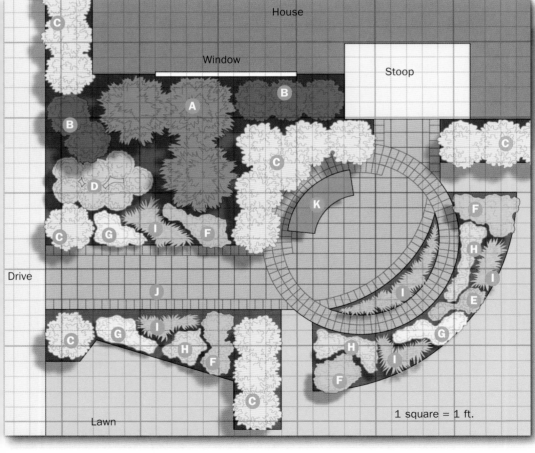

House

Window

Stoop

Drive

Lawn

1 square = 1 ft.

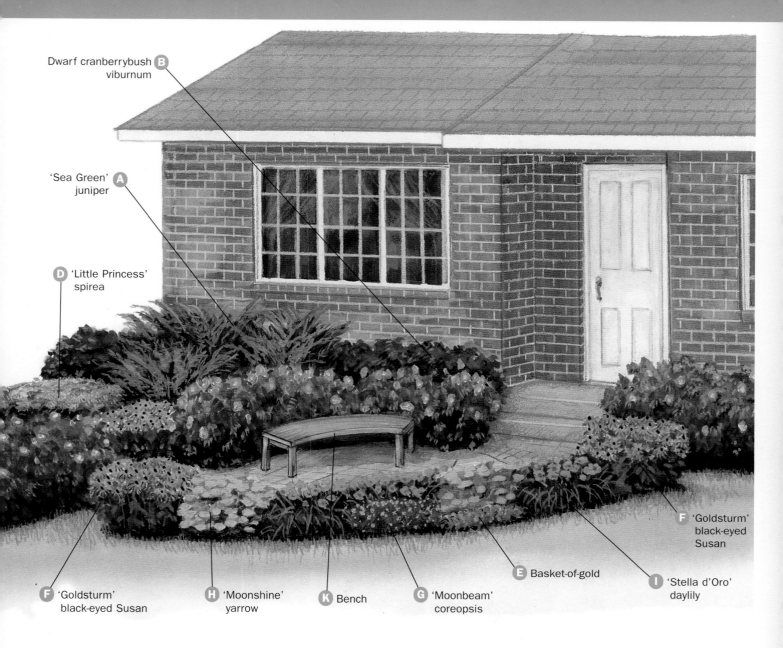

Dwarf cranberrybush **B**
viburnum

'Sea Green' **A**
juniper

D 'Little Princess'
spirea

F 'Goldsturm'
black-eyed Susan

H 'Moonshine'
yarrow

K Bench

G 'Moonbeam'
coreopsis

E Basket-of-gold

F 'Goldsturm'
black-eyed
Susan

I 'Stella d'Oro'
daylily

Note: all plants are appropriate for USDA Hardiness *Zones 4, 5, 6, and 7.*

B **Dwarf cranberrybush**
Viburnum opulus 'Nanum'
(use 5)
This small deciduous shrub
has a dense, bushy habit and
dark green, maplelike leaves
that turn shades of red in fall.
It won't outgrow its place
beneath the windows.

C **'Frau Dagmar Hartop'** *Rosa*
(use 18 or more)
With its crinkly bright green
leaves, fragrant single pink
flowers, and colorful red hips
from autumn into winter, this
easy-to-grow deciduous shrub
puts on quite a show. Flowers
all summer; forms a dense
"natural-looking" hedge.

Extend the planting along the
house as needed.

D **'Little Princess'** *Spiraea japoni-
ca* (use 7)
Another compact deciduous
shrub, with dainty twigs and
leaves. Bears clear pink flowers
in June and July.

E **Basket-of-gold** *Aurinia saxatilis*
(use 4)
The planting's first flowers
appear on this perennial in
spring. After the fragrant yellow
blooms fade, the low mounds of
gray leaves look good through
late fall.

F **'Goldsturm'** *Rudbeckia fulgi-
da* (use 20) A popular prairie
perennial, this bears large

golden yellow flowers (each
with a dark "eye" in the center) that are a cheerful sight
in late summer.

G **'Moonbeam'**
Coreopsis verticillata (use 22)
For months during the summer,
this perennial features masses of
tiny pale yellow flowers on neat
mounds of lacy dark green
foliage.

H **'Moonshine'** *Achillea* (use 17)
A perennial offering flat heads
of sulphur yellow flowers for
much of the summer. The fine
gray-green leaves contrast nicely with surrounding foliage.

I **'Stella d'Oro' daylily**
Hemerocallis (use 30)

Distinctive golden yellow
flowers hover over this perennial's attractive grassy foliage
from mid-June until fall.

J **Walk**
Made of precast concrete
pavers, the walk and decorative edgings require careful
layout and installation.
Consider renting a mason's
saw to ensure accuracy when
cutting pavers.

K **Bench**
A nursery or garden center
can usually order a simple
curved bench like the one
shown here, although a
straight, simple bench will
do, too.

A Warm Welcome
Make a Pleasant Passage to Your Front Door

Why wait until a visitor reaches the front door to extend a cordial greeting? Have your landscape offer a friendly welcome and a helpful "Please come this way." Well-chosen plants and a revamped walkway not only make a visitor's short journey a pleasant one, but they can also enhance your home's most public face.

This simple arrangement of plants and paving produces an elegant entrance that deftly mixes formal and informal elements. A wide walk of neatly fitted flagstones and a rectangular bed of roses have the feel of a small formal courtyard, complete with a pair of "standard" roses in planters, each displaying a mound of flowers atop a single stem. Clumps of ornamental grass rise from the paving like leafy fountains.

Gently curving beds of low-growing evergreens and shrub roses edge the flagstones, softening the formality and providing a comfortable transition to the lawn. Morning glories and clematis climb simple trellises to brighten the walls of the house.

Flowers in pink, white, purple, and violet are abundant from early summer until frost. They are set off by the rich green foliage of the junipers and roses and the gray leaves of the catmint edging.

Add a bench, as shown here, so you can linger and enjoy the scene; in later years, the lovely star magnolia behind it will provide comfortable dappled shade.

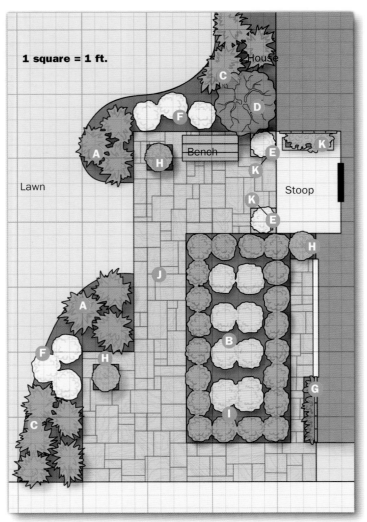

1 square = 1 ft.

House

Lawn

Bench

Stoop

Plants & Projects

Once established, these shrubs and perennials require little care beyond deadheading and an annual pruning. Ask the nursery where you buy the standard roses for advice on how to protect the plants in winter.

A **'Blue Star' juniper** *Juniperus squamata* (use 6 plants)
The sparkly blue foliage of this low-growing evergreen shrub neatly edges the opening onto the lawn.

B **'Bonica' rose** *Rosa* (use 8)
This deciduous shrub blooms from June until frost, producing clusters of double, soft pink flowers.

C **Dwarf creeping juniper** *Juniperis procumbens* 'Nana' (use 8)
This low, spreading evergreen with prickly green foliage makes a tough, handsome ground cover.

D **Star magnolia** *Magnolia stellata* (use 1)
This small, multitrunked deciduous tree graces the entry with lightly scented white flowers in early spring.

E **'The Fairy' rose** *Rosa* (use 2)
Clusters of small, double pale-pink roses appear in abundance from early summer to frost. Buy plants trained as standards at a nursery. Underplant with impatiens.

F **'White Meidiland' rose** *Rosa* (use 6)
A low, spreading shrub, it is covered with clusters of lovely single white flowers all summer.

G **Jackman clematis** *Clematis × Jackmanii* (use 2)
Trained to a simple lattice, this deciduous vine produces large, showy, dark purple flowers for weeks in summer.

H **'Gracillimus' Japanese silver grass** *Miscanthus* (use 3)
The arching leaves of this perennial grass are topped by fluffy seed heads from late summer through winter.

I **'Six Hills Giant' catmint** *Nepeta × faassenii* (use 20)
A perennial with violet-blue flowers and aromatic gray-green foliage edges the roses.

J **Flagstone paving**
Rectangular flagstones in random sizes.

K **Planters**
Simple wooden boxes contain blue-flowered annual morning glories (on the stoop, trained to a wooden lattice) and standard roses (in front of the stoop).

Note: all plants are appropriate for USDA Hardiness *Zones 5, 6, and 7.*

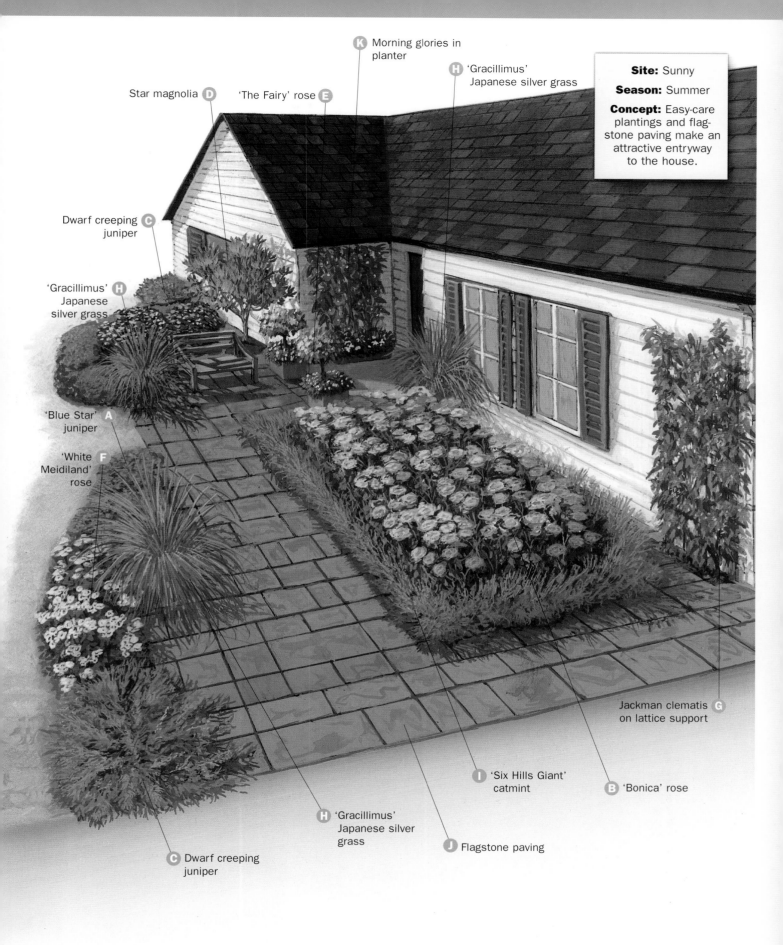

Morning glories in planter **K**

H 'Gracillimus' Japanese silver grass

Star magnolia **D**

'The Fairy' rose **E**

Site: Sunny

Season: Summer

Concept: Easy-care plantings and flagstone paving make an attractive entryway to the house.

Dwarf creeping juniper **C**

'Gracillimus' **H** Japanese silver grass

'Blue Star' **A** juniper

'White **F** Meidiland' rose

Jackman clematis **G** on lattice support

I 'Six Hills Giant' catmint

B 'Bonica' rose

H 'Gracillimus' Japanese silver grass

J Flagstone paving

C Dwarf creeping juniper

Around Back

Dress Up the Area between House and Detached Garage

When people think of landscaping the entrance to their home, the public entry at the front of the house comes immediately to mind. It's easy to forget that the back door often gets more use. If you make the journey between back door and driveway or garage many times each day, why not make it as pleasant a trip as possible? For many properties, a simple planting can transform the space bounded by the house, garage, and driveway, making it at once more inviting and more functional.

In a high-traffic area frequented by ball-bouncing, bicycle-riding children as well as busy adults, delicate, fussy plants have no place. The design shown here employs a few types of tough low-care plants, all of which look good year-round. The low yew hedge links the house and the garage and separates the more private backyard from the busy driveway. The star magnolia is just the right size for its spot. Its early-spring flowers will be a delight whether viewed coming up the driveway or from a window overlooking the backyard. The wide walk makes passage to and from the car easy—even with your arms full of groceries.

Note: all plants are appropriate for USDA Hardiness Zones 5, 6, and 7

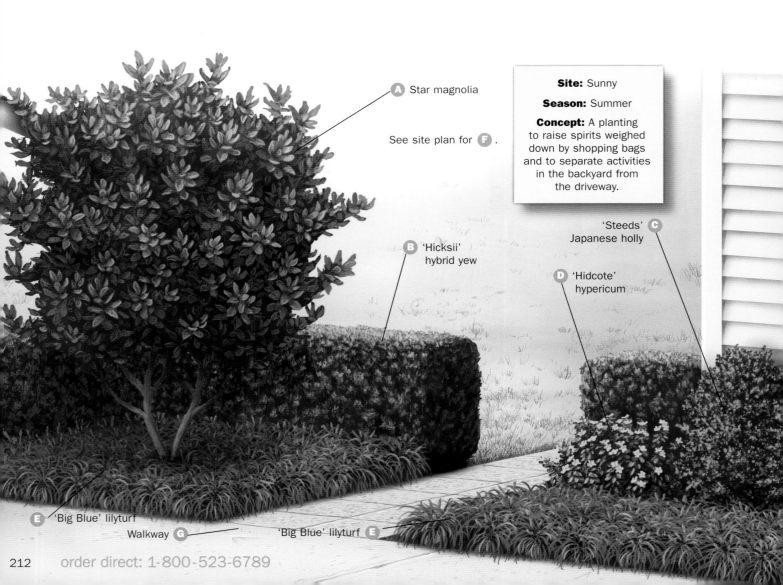

A Star magnolia

See site plan for **F** .

Site: Sunny

Season: Summer

Concept: A planting to raise spirits weighed down by shopping bags and to separate activities in the backyard from the driveway.

C 'Steeds' Japanese holly

B 'Hicksii' hybrid yew

D 'Hidcote' hypericum

E 'Big Blue' lilyturf

Walkway **G**   'Big Blue' lilyturf **E**

Plants & Projects

The watchword in this planting is evergreen. Except for the magnolia, all the plants here are fully evergreen or are nearly so. Spring and summer see lovely flowers from the magnolia and hypericum, and the carpet of lilyturf turns a handsome blue in August. For a bigger splash in spring, underplant the lilyturf with daffodils. Choose a single variety for uniform color, or select several varieties for a mix of colors and bloom times. Other than shearing the hedge, the only maintenance required is cutting back the lilyturf and hypericum in late winter.

A **Star magnolia** *Magnolia stellata* (use 1 plant)
Lovely white flowers cover this small deciduous tree before the leaves appear. Starlike blooms, slightly fragrant and sometimes tinged with pink, appear in early spring and last up to two weeks. In summer, the dense leafy crown of dark green leaves helps provide privacy in the backyard. A multitrunked specimen will fill the space better and display more of the interesting winter bark.

B **'Hicksii' hybrid yew** *Taxus x media* (use 9)
A fast-growing evergreen shrub that is ideal for this 3-ft.-tall neatly sheared hedge. Needles are glossy dark green and soft, not prickly. Eight plants form the L-shaped portion, while a single sheared plant extends the hedge on the other side of the walk connecting it to the house. (If the hedge needs to play a part in confining a family pet, you could easily set posts either side of the walk and add a gate.)

C **'Steeds' Japanese holly** *Ilex crenata* (use 3 or more)
Several of these dense, upright evergreen shrubs can be grouped at the corner as specimen plants or to tie into an existing foundation planting. You could also extend them along the house to create a foundation planting, as shown here. The small dark green leaves are thick and leathery and have tiny spines. Plants attain a pleasing form when left to their own devices. Resist the urge to shear them; just prune to control size if necessary.

D **'Hidcote' hypericum** *Hypericum* (use 1)
All summer long, clusters of large golden flowers cover the arching stems of this tidy semievergreen shrub, brightening the entrance to the backyard.

E **'Big Blue' lilyturf** *Liriope muscari* (use 40 or more)
Grasslike evergreen clumps of this perennial ground cover grow together to carpet the ground flanking the driveway and walk. (Extend the planting as far down the drive as you like.) Slim spires of tiny blue flowers rise above the dark green leaves in June. Lilyturf doesn't stand up to repeated tromping. If the drive is also a basketball court, substitute periwinkle (*Vinca minor*), a tough ground cover with latespring lilac flowers.

F **Stinking hellebore** *Helleborus foetidus* (use 5 or more)
This clump-forming perennial is ideal for filling the space between the walk and house on the backyard side of the hedge. (You might also consider extending the planting along the L-shaped side of the hedge.) Its pale green flowers are among the first to bloom in the spring and continue for many weeks; dark green leaves are attractive year-round.

G **Walkway**
Precast concrete pavers, 2 ft. by 2 ft., replace an existing walk or form a new one.

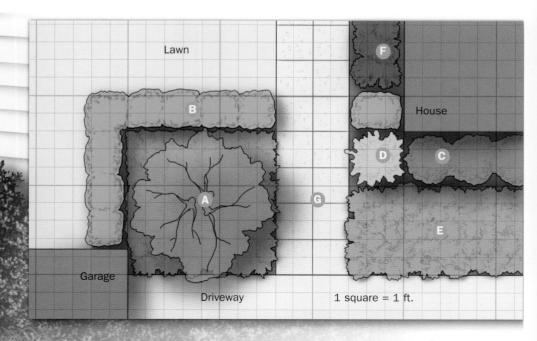

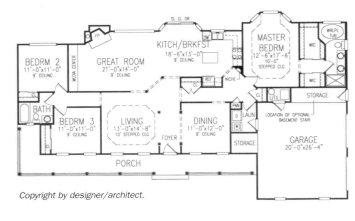

Plan #131016

Dimensions: 75' W x 45' D
Levels: 1
Square Footage: 1,902
Bedrooms: 3
Bathrooms: 2
Foundation: Crawl space, slab, or basement
Materials List Available: Yes
Price Category: E

Images provided by designer/architect.

Great Room

Plan #141011

Dimensions: 54' W x 60'6" D
Levels: 1
Square Footage: 1,869
Bedrooms: 3
Bathrooms: 2
Foundation: Crawl space, slab, or basement
Materials List Available: Yes
Price Category: D

Images provided by designer/architect.

This home, as shown in the photograph, may differ from the actual blueprints. For more detailed information, please check the floor plans carefully.

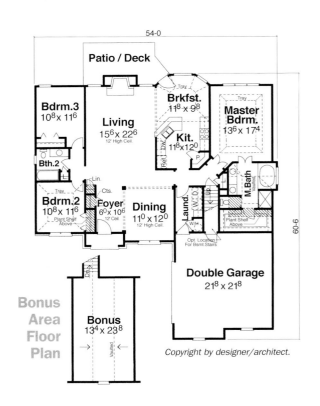

Plan #141007

Dimensions: 65' W x 56'5" D
Levels: 1
Square Footage: 1,854
Bedrooms: 3
Bathrooms: 2½
Foundation: Basement
Materials List Available: No
Price Category: D

Images provided by designer/architect.

Master Bdrm. 13⁶ x 17⁶ Tray Ceil.

Brkfst. 11⁴ x 11⁰

Sundeck

Bdrm.3 11¹⁰ x 13²

M. Bath Tray Ceil.

Kit. 13⁴ x 10⁴ Island

Living Area 17⁶ x 15⁴ 12' High Ceil.

Bth.2

W.D. Lnd. Pant. Up Dn.

Foyer 5⁶ x 9⁶ 12' Ceil.

Dbl. Garage 19⁴ x 21⁸

Dining 11⁶ x 13⁶ 12' High Ceil.

Bdrm.2 11¹⁰ x 13²

Copyright by designer/architect.

SMARTtip

Painting Walls

Paint won't hide imperfections. Rather, it will make them stand out. So shine a bright light at a low angle across the surface to spot problem areas before painting.

Plan #281029

Dimensions: 48' W x 59' D
Levels: 1
Square Footage: 1,833
Bedrooms: 3
Bathrooms: 2
Foundation: Basement
Materials List Available: Yes
Price Category: D

Images provided by designer/architect.

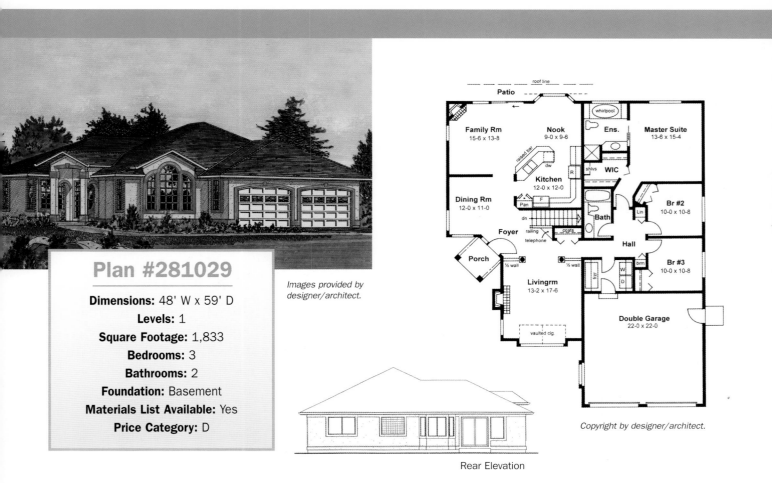

Rear Elevation

Copyright by designer/architect.

Plan #121125

Dimensions: 54' W x 58'8" D
Levels: 1
Square Footage: 1,978
Bedrooms: 3
Bathrooms: 2½
Foundation: Basement; crawl space for fee
Material List Available: Yes
Price Category: D

Images provided by designer/architect.

Copyright by designer/architect.

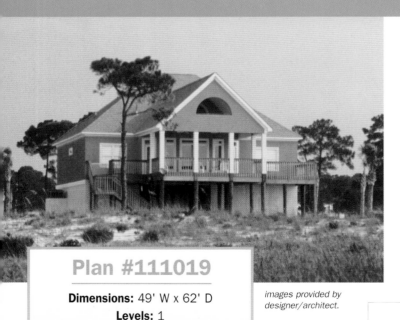

Plan #111019

Dimensions: 49' W x 62' D
Levels: 1
Square Footage: 1,936
Bedrooms: 4
Bathrooms: 2
Foundation: Pier
Materials List Available: No
Price Category: D

images provided by designer/architect.

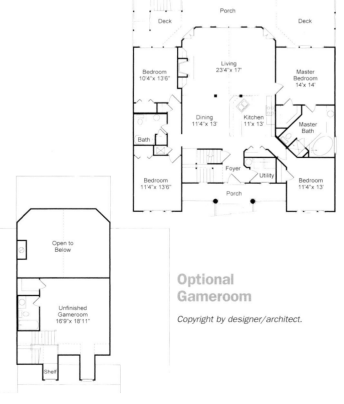

Optional Gameroom

Copyright by designer/architect.

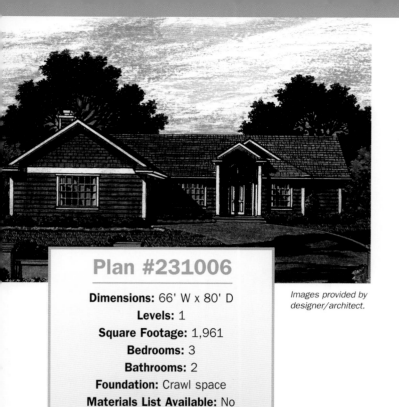

Plan #231006

Dimensions: 66' W x 80' D

Levels: 1

Square Footage: 1,961

Bedrooms: 3

Bathrooms: 2

Foundation: Crawl space

Materials List Available: No

Price Category: D

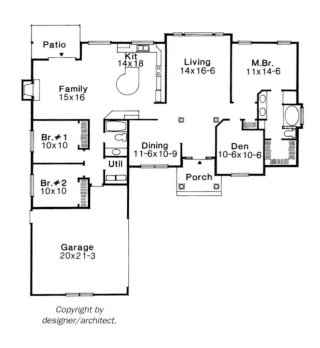

Images provided by designer/architect.

Copyright by designer/architect.

Plan #371075

Dimensions: 49'8" W x 54'6" D

Levels: 1

Square Footage: 1,904

Bedrooms: 4

Bathrooms: 2

Foundation: Crawl space or slab

Materials List Available: No

Price Category: D

Images provided by designer/architect.

CAD FILE AVAILABLE

Copyright by designer/architect.

Plan #371109

Dimensions: 53'6" W x 63' D
Levels: 1
Square Footage: 1,839
Bedrooms: 4
Bathrooms: 2
Foundation: Crawl space or slab
Material List Available: No
Price Category: D

Images provided by designer/architect.

CAD FILE AVAILABLE

Copyright by designer/architect.

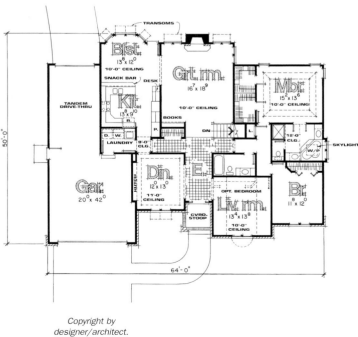

Plan #121050

Dimensions: 64' W x 50' D
Levels: 1
Square Footage: 1,996
Bedrooms: 2
Bathrooms: 2
Foundation: Basement
Materials List Available: Yes
Price Category: D

Images provided by designer/architect.

Copyright by designer/architect.

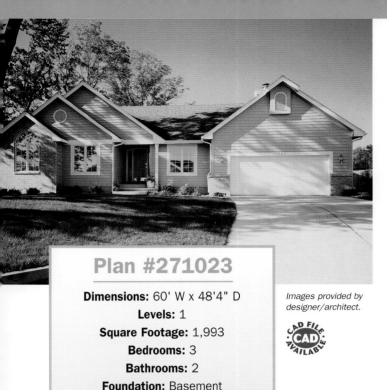

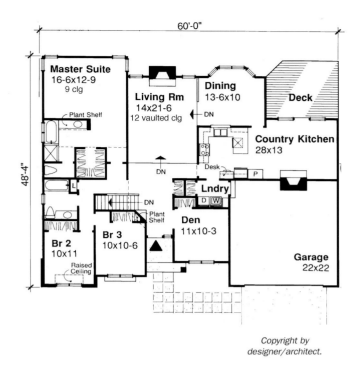

Master Suite
16-6x12-9
9 clg

Plant Shelf

Living Rm
14x21-6
12 vaulted clg

Dining
13-6x10

Deck

Country Kitchen
28x13

Desk

Lndry
D W

Den
11x10-3

Br 2
10x11

Br 3
10x10-6

Raised Ceiling

Plant Shelf

Garage
22x22

60'-0"

48'-4"

Copyright by designer/architect.

Plan #271023

Dimensions: 60' W x 48'4" D

Levels: 1

Square Footage: 1,993

Bedrooms: 3

Bathrooms: 2

Foundation: Basement

Materials List Available: Yes

Price Category: D

Images provided by designer/architect.

CAD FILE AVAILABLE

34'-10"

GARAGE
21'-0" X 19'-8"

8' GRILLING PORCH

GAS

MASTER SUITE
14'-0" X 13'-2"
10' BOXED CEILING

LAU.
8'-8" X 6'-0"

PAN

REF

KITCHEN
16'-10" X 11'-6"

RG

DW

M. BATH
17'-0" X 10'-0"

WHP TUB

DINING
14'-10" X 12'-0"
10' BOXED CEILING

BEDROOM 2
14'-0" X 10'-0"

10' BOXED COLUMNS

83'-0"

GREAT RM.
19'-10" X 17'-2"
10' BOXED CEILING

BEDROOM 3 / STUDY
14'-0" X 10'-0"

8' COVERED PORCH

Copyright by designer/architect.

Plan #151069

Dimensions: 34'10" W x 83' D

Levels: 1

Square Footage: 1,811

Bedrooms: 3

Bathrooms: 2

Foundation: Crawl space or slab

CompleteCost List Available: Yes

Price Category: D

Images provided by designer/architect.

CAD FILE AVAILABLE

Plan #351001

Dimensions: 72'8" W x 51' D

Levels: 1

Square Footage: 1,855

Bedrooms: 3

Bathrooms: 2½

Foundation: Crawl space, slab, or basement

Materials List Available: Yes

Price Category: D

Images provided by designer/architect.

From the lovely arched windows on the front to the front and back covered porches, this home is as comfortable as it is beautiful.

Features:

- **Great Room:** Come into this room with 12-ft. ceilings, and you're sure to admire the corner gas fireplace and three windows overlooking the porch.

- **Dining Room:** Set off from the open design, this room is designed to be used formally or not.

- **Kitchen:** You'll love the practical walk-in pantry, broom closet, and angled snack bar here.

- **Breakfast Room:** Brightly lit and leading to the covered porch, this room will be a favorite spot.

- **Bonus Room:** Develop a playroom or study in this area.

- **Master Suite:** The large bedroom is complemented by the private bath with garden tub, separate shower, double vanity, and spacious walk-in closet.

Copyright by designer/architect.

Bonus Area Floor Plan

Kitchen/Great Room

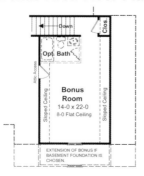

Plan #131057

Dimensions: 79'2" W x 37'8" D
Levels: 1
Square Footage: 1,843
Bedrooms: 3
Bathrooms: 2
Foundation: Crawl space, slab, or basement
Material List Available: Yes
Price Category: D

Images provided by designer/architect.

The size of this traditionally styled brick ranch is deceiving; it more than accommodates all of the modern family's needs. Vaulted ceilings and an abundance of windows open the home up from the inside out.

Features:

- Covered Porch: Sit in peaceful privacy, looking out on your backyard while enjoying coffee on cool summer mornings.
- Great Room: Family and friends alike will be drawn to this expansive, window-lined room to sit by the fireplace on frosty winter days.
- Kitchen: Featuring lots of workspace and a raised bar, this kitchen is great for the family gourmet. The hub of the home, it links together the breakfast room, dining room, and great room, giving you plenty of convenient choices for formal or informal dining.
- Master Bedroom: A large area, bay windows, his and her walk-in closets, and a fully equipped master bath combine to make a relaxing, romantic escape from everyday life. The compartmentalized master bath features a vaulted ceiling, his and her sinks, a standing shower, and a bathtub.

Optional Laundry Room Floor Plan

Copyright by designer/architect.

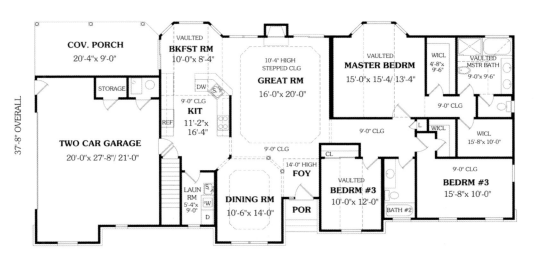

Plan #161002

Dimensions: 64'2" W x 44'2" D
Levels: 1
Square Footage: 1,860
Bedrooms: 3
Bathrooms: 2
Foundation: Basement
Materials List Available: Yes
Price Category: D

CAD FILE AVAILABLE

Images provided by designer/architect.

The brick, stone, and cedar shake facade provides color and texture to the exterior, while the unique nooks and angles inside this delightful one-level home give it character.

Features:

- **Great Room/Dining Room:** This spacious great room is furnished with a wood-burning fireplace, a high ceiling, and French doors. Wide entrances to the breakfast room and dining room expand its space to comfortably hold large gatherings.

- **Kitchen:** The breakfast bar offers additional seating. The covered porch lets you enjoy a view of the landscape and is conveniently located for outdoor meals off this kitchen and breakfast area.

- **Master Bedroom:** The master bedroom is a private retreat. An alcove creates a comfortable sitting area, and an angled entry leads to the bath with whirlpool and a double-bowl vanity.

Left Side Elevation

Rear Elevation

Right Side Elevation

Copyright by designer/architect.

Dining Room

Living Room / Dining Room

Great Room/Breakfast Area

Great Room

Installing Rods and Poles

The way to install a rod or pole depends on the type it is, the brackets that will hold it, the weight of the window treatment, and the surface to which it is being fastened. Given below are some general guidelines, but for specific installation procedures, refer to the instructions that accompany the rod or pole.

- Use a stepladder to reach high places.

- Use the proper tools.

- Take accurate measurements.

- Work with a helper.

- If attaching a bracket to wood, first drill small pilot holes to avoid splitting the wood.

- Consider using wall anchors, particularly for the heavier window treatments.

- Use a level as needed to help you position the brackets for the pole or rod.

- Take care not to drill or hammer into any pipes or electrical wiring.

Because they're designed to stand out, decorative poles and their finials require more room for installation than conventional drapery rods. Finials add inches to the ends of a window treatment, so make sure you have enough wall room to display your hardware to its full advantage. And because decorative rods are often heavy, be certain your window frames and walls can support the weight.

Plan #241028

Dimensions: 56' W x 63' D

Levels: 1

Square Footage: 1,970

Bedrooms: 3

Bathrooms: 2

Foundation: Slab

Materials List Available: No

Price Category: D

Images provided by designer/architect.

Copyright by designer/architect.

Plan #511021

Dimensions: 65'9" W x 49'10" D

Levels: 1

Square Footage: 1,821

Bedrooms: 3

Bathrooms: 2

Foundation: Crawl space or slab

Material List Available: No

Price Category: D

Images provided by designer/architect.

Bonus Area Floor Plan

Copyright by designer/architect.

Images provided by designer/architect.

Plan #511020

Dimensions: 60' W x 55'6" D

Levels: 1

Square Footage: 1,801

Bedrooms: 3

Bathrooms: 2

Foundation: Crawl space or slab

Material List Available: No

Price Category: D

Bonus Area Floor Plan

Copyright by designer/architect.

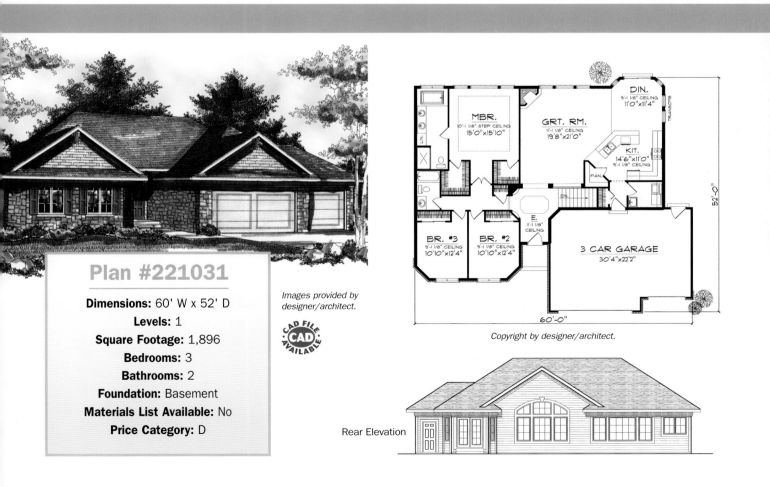

Plan #221031

Dimensions: 60' W x 52' D

Levels: 1

Square Footage: 1,896

Bedrooms: 3

Bathrooms: 2

Foundation: Basement

Materials List Available: No

Price Category: D

Images provided by designer/architect.

CAD FILE AVAILABLE

Copyright by designer/architect.

Rear Elevation

Plan #181724

Dimensions: 55'4"W x 58' D
Levels: 1
Square Footage: 1,808
Bedrooms: 3
Bathrooms: 2
Foundation: Basement
Material List Available: Yes
Price Category: D

Images provided by designer/architect.

Copyright by designer/architect.

58'-0"
17,4 m

55'-4"
16,6 m

Plan #221061

Dimensions: 52' W x 59' D
Levels: 1
Square Footage: 1,867
Bedrooms: 3
Bathrooms: 2
Foundation: Basement
Material List Available: No
Price Category: D

Images provided by designer/architect.

Copyright by designer/architect.

Rear Elevation

Plan #181722

Dimensions: 68'8" W x 41'8" D
Levels: 1
Square Footage: 1,883
Bedrooms: 3
Bathrooms: 2
Foundation: Basement
Material List Available: Yes
Price Category: D

CAD FILE AVAILABLE

Images provided by designer/architect.

Copyright by designer/architect.

Plan #131035

Dimensions: 65'4" W x 45'10" D
Levels: 1
Square Footage: 1,892
Bedrooms: 3
Bathrooms: 2½
Foundation: Crawl space, slab, or basement
Materials List Available: Yes
Price Category: D

Images provided by designer/architect.

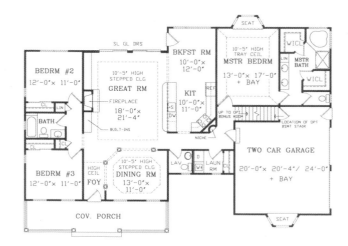

Rear Elevation

Bonus Area

Copyright by designer/architect.

Plan #151104

Dimensions: 43' W x 55' D
Levels: 1
Square Footage: 1,860
Bedrooms: 3
Bathrooms: 2
Foundation: Crawl space or slab;
basement for fee
CompleteCost List Available: Yes
Price Category: D

Images provided by designer/architect.

If you're just starting a family or the
children have left the nest, this is the
ideal home for you.

Features:

• Great Room: Set off by 8-in. columns, this
gathering area features a fireplace and access to
the backyard.

• Kitchen: This U-shaped kitchen has a raised
bar that's open to the breakfast room. The
built-in computer desk will be a great asset to
today's family.

• Master Suite: This private retreat offers a large
sleeping area with access to the rear yard.
The master bath features dual vanities and a
whirlpool tub.

• Garage: This front-loading two-car garage has
room for cars plus storage.

Main Level Floor Plan

43'-0"

55'-0"

GREAT RM.
17'-8" X 17'-4"

MASTER BEDROOM
14'-4" X 17'-0"

WHIP TUB

M.BATH
8'-6" X 10'-8"

8" COLUMNS

LIN

BRKFAST RM.
14'-8" X 12'-0"

BEDROOM 2
12'-0" X 11'-10"

PAN

W   D

KITCHEN
14'-8" X 13'-6"

DW

REF.

COMPUTER DESK

RG

FOYER
7'-4" X 12'-6"

GARAGE
19'-8" X 19'-2"

DINING
14'-8" X 13'-6"

ENTRY PORCH

Bonus Area Floor Plan

Copyright by designer/architect.

LIN

DN

OPT. BEDROOM 3
14'-8" X 13'-0"

OPT. BONUS RM.
23'-6" X 23'-8"

8" LINE

Plan #361538

Dimensions: 46'8"W x 73' D
Levels: 1
Square Footage: 2,011
Bedrooms: 3
Bathrooms: 2½
Foundation: Crawl space
Material List Available: No
Price Category: D

Images provided by designer/architect.

CAD FILE AVAILABLE

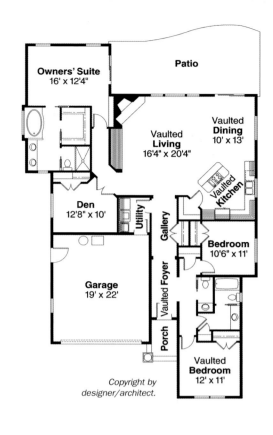

Copyright by designer/architect.

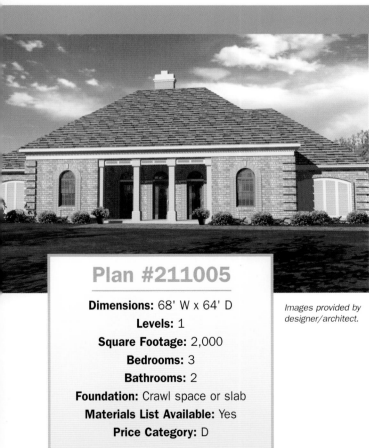

Plan #211005

Dimensions: 68' W x 64' D
Levels: 1
Square Footage: 2,000
Bedrooms: 3
Bathrooms: 2
Foundation: Crawl space or slab
Materials List Available: Yes
Price Category: D

Images provided by designer/architect.

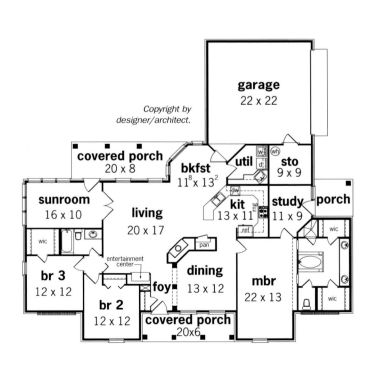

Copyright by designer/architect.

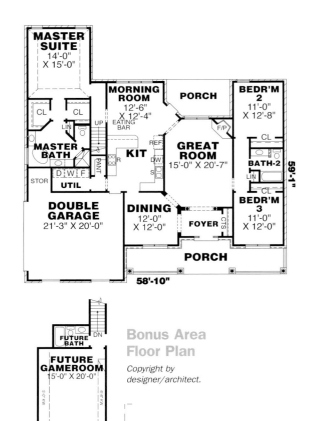

Plan #241007

Dimensions: 58'10" W x 59'1" D

Levels: 1

Square Footage: 2,036

Bedrooms: 3

Bathrooms: 2

Foundation: Crawl space, slab

Materials List Available: No

Price Category: D

Bonus Area Floor Plan

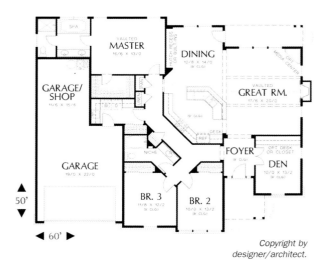

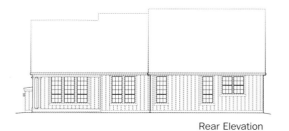

Rear Elevation

Plan #441008

Dimensions: 60' W x 50' D

Levels: 1

Square Footage: 2,001

Bedrooms: 3

Bathrooms: 2

Foundation: Crawl space; slab or basement available for fee

Materials List Available: No

Price Category: D

Plan #351008

Dimensions: 64'6" W x 61'4" D
Levels: 1
Square Footage: 2,002
Bedrooms: 3
Bathrooms: 2
Foundation: Crawl space or basement
Materials List Available: Yes
Price Category: E

This home has the charming appeal of a quaint cottage that you might find in an old village in the English countryside. It's a unique design that maximizes every inch of its usable space.

Features:

- **Great Room:** This room has a vaulted ceiling and built-in units on each side of the fireplace.

- **Kitchen:** This kitchen boasts a raised bar open to the breakfast area; the room is also open to the dining room.

- **Master Bedroom:** This bedroom retreat features a raised ceiling and a walk-in closet.

- **Master Bath:** This bathroom has a double vanity, large walk-in closet, and soaking tub.

- **Bedrooms:** Two bedrooms share a common bathroom and have large closets.

Plan #131009

Dimensions: 64'10" W x 57'8" D
Levels: 1
Square Footage: 2,018
Bedrooms: 3
Bathrooms: 2
Foundation: Crawl space, slab, or basement
Materials List Available: Yes
Price Category: E

The pavilion-styled great room at the heart of this H-shaped ranch gives it an unusual elegance that you're sure to enjoy.

Features:

- Great Room: The tray ceiling sets off this room, and a fireplace warms it on chilly nights and cool days. Two sets of sliding glass doors leading to the backyard terrace let in natural light and create an efficient traffic flow.

- Kitchen: Designed for a gourmet cook, this kitchen features a snack bar that everyone will enjoy and easy access to the breakfast room.

- Breakfast Room: Open to the columned rear porch, this breakfast room is an ideal spot for company or family brunches.

- Master Suite: A sitting area and access to the porch make the bedroom luxurious, while the private bath featuring a whirlpool tub creates a spa atmosphere.

VAULTED
BEDRM #2
14'-8"x 11'-0"

CL CL

BEDRM #3
11'-0"x
13'-0"

BATH #2

STOR UTIL

LOCATION OF
OPT. BSMT STAIR

TWO CAR
GARAGE
20'-0"x 21'-0"

ALT. FRONT ENTRY
GARAGE

TERRACE

BUILT-IN

11'-6" HIGH
STEPPED CLG
GREAT RM
21'-0"x 16'-0"

TV

CL

HIGH CEIL
GALLERY

COV. PORCH

COV. PORCH
24'-8"x 10'-2"

9'-6" HIGH
CEILING
BKFST RM
13'-0"x
20'-2"

KITCHEN

DW

REF

PANT

SITTING
CL. OR
BUILT-IN

11'-6" HIGH
STEPPED CLG
MSTR
BEDRM
13'-0"x
18'-0"

DRSG WICL

WICL

LIN

9'-6" HIGH
STEPPED CLG
DINING RM
12'-0"x
14'-0"

MSTR
BATH

STEAM
SHOWER

SEAT

Copyright by designer/architect.

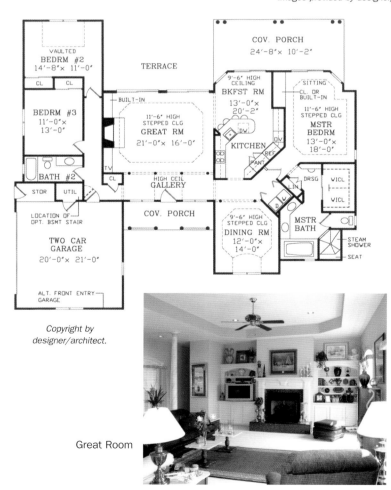

Great Room

Main Level Floor Plan

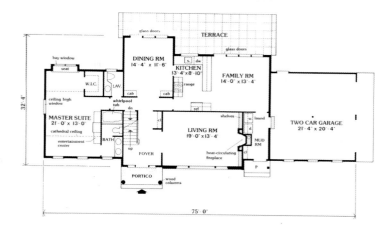

Images provided by designer/architect.

Upper Level Floor Plan

Copyright by designer/architect.

Plan #131072

Dimensions: 75' W x 32' D

Levels: 1.5

Square Footage: 2,053

Main Floor Sq. Ft.: 1,440

Upper Level Sq. Ft.: 613

Bedrooms: 3

Bathrooms: 2½

Foundation: Crawl space, slab, or basement

Material List Available: Yes

Price Category: E

Plan #311056

Dimensions: 56' W x 71'10" D

Levels: 1

Square Footage: 2,053

Bedrooms: 3

Bathrooms: 2

Foundation: Crawl space, slab, or basement

Material List Available: Yes

Price Category: D

Images provided by designer/architect.

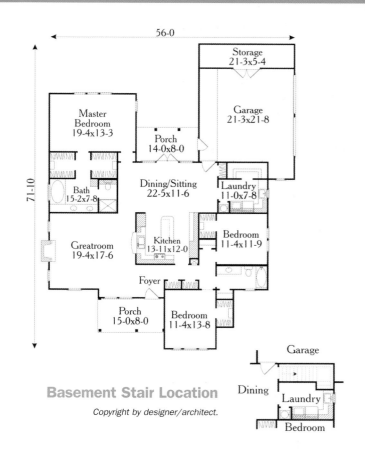

Basement Stair Location

Copyright by designer/architect.

Images provided by designer/architect.

Bonus Area Floor Plan
Copyright by designer/architect.

Plan #361505

Dimensions: 58' W x 62' D
Levels: 1
Square Footage: 2,066
Bedrooms: 3
Bathrooms: 2
Foundation: Crawl space
Material List Available: No
Price Category: D

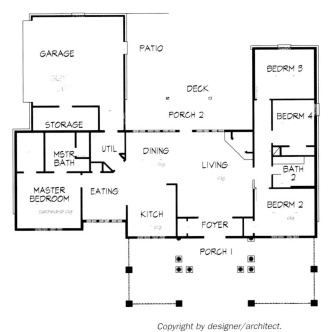

Images provided by designer/architect.

Copyright by designer/architect.

Plan #271082

Dimensions: 71' W x 62' D
Levels: 1
Square Footage: 2,074
Bedrooms: 4
Bathrooms: 2
Foundation: Crawl space or slab
Materials List Available: No
Price Category: D

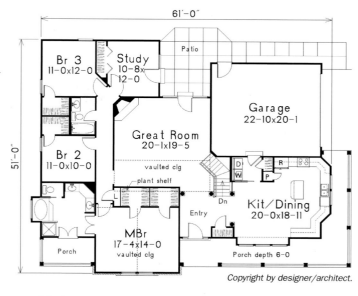

Images provided by designer/architect.

Copyright by designer/architect.

Plan #321030

Dimensions: 61' W x 51' D
Levels: 1
Square Footage: 2,029
Bedrooms: 4
Bathrooms: 2
Foundation: Crawl space, slab, basement, or walkout
Materials List Available: Yes
Price Category: D

SMARTtip
Measuring Angles

A sure-fire way to accurately measure the wall-frame acute angle is to cut a piece of scrap lumber to emulate the angle, and then measure it.

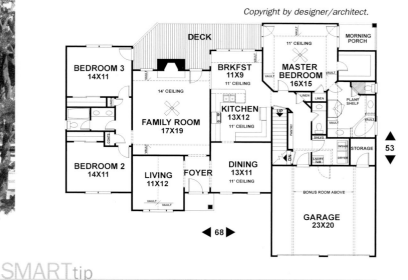

Copyright by designer/architect.

Images provided by designer/architect.

CAD FILE AVAILABLE

Plan #101008

Dimensions: 68' W x 53' D
Levels: 1
Square Footage: 2,088
Bedrooms: 3
Bathrooms: 2½
Foundation: Crawl space, slab, or basement
Materials List Available: Yes
Price Category: D

SMARTtip
Accentuating Your Bathroom with Details

No matter how big or small the room, details will pull the style together. Some of the best details that you can include are the smallest—drawer pulls from an antique store or shells in a glass jar or just left on the countertop. Add period flavor with crown molding, or dress up contemporary fixtures with polished stone fittings.

Plan #391059

Dimensions: 68' W x 46' D
Levels: 1
Square Footage: 2,020
Bedrooms: 3
Bathrooms: 2½
Foundation: Basement
Materials List Available: Yes
Price Category: C

Images provided by designer/architect.

A small porch and inviting entry draw folks inside to a central dining room with elegant ceiling treatment.

Features:

• Kitchen: This clever kitchen with island boasts a corner-window breakfast area with the aura of a café.

• Great Room: This room with fireplace heads out to a large deck.

• Bedrooms: Two secondary bedrooms share a full bath.

• Master Suite: This area (with tiled tub and dual vanities) is located on the opposite side of the house from the living areas for more intimacy.

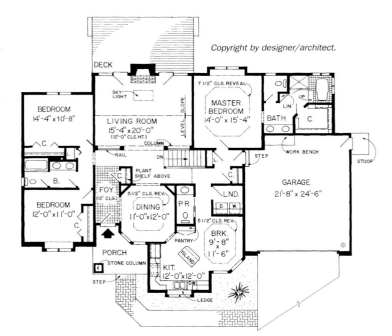

Copyright by designer/architect.

Front View/Side View

Rear View

Plan #291023

Dimensions: 34'3" W x 60'8" D
Levels: 1
Square Footage: 2,047
Main Level Sq. Ft.: 1,284
Lower Level Sq. Ft.: 763
Bedrooms: 2
Bathrooms: 2½
Foundation: Walkout basement
Material List Available: No
Price Category: D

Images provided by designer/architect.

Copyright by designer/architect.

Side View

Plan #121052

Dimensions: 56' W x 70' D
Levels: 1
Square Footage: 2,093
Bedrooms: 4
Bathrooms: 2
Foundation: Basement
Materials List Available: Yes
Price Category: D

Images provided by designer/architect.

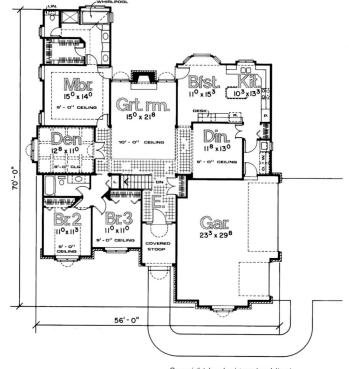

Copyright by designer/architect.

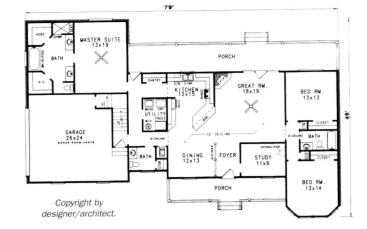

Images provided by designer/architect.

Copyright by designer/architect.

Bonus Area

Plan #171015

Dimensions: 79' W x 52' D

Levels: 1

Square Footage: 2,089

Bedrooms: 3

Bathrooms: 2½

Foundation: Crawl space, slab

Materials List Available: Yes

Price Category: D

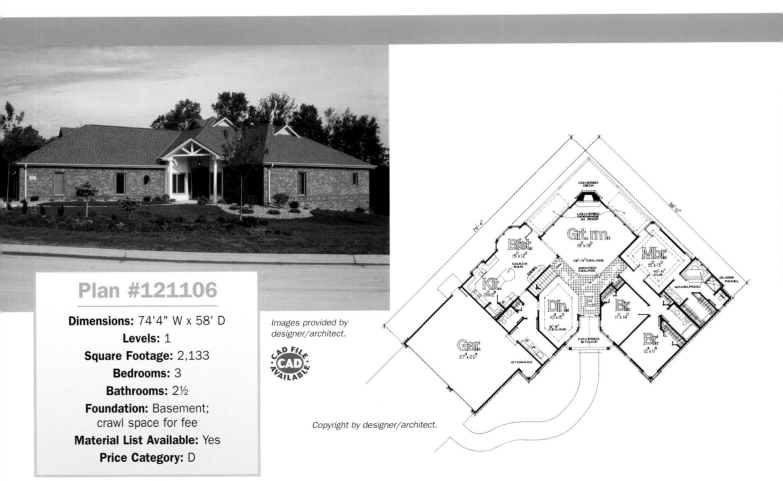

Images provided by designer/architect.

Copyright by designer/architect.

Plan #121106

Dimensions: 74'4" W x 58' D

Levels: 1

Square Footage: 2,133

Bedrooms: 3

Bathrooms: 2½

Foundation: Basement; crawl space for fee

Material List Available: Yes

Price Category: D

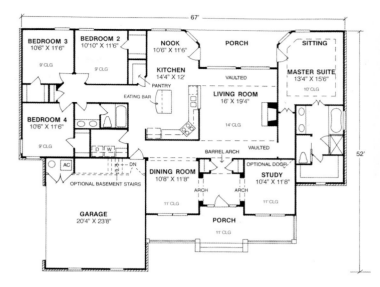

Plan #121176

Dimensions: 67' W x 52' D
Levels: 1
Square Footage: 2,144
Bedrooms: 4
Bathrooms: 2
Foundation: Slab; basement for fee
Material List Available: Yes
Price Category: D

Images provided by designer/architect.

Copyright by designer/architect.

Plan #161118

Dimensions: 70'2" W x 50'8" D
Levels: 1
Square Footage: 2,154
Main Level Sq. Ft.: 1,483
Basement Level Sq. Ft.: 671
Bedrooms: 3
Bathrooms: 3
Foundation: Basement
Material List Available: Yes
Price Category: D

Images provided by designer/architect.

Copyright by designer/architect.

Basement Level Floor Plan

Plan #311001

Dimensions: 65'11" W x 67'9" D
Levels: 1
Square Footage: 2,085
Bedrooms: 3
Bathrooms: 2½
Foundation: Crawl space, slab, or basement
Materials List Available: No
Price Category: D

Images provided by designer/architect.

Rear View

Copyright by designer/architect.

Optional Bonus Area

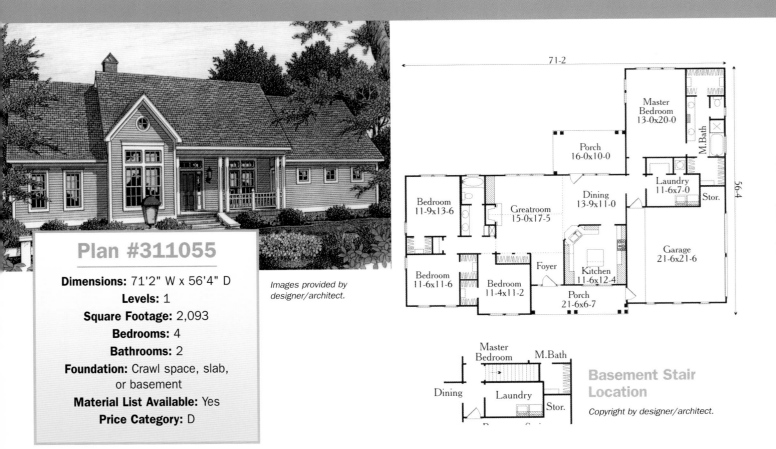

Plan #311055

Dimensions: 71'2" W x 56'4" D
Levels: 1
Square Footage: 2,093
Bedrooms: 4
Bathrooms: 2
Foundation: Crawl space, slab, or basement
Material List Available: Yes
Price Category: D

Images provided by designer/architect.

Basement Stair Location

Copyright by designer/architect.

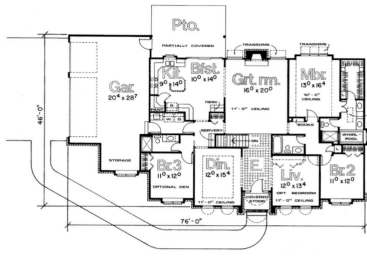

Images provided by designer/architect.

Plan #121117

Dimensions: 76' W x 46' D

Levels: 1

Square Footage: 2,172

Bedrooms: 4

Bathrooms: 3

Foundation: Basement; crawl space for fee

Material List Available: Yes

Price Category: D

Copyright by designer/architect.

Images provided by designer/architect.

Plan #151004

Dimensions: 64'8" W x 62'1" D

Levels: 1

Square Footage: 2,107

Bedrooms: 4

Bathrooms: 2½

Foundation: Crawl space, slab, or basement

CompleteCost List Available: Yes

Price Category: D

Copyright by designer/architect.

Plan #151034

Dimensions: 58'6" W x 64'6" D

Levels: 1

Square Footage: 2,133

Bedrooms: 3

Bathrooms: 2

Foundation: Crawl space, slab, or basement

CompleteCost List Available: Yes

Price Category: D

Images provided by designer/architect.

This home, as shown in the photograph, may differ from the actual blueprints. For more detailed information, please check the floor plans carefully.

Copyright by designer/architect.

Plan #191001

Dimensions: 62' W x 72' D

Levels: 1

Square Footage: 2,156

Bedrooms: 4

Bathrooms: 3

Foundation: Crawl space, slab, or basement

Materials List Available: No

Price Category: D

Images provided by designer/architect.

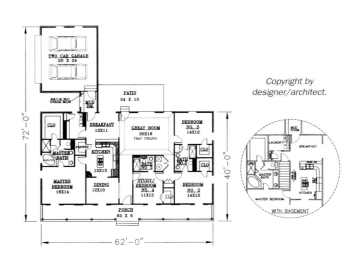

Copyright by designer/architect.

Front View

Plan #221018

Dimensions: 67' W x 53' D
Levels: 1
Square Footage: 2,007
Bedrooms: 3
Bathrooms: 2
Foundation: Basement
Materials List Available: No
Price Category: D

You'll love this ranch design, with its traditional stucco facade and interesting roofline.

Features:

- Ceiling Height: 9 ft.

- Great Room: A cathedral ceiling points up the large dimensions of this room, and the handsome fireplace with tall flanking windows lets you decorate for a formal or a casual feeling.

- Dining Room: A tray ceiling imparts elegance to this room, and a butler's pantry just across from the kitchen area lets you serve in style.

- Kitchen: You'll love the extensive counter space in this well-designed kitchen. The adjoining nook is large enough for a full-size dining set and features a door to the outside deck, where you can set up a third dining area.

- Master Suite: Located away from the other bedrooms for privacy, this suite includes a huge walk-in closet, windows overlooking the backyard, and a large bath with a whirlpool tub, standing shower, and dual-sink vanity.

Images provided by designer/architect.

Rear Elevation

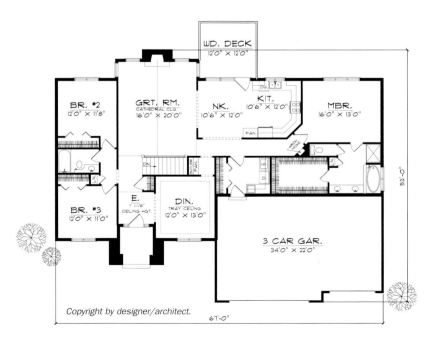

Copyright by designer/architect.

Plan #351007

Dimensions: 73'8"W x 53'2" D

Levels: 1

Square Footage: 2,251

Bedrooms: 3

Bathrooms: 2½

Foundation: Crawl space, slab, or basement

Materials List Available: Yes

Price Category: E

Images provided by designer/architect.

This three-bedroom brick home with arched window offers traditional styling that features an open floor plan.

Features:

• **Great Room:** This room has a 12-ft.-high ceiling and a corner fireplace.

• **Kitchen:** This kitchen boasts a built-in pantry and a raised bar open to the breakfast area.

• **Dining Room:** This area features a vaulted ceiling and a view of the front yard.

• **Master Bedroom:** This private room has an office and access to the rear porch.

• **Master Bath:** This bathroom has a double vanity, large walk-in closet, and soaking tub.

Bonus Room

Copyright by designer/architect.

Plan #211006

Dimensions: 61' W x 77' D
Levels: 1
Square Footage: 2,177
Bedrooms: 3
Bathrooms: 2
Foundation: Crawl space or slab
Materials List Available: Yes
Price Category: D

Images provided by designer/architect.

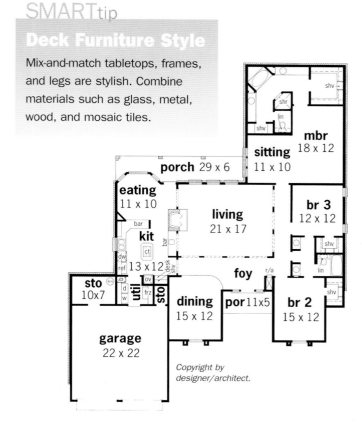
Copyright by designer/architect.

Plan #271076

Dimensions: 69' W x 57' D
Levels: 1
Square Footage: 2,188
Bedrooms: 2-4
Bathrooms: 1½-2½
Foundation: Daylight basement
Materials List Available: No
Price Category: D

Images provided by designer/architect.

Optional Basement Level Floor Plan

Copyright by designer/architect.

Plan #151050

Dimensions: 69'2" W x 74'10" D

Levels: 1

Square Footage: 2,096

Bedrooms: 3

Bathrooms: 2½

Foundation: Crawl space, slab, or basement

CompleteCost List Available: Yes

Price Category: D

You'll love this spacious home for both its elegance and its convenient design.

Features:

- Ceiling Height: 8 ft.

- Great Room: A 9-ft. boxed ceiling complements this large room, which sits just beyond the front gallery. A fireplace and door to the rear porch make it a natural gathering spot.

- Kitchen: This well-designed kitchen includes a central work island and shares an angled eating bar with the adjacent breakfast room.

- Breakfast Room: This room's bay window is gorgeous, and the door to the garage is practical.

- Master Suite: You'll love the 9-ft. boxed ceiling in the bedroom and the vaulted ceiling in the bath, which also includes two walk-in closets, a corner whirlpool tub, split vanities, a shower, and a compartmentalized toilet.

- Workshop: A huge workshop with half-bath is ideal for anyone who loves to build or repair.

Images provided by designer/architect.

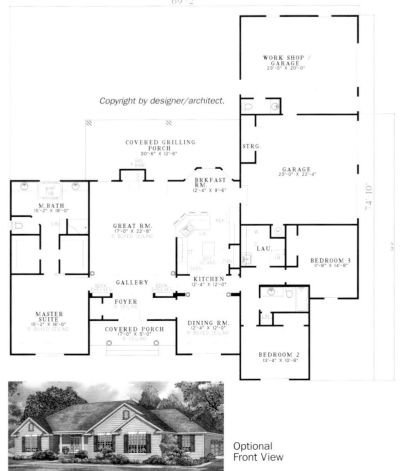

Optional Front View

Plan #101010

Dimensions: 70' W x 47' D
Levels: 1
Square Footage: 2,187
Bedrooms: 4
Bathrooms: 2½
Foundation: Crawl space, slab, or basement
Materials List Available: Yes
Price Category: D

CAD FILE AVAILABLE

Images provided by designer/architect.

This stately ranch features a brick-and-stucco exterior, layered trim, and copper roofing returns.

Features:

- Ceiling Height: 11 ft. unless otherwise noted.

- Special Ceilings: Vaulted and raised ceilings adorn the living room, family room, dining room, foyer, kitchen, breakfast room, and master suite.

- Kitchen: This roomy kitchen is brightened by an abundance of windows.

- Breakfast Room: Located off the kitchen, this breakfast room is the perfect spot for informal family meals.

- Master Suite: This truly exceptional master suite features a bath, and a spacious walk in closet.

- Morning Porch: Step out of the master bedroom, and greet the day on this lovely porch.

- Additional Bedrooms: The three additional bedrooms each measure approximately 11 ft. x 12 ft. Two of them have walk-in closets.

Copyright by designer/architect.

SMARTtip
Using Slipcovers in Your Dining Area

Change the look of your dining room by slipcovering chairs. Short-skirted slipcovers give a more informal appearance; fabrics in graphic patterns, such as checks or floral prints, complement this style of slipcover best. Long-skirted covers are elegant additions to a formal dining room, particularly in solid color or tone-on-tone fabrics. Ties, buttons, or trim can add personality.

Copyright by designer/architect.

Images provided by designer/architect.

Plan #131006

Dimensions: 61' W x 53'6" D

Levels: 1

Square Footage: 2,193

Bedrooms: 3

Bathrooms: 2

Foundation: Crawl space, slab, or basement

Materials List Available: Yes

Price Category: E

Alternate Floor Plan

Plan #111015

Dimensions: 64' W x 58' D

Levels: 1

Square Footage: 2,208

Bedrooms: 4

Bathrooms: 2

Foundation: Slab

Materials List Available: No

Price Category: E

Images provided by designer/architect.

Copyright by designer/architect.

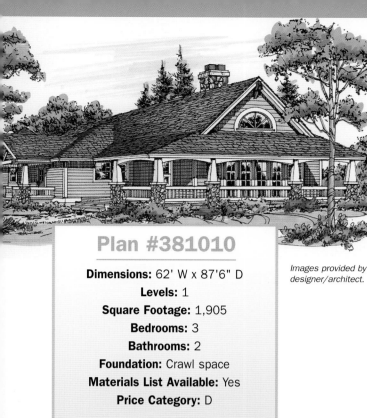

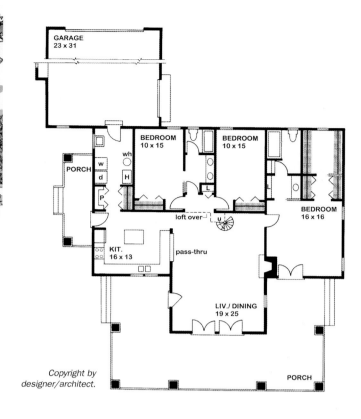

Plan #381010

Dimensions: 62' W x 87'6" D

Levels: 1

Square Footage: 1,905

Bedrooms: 3

Bathrooms: 2

Foundation: Crawl space

Materials List Available: Yes

Price Category: D

Images provided by designer/architect.

Copyright by designer/architect.

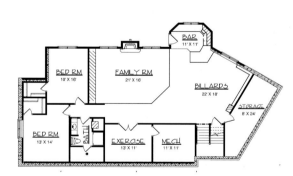

Optional Basement Level Floor Plan

Plan #271079

Dimensions: 104' W x 55' D

Levels: 1

Square Footage: 2,228

Bedrooms: 1-3

Bathrooms: 1½

Foundation: Daylight basement

Materials List Available: No

Price Category: E

Images provided by designer/architect.

CAD FILE AVAILABLE

Copyright by designer/architect.

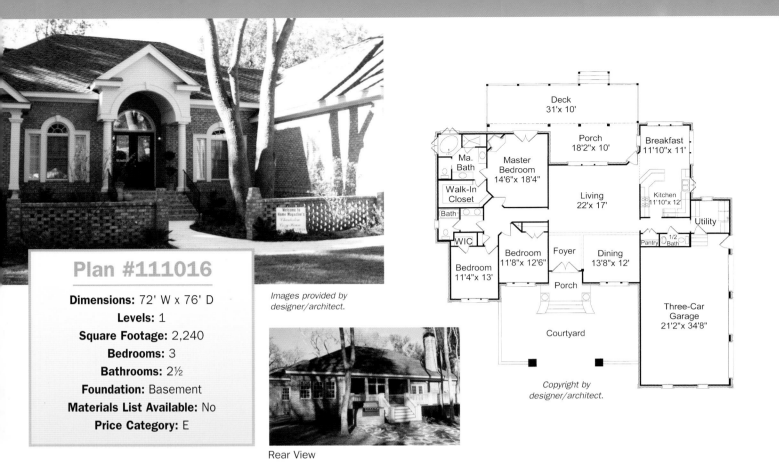

Plan #111016

Dimensions: 72' W x 76' D
Levels: 1
Square Footage: 2,240
Bedrooms: 3
Bathrooms: 2½
Foundation: Basement
Materials List Available: No
Price Category: E

Images provided by designer/architect.

Rear View

Copyright by designer/architect.

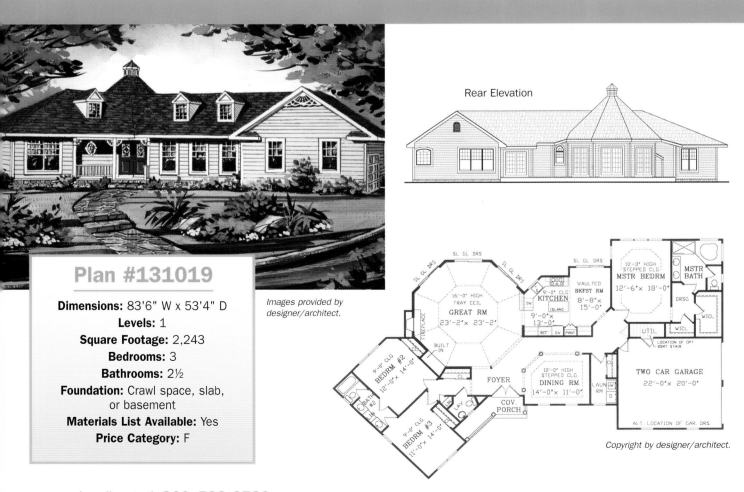

Plan #131019

Dimensions: 83'6" W x 53'4" D
Levels: 1
Square Footage: 2,243
Bedrooms: 3
Bathrooms: 2½
Foundation: Crawl space, slab, or basement
Materials List Available: Yes
Price Category: F

Images provided by designer/architect.

Rear Elevation

Copyright by designer/architect.

Plan #441007

Dimensions: 70' W x 64' D
Levels: 1
Square Footage: 2,197
Bedrooms: 4
Bathrooms: 2½
Foundation: Crawl space
Materials List Available: No
Price Category: D

Welcome to this roomy ranch, embellished with a brick facade, intriguing roof peaks, and decorative quoins on all the front corners.

Features:

- **Great Room:** There's a direct sightline from the front door through the trio of windows in this room. The rooms are defined by columns and changes in ceiling height rather than by walls, so light bounces from dining room to breakfast nook to kitchen.

- **Kitchen:** The primary workstation in this kitchen is a peninsula, which faces the fireplace. The peninsula is equipped with a sink, dishwasher, downdraft cooktop, and snack counter.

- **Den/Home Office:** Conveniently located off the foyer, this room would work well as a home office.

- **Master Suite:** The double doors provide an air of seclusion for this suite. The vaulted bedroom features sliding patio doors to the backyard and an arch-top window. The adjoining bath is equipped with a whirlpool tub, shower, double vanity, and walk-in closet.

- **Secondary Bedrooms:** The two additional bedrooms, each with direct access to the shared bathroom, occupy the left wing of the ranch.

Rear Elevation

Copyright by designer/architect.

Plan #351086

Dimensions: 82'6" W x 65' D
Levels: 1
Square Footage: 2,201
Bedrooms: 3
Bathrooms: 2½
Foundation: Crawl space or slab
Material List Available: Yes
Price Category: E

CAD FILE AVAILABLE

This stunning European country home is designed with the contemporary family in mind.

Features:

- **Porches:** Beautiful brick arches welcome guests into your covered front porch, indicating the warmth and hospitality within the home. A screened back porch, accessible from the dining area, is ideal for enjoying meals in the fresh air.

- **Great Room:** Three entrances from the covered porch, elegant archways into the kitchen and dining area, raised ceilings, a fireplace, and built-in cabinets combine to make this an ideal space for entertaining.

- **Kitchen:** The efficient L-shaped design of this work area includes an island with a vegetable sink and raised bar. The kitchen is open to the dining area and great room to provide a feeling of openness and informality.

- **Master Suite:** This suite features vaulted ceilings and a walk-in closet. But the compartmentalized master bath, with its second walk-in closet, his and her sinks and linen cabinets, standing shower, vanity, and jetted tub, really makes the suite special.

- **Secondary Bedrooms:** The secondary bedrooms have a wing of their own, and both include computer desks, large closets, and shared access to a bathtub through their individual half-baths.

- **Garages:** Two separate garages house up to three cars, or use the one-car bay for storage or hobby needs.

Rear Elevation

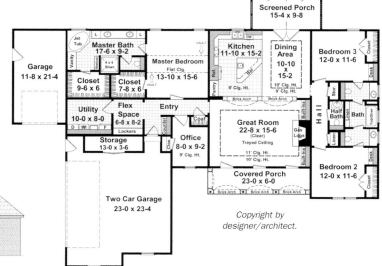

Copyright by designer/architect.

Plan #121034

Dimensions: 92'8" W x 59'4" D

Levels: 1

Square Footage: 2,223

Bedrooms: 1

Bathrooms: 2½

Foundation: Basement;
crawl space for fee

Materials List Available: Yes

Price Category: E

This home features a flowing, open floor plan coupled with an abundance of amenities.

Features:

- Ceiling Height: 8 ft. unless otherwise noted.
- Foyer: This elegant entry features a curved staircase and a view of the formal dining room.
- Formal Dining Room: Magnificent arched openings lead from the foyer into this dining room. The boxed ceiling adds to the architectural interest.

- Great Room: A wall of windows, a see-through fireplace, and built-in entertainment center make this the perfect gathering place.
- Covered Deck: The view of this deck, through the wall of windows in the great room, will lure guests out to this large deck.
- Hearth Room: This room share a panoramic view with the eating area.
- Kitchen: This kitchen features a corner pantry, a built-in desk, and a curved island.

Main Level Floor Plan

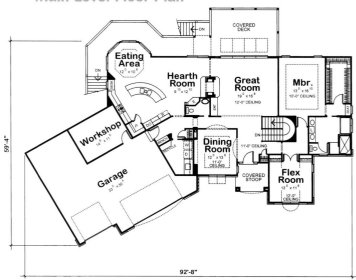

Optional Basement Level Floor Plan

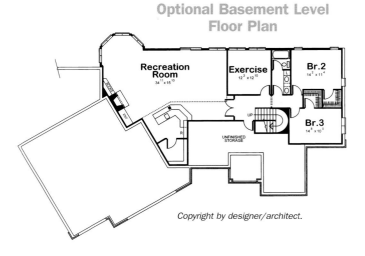

Copyright by designer/architect.

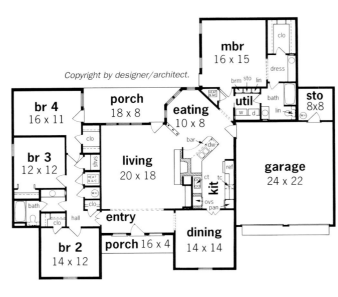

Copyright by designer/architect.

mbr
16 x 15

clo

dress

br 4
16 x 11

porch
18 x 8

eating
10 x 8

util

bath

sto
8 x 8

clo

living
20 x 18

kit

garage
24 x 22

br 3
12 x 12

bath

entry

dining
14 x 14

br 2
14 x 12

porch 16 x 4

Images provided by designer/architect.

Plan #211007

Dimensions: 72' W x 60' D

Levels: 1

Square Footage: 2,252

Bedrooms: 4

Bathrooms: 2

Foundation: Slab

Materials List Available: Yes

Price Category: E

Front View

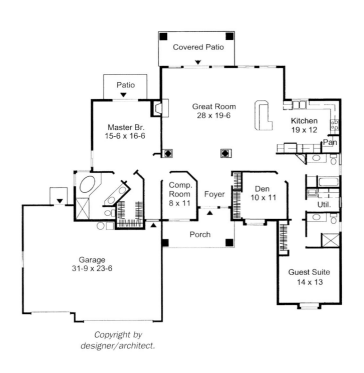

Covered Patio

Patio

Great Room
28 x 19-6

Kitchen
19 x 12

Pan

Master Br.
15-6 x 16-6

Comp.
Room
8 x 11

Foyer

Den
10 x 11

Util.

Porch

Garage
31-9 x 23-6

Guest Suite
14 x 13

Illustration provided by designer/architect.

Plan #231003

Dimensions: 74' W x 69' D

Levels: 1

Square Footage: 2,254

Bedrooms: 2

Bathrooms: 3

Foundation: Crawl space

Materials List Available: No

Price Category: E

Copyright by designer/architect.

Plan #111006

Dimensions: 56' W x 67' D
Levels: 1
Square Footage: 2,241
Bedrooms: 4
Bathrooms: 2½
Foundation: Slab
Materials List Available: No
Price Category: E

You'll love this plan if you're looking for a home with fantastic curb appeal on the outside and comfortable amenities on the inside.

Features:

- Foyer: This lovely foyer opens to both the living and dining rooms.

- Dining Room: Three columns in this room accentuate both its large dimensions and its slightly formal air.

- Living Room: This room gives an airy feeling, and the fireplace here makes it especially inviting when the weather's cool.

- Kitchen: This G-shaped kitchen is designed to save steps while you're working, and the ample counter area adds even more to its convenience. The breakfast bar is a great gathering area.

- Master Suite: Two walk-in closets provide storage space, and the bath includes separate vanities, a standing shower, and a deluxe corner bathtub.

Front Elevation

Copyright by designer/architect.

Family Kitchens

From every standpoint, the importance of the kitchen and its design cannot be underestimated. The heart of the home beats in the kitchen. There's the hum of the refrigerator, the whir of the food processor, the crunch of the waste-disposal unit, and the bubbling of dinner simmering on the stove. These are the reassuring sounds of a home in action. The kitchen is also a warehouse, a communications center, a place to socialize, and the hub of family life. According to industry studies, 90 percent of American families eat some or all of their meals in the kitchen. It is also the command center where household bills are paid and vacations are planned. The kitchen is even a playroom at times. Emotions, as well as tasks, reside here. When you were little, this is where you could find mom whenever you needed her. It's where the cookies were kept. When other rooms were cold and empty, the kitchen was a place of warmth and companionship. It is from the kitchen that the family sets off into the day. And it is to the kitchen that they return at nightfall.

The Great Room Concept

Today, the family life that was once contained by the kitchen is spilling into an adjoining great room. Usually a large, open room, great rooms and kitchens are often considered part of the same space. It is here where the family gathers to watch TV, share meals, and do homework. In short, great rooms/kitchens are the new heart of the home and the places where families do most of their living. In most designs, a kitchen and great room are separated by a snack counter, an island, or a large pass-through.

Kitchen Layouts That Work

The basic layout of your kitchen will depend on the home design you choose. Look for aisles that have at least 39 inches between the front of the cabinets and appliances or an opposite-facing island. If it's possible, a clearance of 42 inches is better. And given more available space, a clear-

Below: Large kitchen/great rooms are now considered the true heart of the family home.

Opposite: In large kitchens, look for plenty of counter and storage space, but insist on compact, efficient work areas.

ance of 48 to 49 inches is ideal. It means that you can open the dishwasher to load or unload it, and someone will still be able to walk behind you without doing a side-to-side shuffle or a crab walk. It also means that two people can work together in the same area. Any more than 49 inches, and the space is too much and involves a lot of walking back and forth. Fifty-four inches, for example, is too big a stretch. In large kitchens, look for balance; the work areas should have generous proportions, but to be truly efficient they should be compact and well designed.

Food Prep Areas and Surfaces. In many families, much of the food preparation takes place between the sink and the refrigerator. When you think of the work triangle, think of how much and how often you use an appliance. For example, sinks are generally used the most, followed by the refrigerator. The use of the cooktop is a matter of personal habit. Some families use it everyday, others use it sporadically. How close does it really need to be in relation to

the sink and refrigerator? Make your primary work zone the link between the sink and the refrigerator; then make the cooktop a secondary zone that's linked to them.

Cabinets Set the Style

Cabinets are the real furniture of a kitchen, making their selection both an aesthetic and functional choice. They are also likely to account for the largest portion of the budget.

Laminate. There are different brands and grades of plastic laminate, but cabinets made from this material generally are the least expensive you can buy. For the most part, they are devoid of detail and frameless, so don't look for raised panels, moldings, or inlaid beads on plastic laminate cabinets.

Although the surface is somewhat vulnerable (depending on the quality) to scratches and chips, plastic laminate cabinets can be refaced relatively inexpensively. Laminates come in a formidable range of

colors and patterns. Some of the newer speckled and patterned designs, which now even include denim and canvas, not only look great but won't show minor scratches and scars.

Wood. Wood cabinets offer the greatest variety of type, style, and finish. Framed cabinets (the full frame across the face of the cabinets may show between the doors) are popular for achieving a traditional look, but they are slightly less roomy inside. That's because you lose the width of the frame, which can be as much as an inch on each side. Frameless cabinets have full overlay doors and drawer fronts. With frameless cabinets, you gain about 2 inches of interior space per cabinet unit. Multiply that by the number of cabinet doors or drawer units you have, and add it up. It's easy to see that if space is at a premium, choose the frameless or full-overlay type. Besides, most cabinet companies now offer enough frameless styles to give you a traditional look in cabinetry, if that's your style.

Above: Be creative with storage. Here a tall cabinet tops a drawer unit that holds dish towels and tablecloths.

Below: A great room works best when a well-defined kitchen area flows effortlessly into the living area.

The Decorative Aspect of Cabinets

While the trend in overall kitchen style is toward more decorative moldings and carvings, the trend in cabinet doors is toward simpler designs. Plain panels, for instance, are now more popular than raised panels. They allow you to have more decoration elsewhere. Ornamentation is effective when it is used to provide a focal point over a hood, fridge, or sink. Instead of installing a single crown profile, you might create a three- or four-piece crown treatment, or add a carving of grapevines, acanthus leaves, or another decorative motif. In the traditional kitchen, add them, but sparingly.

Finishes. Of all of the choices you will need to make regarding wood cabinets, the selection of the finish may be the hardest. Wood can be stained, pickled, painted, or oiled. Your selection will be determined in part by whether you order stock or custom cabinets. Finishing options on stock cabinets are usually limited, and variations are offered as an upgrade. Translation: more money. Try working with the manufacturer's stock cabinets. It not only costs less but also speeds up the process. There is usually

a reason why manufacturers offer certain woods in certain choices: it's because those choices work best with other elements in the room.

Wood Stains. Today, stains that are close to natural wood tones are popular, particularly natural wood finishes. Cherry is quickly becoming the number-one wood in the country. Pickled finishes, very popular in the early 1990s, are now looking dated. Some woods, particularly oak, have more grain than others. Some, such as maple, are smoother. And others, such as birch, dent more easily. The quality and inherent characteristics of the wood you choose will help determine whether it is better to stain, pickle, or paint. For staining, you need a good-quality clear wood. Pickling, because it has pigment in the stain, masks more of the grain but is still translucent. Because paint completely covers the grain, painted wood cabinets are usually made of lesser-quality paint-grade wood.

Painted Wood. Paint gives wood a smooth, clean finish. You can paint when you want a change or if the finish starts to show wear. This comes at no small expense, though, because the painter will have to sand the surfaces well before applying several coats of paint. If you choose painted cabinets, be sure to obtain a small can of the exact same paint from your kitchen vendor. There is usually a charge for this, but it allows you to do small touch-ups yourself, ridding your cabinets of particularly hideous scars without a complete repainting. While in theory the color choice for painted cabinets is infinite, manufacturers generally offer four shades of white and a few other standard color options from which to choose.

Pickled Wood. Pickled cabinets fall midway between full-grain natural cabinets and painted ones. Pickling is a combination of stain and paint, allowing some of the grain to show. It subdues the strongest patterns, while it covers over the lesser ones. The degree depends on your choice and on the options available from the manufacturer.

Hardware. Handles are easier to maneuver than knobs. Advocates of universal design, which takes into consideration the capabilities of all people—young and old, with and without physical limitations—recommend them. Knobs do not work easily for children or elderly people with arthritis. A handle with a backplate will keep fingerprints off the cabinet door.

Fitting Cabinets into Your Layout

This calls for attention to the kitchen layout. In specifying cabinets, first let common sense and budget be your guide. Kitchen geography can help you determine how much storage you need and where it should be. Mentally divide your kitchen into zones: food preparation, food consumption, and so on. And don't forget about the nonfood areas. Do you see yourself repotting plants or working on a hobby in the kitchen? You'll need work space and cabinet space for those extra activities.

A kitchen workhorse, the island, is not new to kitchen design. It's as old as the solid, slightly elevated, central table of medieval kitchens in England. But where that table was a work surface, today's island can hold cabinets, a sink, a cooktop, a beverage refrigerator, and it can serve to divide areas of the kitchen.

How Tall Is Too Tall?

Upper cabinets are typically 12 inches deep; base, or lower, cabinets are 24 inches deep. With the exception of a desk unit, standard base cabinets are always the same height, 36 inches. Although most people prefer clean lines and planes as much as possible, some circumstances call for variations in the height of lower cabinets. There may be an often-used area where you want a countertop at which you can work while seated, for example.

Upper cabinets come in two or three standard heights: 30, 36, and 42 inches. The 30-inch ones look short; 36-inch cabinets look standard, and 42-inch ones can look too tall if your ceiling is not unusually high. In general, there is a slight up-charge for 30-inch cabinets and a big jump in price for 42-inch units. Order another size and you will pay double-custom prices. But you don't need to. For greater variation, install upper cabinets at varying heights. The old standard was to install 30-inch upper cabinets under a soffit—the often,

but not always, boxed-in area just under the ceiling and above the wall cabinets. Now, unless you have very tall ceilings, soffits are practically obsolete. Provided you have standard-height, 8-foot ceilings, the way to go now seems to be 36-inch cabinets with the remaining space of 6 inches or so filled with decorative trim up to the ceiling. It is a nicer, more refined look than cabinets that extend all the way to the ceiling, unless you prefer something contemporary and totally sleek and without ornament.

Size and Space. You don't want a massive bank of cabinets, either. Add up the dimensions wherever you're considering wall units. The counter is 36 inches high; backsplashes typically range from 15 to 17 inches. So with 36-inch-high upper cabinets, we're talking 7½ feet in all, 8 feet if you chose 42-inch-high wall units. Your own size can help determine which ones to choose. Determine what's comfortable by measuring your reach. A petite person will lose access to the top third of a cabinet. An inch or two can make a very big difference.

Also, be sure that the small appliances you keep on the countertop fit under the wall cabinets. Having them sit at the front edge of a countertop is an accident waiting to happen. A lot of people who have "appliance garages" discovered this. Whenever they pulled out the appliance, which places it nearer the counter's edge, they watched their mixer or coffeemaker tumble to the floor.

Often people need extra storage, so they extend the cabinets up to the ceiling. This provides the added extra storage space, but it can only be reached by a step stool. An open soffit above the upper cabinets provides just as much space for oversize, infrequently used objects, and it is equally accessible by stepladder. Plus it can be both a display area and perfect home for hard-to-store items: pitchers, trays, salad bowls, vases, collectibles, platters, covered servers, and so forth.

Left: Natural wood finishes are a popular cabinet choice.

Just remember to allow plenty of room for air to circulate around the TV.

Kitchen Storage Solutions

There are many storage options that are extremely useful. At the top of the list is a spice drawer or rack attached to an upper cabinet or door. Both drawer and door spice racks are offered as factory options when you order cabinets, or you can retrofit them into existing cabinets. They provide visible access to all spices, so you don't end up with three tins of cinnamon, nine jars of garlic salt, four tiny bottles of vanilla, and no red pepper.

Lazy Susans. These rotating trays make items in the back of corner cabinets accessible. Consider adding inexpensive, plastic lazy Susans in a small upper cabinet. They will make the seasonings and cooking items you use everyday easily accessible.

Pie-cut door attachments can provide the same accessibility as a lazy Susan. Your choice depends on how much and what kind of storage you need. If a corner cabinet is home to sodas, chips, and cooking materials, install a pie-cut. A lazy Susan is more stable, best for pots, bowls, and larger, heavier objects.

Pullouts, Rollouts, and Dividers.

Pullout fittings maximize the use of very narrow spaces. There are just two options for these areas: vertical tray-storage units or pullout pantries. You can find a 12-inch-wide base cabinet that is a pullout pantry with storage for canned goods and boxed items.

Pullout racks for cabinets and lid-rack dividers for drawers are also available from some cabinet suppliers. They are handy, but if you have enough cabinet storage space, the best thing is to store pots and pans with the lids on them in a couple of large cabinets.

Rollout cabinets are great and offer a lot of flexibility. They are adjustable to accommodate bulky countertop appliances and

The Kitchen Desk

Consider whether you will actually sit at a kitchen desk. Many people don't. Instead, they use it as the family message center and generally stand or perch on a stool. An additional, taller counter simply introduces more clutter to a room that is already overburdened with paraphernalia. And forget a desk-high cabinet, too. Instead use a standard counter-height cabinet to streamline whenever and wherever you can in the room.

Think about outfitting the desk area with a phone and answering machine and a corkboard for notes, your family's social schedule, invitations, and reminders. If you have room, a file drawer makes sense for storing school and business papers that need to be easy to retrieve. Also, if you don't have a separate study, and there's room, the kitchen may be a place to keep the family computer. Not only will you likely be using it more in the future for household record-keeping, but you can also help the kids with their homework and monitor their Internet use. In those cases, it makes sense to add a desk for comfort.

A Niche for the TV. Many people also want a TV in the kitchen. Plan for it. Who wants to see the back of the set or look at cords stretching across work areas, atop the refrigerator or the stove? Space and an outlet can be built into the lower portion of a well-placed wall cabinet or an open unit.

Above Left: Pullout cutting boards increase usable counter space.

Left: Accessories for tall narrow cabinets, come in handy for storing cookie sheets and trays.

Above: Decorative molding can enhance any cabinet. Most manufacturers offer a variety of molding options.

stock pots, and they can save a lot of steps and banging around.

You can also divide a base cabinet vertically into separate parts. Some of the vertical spaces are further subdivided horizontally—good places for storing cutting boards, cookie trays, baking tins, and big glass baking dishes.

Other Organizers

Buy cutlery drawers carefully. They are often too big and too clumsy, and they fail to take advantage of the full interior of the drawer. They are as bad as bookshelves spread too far apart. Consider cutlery dividers that are almost no wider than a spoon, with separate sections for teaspoons, cereal spoons, breakfast and dinner knives, lunch forks, dinner forks, and serving pieces. Add to this a section for miscellaneous utensils such as spoons for iced tea, chopsticks, and so on. Drawer dividers should be adjustable in case your needs, or your cutlery, change.

Knife, Towel, and Bread Storage. If you want a place to store knives, use slotted storage on a countertop. Frequently islands have false backs because they are deeper than base cabinets. Slots for knives can be cut into the area of the countertop that covers the void behind the base cabinet.

You can obtain all these storage options at the time you buy your cabinets. But you don't have to and may not even want to until you see how you really end up using your kitchen. A carpenter or handyman can often make them or install off-the-shelf units. Think outside of the box. We get in a rut; it is hard to be objective. Ask friends where they keep their kitchen stuff, and analyze every aspect of how you use your kitchen. Store things at point of use, such as leftover containers and sandwich bags near the refrigerator; mixing bowls and carving knives near the sink.

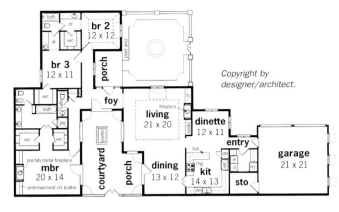

Plan #211008

Dimensions: 56' W x 93' D
Levels: 1
Square Footage: 2,259
Bedrooms: 3
Bathrooms: 2½
Foundation: Slab
Material List Available: Yes
Price Category: E

Images provided by designer/architect.

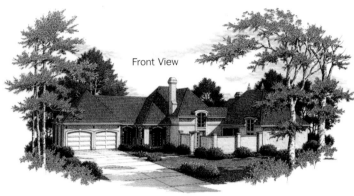

Front View

Plan #361513

Dimensions: 107' W x 63'3" D
Levels: 1
Square Footage: 2,260
Bedrooms: 3
Bathrooms: 2
Foundation: Crawl space
Material List Available: No
Price Category: E

Images provided by designer/architect.

CAD FILE AVAILABLE

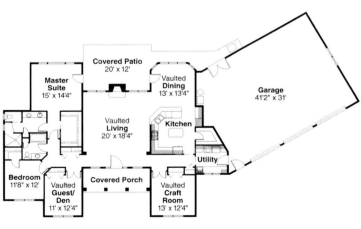

Plan #351067

Dimensions: 78' W x 58'6" D

Levels: 1

Square Footage: 2,200

Bedrooms: 3

Bathrooms: 3½

Foundation: Crawl space or slab

Material List Available: Yes

Price Category: F

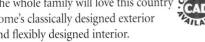

The whole family will love this country home's classically designed exterior and flexibly designed interior.

Features:

- **Porches:** A covered porch is great for welcoming guests or sitting out with neighbors. A door from the great room opens onto the back covered porch, perfect for out door meals or relaxing afternoons enjoying the unfettered breeze. This leads down onto the back patio, with plenty of room for barbecuing and soaking up the sun.

- **Kitchen:** Featuring an L-shaped design with an island, this kitchen has plenty of work space and storage and is separated from the dining area only by a raised bar.

- **Master Bedroom:** This room plays two roles: preparing you for everyday life while giving you an escape from it when needed. Vaulted ceilings and a sitting area give you the space you need to relax. The master bath features his and her closets and sinks, as well as linen cabinets, a standing shower, a jetted tub, and a compartmentalized toilet.

- **Secondary Bedrooms:** In a wing of their own, the other two bedrooms each feature a large closet and private full bathroom. Between the two is a media room with built-in entertainment space.

- **Bonus Area:** Above the garage is this flexible space, which can easily be used as a spare bedroom.

Bonus Area Floor Plan

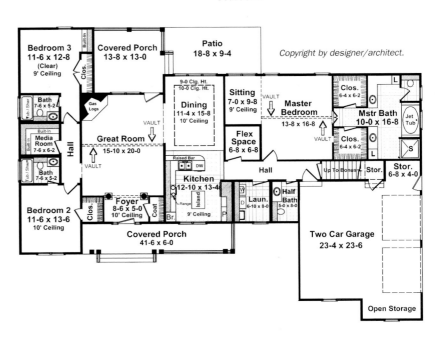

Copyright by designer/architect.

Plan #161115

Dimensions: 79'8" W x 44'2" D
Levels: 1
Square Footage: 2,253
Bedrooms: 4
Bathrooms: 3
Foundation: Walkout basement
Material List Available: Yes
Price Category: E

Images provided by designer/architect.

This one-level home offers a beautiful exterior of brick and stone with shake siding.

CAD FILE AVAILABLE

Features:

- **Great Room:** This open gathering area features an 11-foot-high ceiling and access to the rear yard. Turn on the corner gas fireplace, and fill the room with warmth and charm.

- **Kitchen:** This peninsula kitchen with built-in pantry and counter seating offers easy access to both formal and informal dining. The laundry facilities and the garage are just a few steps away. A magnificent bay window decorates the breakfast room and brings natural light into the area.

- **Master Suite:** This retreat offers a furniture alcove in the sleeping area and a walk-in closet. The private bath features a double-bowl vanity and a whirlpool tub.

- **Guest Suite:** This private bedroom suite is located behind the three-car garage and offers a welcoming environment for your overnight guests.

- **Basement:** This full walkout basement expands the living space of the delightful home.

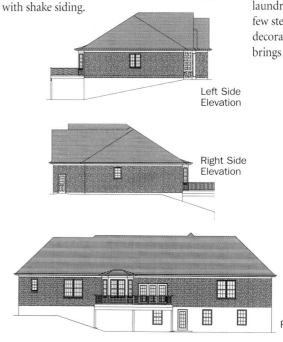

Left Side Elevation

Right Side Elevation

Rear Elevation

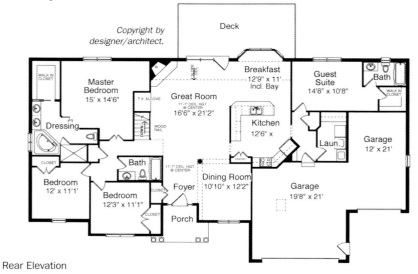

Copyright by designer/architect.

Plan #161098

Dimensions: 72' W x 55'10" D
Levels: 1
Square Footage: 2,283
Bedrooms: 3
Bathrooms: 2
Foundation: Basement
Material List Available: No
Price Category: E

This home, as shown in the photograph, may differ from the actual blueprints. For more detailed information, please check the floor plans carefully.

Images provided by designer/architect.

This spacious single-level home with 9-ft.-high ceiling heights is designed with formal and informal spaces.

Features:

- Dining Room: This open room and the great room are defined by columns and dropped ceilings.

- Great Room: This gathering area features a fireplace and a triple sliding glass door to the rear yard.

- Kitchen: This spacious kitchen with large pantry and angled counter serves the informal dining area and solarium, creating a comfortably relaxed gathering place.

- Master Suite: Designed for luxury, this suite, with its high-style tray ceiling, offers a whirlpool tub, double-bowl vanity, and large walk-in closet.

Rear Elevation

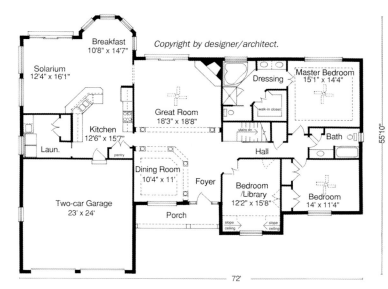

Copyright by designer/architect.

Kitchen

Plan #321009

Dimensions: 55'8" W x 46'4" D

Levels: 1

Square Footage: 2,295

Bedrooms: 3

Bathrooms: 2

Foundation: Basement

Materials List Available: Yes

Price Category: E

Images provided by designer/architect.

If you've got a site with great views, you'll love this home, which is designed to make the most of them.

Features:

- Porch: This wraparound porch is an ideal spot to watch the sun come up or go down. Add potted plants to create a lush atmosphere or grow some culinary herbs.

- Great Room: You couldn't ask for more luxury than this room provides, with its vaulted ceiling, large bay window, fireplace, dining balcony, and atrium window wall.

- Kitchen: No matter whether you're an avid cook or not, you'll relish the thoughtful design of this room.

- Master Suite: This suite is truly a retreat you'll treasure. It has two large walk-in closets for good storage space, and sliding doors that open to an exterior balcony where you can sit out to enjoy the stars. The amenity-filled bath adds to your enjoyment of this suite.

Rear View

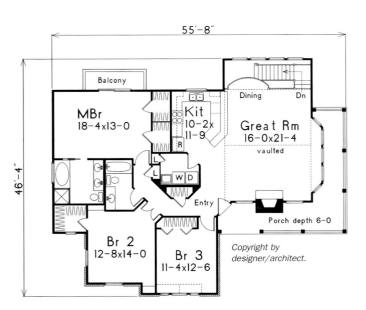

Copyright by designer/architect.

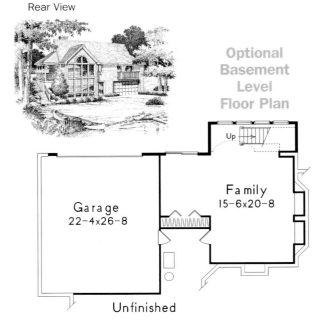

Optional Basement Level Floor Plan

Plan #131059

Dimensions: 57' W x 62' D
Levels: 1
Square Footage: 2,315
Bedrooms: 3
Bathrooms: 2½
Foundation: Crawl space, slab, or basement
Material List Available: Yes
Price Category: E

A front bay and an arched window prove that a house needn't be big to be beautiful.

Features:

- Living Room: This room is located just off the foyer, with columns accenting the entry. The vaulted ceiling and the bay window add elegance to the formal gathering area.

- Great Room: This informal gathering area boasts a stepped ceiling and a cozy fireplace. Family and friends are able to mingle between the breakfast room and the kitchen, creating one big open area.

- Kitchen: This fully equipped kitchen is great for preparation of a quick meal or a gourmet feast. The island features an eating counter, which is perfect for popcorn while watching a movie in the great room.

- Master Suite: This private retreat boasts a large sleeping area, two walk-in closets, and a bay window for enjoying the view of the

backyard. The master bath features his and her vanities and a compartmentalized toilet area.

- Bedrooms: Two secondary bedrooms with walk-in closets share a common full bathroom. Large windows flood these rooms with natural light.

Images provided by designer/architect.

Copyright by designer/architect.

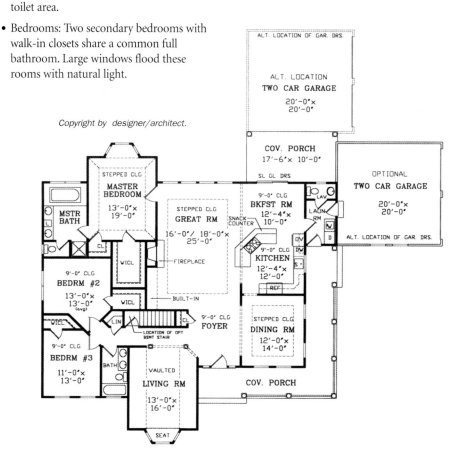

Plan #521017

Dimensions: 94'11" W x 94'10" D
Levels: 1
Square Footage: 2,359
Bedrooms: 3
Bathrooms: 3
Foundation: Slab
Material List Available: No
Price Category: E

This country-style ranch home is ideal for a growing family. The covered front porch houses a window-lined exterior, illustrating to guests how open and welcoming the home is.

CAD FILE AVAILABLE · CAD

Features:

- **Living Room:** This large space features a fireplace and built-in storage, and it opens onto the large deck, which is perfect for barbecues and soaking up the sun.

- **Kitchen:** An efficient and convenient design, this L-shaped kitchen includes an island with sinks and a raised bar. It opens into the breakfast room and open dining area and onto the screened porch. The space is ideal for warm indoor meals or fun, insect-free meals outside.

- **Master Suite:** Lined with windows, this already-spacious area opens up in sunlit comfort. Amenities include a walk-in closet and full master bath, which includes dual sinks, a large standing shower, and an over-sized tub set beneath bay windows.

- **Secondary Bedrooms:** Both bedrooms include a large closet, access to a full bathroom, and enough space to accommodate any design you can create.

- **Garage:** This two-car garage includes extra space for storage or hobbies and is far enough from the house for all the hammer strokes and buzzing saws of a busy workshop without disturbing the household.

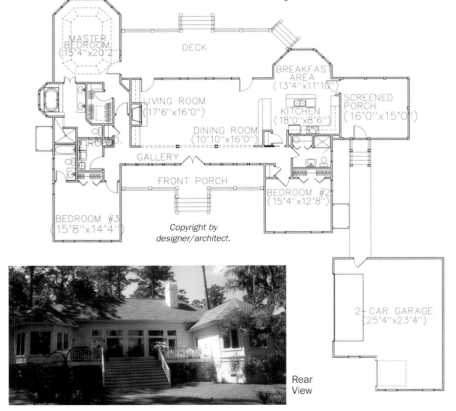

Rear View

Plan #131045

Dimensions: 81'4" W x 68'3" D
Levels: 1
Square Footage: 2,347
Bedrooms: 4
Bathrooms: 2½
Foundation: Crawl space, slab, or basement
Materials List Available: Yes
Price Category: E

Images provided by designer/architect.

You'll love the character and flexibility in siting that the angled design gives to this contemporary ranch-style home.

Features:

- Porch: A wraparound rear porch adds distinction to this lovely home.

- Great Room: Facing the rear of the house, this great room has a high, stepped ceiling, fireplace, and ample space for built-ins.

- Kitchen: This large room sits at an angle to the great room and is adjacent to both a laundry room and extra powder room.

- Office: Use the 4th bedroom as a home office, study, or living room, depending on your needs.

- Master Suite: This area is separated from the other bedrooms in the house to give it privacy. The beautiful bay window at the rear, two large walk-in closets, and luxurious bath make it an ideal retreat after a hectic day.

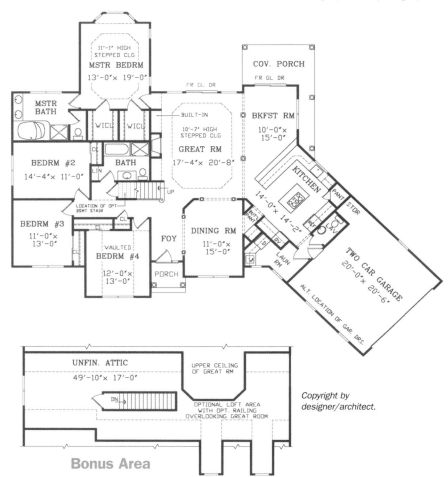

Copyright by designer/architect.

Plan #321037

Dimensions: 78'8" W x 50'6" D

Levels: 1

Square Footage: 2,397

Bedrooms: 3

Bathrooms: 2

Foundation: Basement or walkout

Materials List Available: Yes

Price Category: E

Come home to this three-bedroom stucco home with arched windows.

Features:

• **Dining Room:** Just off the entry is this formal room, with its vaulted ceiling.

• **Great Room:** This large room has a vaulted ceiling and a fireplace.

• **Kitchen:** A large pantry and an abundance of counter space make this kitchen a functional work space.

• **Master Suite:** This suite has a large walk-in closet and a private bath.

• **Bedrooms:** The two additional bedrooms share a common bathroom.

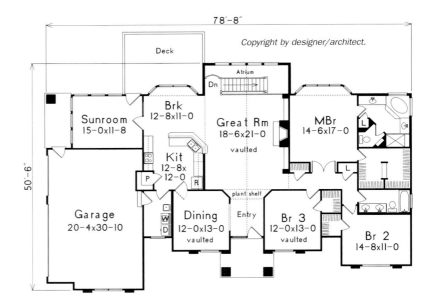

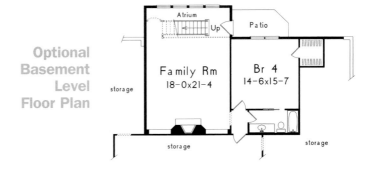

Optional Basement Level Floor Plan

Plan #101012

Dimensions: 69'4" W x 62'9" D

Levels: 1

Square Footage: 2,288

Bedrooms: 3

Bathrooms: 2½

Foundation: Crawl space, slab, basement, or walkout

Materials List Available: No

Price Category: E

This classic brick ranch boasts traditional styling and an exciting up-to-date floor plan.

CAD FILE AVAILABLE

Features:

- Ceiling Height: 9 ft. unless otherwise noted.
- Front Porch: Guests will be welcome by this inviting front porch, which features a 12-ft. ceiling.

- Family Room: This warm and inviting room measures 16 ft. x 19 ft. It features a 14-ft. ceiling and a rear wall of windows. French doors lead to an enormous deck.
- Kitchen: This unique angled kitchen is open to the hearth room and eating areas, all of which enjoy vaulted ceilings and are surrounded by windows. The hearth room has a TV niche.
- Master Suite: This 16-ft. x 15-ft. master suite is truly sumptuous, with its

12-ft. ceiling, sitting area, two walk-in closets, and full-featured bath.

- Bonus Room: Here is plenty of storage or room for future expansion. Just beyond the entry are stairs leading to a bonus room measuring approximately 12 ft. x 21 ft.

Living Room

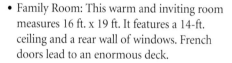

Plan #211009

Dimensions: 72' W x 60' D
Levels: 1
Square Footage: 2,396
Bedrooms: 4
Bathrooms: 2
Foundation: Slab
Materials List Available: Yes
Price Category: E

Beautiful arched windows lend a luxurious feeling to the exterior of this one-story home.

Features:

- Ceiling Height: 9 ft. unless otherwise noted.

- Entry: Guests will be greeted by a dramatic 12-ft. ceiling in this elegant foyer.

- Living Room: The 12-ft. ceiling continues through the foyer into this inviting living room. Everyone will feel welcomed by the crackling fire in the handsome fireplace.

- Covered Porch: When the weather is warm, invite guests to step out of the living room directly into this covered porch.

- Kitchen: This bright and cheery kitchen is designed for the way we live today. It includes a pantry and an angled eating bar that will see plenty of impromptu family meals.

- Energy-Efficient Walls: All the outside walls are framed with 2x6 lumber instead of 2x4. The extra thickness makes room for more insulation to lower your heating and cooling bills.

Images provided by designer/architect.

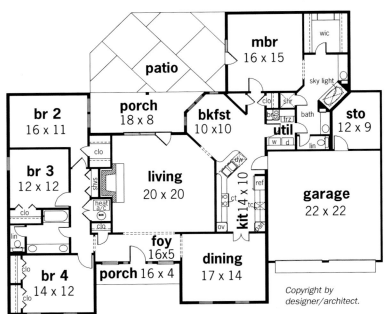

Copyright by designer/architect.

SMARTtip

Ornaments in a Garden

Placement is everything with ornaments in a garden. Some elements are best sitting by themselves. Others are better when they are part of a cohesive whole, perhaps placed in the greenery at a corner or flanking a structure.

Plan #101009

Dimensions: 70'2" W x 59' D
Levels: 1
Square Footage: 2,097
Bedrooms: 3
Bathrooms: 3
Foundation: Crawl space, slab, or basement
Materials List Available: Yes
Price Category: D

Round columns enhance this country porch design, which will nestle into any neighborhood.

Features:

- Ceiling Height: 9 ft. unless otherwise noted.

- Family Room: This large family room seems even more spacious, thanks to the vaulted ceiling. It's the perfect spot for all kinds of family activities.

- Dining Room: This elegant dining room is adorned with a decorative round column and a tray ceiling.

- Kitchen: You'll love the convenience of this enormous 14-ft.-3-in. x 22-ft.-6-in. country kitchen, which is open to the living room.

- Screened Porch: A French door leads to this breezy porch, with its vaulted ceiling.

- Master Suite: This sumptuous suite includes a double tray ceiling, a sitting area, a large walk-in closet, and a luxurious bath.

- Patio or Deck: This area is accessible from both the screened porch and master bedroom.

Images provided by designer/architect.

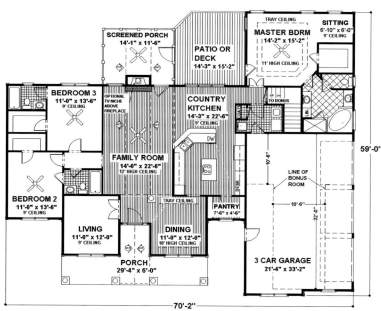

Copyright by designer/architect.

SMARTtip

Single-Level Decks

A single-level deck can use a strong vertical element, such as a pergola or a gazebo, to make it interesting. A simple and less-expensive option is a potted conical shrub or a clematis growing on a trellis.

Plan #161026

Dimensions: 67'6" W x 63'6" D
Levels: 1
Square Footage: 2,041
Bedrooms: 3
Bathrooms: 2
Foundation: Basement
Materials List Available: No
Price Category: D

You'll love the special features of this home, which has been designed for efficiency and comfort.

CAD FILE AVAILABLE

Features:

• Foyer: This raised foyer offers a view through the great room and beyond it to the covered deck.

• Great Room: Elegant windows allow versatility — decorate casually or more formally.

• Kitchen: You'll find ample counter space and cabinets in this spacious room, which adjoins the dining room and opens onto the rear yard.

• Library: Curl up on the window seat that wraps around the tower in this quiet spot.

• Laundry Room: A tub makes this large room practical for crafts as well as laundry.

• Master Suite: A vaulted ceiling gives grace to the sitting area, and the garden bath with a walk-in closet and whirlpool tub adds luxury.

Rear Elevation

Main Level Floor Plan

Basement Level Floor Plan

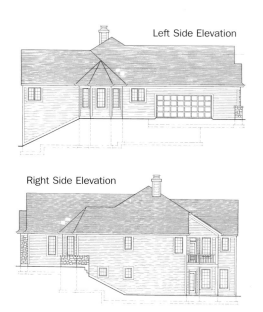

Left Side Elevation

Right Side Elevation

Front View

Living Room

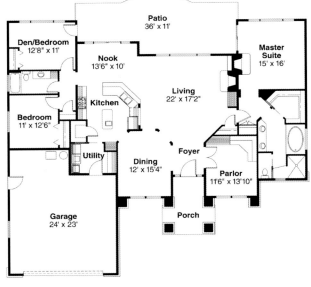

Images provided by designer/architect.

CAD FILE AVAILABLE

Plan #361470

Dimensions: 68' W x 60' D

Levels: 1

Square Footage: 2,313

Bedrooms: 3

Bathrooms: 2

Foundation: Crawl space

Material List Available: No

Price Category: E

Copyright by designer/architect.

Images provided by designer/architect.

CAD FILE AVAILABLE

Plan #151168

Dimensions: 66' W x 65'2" D

Levels: 1

Square Footage: 2,261

Bedrooms: 4

Bathrooms: 2½

Foundation: Crawl space, slab, basement, or daylight basement

CompleteCost List Available: Yes

Price Category: E

Copyright by designer/architect.

Bonus Room

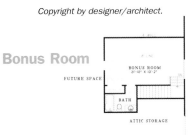

Plan #101011

Dimensions: 71'2" W x 58'1" D
Levels: 1
Square Footage: 2,184
Bedrooms: 3
Bathrooms: 3
Foundation: Crawl space, slab, basement, or walkout
Materials List Available: Yes
Price Category: D

A classic design and spacious interior add up to a flexible design suitable to any modern lifestyle.

CAD FILE AVAILABLE

Features:

- Ceiling Height: 9 ft. unless otherwise noted.

- Formal Dining Room: A decorative square column and a tray ceiling adorn this elegant dining room.

- Screened Porch: Enjoy summer breezes in style by stepping out of the French doors into this vaulted screened porch.

- Kitchen: Does everyone want to hang out in the kitchen while you are cooking? No problem. True to the home's country style, this huge 14-ft.-3-in. x 22-ft.-6-in. has plenty of room for helpers.

- The kitchen is open to the vaulted family room.

- Patio or Deck: This pleasant outdoor area is accessible from both the screened porch and the master bedroom.

- Master Suite: This luxurious suite includes a double tray ceiling, a sitting area, two walk-in closets, and an exquisite bath.

Kitchen

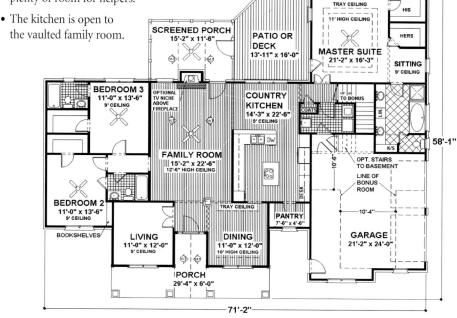

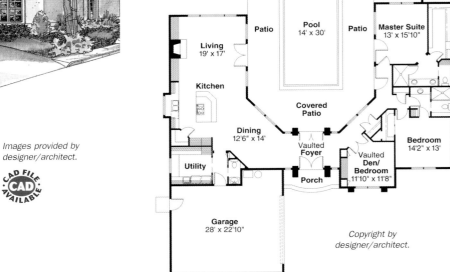

Plan #361469

Dimensions: 74'6" W x 78'6" D

Levels: 1

Square Footage: 2,261

Bedrooms: 3

Bathrooms: 2½

Foundation: Crawl space

Material List Available: No

Price Category: E

Images provided by designer/architect.

Copyright by designer/architect.

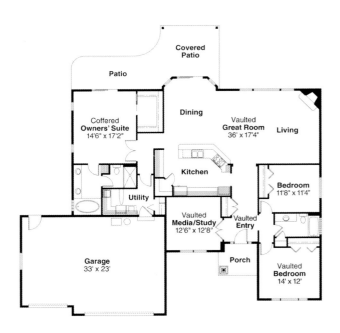

Plan #361545

Dimensions: 70' W x 69' D

Levels: 1

Square Footage: 2,270

Bedrooms: 3

Bathrooms: 2

Foundation: Crawl space

Material List Available: No

Price Category: E

Images provided by designer/architect.

Copyright by designer/architect.

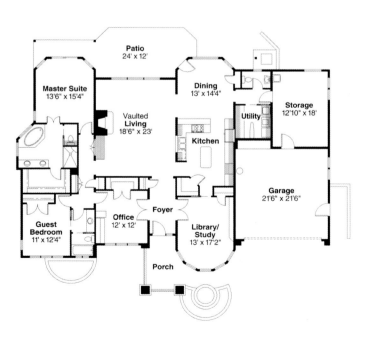

Plan #111017

Dimensions: 61' W x 70' D

Levels: 1

Square Footage: 2,323

Bedrooms: 3

Bathrooms: 2½

Foundation: Monolithic slab

Materials List Available: No

Price Category: E

Images provided by designer/architect.

Copyright by designer/architect.

Bedroom 12'x 12'
Breakfast 12'6"x 12'
Porch 20'6"x 10'
Sunroom 14'4"x 10'
Bath
Kitchen 12'x 16'
Living 20'6"x 20'2"
Master Bedroom 14'4"x 16'
Bedroom 12'x 12'
Utility | 1/2 Bath
Dining 12'8"x 12'
Foyer
WIC
Ext. Storage 12'x 4'6"
Porch
Master Bath
Two-Car Garage 20'8"x 23'2"

Plan #361493

Dimensions: 73' W x 60'8" D

Levels: 1

Square Footage: 2,350

Bedrooms: 2

Bathrooms: 2½

Foundation: Crawl space

Material List Available: No

Price Category: E

Images provided by designer/architect.

Patio 24' x 12'
Master Suite 13'6" x 15'4"
Dining 13' x 14'4"
Storage 12'10" x 18'
Vaulted Living 18'6" x 23'
Utility
Kitchen
Garage 21'6" x 21'6"
Guest Bedroom 11' x 12'4"
Office 12' x 12'
Foyer
Library/ Study 13' x 17'2"
Porch

Copyright by designer/architect.

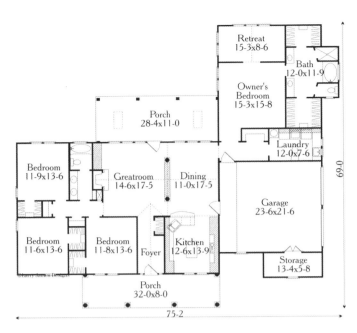

Plan #311054

Dimensions: 75'2" W x 69' D
Levels: 1
Square Footage: 2,360
Bedrooms: 4
Bathrooms: 2
Foundation: Crawl space, slab, or basement
Material List Available: Yes
Price Category: E

Images provided by designer/architect.

Copyright by designer/architect.

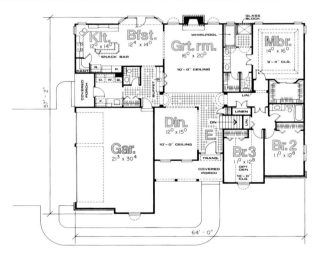

Plan #121057

Dimensions: 64' W x 57'2" D
Levels: 1
Square Footage: 2,311
Bedrooms: 3
Bathrooms: 2½
Foundation: Basement
Materials List Available: Yes
Price Category: E

Images provided by designer/architect.

Copyright by designer/architect.

SMARTtip

Installing Crown Molding

Test for the direction and location of ceiling joists with a stud sensor, by tapping with a hammer to hear the sound of hollow or solid areas or by tapping in test finishing nails.

Plan #271074

Dimensions: 68' W x 86' D
Levels: 1
Square Footage: 2,400
Bedrooms: 4
Bathrooms: 3
Foundation: Crawl space or slab
Materials List Available: No
Price Category: E

Perfect for families with aging relatives or boomerang children, this home includes a completely separate suite at the rear.

Features:

• Living Room: A corner fireplace casts a friendly glow over this gathering space.

• Kitchen: This efficient space offers a serving bar that extends toward the eating nook and the formal dining room.

• Master Suite: A cathedral ceiling presides over this deluxe suite, which boasts a whirlpool tub, dual-sink vanity, and walk-in closet.

• In-law Suite: This separate wing has its own vaulted living room, plus a kitchen, a dining room, and a bedroom suite.

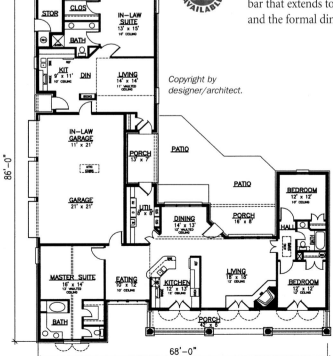

Copyright by designer/architect.

SMARTtip

Adding Professional Flair to Window Treatments

You can give your window treatment designs a professional look by using decorator tricks to customize readymades or dress your own home-sewn designs. These could include contrast linings, tassels, cording, ribbons, or couture trimmings such as buttons, coins,or bows applied to edges. Another trick is to sew a fine wire into the hem of curtains or valances to create a pliable edge that you can shape yourself. Small weights that you can sew into the hem of drapery panels or jabots will make them hang better. For more inspiration look at fashion magazines and visit showrooms.

Plan #441011

Dimensions: 67' W x 46' D
Levels: 1
Square Footage: 2,898
Main Level Sq. Ft.: 1,744
Basement Level Sq. Ft.: 1,154
Bedrooms: 3
Bathrooms: 2½
Foundation: Walkout basement
Materials List Available: No
Price Category: F

Images provided by designer/architect.

Think one-story, then think again—it's a hillside home designed to make the best use of a sloping lot. Elegant in exterior appeal, this home uses high arches and a hipped room to promote a sense of style.

Features:

- Dining Room: Box beams and columns define this formal space, which is just off the foyer.

- Kitchen: This fully equipped kitchen has everything the chef in the family could want. Nearby is the breakfast nook with sliding glass doors to the deck, which acts as the roof for the patio below.

- Master Suite: This suite is located on the right side of the main level. The master bath is

replete with a spa tub, compartmented toilet, separate shower, and dual lavatories.

- Lower Level: The two extra bedrooms, full bathroom, and games room are on this lower floor, which adds to the great livability of the home. The wet bar in the games room is a bonus.

Rear Elevation

Main Level Floor Plan

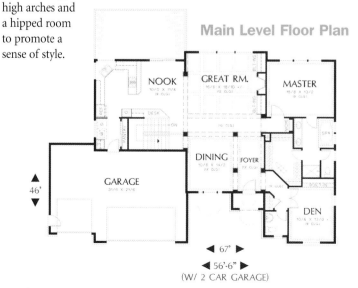

◀ 67' ▶

◀ 56'-6" ▶
(W/ 2 CAR GARAGE)

Basement Level Floor Plan

Copyright by designer/architect.

Plan #521015

Dimensions: 69'10" W x 80'10" D
Levels: 1
Square Footage: 2,425
Bedrooms: 3
Bathrooms: 2½
Foundation: Slab
Material List Available: No
Price Category: E

Images provided by designer/architect.

Bonus Area Floor Plan

Copyright by designer/architect.

Plan #461081

Dimensions: 85'6" W x 56'6" D
Levels: 1
Square Footage: 2,464
Bedrooms: 3
Bathrooms: 2½
Foundation: Slab or basement;
crawl space for fee
Material List Available: No
Price Category: E

Images provided by designer/architect.

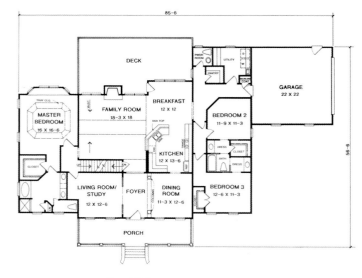

Copyright by designer/architect.

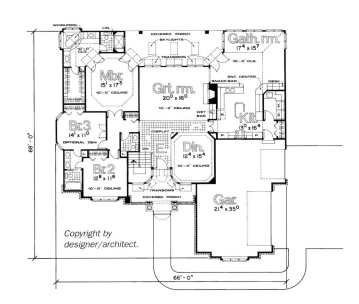

Plan #121053

Dimensions: 66' W x 68' D
Levels: 1
Square Footage: 2,456
Bedrooms: 3
Bathrooms: 2½
Foundation: Basement
Materials List Available: Yes
Price Category: E

Images provided by designer/architect.

This home, as shown in the photograph, may differ from the actual blueprints. For more detailed information, please check the floor plans carefully.

SMARTtip

Installing Plastic Molding

Foam trim is best cut with a backsaw. Power miter saws with fine-toothed blades also work. Larger-toothed blades tend to tear the foam unevenly.

Plan #521007

Dimensions: 67' W x 69'4" D
Levels: 1.5
Square Footage: 2,810
Main Level Sq. Ft.: 2,420
Upper Level Sq. Ft.: 390
Bedrooms: 3
Bathrooms: 3½
Foundation: Crawl space
Material List Available: No
Price Category: F

Images provided by designer/architect.

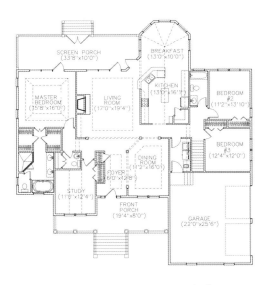

Bonus Area Floor Plan

Copyright by designer/architect.

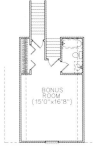

Plan #461045

Dimensions: 69' W x 65'6" D
Levels: 1
Square Footage: 2,889
Bedrooms: 3
Bathrooms: 2½
Foundation: Slab or basement; crawl space for fee
Material List Available: No
Price Category: F

Images provided by designer/architect.

Copyright by designer/architect.

Plan #451263

Dimensions: 89'8" W x 66' D
Levels: 1
Square Footage: 2,709
Bedrooms: 3
Bathrooms: 2½
Foundation: Walkout basement
Material List Available: No
Price Category: F

Images provided by designer/architect.

CAD FILE AVAILABLE

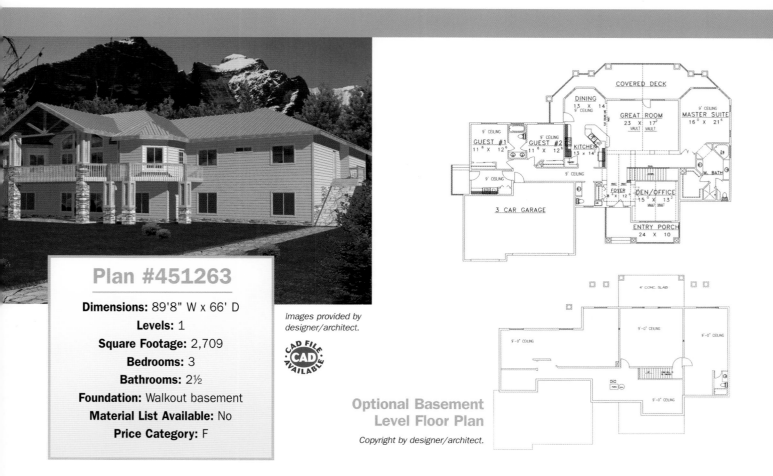

Optional Basement Level Floor Plan

Copyright by designer/architect.

Plan #121007

Dimensions: 74' W x 67'8" D
Levels: 1
Square Footage: 2,512
Bedrooms: 3
Bathrooms: 2½
Foundation: Basement
Materials List Available: Yes
Price Category: E

A series of arches brings grace to this home's interior and exterior.

Features:

• Ceiling Height: 8 ft.

• Formal Dining Room: Tapered columns give this dining room a classical look that lends elegance to any dinner party.

• Great Room: Just beyond the dining room is this light-filled room, with its wall of arched windows and see-through fireplace.

• Hearth Room: On the other side of the fire place you will find this cozy area, with its corner entertainment center.

• Dinette: A gazebo-shaped dinette is the architectural surprise of the house layout.

• Kitchen: This well-conceived working kitchen features a generous center island.

• Garage: With three garage bays you'll never be short of parking space or storage.

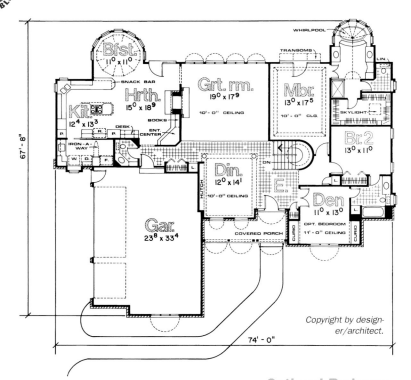

Copyright by designer/architect.

Optional Bedroom

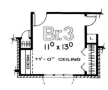

Plan #311006

Dimensions: 65'1" W x 73'7" D
Levels: 1
Square Footage: 2,465
Bedrooms: 4
Bathrooms: 2½
Foundation: Crawl space, slab, or basement
Materials List Available: Yes
Price Category: E

Images provided by designer/architect.

Wide steps and a columned front porch, combined with an exterior full of large, glowing windows, provide a warm welcome for friends and family.

Features:

- **Great Room:** This spacious room is central to the house, open in every direction, and features a fireplace flanked by doors that open onto the back covered porch. Relax inside by the warmth of the fire, or take your conversation out to rocking chairs under the stars on pleasant evenings.

- **Kitchen:** Two pantries, an island with a dining bar, and extra counter space give the gourmet organized room to breathe in this workspace. The kitchen is also open to the dining room and a generous breakfast room for convenient meal transitions.

- **Master Suite:** This suite becomes a retreat from the everyday, with its comfortable sitting room lined by windows, his and her walk-in closets and vanities, a standing shower, large tub, and compartmentalized toilet.

- **Secondary Bedrooms:** Each of three additional bedrooms includes a walk-in closet and access to the centralized second full bathroom.

Rear View

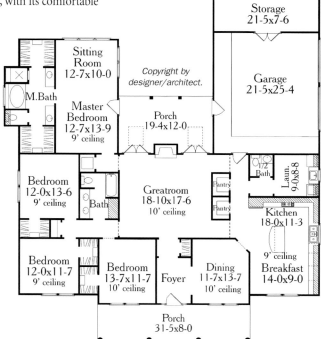

Plan #151711

Dimensions: 64' W x 60'2" D
Levels: 1
Square Footage: 2,554
Bedrooms: 4
Bathrooms: 2½
Foundation: Crawl space or slab
CompleteCost List Available: Yes
Price Category: E

Images provided by designer/architect.

An alluring arched entry welcomes guests into your home, giving them a taste of the lavishness they'll find once inside.

Features:

- Kitchen: Counter space on all sides and a center island provide ample space for the budding chef. This kitchen is located across the hall from the dining room and opens into the hearth room, providing easy transitions between preparing and serving. A snack bar acts as a shift between the kitchen and hearth room.

- Hearth Room: This spacious area is lined with windows on one side, shares a gas fire place with the great room, and opens onto the grilling porch, which makes it ideal for gatherings of all kinds and sizes.

- Master Suite: Larger than any space in the house, this room will truly make you feel like the master. The bedroom is a blank canvas waiting for your personal touch and has a door opening to the backyard. The compartmentalized master bath includes his and her walk-in closets and sinks, a glass shower stall, and a whirlpool bathtub.

- Secondary Bedrooms: If three bedrooms is one too many, the second bedroom can easily be used as a study with optional French doors opening from the foyer. Every additional bedroom has a large closet and access to the central full bathroom.

Front View

This home, as shown in the photograph, may differ from the actual blueprints. For more detailed information, please check the floor plans carefully.

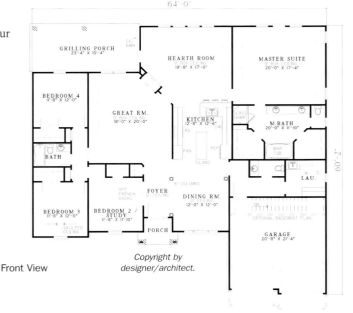

Copyright by designer/architect.

Plan #351089

Dimensions: 79'4" W x 53'6" D
Levels: 1
Square Footage: 2,505
Bedrooms: 3
Bathrooms: 3
Foundation: Crawl space or slab
Material List Available: Yes
Price Category: F

Rear View

This colonial farmhouse has beautiful architectural features and a unique interior design, a combination that you'll love to come home to.

Features:

- **Porches:** Columns and arched windows add a graceful touch to the front porch, which opens into a large, inviting foyer. The breakfast area opens on either side to porches, one covered and one you can choose to be covered or screened. Either way, you'll be able to relax over breakfast on the porch.

- **Great Room:** Vaulted ceilings, windows opening to the covered porch, and a gas fireplace provide a warm welcome for guests and make this a great space for gatherings.

- **Kitchen:** Working from the concept of the kitchen as the heart of the home, this design centralizes it between the breakfast room/sunroom, dining room, and great room for easy transitions between preparing and serving. It features plenty of workspace, a raised bar, and a desk area for organizing mail, grocery lists, and the family calendar.

- **Master Suite:** This suite has a unique design, with his and her bathrooms and closets. "Her bath" features a vanity and jetted tub, while "his" has a stall shower with seat and sink. But there's no harm in sharing.

- **Garage:** This attached garage has enough space for two cars, as well as room for his "toys" and a workshop.

Bonus Area Floor Plan

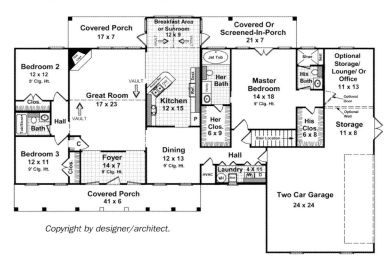

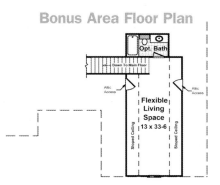

Plan #121003

Dimensions: 76' W x 55'4" D
Levels: 1
Square Footage: 2,498
Bedrooms: 4
Bathrooms: 2½
Foundation: Basement
Materials List Available: Yes
Price Category: E

Images provided by designer/architect.

Repeated arches bring style and distinction to the interior and exterior of this spacious home.

Features:

- Ceiling Height: 8 ft. except as noted.

- Den: A decorative volume ceiling helps make this spacious retreat the perfect place to relax after a long day.

- Formal Living Room: The decorative volume ceiling carries through to the living room that invites large formal gatherings.

- Formal Dining Room: There's plenty of room for all the guests to move into this gracious formal space that also features a decorative volume ceiling.

- Master Suite: Retire to this suite with its glamorous bayed whirlpool, his and her vanities, and a walk-in closet.

- Optional Sitting Room: With the addition of French doors, one of the bedrooms can be converted into a sitting room for the master suite.

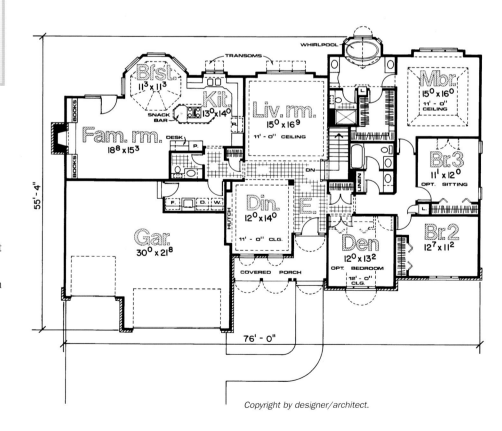

Copyright by designer/architect.

Plan #241008

Dimensions: 65' W x 56'8" D
Levels: 1
Square Footage: 2,526
Bedrooms: 4
Bathrooms: 3
Foundation: Crawl space, slab, or basement
Materials List Available: No
Price Category: E

Images provided by designer/architect.

A covered back porch—with access from the master suite and the breakfast area—makes this traditional home ideal for siting near a golf course or with a backyard pool.

Features:

- **Great Room:** From the foyer, guests enter this spacious and comfortable great room, which features a handsome fireplace.

- **Kitchen:** This kitchen—the hub of this family-oriented home—is a joy in which to work, thanks to abundant counter space, a pantry, a convenient eating bar, and an adjoining breakfast area and sunroom.

- **Master Suite:** Enjoy the quiet comfort of this coffered-ceiling master suite, which features dual vanities and separate walk-in closets.

- **Additional Bedrooms:** Two secondary bedrooms, which share a full bath, are located at the opposite end of the house from the master suite. Bedroom 4—in front of the house—can be converted into a study.

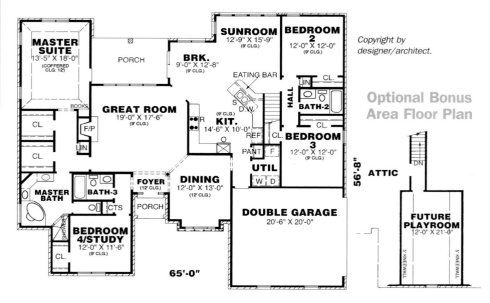

Copyright by designer/architect.

Optional Bonus Area Floor Plan

SMARTtip
Traditional-Style Kitchen Cabinetry

You can modify stock kitchen cabinetry to enjoy fine furniture-quality details. Prefabricated trims may be purchased at local lumber mills and home centers. For example, crown molding, applied to the top of stock cabinetry and stained or painted to match the door style, may be all you need. Likewise, you can replace hardware with reproduction polished-brass door and drawer knobs or pulls for a finishing touch.

Plan #271080

Dimensions: 71' W x 83' D

Levels: 1

Square Footage: 2,581

Bedrooms: 3

Bathrooms: 3

Foundation: Basement

Materials List Available: Yes

Price Category: E

An open floor plan and beautiful adornments promise comfortable living within this appealing one-story home.

Features:

- **Living Room:** Beyond the sidelighted entry, this spacious living room is bordered on two sides by striking arched openings.

- **Kitchen:** This island kitchen flows into a bayed eating nook, which shares a two-sided fireplace with the living room.

- **Master Suite:** A bright sitting room is a nice feature in this luxurious suite, which is secluded to the rear of the home. The private bath boasts a corner tub, a separate shower, two vanities, and a walk-in closet.

Images provided by designer/architect.

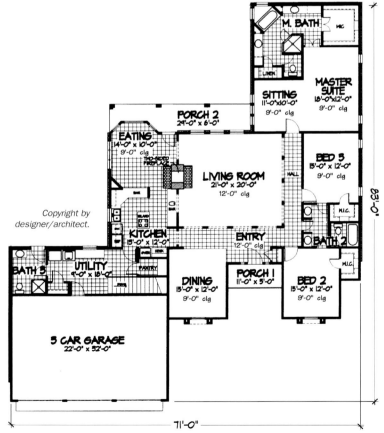

Copyright by designer/architect.

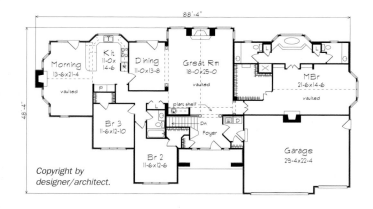

Copyright by designer/architect.

Plan #321018

Dimensions: 88'4" W x 48'4" D
Levels: 1
Square Footage: 2,523
Bedrooms: 3
Bathrooms: 2
Foundation: Basement
Materials List Available: Yes
Price Category: E

Images provided by designer/architect.

Plan #151383

Dimensions: 70'4" W x 57'2" D
Levels: 1
Square Footage: 2,534
Bedrooms: 3
Bathrooms: 2
Foundation: Crawl space or slab
CompleteCost List Available: Yes
Price Category: E

Images provided by designer/architect.

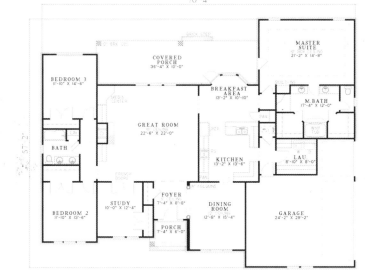

Copyright by designer/architect.

Front View

Plan #451230

Dimensions: 59'9" W x 56'2" D
Levels: 1
Square Footage: 2,685
Main Level Sq. Ft.: 1,462
Lower Level Sq. Ft.: 1,223
Bedrooms: 3
Bathrooms: 2
Foundation: Walkout basement
Material List Available: No
Price Category: F

Images provided by designer/architect.

CAD FILE AVAILABLE

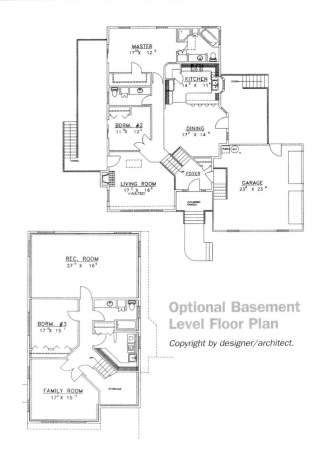

Optional Basement Level Floor Plan

Copyright by designer/architect.

Plan #311059

Dimensions: 66'1" W x 77'7" D
Levels: 1
Square Footage: 2,555
Bedrooms: 4
Bathrooms: 2½
Foundation: Crawl space, slab, or basement
Material List Available: Yes
Price Category: E

Images provided by designer/architect.

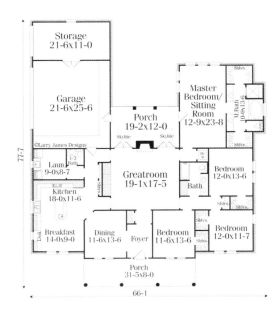

Basement Stair Location

Copyright by designer/architect.

Plan #151063

Dimensions: 64' W x 60'2" D
Levels: 1
Square Footage: 2,554
Bedrooms: 4
Bathrooms: 2½
Foundation: Crawl space or slab; basement or walkout for a fee
CompleteCost List Available: Yes
Price Category: E

Images provided by designer/architect.

This home, as shown in the photograph, may differ from the actual blueprints. For more detailed information, please check the floor plans carefully.

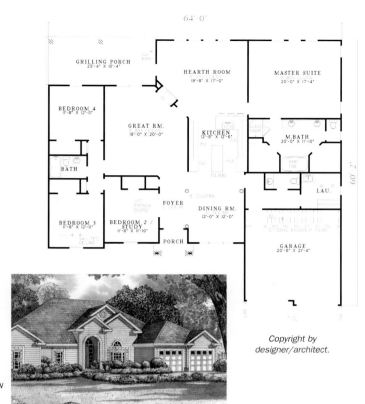

Copyright by designer/architect.

Rear View

Plan #521002

Dimensions: 58'10" W x 70'4" D
Levels: 1.5
Square Footage: 2,793
Main Level Sq. Ft.: 2,265
Upper Level Sq. Ft.: 528
Bedrooms: 3
Bathrooms: 3 full, 2 half
Foundation: Crawl space
Material List Available: No
Price Category: F

Images provided by designer/architect.

Bonus Area Floor Plan
Copyright by designer/architect.

Plan #151002

Dimensions: 67' W x 66' D
Levels: 1
Square Footage: 2,444
Bedrooms: 3
Bathrooms: 2½
Foundation: Crawl space, slab, or basement
CompleteCost List Available: Yes
Price Category: E

Images provided by designer/architect.

This gracious, traditional home is designed for practicality and convenience.

Features:

• Ceiling Height: 9 ft. except as noted below.

• Great Room: This room is ideal for entertaining, thanks to its lovely fireplace and French doors that open to the covered rear porch. Built-in cabinets give convenient storage space.

• Family Room: With access to the kitchen as well as the rear porch, this room will become your family's "headquarters."

• Study: Enjoy the quiet in this room with its 12-ft. ceiling and doorway to a private patio on the side of the house.

• Dining Room: Take advantage of the 8-in. wood columns and 12-ft. ceilings to create a formal dining area.

• Kitchen: An eat-in bar is a great place to snack, and the handy computer nook allows the kids to do their homework while you cook.

• Breakfast Room: Opening from the kitchen, this area gives added space for the family to gather any time.

• Master Suite: Featuring a 10-ft. boxed ceiling, the master bedroom also has a door way that opens onto the covered rear porch. The master bathroom has a step-up whirlpool tub, separate shower, and twin vanities with a makeup area.

Copyright by designer/architect.

Plan #271081

Dimensions: 86' W x 54' D
Levels: 1
Square Footage: 2,539
Bedrooms: 3
Bathrooms: 2
Foundation: Slab
Materials List Available: No
Price Category: E

This traditional home is sure to impress your guests and even your neighbors.

Features:

- **Living Room:** This quiet space off the foyer is perfect for pleasant conversation.

- **Family Room:** A perfect gathering spot, this room is nicely enhanced by a fireplace.

- **Kitchen:** This room easily serves the bayed morning room and the formal dining room.

- **Master Suite:** The master bedroom overlooks a side patio, and boasts a private bath with a skylight and a whirlpool tub.

- **Library:** This cozy room is perfect for curling up with a good novel. It would also make a great extra bedroom.

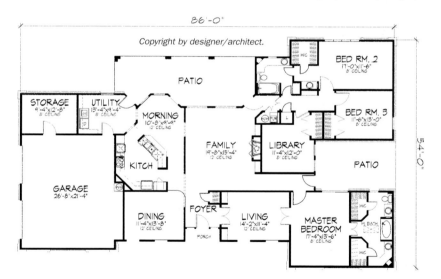

SMARTtip
Determining Curtain Length

Follow length guidelines for foolproof results, but remember that they're not rules. Go ahead and play with curtain and drapery lengths. Instead of shortening long panels at the hem, for instance, take up excess material by blousing them over tiebacks for a pleasing effect.

Plan #321017

Dimensions: 77' W x 36'8" D
Levels: 1
Square Footage: 2,531
Main Level Sq. Ft.: 1,297
Lower Level Sq. Ft.: 1,234
Bedrooms: 4
Bathrooms: 2½
Foundation: Walkout basement
Material List Available: Yes
Price Category: E

This charming home with stone accent, is an inviting place to call home.

Features:

- Porches and Decks: The covered front porch welcomes you and your guests to the home. Relax in the rear-covered porch, or enjoy the sun on the rear deck. Just off the rear deck would be a perfect spot for a swimming pool.

- Dining Room: This eating area is for daily meals and for formal gatherings. The railing overlooking into the two-story atrium adds a dramatic feeling of open space.

- Master Suite: This main-level retreat features a vaulted ceiling and a large walk-in closet. Walking under the plant shelf brings you into the luxurious master bath. This space boasts his and her vanities and a large tub with separate shower.

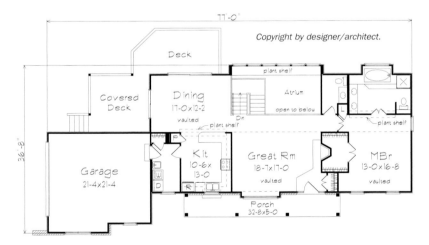

Basement Level Floor Plan

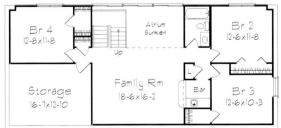

- Lower Level: In addition to the lower part of the two-story atrium, there are three additional bedrooms, the family room with bar, and the second full bathroom.

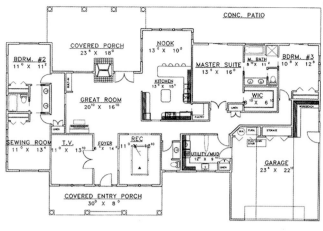

Copyright by designer/architect.

Plan #451210

Dimensions: 83'6" W x 53'3" D
Levels: 1
Square Footage: 2,646
Bedrooms: 3
Bathrooms: 2½
Foundation: Crawl space
Material List Available: No
Price Category: F

Images provided by designer/architect.

CAD FILE AVAILABLE

Rear Elevation

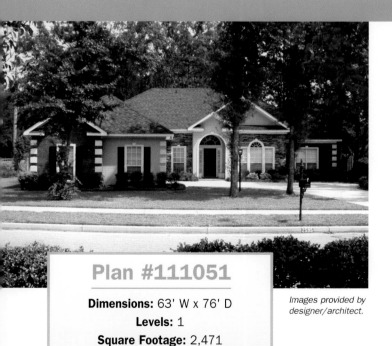

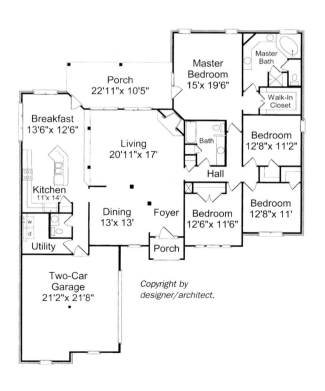

Images provided by designer/architect.

Copyright by designer/architect.

Plan #111051

Dimensions: 63' W x 76' D
Levels: 1
Square Footage: 2,471
Bedrooms: 4
Bathrooms: 2½
Foundation: Slab
Materials List Available: No
Price Category: E

Plan #361483

Dimensions: 71' W x 76'6" D
Levels: 1
Square Footage: 2,507
Bedrooms: 5
Bathrooms: 3
Foundation: Crawl space
Material List Available: No
Price Category: E

Images provided by designer/architect.

CAD FILE AVAILABLE

Copyright by designer/architect.

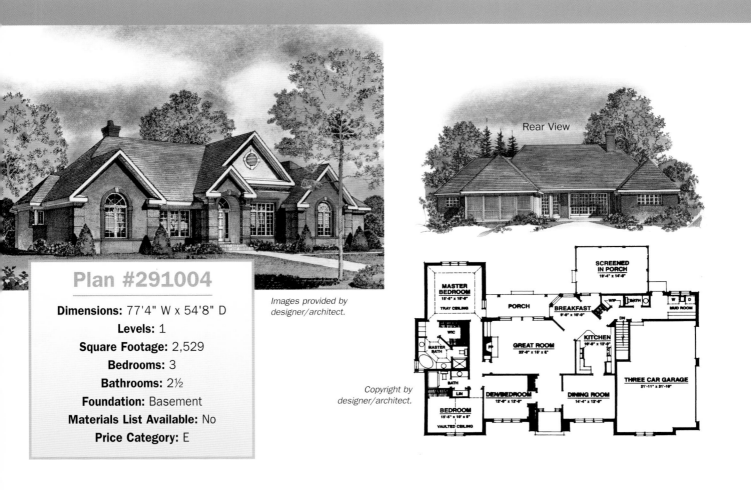

Plan #291004

Dimensions: 77'4" W x 54'8" D
Levels: 1
Square Footage: 2,529
Bedrooms: 3
Bathrooms: 2½
Foundation: Basement
Materials List Available: No
Price Category: E

Images provided by designer/architect.

Rear View

Copyright by designer/architect.

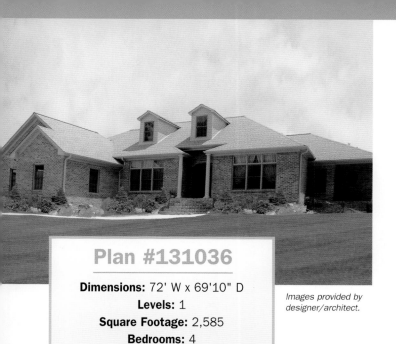

COV. PORCH
14'-0"x 12'-0"

BEDRM #2
9' CLG
13'-0"x 11'-0"

BATH

9' CLG
BKFST RM
10'-0"x 11'-0"

10'-7" HIGH
STEPPED CLG
GREAT RM
17'-0"x 18'-0"

SITTING

10'-7" HIGH
STEPPED
CEIL
MSTR BEDRM
12'-0"x
23'-0"

MSTR
BATH

BEDRM #3
9' CLG
11'-4"x 14'-0"

KITCHEN

ISLAND
13'-6"

SNACK
COUNTER

FIREPLACE

BUILT-INS

WICL

9' CLG
STUDY/
OFFICE
11'-0"x
11'-0"

COV.
PORCH

PANT

DN TO
OPT BSMT

BATH

LAUN RM
DN

PORCH

S W D

14'-0" HIGH
STEPPED
CEIL
FOYER

11'-4" HIGH
STEPPED CEIL
DINING RM
14'-0"x 11'-0"

11'-4" HIGH
STEPPED CEIL
LIVING RM
15'-0"x 13'-0"

TWO CAR GARAGE
20'-4"x 26'-0/ 22'-0"

PORCH

WORK SHOP

Copyright by designer/architect.

Plan #131036

Dimensions: 72' W x 69'10" D
Levels: 1
Square Footage: 2,585
Bedrooms: 4
Bathrooms: 3
Foundation: Crawl space, slab, or basement
Materials List Available: Yes
Price Category: F

Images provided by designer/architect.

**Optional
Upper Level
Floor Plan**

UNFIN. ATTIC
12'-0"x 12'-0"

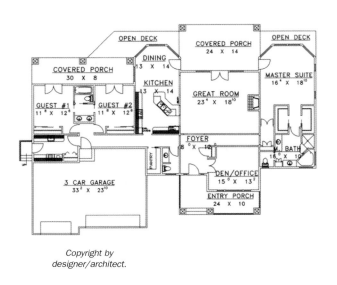

OPEN DECK

COVERED PORCH
24 X 14

OPEN DECK

COVERED PORCH
30 X 8

DINING
13 X 14

KITCHEN
13 X 14

MASTER SUITE
16⁴ X 18¹⁰

GUEST #1
11⁸ X 12⁴

GUEST #2
11⁸ X 12⁴

GREAT ROOM
23⁴ X 18¹⁰

M. BATH

PANTRY

FOYER

3 CAR GARAGE
33² X 23¹⁰

DEN/OFFICE
15⁰ X 13²

ENTRY PORCH
24 X 10

Copyright by designer/architect.

Plan #451194

Dimensions: 87'8" W x 58' D
Levels: 1
Square Footage: 2,618
Bedrooms: 3
Bathrooms: 2½
Foundation: Crawl space
Materials List Available: No
Price Category: F

Images provided by designer/architect.

CAD FILE AVAILABLE

Plan #311005

Dimensions: 87' W x 57'3" D
Levels: 1
Square Footage: 2,497
Bedrooms: 3
Bathrooms: 2½
Foundation: Crawl space, slab, or basement
Materials List Available: Yes
Price Category: E

You'll love this home, which mixes practical features with a gracious appearance.

Features:

- Great Room: A handsome fireplace and flanking windows that give a view of the back patio are the highlights of this gracious room.

- Kitchen: A curved bar defines the perimeter of this well-planned kitchen.

- Breakfast Room: Open to both the great room and the kitchen, this sunny spot leads to the rear porch, which in turn, leads to the patio beyond.

- Master Suite: Vaulted ceilings, a huge walk-in closet, and deluxe bath create luxury here.

- Bonus Room: Finish this 966-sq.-ft. area as a huge game room, or divide it into a game room, study, and sewing or craft room.

- Additional Bedrooms: Each bedroom has a private bath and good closet space.

Images provided by designer/architect.

Copyright by designer/architect.

Main Level Floor Plan

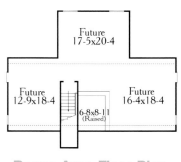

Bonus Area Floor Plan

Plan #101013

Dimensions: 72' W x 66' D
Levels: 1
Square Footage: 2,564
Bedrooms: 3
Bathrooms: 2½
Foundation: Crawl space, slab, basement, or walkout
Materials List Available: Yes
Price Category: E

Images provided by designer/architect.

This exciting design combines a striking classic exterior with a highly functional floor plan.

Features:

• Ceiling Height: 9 ft. unless otherwise noted.

• Family Room: This warm and inviting room measures 18 ft. x 22 ft. It features a 14-ft. ceiling and a rear wall of windows. French doors lead to an enormous deck.

• Kitchen: This unique angled kitchen is open to the hearth room and eating areas, all of which enjoy vaulted ceilings and are surrounded by windows. The hearth room has a TV niche.

• Master Suite: This 19-ft. x 18-ft. master suite is truly sumptuous, with its 12-ft. ceiling, sitting area, two walk-in closets, and full-featured bath.

• Secondary Bedrooms: Each of the secondary bedrooms measures 11 ft. x 14 ft. and has direct access to a shared bath.

• Bonus Room: Just beyond the entry are stairs leading to this bonus room, which measures approximately 12 ft. x 21 ft.—plenty of room for storage or future expansion.

Master Bedroom

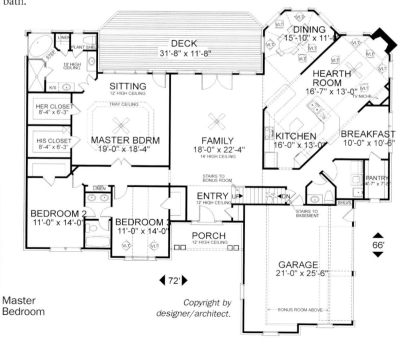

Copyright by designer/architect.

Plan #351088

Dimensions: 66'8" W x 73'2" D
Levels: 1
Square Footage: 2,500
Bedrooms: 4
Bathrooms: 3
Foundation: Crawl space or slab
Material List Available: Yes
Price Category: F

The dashing contemporary-country style of brick and siding with attractive architectural details, like a string of dormers, makes this home's exterior as lovely as its interior.

CAD FILE AVAILABLE — CAD

Features:

• Great Room: Opening onto the rear covered porch for the overflow of relaxing warm-weather gatherings and enjoyment of the outdoor kitchen, this great room also features a fireplace and built-in storage for when you'd rather stay comfortably inside. Vaulted ceilings give the an even greater amount of freedom.

• Kitchen: This efficiently designed space features an L-shaped work area, a pantry, and an island with a raised eating bar.

Opening into the formal dining room, fireplace-warmed breakfast room, and large great room gives mealtime plenty of possibilities.

• Master Suite: In a space of its own, this retreat exudes relaxation and privacy. A hallway leads to the expansive space, which features an extensive master bath with dual sinks, an oversized jetted tub, a stall shower, and his and her walk-in closets.

• Secondary Bedrooms: The other bedrooms have hallways of their own and are all just steps away from full bathrooms.

• Flex Space: A small room adjacent to the master suite is in perfect proximity for use as a home office, a nursery, or extra storage space. Above the garage is an unfinished bonus space that can be used however you like.

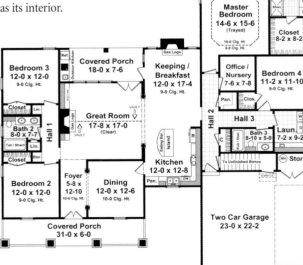

Bonus Room Floor Plan

Copyright by designer/architect.

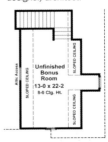

Rear Elevation

Plan #271063

Dimensions: 61'4" W x 70' D
Levels: 1
Square Footage: 2,572
Bedrooms: 3
Bathrooms: 2
Foundation: Daylight basement
Materials List Available: No
Price Category: E

Images provided by designer/architect.

CAD FILE AVAILABLE

Basement Level Floor Plan
Copyright by designer/architect.

Plan #481014

Dimensions: 100'2" W x 61'8" D
Levels: 1
Square Footage: 2,706
Main Level Sq. Ft.: 1,623
Lower Level Sq. Ft.: 1,083
Bedrooms: 4
Bathrooms: 2½
Foundation: Walkout basement
Material List Available: No
Price Category: F

Images provided by designer/architect.

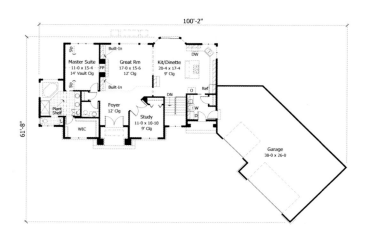

Basement Level Floor Plan
Copyright by designer/architect.

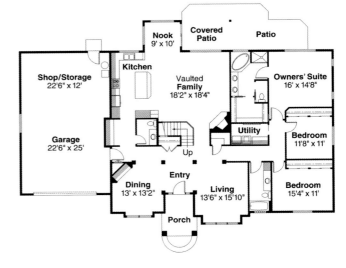

Images provided by designer/architect.

Plan #361537

Dimensions: 80' W x 57' D
Levels: 1
Square Footage: 2,551
Bedrooms: 3
Bathrooms: 2½
Foundation: Crawl space
Material List Available: No
Price Category: E

Bonus Area Floor Plan

Copyright by designer/architect.

Plan #311061

Dimensions: 73' W x 71' D
Levels: 1
Square Footage: 2,570
Bedrooms: 3
Bathrooms: 2½
Foundation: Crawl space, slab, or basement
Material List Available: Yes
Price Category: E

Images provided by designer/architect.

Rear View

Copyright by designer/architect.

Plan #321027

Dimensions: 72' W x 68' D
Levels: 1
Square Footage: 2,758
Bedrooms: 4
Bathrooms: 2½
Foundation: Basement
Materials List Available: Yes
Price Category: F

Images provided by designer/architect.

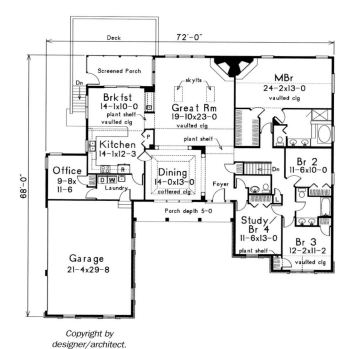

Copyright by designer/architect.

Plan #421009

Dimensions: 64'9" W x 59' D
Levels: 1
Square Footage: 2,649
Bedrooms: 3
Bathrooms: 2
Foundation: Crawl space, slab, or basement
Materials List Available: Yes
Price Category: F

Images provided by designer/architect.

CAD FILE AVAILABLE

Main Level Floor Plan

Alternate Floor Plan

Copyright by designer/architect.

Plan #121163

Dimensions: 65'10" W x 75'6" D
Levels: 1
Square Footage: 2,679
Bedrooms: 4
Bathrooms: 3
Foundation: Slab; basement for fee
Material List Available: Yes
Price Category: F

Large rooms give this home a spacious feel in a modest footprint.

Features:

- Family Room: This area is the central gathering place in the home. The windows to the rear fill the area with natural light. The fireplace take the chill off on cool winter nights.

- Kitchen: This peninsula kitchen with raised bar is open into the family room and the breakfast area. The built-in pantry is a welcomed storage area for today's family.

- Master Suite: This secluded area features large windows with a view of the backyard. The master bath boasts a large walk-in closet, his and her vanities and a compartmentalized lavatory area.

- Secondary Bedrooms: Bedroom 2 has its own access to the main bathroom, while bedrooms 3 and 4 share a Jack-and-Jill bathroom. All bedrooms feature walk-in closets.

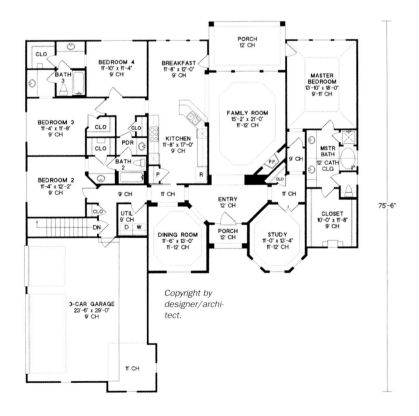

Copyright by designer/architect.

Plan #321007

Dimensions: 76' W x 55'2" D
Levels: 1
Square Footage: 2,695
Bedrooms: 3
Bathrooms: 2½
Foundation: Basement
Materials List Available: Yes
Price Category: F

You'll love the way this spacious ranch reminds you of a French country home.

Features:

- **Foyer:** Come into this lovely home's foyer, and be greeted with a view of the gracious staircase and the great room just beyond.

- **Great Room:** Settle down by the cozy fireplace in cool weather, and reach for a book on the built-in shelves that surround it.

- **Kitchen:** Designed for efficient work patterns, this large kitchen is open to the great room.

- **Breakfast Room:** Just off the kitchen, this sunny room will be a family favorite all through the day.

- **Master Suite:** A bay window, walk-in closet, and shower built for two are highlights of this area.

- **Additional Bedrooms:** These large bedrooms both have walk-in closets and share a Jack-and-Jill bath for total convenience.

Images provided by designer/architect.

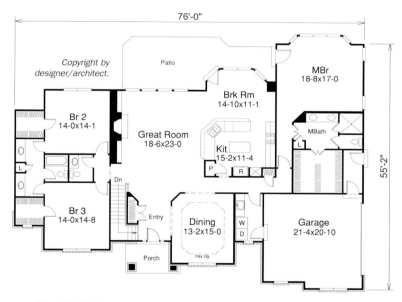

SMARTtip

Decorative Poles

Drapery poles are supported by the brackets fastened to the window frame or wall. The brackets that are provided with the poles generally coordinate and blend in with the pole finish. Brackets can be simple but also decorative. If you opt for a spectacular, attention-grabbing bracket, consider choosing less showy finials for the ends of the pole.

Images provided by designer/architect. Living Room

Plan #111004

Dimensions: 76' W x 85' D
Levels: 1
Square Footage: 2,968
Bedrooms: 4
Full Bathrooms: 3½
Foundation: Slab;
crawl space available for fee
Materials List Available: No
Price Category: F

If you've been looking for a home that includes a special master suite, this one could be the answer to your dreams.

Features:

• **Living Room:** Make a sitting area around the fireplace here so that the whole family can enjoy the warmth on chilly days and winter evenings. A door from this room leads to the rear covered porch, making this room the heart of your home.

• **Kitchen:** An island with a cooktop makes cooking a pleasure in this well-designed kitchen, and the breakfast bar invites visitors at all times of day.

• **Utility Room:** A sink and a built-in ironing board make this room totally practical.

• **Master Suite:** A private fireplace in the corner sets a romantic tone for this bedroom, and the door to the covered porch allows you to sit outside on warm summer nights. The bath has two vanities, a divided walk-in closet, a standing shower, and a deluxe corner bathtub.

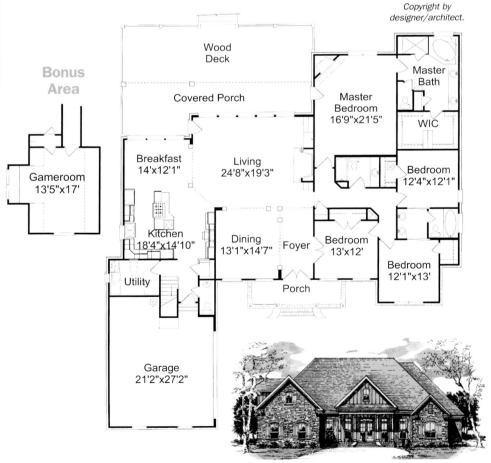

Bonus Area

Gameroom 13'5"x17'

Wood Deck

Covered Porch

Master Bedroom 16'9"x21'5"

Master Bath

WIC

Breakfast 14'x12'1"

Living 24'8"x19'3"

Bedroom 12'4"x12'1"

Kitchen 18'4"x14'10"

Dining 13'1"x14'7"

Foyer

Bedroom 13'x12'

Bedroom 12'1"x13'

Utility

Porch

Garage 21'2"x27'2"

Kitchen

Dining Room

Master Bath

Master Bath

SMARTtip

How to Quit Smoking — Lighting Your Fireplace

Before attempting to light a wood fire, make certain that the damper is open all the way. This allows a good draft (flow of air up the chimney) to prevent smoke from blowing back into the room. To ensure a good draft—particularly if your home is well insulated —open a window a bit when lighting a fire.

The opposite of draft is downdraft, which occurs when cold air flows down the chimney and into the room. If the fireplace is properly designed and maintained, the smoke shelf will prevent backpuffing from downdraft most of the time by redirecting cold air currents back up the chimney. The open damper also helps prevent backpuffing.

Also, build a fire slowly to let the chimney liner heat up, which will create a good draft and minimize the chances of downdraft.

Don't wait until fall to inspect the chimney. Do this job, or call a chimney sweep, when the weather is mild. Because some repairs take a while to make, it's best to have them done when the fireplace is not normally in use. If you do the inspection yourself, wear old clothes, eye goggles, and a mask.

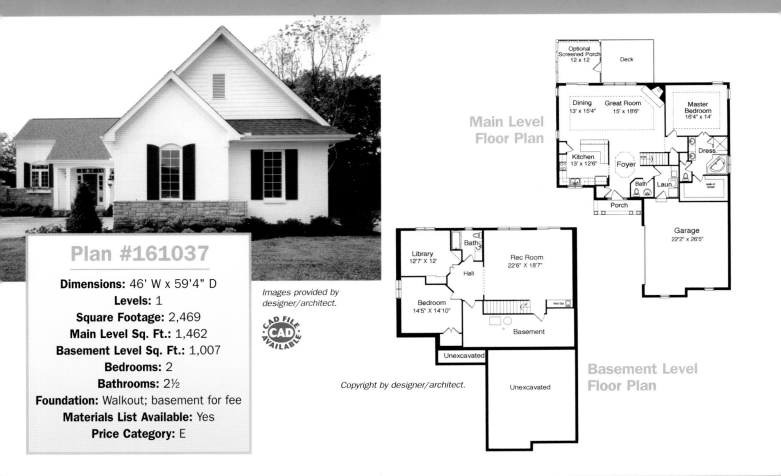

Plan #161037

Dimensions: 46' W x 59'4" D
Levels: 1
Square Footage: 2,469
Main Level Sq. Ft.: 1,462
Basement Level Sq. Ft.: 1,007
Bedrooms: 2
Bathrooms: 2½
Foundation: Walkout; basement for fee
Materials List Available: Yes
Price Category: E

Images provided by designer/architect.

CAD FILE AVAILABLE

Main Level Floor Plan

Optional Screened Porch 12 x 12
Deck
Dining 13' x 15'4"
Great Room 15' x 18'6"
Master Bedroom 16'4" x 14'
Kitchen 13' x 12'6"
Foyer
Dress.
walk-in closet
Bath
Laun.
Porch
Garage 22'2" x 26'5"

Copyright by designer/architect.

Basement Level Floor Plan

Library 12'7" X 12'
Bath
Rec Room 22'6" X 18'7"
Hall
Bedroom 14'5" X 14'10"
Wet Bar
Basement
Unexcavated
Unexcavated

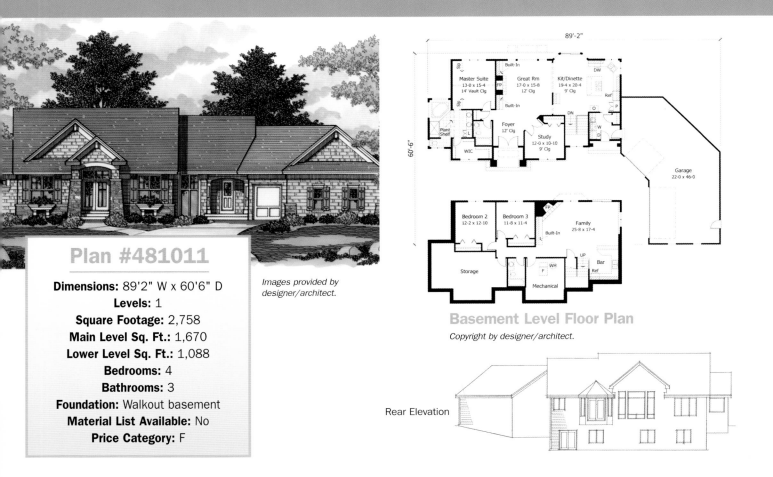

Plan #481011

Dimensions: 89'2" W x 60'6" D
Levels: 1
Square Footage: 2,758
Main Level Sq. Ft.: 1,670
Lower Level Sq. Ft.: 1,088
Bedrooms: 4
Bathrooms: 3
Foundation: Walkout basement
Material List Available: No
Price Category: F

Images provided by designer/architect.

89'-2"

Master Suite 13-0 x 15-4 14' Vault Clg
Great Rm 17-0 x 15-8 12' Clg
Kit/Dinette 19-4 x 20-4 9' Clg
Plant Shelf
Foyer 12' Clg
Study 12-0 x 10-10 9' Clg
W1C
Garage 22-0 x 46-0

Bedroom 2 12-2 x 12-10
Bedroom 3 11-8 x 11-4
Family 25-8 x 17-4
Built-In
Storage
Mechanical
WH
UP
Bar

Basement Level Floor Plan

Copyright by designer/architect.

Rear Elevation

Plan #451113

Dimensions: 70'2" W x 43' D

Levels: 1

Square Footage: 2,542

Bedrooms: 3

Bathrooms: 2½

Foundation: Slab

Material List Available: No

Price Category: E

Rear Elevation

Images provided by designer/architect.

CAD FILE AVAILABLE

Optional Basement Level Floor Plan

Copyright by designer/architect.

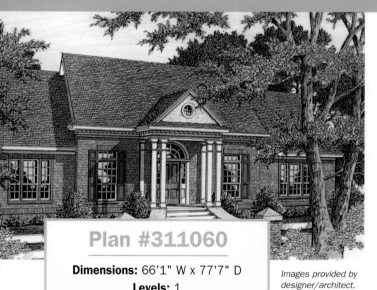

Plan #311060

Dimensions: 66'1" W x 77'7" D

Levels: 1

Square Footage: 2,585

Bedrooms: 4

Bathrooms: 2½

Foundation: Crawl space, slab, or basement

Material List Available: Yes

Price Category: E

Images provided by designer/architect.

Rear View

Basement Stair Location

Copyright by designer/architect.

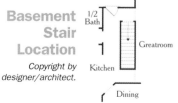

Plan #441009

Dimensions: 94' W x 53' D
Levels: 1
Square Footage: 2,650
Bedrooms: 4
Bathrooms: 2½
Foundation: Crawl space; slab or basement available for fee
Materials List Available: No
Price Category: F

You'll love to call this plan home. It's large enough for the whole family and has a façade that will make you the envy of the neighborhood.

Images provided by designer/architect.

Features:

- Foyer: The covered porch protects the entry, which has a transom and sidelights to brighten this space.

- Great Room: To the left of the foyer, beyond decorative columns, lies this vaulted room, with its fireplace and media center. Additional columns separate the room from the vaulted formal dining room.

- Kitchen: A casual nook and this island work center are just around the corner from the great room. The second covered porch can be reached via a door in the nook.

- Master Suite: This luxurious space boasts a vaulted salon, a private niche that could be a small study, and a view of the front yard. The master bath features a spa tub, separate shower, compartmented toilet, huge walk-in closet, and access to the laundry room.

- Bedrooms: The two additional bedrooms are located at the back of the plan and share the Jack-and-Jill bathroom.

Copyright by designer/architect.

Plan #151040

Dimensions: 70' W x 51'10" D
Levels: 1
Square Footage: 2,444
Bedrooms: 4
Bathrooms: 2½
Foundation: Crawl space or slab; basement for fee
CompleteCost List Available: Yes
Price Category: E

Images provided by designer/architect.

This is the perfect brick ranch home for any family

Features:

- Entry: Enter from the front porch into this classically designed foyer, with the formal living room to the left and formal dining room to right, and you get the feeling that you can live here forever.

- Great Room: This large gathering area features a 10-ft.-high boxed ceiling and an eye-catching fireplace. Step through either of the two doors flanking the fireplace for fresh air on the rear grilling porch.

- Kitchen: A superb breakfast room is the perfect accent to this spacious kitchen, with its functional eat-at bar.

- Garage: This two-car garage has room for the cars and an extra storage area.

Copyright by designer/architect.

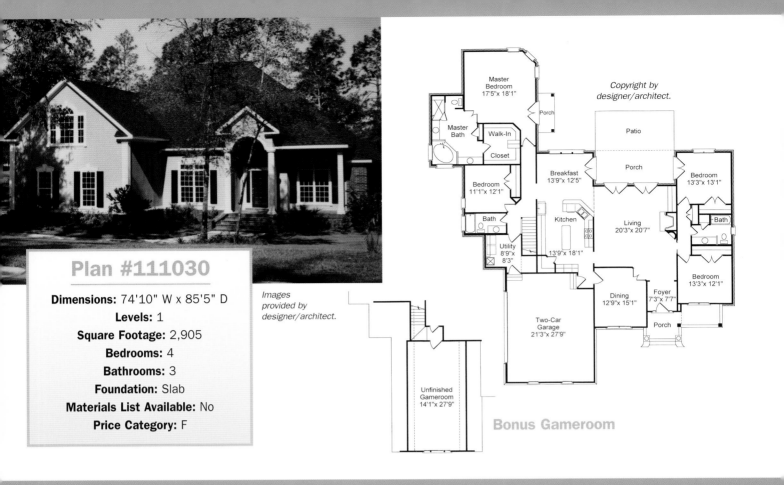

Plan #111030

Dimensions: 74'10" W x 85'5" D

Levels: 1

Square Footage: 2,905

Bedrooms: 4

Bathrooms: 3

Foundation: Slab

Materials List Available: No

Price Category: F

Images provided by designer/architect.

Bonus Gameroom

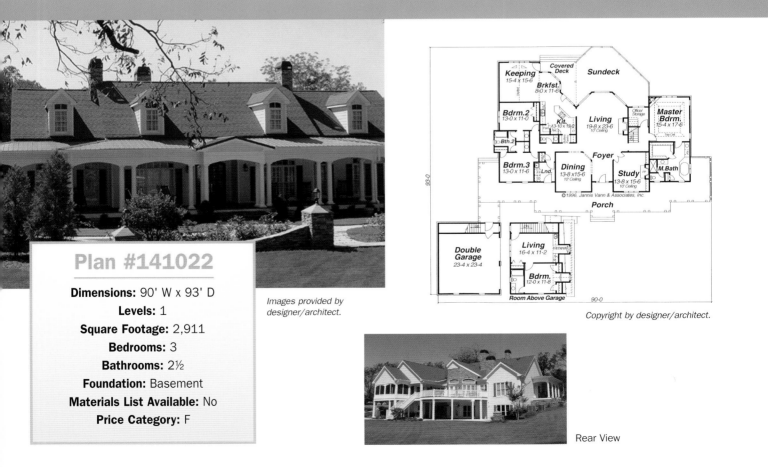

Plan #141022

Dimensions: 90' W x 93' D

Levels: 1

Square Footage: 2,911

Bedrooms: 3

Bathrooms: 2½

Foundation: Basement

Materials List Available: No

Price Category: F

Images provided by designer/architect.

Copyright by designer/architect.

Rear View

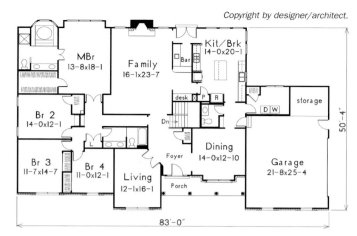

Images provided by designer/architect.

Plan #321011

Dimensions: 83' W x 50'4" D
Levels: 1
Square Footage: 2,874
Bedrooms: 4
Bathrooms: 2½
Foundation: Basement
Materials List Available: Yes
Price Category: F

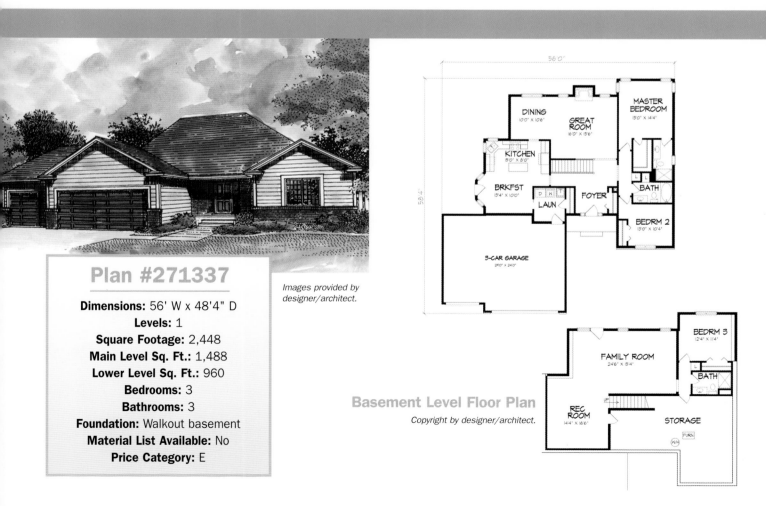

Plan #271337

Dimensions: 56' W x 48'4" D
Levels: 1
Square Footage: 2,448
Main Level Sq. Ft.: 1,488
Lower Level Sq. Ft.: 960
Bedrooms: 3
Bathrooms: 3
Foundation: Walkout basement
Material List Available: No
Price Category: E

Images provided by designer/architect.

Basement Level Floor Plan

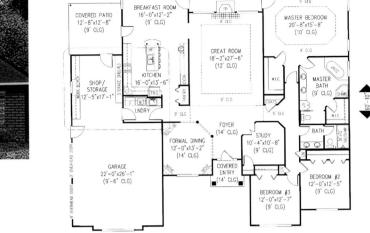

Plan #421021

Dimensions: 69'8" W x 60'10" D
Levels: 1
Square Footage: 2,836
Bedrooms: 3
Bathrooms: 2
Foundation: Crawl space, slab, or basement
Material List Available: Yes
Price Category: F

Images provided by designer/architect.

CAD FILE AVAILABLE

Optional Basement Level Floor Plan

Copyright by designer/architect.

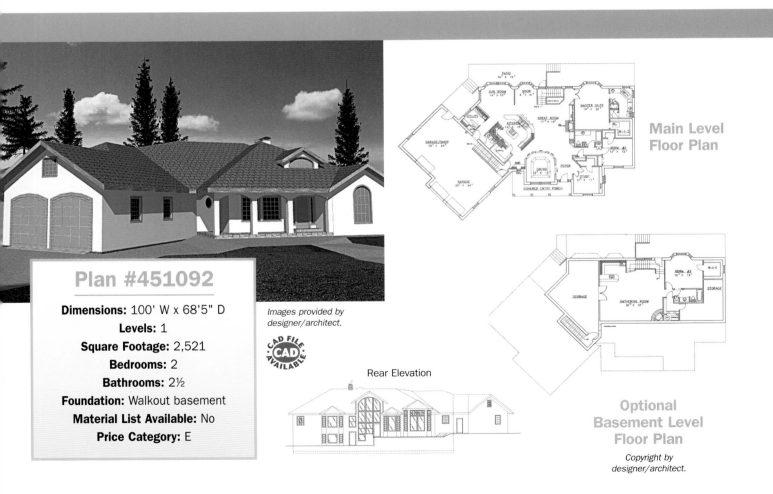

Main Level Floor Plan

Rear Elevation

Optional Basement Level Floor Plan

Copyright by designer/architect.

Plan #451092

Dimensions: 100' W x 68'5" D
Levels: 1
Square Footage: 2,521
Bedrooms: 2
Bathrooms: 2½
Foundation: Walkout basement
Material List Available: No
Price Category: E

Images provided by designer/architect.

CAD FILE AVAILABLE

Plan #321036

Dimensions: 78'4" W x 68'6" D
Levels: 1
Square Footage: 2,900
Bedrooms: 4
Bathrooms: 2½
Foundation: Basement
Materials List Available: No
Price Category: F

Images provided by designer/architect.

This classic contemporary is wrapped in brick.

Features:

- **Great Room:** This grand-scale room offers a vaulted ceiling and Palladian windows flanking an 8-ft.-wide brick fireplace.

- **Kitchen:** This built-in-a-bay room features a picture window above the sink, a huge pantry, and a cooktop island. It opens to the large morning room.

- **Breakfast Area:** Open to the kitchen, this area features 12 ft. of cabinetry.

- **Master Bedroom:** This room features a coffered ceiling, and a walk-in closet gives you good storage space in this luxurious bedroom.

- **Garage:** This area can fit three cars with plenty of room to spare.

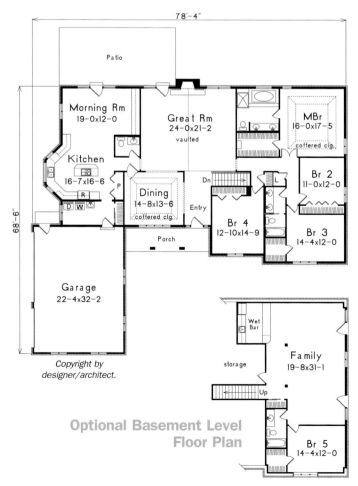

Copyright by
designer/architect.

Optional Basement Level Floor Plan

Plan #321028

Dimensions: 79' W x 64'2" D
Levels: 1
Square Footage: 2,723
Bedrooms: 3
Bathrooms: 2½
Foundation: Basement
Materials List Available: Yes
Price Category: F

This dream brick three-bedroom home with a three-car garage has everything you are looking for in a new home.

Features:

- Great Room: This large room has a vaulted ceiling and a fireplace.

- Dining Room: Just off the entry is this formal space, with its tray ceiling.

- Kitchen: This island kitchen has a large pantry and an abundance of counter space.

- Master Suite: This retreat features a vaulted ceiling and a large walk-in closet. The master bath has a double vanity and a soaking tub.

- Bedrooms: Two additional bedrooms share a common bathroom.

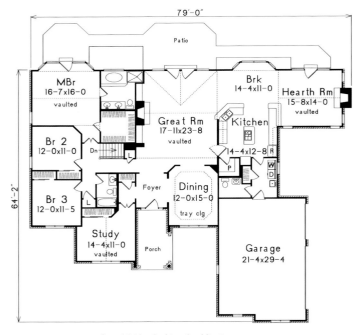

Plan #401023

Dimensions: 76' W x 63'4" D
Levels: 1
Square Footage: 2,806
Bedrooms: 3
Bathrooms: 2½
Foundation: Basement, walkout
Materials List Available: Yes
Price Category: F

The lower level of this magnificent home includes unfinished space that could have a future as a den and a family room with a fireplace. This level could also house extra bedrooms or an in-law suite.

Features:

- Foyer: On the main level, this foyer spills into a tray ceiling living room with a fireplace and an arched, floor-to-ceiling window wall.

- Family Room: Up from the foyer, a hall introduces this vaulted room with built-in media center and French doors that open to an expansive railed deck.

- Kitchen: Featured in this gourmet kitchen are a food-preparation island with a salad sink, double-door pantry, corner-window sink, and breakfast bay.

- Master Bedroom: The vaulted master bedroom opens to the deck, and the deluxe bath offers a raised whirlpool spa and a double-bowl vanity under a skylight.

- Bedroom: Two family bedrooms share a compartmented bathroom.

Rear Elevation

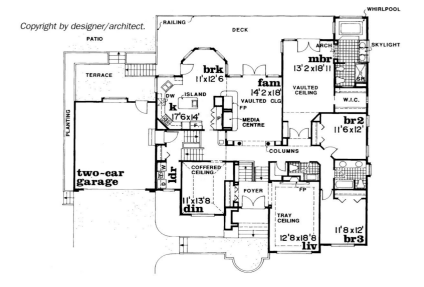

Copyright by designer/architect.

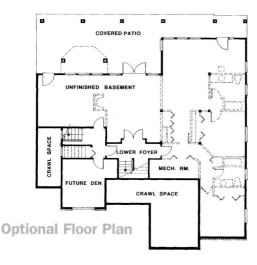

Optional Floor Plan

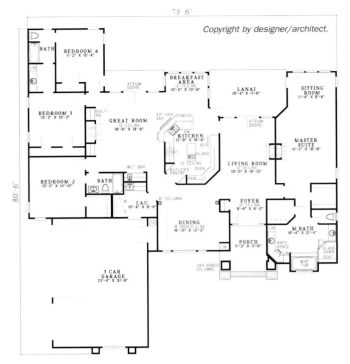

Images provided by designer/architect.

Plan #151057

Dimensions: 73'6" W x 80'6" D

Levels: 1

Square Footage: 2,951

Bedrooms: 4

Bathrooms: 3

Foundation: Crawl space, slab, or basement

CompleteCost List Available: Yes

Price Category: F

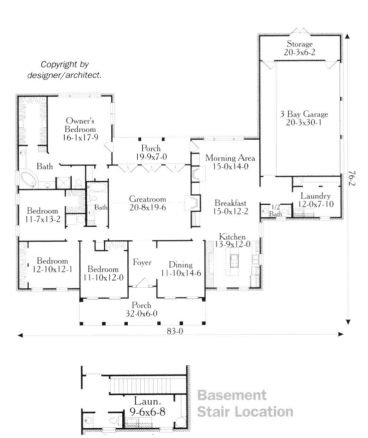

Images provided by designer/architect.

Plan #311053

Dimensions: 83' W x 76'2" D

Levels: 1

Square Footage: 2,925

Bedrooms: 4

Bathrooms: 2½

Foundation: Crawl space, slab, or basement

Material List Available: Yes

Price Category: F

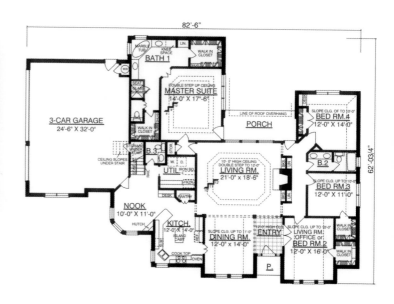

Plan #371095

Dimensions: 82'6" W x 62'0 3/4" D

Levels: 1

Square Footage: 2,725

Bedrooms: 4

Bathrooms: 2½

Foundation: Crawl space, slab, or basement

Material List Available: No

Price Category: F

Images provided by designer/architect.

CAD FILE AVAILABLE

Bonus Area Floor Plan

Copyright by designer/architect.

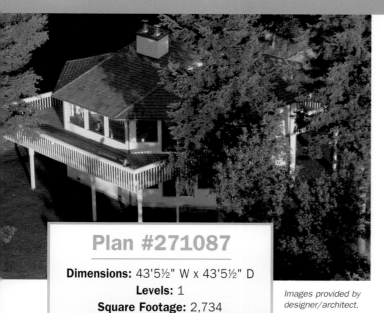

Plan #271087

Dimensions: 43'5½" W x 43'5½" D

Levels: 1

Square Footage: 2,734

Main Level Sq. Ft.: 1,564

Lower Level Sq. Ft.: 1,170

Bedrooms: 4

Bathrooms: 3

Foundation: Crawl space or walkout basement

Material List Available: No

Price Category: F

Images provided by designer/architect.

Main Level Floor Plan

Basement Level Floor Plan

Copyright by designer/architect.

Plan #151015

Dimensions: 72'4" W x 48'4" D
Levels: 2
Square Footage: 2,789
Main Level Sq. Ft.: 1,977
Upper Level Sq. Ft.: 812
Bedrooms: 4
Bathrooms: 3
Foundation: Crawl space, slab, or basement
CompleteCost List Available: Yes
Price Category: F

Images provided by designer/architect.

The spacious kitchen that opens to the breakfast room and the hearth room make this family home ideal for entertaining.

Features:

- Great Room: The fireplace will make a cozy winter focal point in this versatile space.

- Hearth Room: Enjoy the built-in entertainment center, built-in shelving, and fireplace here.

- Dining Room: A swing door leading to the kitchen is as attractive as it is practical.

- Study: A private bath and walk-in closet make this room an ideal spot for guests when needed.

- Kitchen: An island work area, a computer desk, and an eat-in bar add convenience and utility.

- Master Bath: Two vanities, two walk-in closets, a shower with a seat, and a whirlpool tub highlight this private space.

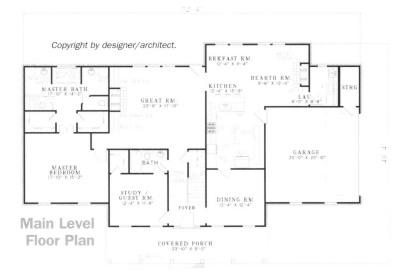

Main Level Floor Plan

Upper Level Floor Plan

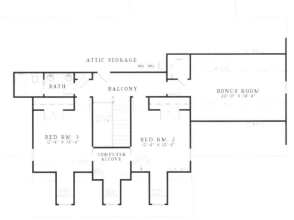

Plan #211011

Dimensions: 84' W x 54' D
Levels: 1
Square Footage: 2,791
Bedrooms: 3 or 4
Bathrooms: 2
Foundation: Slab or crawl space
Materials List Available: Yes
Price Category: F

SMARTtip

Types of Decks

Ground-level decks resemble a low platform and are best for flat locations. They can be the most economical type to build because they don't require stairs.

Raised decks can rise just a few steps up or meet the second story of a house. Lifted high on post supports, they adapt well to uneven or sloped locations.

Multilevel decks feature two or more stories and are connected by stairways or ramps. They can follow the contours of a sloped lot, unifying the deck with the outdoors.

Images provided by designer/architect.

Plenty of room plus an open, flexible floor plan make this a home that will adapt to your needs.

Features:

- Ceiling Height: 8 ft. unless otherwise noted.

- Living Room: This distinctive room features a 12-ft. ceiling and is designed so that it can also serve as a master suite with a sitting room.

- Family Room: The whole family will want to gather in this large, inviting family room.

- Morning Room: The family room blends

into this sunny spot, which is perfect for informal family meals.

- Kitchen: This spacious kitchen offers a smart layout. It is also contiguous to the family room.

- Master Suite: You'll look forward to the end of the day when you can enjoy this master suite. It includes a huge, luxurious master bath with two large walk-in closets and two vanity sinks.

- Optional Bedroom: This optional fourth bedroom is located so that it can easily serve as a library, den, office, or music room.

Copyright by designer/architect.

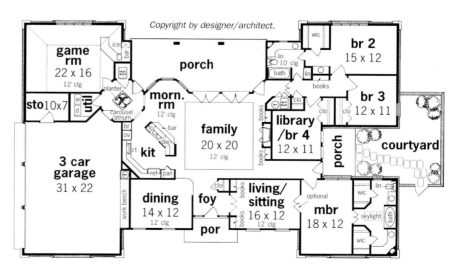

Plan #241050

Dimensions: 79'9" W x 49'9" D
Levels: 1
Square Footage: 2,498
Bedrooms: 3
Bathrooms: 2½
Foundation: Slab
Material List Available: No
Price Category: E

This brick ranch will be an elegant addition to any neighborhood.

Features:

- Great Room: Enter the home through the foyer, and you'll find yourself in this great room. The large gathering area boasts a coffered ceiling and a cozy fireplace.

- Kitchen: This island kitchen has an abundance of counter space and storage for the needs of the family. The raised bar is open to the great room and the breakfast nook.

- Master Suite: The split floor plan provides privacy in this area. The coffered ceiling adds to the elegance in the sleeping area. The master bath boasts his and her walk-in closets, dual vanities, a separate shower, and a compartmentalized lavatory.

- Secondary Bedrooms: Two large bedrooms with ample closet space share the second full bathroom.

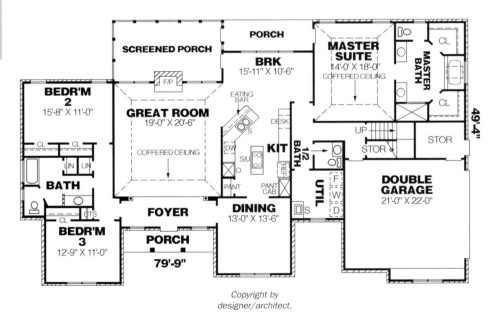

Copyright by designer/architect.

Plan #371122

Dimensions: 88'2" W x 63'2½" D
Levels: 1
Square Footage: 2,774
Bedrooms: 3
Bathrooms: 2½
Foundation: Crawl space, slab, or basement
Material List Available: No
Price Category: F

Images provided by designer/architect.

Bonus Area Floor Plan

Copyright by designer/architect.

Plan #311057

Dimensions: 68'2" W x 67'6" D
Levels: 1
Square Footage: 2,424
Bedrooms: 3
Bathrooms: 2½
Foundation: Crawl space, slab, or basement
Material List Available: Yes
Price Category: E

Images provided by designer/architect.

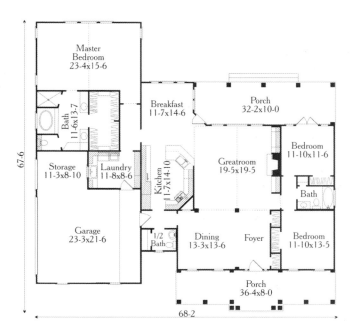

Copyright by designer/architect.

Plan #221001

Dimensions: 87' W x 60' D
Levels: 1
Square Footage: 2,600
Bedrooms: 3
Bathrooms: 2½
Foundation: Basement
Materials List Available: No
Price Category: F

Images provided by designer/architect.

Rear Elevation

Kitchen

Plan #141021

Dimensions: 70'10" W x 78'9" D
Levels: 1
Square Footage: 2,614
Bedrooms: 3
Bathrooms: 2½
Foundation: Basement
Materials List Available: Yes
Price Category: F

Images provided by designer/architect.

Living Room

Dining Room

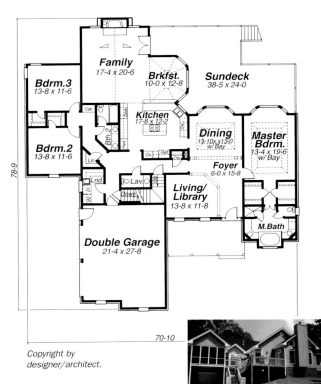

Copyright by designer/architect.

Rear View

Plan #321005

Dimensions: 69' W x 53'8" D
Levels: 1
Square Footage: 2,483
Bedrooms: 3
Bathrooms: 2
Foundation: Basement
Materials List Available: Yes
Price Category: E

You'll love the grand feeling of this home, which combines with the very practical features that make living in it a pleasure.

Features:

- Porch: The open brick arches and Palladian door set the tone for this magnificent home.

- Great Room: An alcove for the entertainment center and vaulted ceiling show the care that went into designing this room.

- Dining Room: A tray ceiling sets off the formality of this large room.

- Kitchen: The layout in this room is designed to make your work patterns more efficient and to save you steps and time.

- Study: This quiet room can be a wonderful refuge, or you can use it for a fourth bedroom if you wish.

- Master Suite: Made for relaxing at the end of the day, this suite will pamper you with luxuries.

Images provided by designer/architect.

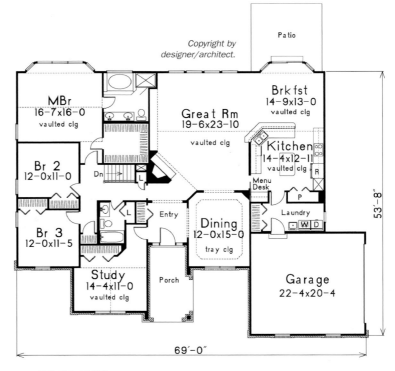

Copyright by designer/architect.

SMARTtip

Art in Pools

The tiled walls and floor of a pool make great canvases for art, so incorporate a serious or whimsical design. Also, make the stairs wide and shallow to form a wading area for kids.

Plan #211010

Dimensions: 81' W x 84' D
Levels: 1
Square Footage: 2,503
Bedrooms: 3
Bathrooms: 2½
Foundation: Slab
Materials List Available: Yes
Price Category: E

A well-designed floor plan makes maximum use of space and creates convenience and comfort.

Features:

- Ceiling Height: 10 ft. unless otherwise noted.

- Living Room: A stepped ceiling gives this living room special architectural interest. There's a full-service wet bar designed to handle parties of any size. When the weather gets warm, step out of the living room into a lovely screened rear porch.

- Master Bedroom: You'll love unwinding at the end of a busy day in this master suite. It's located away from the other bedrooms for more privacy.

- Study: This charming study adjoins the master bedroom. It's the perfect quiet spot to get some work done, surf the internet, or pay the bills.

SMARTtip

Deck Railings

Install caps and post finials to your railings. A rail cap protects the cut ends of the posts from the weather. Finials add another decorative layer to your design, and the styles are endless—ball, chamfered, grooved, and top hat are a few.

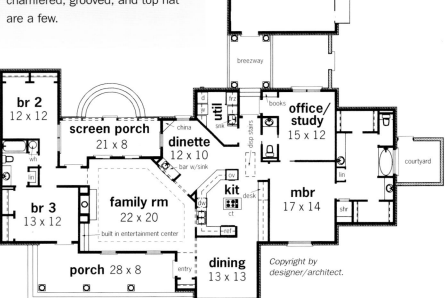

Copyright by designer/architect.

Plan #321004

Dimensions: 91'8" W x 62'4" D
Levels: 1
Square Footage: 2,808
Bedrooms: 3
Bathrooms: 2½
Foundation: Basement
Materials List Available: Yes
Price Category: F

You'll love the sophistication of this design, with its three porches and elegance at every turn.

Features:

- Entry: This impressive space welcomes guests into the living room on one side and the dining room on the other.

- Living Room: This spacious room will be a family favorite, especially in warm weather when you can use the adjoining porch as an outdoor extension of this area.

- Dining Room: Decorate this room to highlight its slightly formal feeling or to create a more casual ambiance for large family dinners.

- Kitchen: The family cooks will appreciate the thought that went into designing the convenient counter space and generous storage areas here.

- Master Suite: A vaulted ceiling, bath with a corner tub, double vanities, walk-in closet, and secluded screened porch make this area a joy.

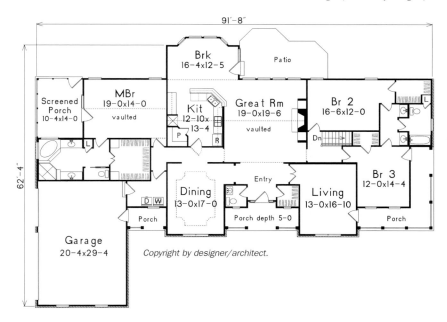

Copyright by designer/architect.

SMARTtip

Ornaments in a Garden

Placement is everything with ornaments in a garden. Some elements are best sitting by themselves. Others are better when they are part of a cohesive whole, perhaps placed in the greenery at a corner or flanking a structure.

Images provided by designer/architect.

Plan #371087

Dimensions: 88'2" W x 62'10" D

Levels: 1

Square Footage: 2,643

Bedrooms: 3

Bathrooms: 2½

Foundation: Crawl space, slab, or basement

Materials List Available: No

Price Category: F

This beautiful country home has a warm look that is all its own.

Features:

- Dining Room: Once inside you will find a tiled entry that leads into this elegant room, with its 11-ft.-high ceiling.

- Living Room: This large gathering area has a 10-ft.-high ceiling, built-in bookcases, and a country fireplace.

- Kitchen: This island kitchen, with a raised bar, is open to the breakfast nook and meets the garage entrance.

- Master Suite: This suite, located in the rear of the home, features a private bathroom, large walk-in closet, marble tub, and double vanities.

- Bedrooms: Two secondary bedrooms have large closets and share a hall bathroom.

Copyright by designer/architect.

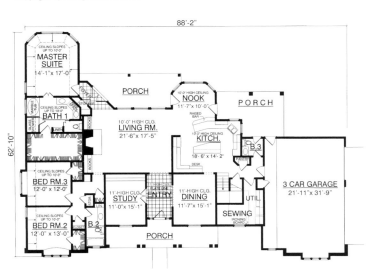

Rear Elevation

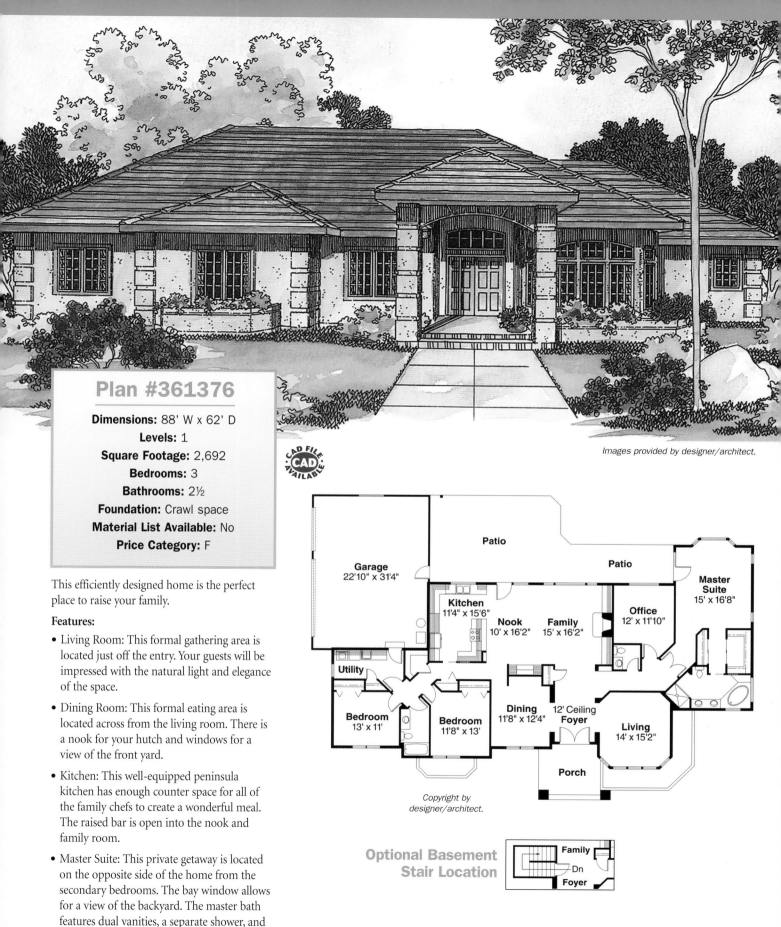

Plan #361376

Dimensions: 88' W x 62' D
Levels: 1
Square Footage: 2,692
Bedrooms: 3
Bathrooms: 2½
Foundation: Crawl space
Material List Available: No
Price Category: F

CAD FILE AVAILABLE — CAD

Images provided by designer/architect.

This efficiently designed home is the perfect place to raise your family.

Features:

- Living Room: This formal gathering area is located just off the entry. Your guests will be impressed with the natural light and elegance of the space.

- Dining Room: This formal eating area is located across from the living room. There is a nook for your hutch and windows for a view of the front yard.

- Kitchen: This well-equipped peninsula kitchen has enough counter space for all of the family chefs to create a wonderful meal. The raised bar is open into the nook and family room.

- Master Suite: This private getaway is located on the opposite side of the home from the secondary bedrooms. The bay window allows for a view of the backyard. The master bath features dual vanities, a separate shower, and a large bathtub.

Garage 22'10" x 31'4"

Patio

Patio

Master Suite 15' x 16'8"

Kitchen 11'4" x 15'6"

Nook 10' x 16'2"

Family 15' x 16'2"

Office 12' x 11'10"

Utility

Bedroom 13' x 11'

Bedroom 11'8" x 13'

Dining 11'8" x 12'4"

12' Ceiling Foyer

Living 14' x 15'2"

Porch

Copyright by designer/architect.

Optional Basement Stair Location

Family

Dn

Foyer

Plan #441010

Dimensions: 108' W x 59' D
Levels: 1
Square Footage: 2,973
Bedrooms: 4
Bathrooms: 4½
Foundation: Crawl space;
slab or basement available for fee
Materials List Available: No
Price Category: F

Images provided by designer/architect.

Features:

- Great Room: This gathering area features a large bay window and a fireplace flanked with built-ins. The vaulted ceiling adds to the large feel of the area.

- Kitchen: This large island kitchen features a walk-in pantry and a built-in desk. The breakfast nook has access to the patio.

- Master Suite: This retreat features a vaulted ceiling in the sleeping area and access to the patio. The master bath boasts dual vanities, a stand-up shower, a spa tub, and a very large walk-in closet.

- Bedrooms: Two family bedrooms, each with its own private bathroom, have large closets.

Bordering on estate-sized, this plan borrows elements from Norman, Mediterranean, and English architecture.

CAD FILE AVAILABLE

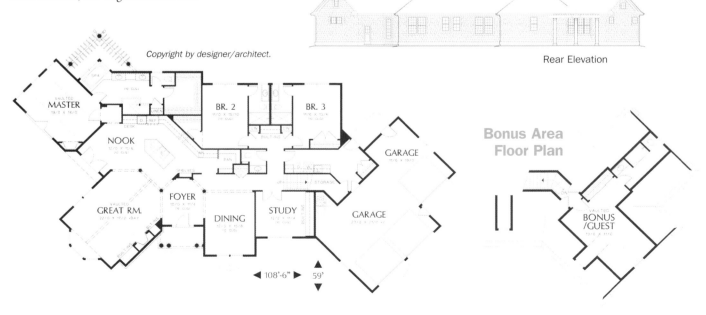

Copyright by designer/architect.

Rear Elevation

Bonus Area Floor Plan

Plan #111001

Dimensions: 66'8" W x 76'11" D

Levels: 1

Square Footage: 2,832

Bedrooms: 4

Bathrooms: 2½

Foundation: Crawl space or slab

Materials List Available: No

Price Category: F

Images provided by designer/architect.

Copyright by designer/architect.

Plan #361498

Dimensions: 88' W x 56'6" D

Levels: 1

Square Footage: 2,778

Bedrooms: 3

Bathrooms: 2½

Foundation: Crawl space

Material List Available: No

Price Category: F

Images provided by designer/architect.

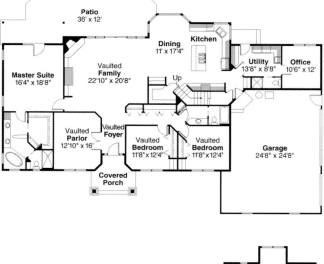

Bonus Area Floor Plan

Copyright by designer/architect.

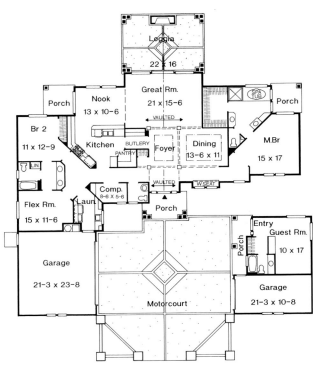

Images provided by designer/architect.

Copyright by designer/architect.

Plan #231002

Dimensions: 79' W x 86' D
Levels: 1
Square Footage: 2,468
Bedrooms: 3
Bathrooms: 3½
Foundation: Crawl space
Material List Available: No
Price Category: E

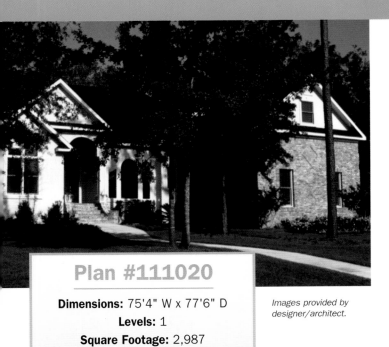

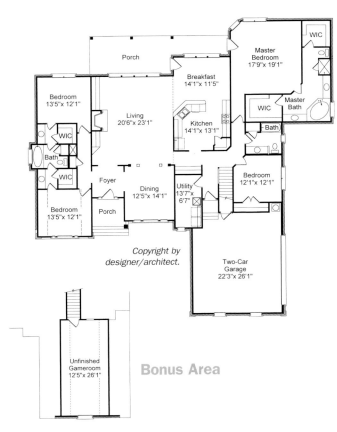

Copyright by designer/architect.

Images provided by designer/architect.

Plan #111020

Dimensions: 75'4" W x 77'6" D
Levels: 1
Square Footage: 2,987
Bedrooms: 4
Bathrooms: 3
Foundation: Slab
Materials List Available: No
Price Category: F

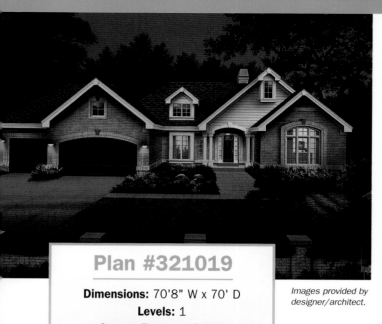

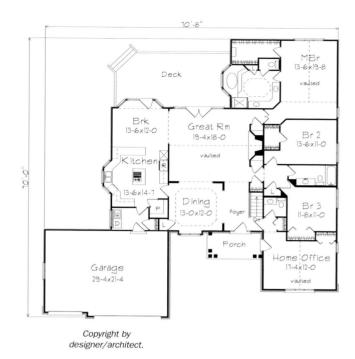

Images provided by designer/architect.

Copyright by designer/architect.

Plan #321019

Dimensions: 70'8" W x 70' D

Levels: 1

Square Footage: 2,452

Bedrooms: 4

Bathrooms: 2½

Foundation: Basement

Materials List Available: Yes

Price Category: E

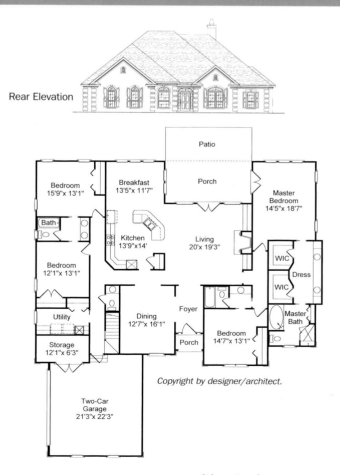

Rear Elevation

Images provided by designer/architect.

Copyright by designer/architect.

Plan #111018

Dimensions: 67' W x 79' D

Levels: 1

Square Footage: 2,745

Bedrooms: 4

Bathrooms: 3½

Foundation: Basement

Materials List Available: No

Price Category: F

Plan #241051

Dimensions: 64'7" W x 68'9" D
Levels: 1
Square Footage: 2,447
Bedrooms: 3
Bathrooms: 2
Foundation: Slab
Material List Available: No
Price Category: E

Images provided by designer/architect.

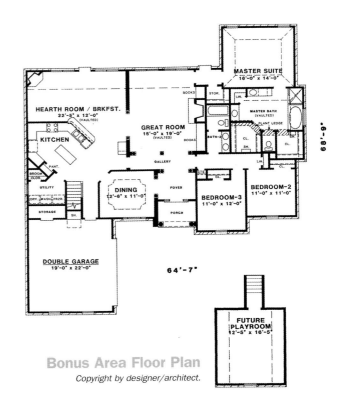

Bonus Area Floor Plan
Copyright by designer/architect.

Plan #271004

Dimensions: 73' W x 56'4" D
Levels: 1
Square Footage: 2,472
Bedrooms: 4
Bathrooms: 2
Foundation: Basement
Material List Available: Yes
Price Category: E

Images provided by designer/architect.

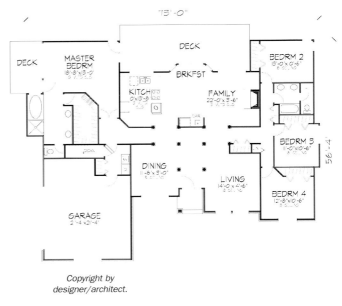

Copyright by designer/architect.

Main Level Floor Plan

Images provided by designer/architect.

CAD FILE AVAILABLE

Plan #101035

Dimensions: 71'4" W x 74'8" D
Levels: 1
Square Footage: 2,461
Bedrooms: 3
Bathrooms: 3½
Foundation: Basement
Material List Available: No
Price Category: E

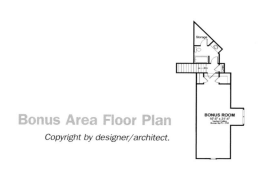

Bonus Area Floor Plan

Copyright by designer/architect.

Plan #121208

Dimensions: 68' W x 65' D
Levels: 1
Square Footage: 2,598
Bedrooms: 3
Bathrooms: 2½
Foundation: Slab; basement for fee
Material List Available: Yes
Price Category: E

Images provided by designer/architect.

CAD FILE AVAILABLE

Optional Dining Room

Optional Stairs

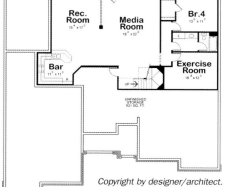

Bonus Area Floor Plan

Optional Basement Level Floor Plan

Copyright by designer/architect.

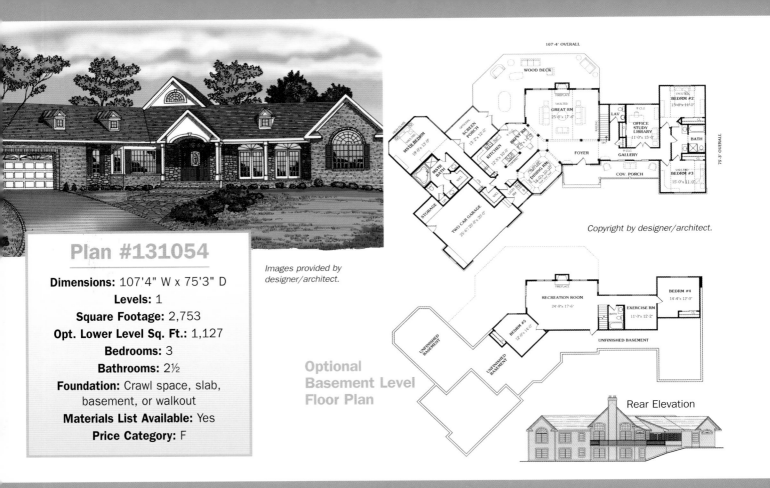

Plan #131054

Dimensions: 107'4" W x 75'3" D
Levels: 1
Square Footage: 2,753
Opt. Lower Level Sq. Ft.: 1,127
Bedrooms: 3
Bathrooms: 2½
Foundation: Crawl space, slab, basement, or walkout
Materials List Available: Yes
Price Category: F

Images provided by designer/architect.

Copyright by designer/architect.

Optional Basement Level Floor Plan

Rear Elevation

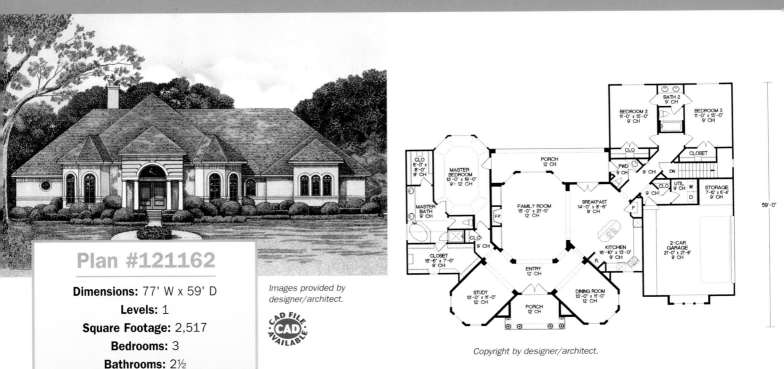

Plan #121162

Dimensions: 77' W x 59' D
Levels: 1
Square Footage: 2,517
Bedrooms: 3
Bathrooms: 2½
Foundation: Slab
Materials List Available: Yes
Price Category: E

Images provided by designer/architect.

CAD FILE AVAILABLE

Copyright by designer/architect.

Plan #161095

Dimensions: 59' W x 49'8" D
Levels: 1
Square Footage: 3,620
Main Level Sq. Ft.: 2,068
Basement Level Sq. Ft.: 1,552
Bedrooms: 3
Bathrooms: 3
Foundation: Walkout basement
Material List Available: No
Price Category: H

This elegant ranch design has everything your family could want in a home.

Features:

- Dining Room: This column-accented formal area has a sloped ceiling and is open to the great room.

- Great Room: Featuring a cozy fireplace, this large gathering area offers a view of the backyard.

- Kitchen: This fully equipped island kitchen has everything the chef in the family could want.

- Master Suite: Located on the main level for privacy, this suite has a sloped ceiling in the sleeping area. The master bath boasts a whirlpool tub, a walk-in closet, and dual vanities.

CAD FILE AVAILABLE

Images provided by designer/architect.

This home, as shown in the photograph, may differ from the actual blueprints. For more detailed information, please check the floor plans carefully.

Main Level Floor Plan

Rear View

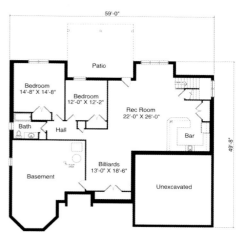

Lower Level Floor Plan

Copyright by designer/architect.

Plan #441012

Dimensions: 65' W x 55' D
Levels: 1
Square Footage: 3,682
Main Level Sq. Ft.: 2,192
Basement Level Sq. Ft.: 1,490
Bedrooms: 4
Bathrooms: 4
Foundation: Slab
Materials List Available: No
Price Category: H

Images provided by designer/architect.

Accommodating a site that slopes to the rear, this home is not only good-looking but practical.

Features:

- Den: Just off the foyer is this cozy space, complete with built-ins.
- Great Room: This vaulted gathering area features a lovely fireplace, a built-in media center, and a view of the back yard.
- Kitchen: This island kitchen is ready to handle the daily needs of your family or aid in entertaining your guests.
- Lower Level: Adding even more livability to the home, this floor contains the games room with media center and corner fireplace, two more bedrooms (each with a full bathroom), and the wide covered patio.

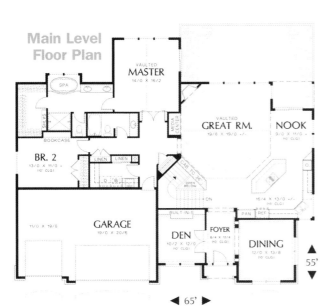

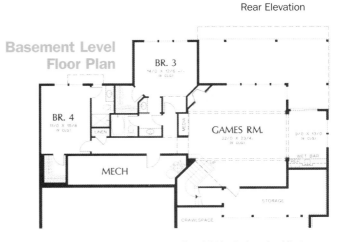

Rear Elevation

Copyright by designer/architect.

Plan #161100

Dimensions: 89' W x 59'2" D
Levels: 1
Square Footage: 5,377
Main Level Sq. Ft.: 2,961
Basement Level Sq. Ft.: 2,416
Bedrooms: 3
Bathrooms: 2 full, 2 half
Foundation: Walkout;
basement for fee
Material List Available: No
Price Category: J

This luxury home is perfect for you and your family.

CAD FILE AVAILABLE

Images provided by designer/architect.

Features:

- **Foyer:** This beautiful foyer showcases the two-sided fireplace, which warms its space, as well as that of the great room.

- **Gathering Areas:** The kitchen, breakfast area, and hearth room will quickly become a favorite gathering area, what with the warmth of the fireplace and easy access to a covered porch. Expansive windows with transoms create a light and airy atmosphere.

- **Master Suite:** This suite makes the most of its circular sitting area and deluxe dressing room with platform whirlpool tub, dual vanities, commode room with closet, and two-person shower.

- **Lower Level:** This lower level is finished with additional bedrooms and areas dedicated to entertaining, such as the wet bar, billiards area, media room, and exercise room

Rear View

Copyright by designer/architect.

Main Level Floor Plan

Basement Level Floor Plan

Plan #481033

Dimensions: 78' W x 73' D
Levels: 1
Square Footage: 5,667
Main Level Sq. Ft.: 3,042
Lower Level Sq. Ft.: 2,625
Bedrooms: 4
Bathrooms: 4 full, 2 half
Foundation: Walkout basement
Material List Available: No
Price Category: J

Images provided by designer/architect.

Basement Level Floor Plan

Copyright by designer/architect.

Plan #481020

Dimensions: 74'8" W x 54' D
Levels: 1
Square Footage: 3,141
Main Level Sq. Ft.: 1,794
Lower Level Sq. Ft.: 1,347
Bedrooms: 5
Bathrooms: 3
Foundation: Walkout basement
Material List Available: No
Price Category: G

Images provided by designer/architect.

Basement Level Floor Plan

Copyright by designer/architect.

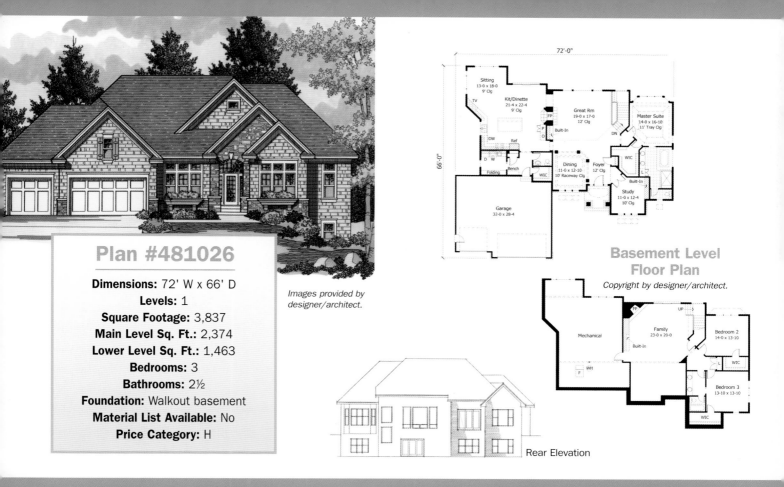

Plan #481026

Dimensions: 72' W x 66' D
Levels: 1
Square Footage: 3,837
Main Level Sq. Ft.: 2,374
Lower Level Sq. Ft.: 1,463
Bedrooms: 3
Bathrooms: 2½
Foundation: Walkout basement
Material List Available: No
Price Category: H

Images provided by designer/architect.

Basement Level Floor Plan
Copyright by designer/architect.

Rear Elevation

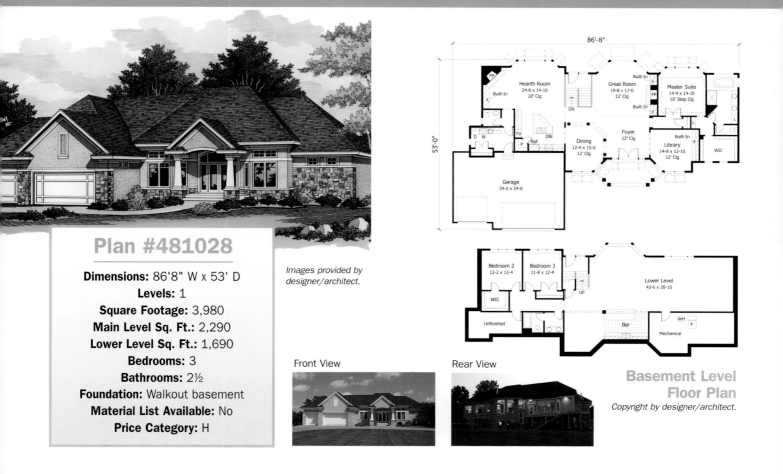

Plan #481028

Dimensions: 86'8" W x 53' D
Levels: 1
Square Footage: 3,980
Main Level Sq. Ft.: 2,290
Lower Level Sq. Ft.: 1,690
Bedrooms: 3
Bathrooms: 2½
Foundation: Walkout basement
Material List Available: No
Price Category: H

Images provided by designer/architect.

Front View

Rear View

Basement Level Floor Plan
Copyright by designer/architect.

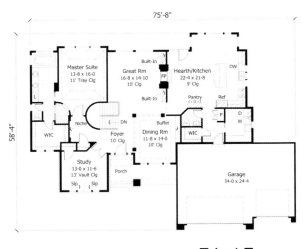

75'-8"

58'-4"

Master Suite
13-8 x 16-0
11' Tray Clg

Great Rm
16-8 x 14-10
10' Clg

Built-In

Hearth/Kitchen
22-4 x 21-8
9' Clg

DW

Built-In

Pantry

Ref

WIC

Niche

DN

Foyer
10' Clg

Buffet

Dining Rm
11-8 x 14-0
10' Clg

WIC

P

D
W

WIC

Study
13-0 x 11-6
13' Vault Clg

Porch

Garage
34-0 x 24-4

Slp   Slp

Images provided by designer/architect.

Plan #481029

Dimensions: 75'8" W x 58'4" D
Levels: 1
Square Footage: 4,048
Main Level Sq. Ft.: 2,147
Lower Level Sq. Ft.: 1,901
Bedrooms: 4
Bathrooms: 3½
Foundation: Walkout basement
Material List Available: No
Price Category: I

Basement Level Floor Plan

Copyright by designer/architect.

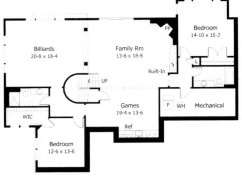

Billiards
20-8 x 18-4

Family Rm
13-6 x 18-8

FP

Bedroom
14-10 x 15-2

Built-In

UP

Games
19-4 x 13-6

F   WH   Mechanical

WIC

Ref

Bedroom
12-6 x 13-6

Plan #391049

Dimensions: 78' W x 52'4" D
Levels: 1
Square Footage: 4,064
Bedrooms: 4
Bathrooms: 3
Foundation: Basement
Material List Available: Yes
Price Category: E

Images provided by designer/architect.

whirlpool

Master Suite
15-0 x 16-0

Deck

Hearth Rm
15-6 x 12-0

3-sided fireplace

Brkfst
12-0 x 13-0

Living Rm
20-0 x 18-10
11'-9" clg.

Kitchen
15-6 x 17-0

Ldry

DN

built-ins

railing

Study / Br 2
13-0 x 12-0

Foyer

Dining Rm
13-0 x 11-2

Garage
31-8 x 21-8

Basement Level Floor Plan

Copyright by designer/architect.

Home Theater
24-0 x 17-0

2-sided fireplace

Br 3
13-8 x 13-10

Br 4
13-0 x 12-4

wet bar

Rec. Rm
20-8 x 15-0

Storage
18-11 x 8-6

W/H

furn.

S

Storage
22-2 x 15-10

UP

Utility
13-0 x 25-10

Images provided by designer/architect.

Plan #481031

Dimensions: 98' W x 72' D
Levels: 1
Square Footage: 4,707
Main Level Sq. Ft.: 2,518
Lower Level Sq. Ft.: 2,189
Bedrooms: 4
Bathrooms: 3½
Foundation: Walkout basement
Material List Available: No
Price Category: I

The stucco-and-stone siding on this home makes it stand out in the neighborhood.

Features:

- Great Room: This large entertaining area features a built-in media center and a see-through fireplace into the hearth and kitchen area. The large bay windows allow an abundance of natural light to illuminate the 12-ft.-high space.

- Kitchen: This open island kitchen boasts an eating area with sliding glass doors leading to a deck. The space is open into the hearth area, and its fireplace adds warmth to the whole space.

- Master Suite: Located on the main floor for privacy and convenience, this retreat boasts a stepped ceiling in the sleeping area. The master bath features dual vanities, a separate shower, and a compartmentalized lavatory.

- Lower Level: This space features three bedrooms, two full bathrooms, the family room, and the bar and game area. The fireplace in the family room will be a cozy place to relax.

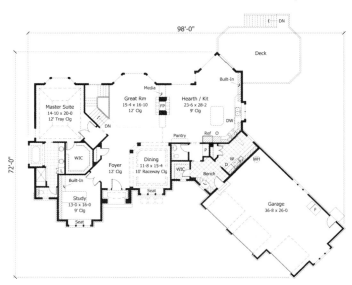

Basement Level Floor Plan

Copyright by designer/architect.

Rear Elevation

Plan #321016

Dimensions: 88' W x 70'8" D
Levels: 1
Square Footage: 3,814
Main Level Sq. Ft.: 3,566
Lower Level Sq. Ft.: 248
Bedrooms: 3
Bathrooms: 2½
Foundation: Daylight basement
Materials List Available: Yes
Price Category: H

Images provided by designer/architect.

Rear View

If you're looking for a design that makes the most of a sloped site, you'll love this gorgeous home.

Features:

- **Great Room:** This fabulous room has a vaulted ceiling, sunken floor, and masonry fireplace, and it opens to the two-story atrium.

- **Dining Room:** Both this room and the living room opposite are naturally lit by two-story arched windows.

- **Kitchen:** Open to the hearth room and breakfast room, this kitchen has a central island, too.

- **Hearth Room/Breakfast Room:** A vaulted ceiling, corner fireplace, and door to one deck highlight this angled space.

- **Master Suite:** The bedroom has a coffered ceiling, corner fireplace, door to one deck, and huge walk-in closet. The bath includes a step-down tub with windows and a fireplace, a linen closet, a separate shower, and two vanities.

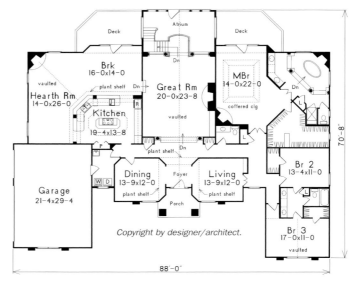

Copyright by designer/architect.

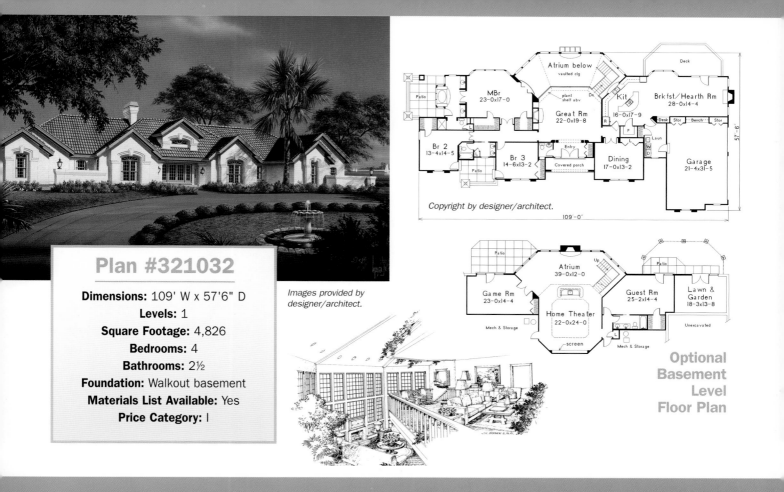

Plan #321032

Dimensions: 109' W x 57'6" D
Levels: 1
Square Footage: 4,826
Bedrooms: 4
Bathrooms: 2½
Foundation: Walkout basement
Materials List Available: Yes
Price Category: I

Images provided by designer/architect.

Optional Basement Level Floor Plan

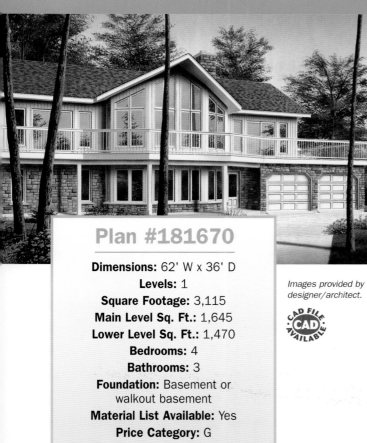

Plan #181670

Dimensions: 62' W x 36' D
Levels: 1
Square Footage: 3,115
Main Level Sq. Ft.: 1,645
Lower Level Sq. Ft.: 1,470
Bedrooms: 4
Bathrooms: 3
Foundation: Basement or walkout basement
Material List Available: Yes
Price Category: G

Images provided by designer/architect.

CAD FILE AVAILABLE

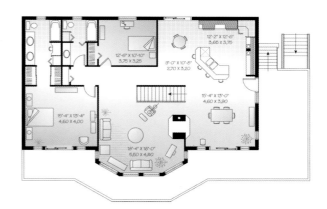

Basement Level Floor Plan

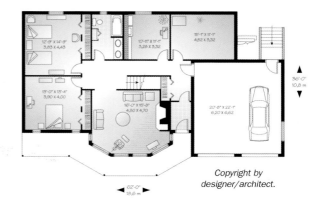

Copyright by designer/architect.

This article was reprinted from *The New Smart Approach to Home Decorating* (Creative Homeowner 2003).

The Right Light

A lighting plan plays a major role in any well-designed home. Not only is a well-lighted house safer and more functional, it also shows off colors, forms, and textures to their best advantage. A lighting plan should include the available natural light at different times of the day and the many different types of artificial light available.

The quality of the light we live with also affects our sense of well being. We learn more quickly and work better in bright, warm light. When we want to rest, dim light relaxes us. All of these considerations point to the importance of thoughtfully planning lighting for the home. Whether you decide to devise a lighting scheme yourself or call in a lighting specialist, remember: good interior designers take advantage of the transformational power of light and so can you. In this chapter, you'll learn how to use light to manipulate the perception of space, casting it up to make a low ceiling seem higher or washing the walls with it to make a small room appear spacious. You'll also learn how to use light in a painterly fashion to emphasize forms or objects. What could be more dramatic than the shadow play of leaves on a nearby wall or ceiling, produced by aiming a small spotlight upwards from underneath a bold, sculptural plant?

Today, at the flick of a switch, you can illuminate your home inside—and out. You can program and store entire lighting schemes thanks to the latest technology. On command, create bright light for work, then change the mood to cozy when you want to relax, or adjust it all over again for TV viewing. Set your lights on timers for safety and security, or activate them by remote control.

Left: When designing a room, be sure to consider the natural light that the room receives. Light levels change with the time of day and the change of the seasons.

Natural Light

Any discussion about lighting your home has to begin with natural light. To the human eye, the desirable norm is sunlight. Part of its appeal is its variety. Consider the clear illumination on a cloudless mountaintop. Compare that to the diffused light on a misty morning or the intense brightness on a tropical beach. Then there's the changeability of sunlight between a cool rainy day, a clear winter afternoon, and a full summer blaze, or the contrast between the color of sunlight at noon and the way it appears as afternoon wears into evening.

The amount and quality of natural light a room receives depends on the size of its windows and its orientation with regard to the sun. South-facing windows get the lion's share of direct sunlight for most of the day. East-facing rooms benefit from early mornings, while rooms that face west are sunny in the afternoon. Because its back is to the sun, a north-facing room receives only indirect natural light and tends to be cool and dim.

When you are renovating or redecorating a room, always look at the existing space and take the seasons, time of day, and orientation of the windows into consideration. Sometimes making a window bigger, or adding another one, doesn't make a room brighter. If the window's siting is toward the north, the room will just get colder. You can make a breakfast nook cheerier with a window that faces east, but don't try to take a late afternoon nap in a room with west-facing windows, unless you can control the light with shades, blinds, or lined curtains.

The natural light in the room will affect any tasks you perform as well. Never arrange furniture, such as a desk or worktable, so that you are facing directly into bright sunlight. But be careful about having your back to a window. This can create shadows on your work surface. Ideally, follow the old

For complicated situations, you may want to consult with a lighting design professional, or you may feel comfortable devising a plan yourself with the help of an electrician. In any case, you need to understand something of the basic science of light, how it is measured, and its effect on color. To make wise choices from among the wide variety of lighting types available, compare them on a level playing field. That's what lighting measurements can help you do.

You'll also need to learn about the types of lighting, the different kinds of bulbs and fixtures, in addition to the terminology. This will help you with planning, and will make you more effective when discussing ideas with experts and sales staff. For instance, many of us use the words "fixture" and "lamp" interchangeably, but when lighting professionals speak of "lamps" they are talking about "bulbs." Learn to speak the language.

Once you have prepared yourself, you can begin sketching out a plan that can cover areas within one room and to create a flow from one space to another.

axiom that recommends "light coming from over the left shoulder." By charting the light, and arranging your room and selecting window treatments accordingly, you can avoid problems.

Types of Artificial Light

Artificial light picks up where natural light leaves off. It is the illumination that you provide, and unlike natural light, you can also fine-tune it. In the daytime, artifi- cial light augments natural light; after dark, it compensates for daylight com- pletely. The key to devising a versatile plan that can change with each activity, as well as with the time of day or the weather, begins with knowing about the different types of artificial light. Here's a review:

Ambient Light

Ambient, or general, light is illumina- tion that fills an entire room. Its source is sometimes an overhead fixture, but the light itself does not appear to come from any one specific direction. Ambient light surrounds a room gener- ally. An obvious example of ambient light is ceiling-hung fluorescent strips in the average office environment. A cover- ing over the strips hides the source and diffuses the light throughout the room.

A wall sconce is another good example of ambient light. The fixture washes light up the wall for an overall glow. The wall reflects the light, which diminishes the

Above: Choose artificial light sources to solve problems. Here a bedside lamp fills two needs: it provides general illumination and serves as a reading lamp.

appearance of a single source. While you can tell the light is coming from the sconce, the overall glow is diffused.

The key to good ambient lighting is making it inconspicuous. Ambient light is merely the backdrop for the rest of the room, not the main feature. It changes with the surrounding environment—always providing light but never becoming obvious. For example, ambient lighting used during the day should blend in with the amount of natural light entering the room. At night, you should be able to diminish the light level so that it doesn't contrast jarringly against the darkness outside.

Task Light

As its name implies, task lighting is purely functional. It illuminates a specific area for a particular job, such as chopping food on a kitchen counter, laboring over a woodworking project, or applying makeup.

Theatrical lighting around vanity mirrors is an excellent example of task lighting. It provides cross-illumination while avoiding the distorting shadows often seen with over-head lighting. Task lighting should always be included in any room where specific functions take place, but its use should be optional. In other words, you can turn it on when you need it and keep it off at other times. Task lights should not be on the same switch with the fixture that provides general illumination. Using both types simultaneously creates a harsh, too-bright effect.

Accent Light

Often overlooked, but always the most dramatic, accent lighting draws attention to a particular element in the room, such as a handsome architectural feature or a work of art. Accent lighting makes a room come alive. It creates a mood. It shapes space. Lights recessed into a soffit above a handsome kitchen countertop cast a downward glow of illumination that offsets the counter without spilling light into the rest of the room. Cove lighting over a bathtub shimmers above the water and delineates a bathing area dramatically.

Without accent lighting, there may be light, but no focus, no character, no show business. With it, a design becomes exciting, theatrical, and rich.

Decorative Light

While accent lighting draws attention to another object or surface, decorative lighting draws attention to itself. It can be kinetic, in the form of candles or flames in a fireplace, or static, such as fixed wall candelabra. It is there to grab attention. It is lighting for the pure sake of lighting.

Because decorative lighting is compelling, it can be a device to indirectly attract or distract. You can use it to draw the eye upward toward a cathedral ceiling, for example. By capturing your eye, decorative lighting forces your focus away from anything else. It doesn't highlight anything, as accent lighting does. And it doesn't provide a great deal of illumination, as ambient lighting does. It is the device that most lighting designers love to use, the final stroke in a complex multilayered plan.

Some types of decorative lighting include candles, chandeliers, neon sculptures or signs, a strip of miniature lights—any

type of light that is deliberate and contrived. Include it to unify a room—to strike a balance among the various types of lighting, including natural light from the sun and moon.

Contrast and Diffusion

Task lighting and accent lighting are examples of high-contrast lighting—they eliminate shadows and bring an object into sharp, crisp focus. Ambient lighting and decorative lighting are more diffused. They are softer, more forgiving lights that are comfortable and relaxing. Most rooms benefit from a combination of contrast lighting and diffused light, so incorporate both in your plan.

Selecting Light Levels

Design professionals have established a set of ideal lighting levels for performing the various activities and tasks that take place in any house. Your own personal preferences should lie within the

Clockwise (from above): Backlighting draws the eye to the decorative objects on the shelves. Recessed ceiling fixtures wash the wall with light. The fixture over the pool table provides adequate task lighting for players. This hall contains both ambient light and accent lighting over the statue.

Using a reading light in an otherwise dark room strains your eyes by forcing them to adjust frequently from light to darkness. The greatest range of light in any room should be a four-to-one ratio at most.

Direct Glare. Bare-bulb glare is obvious. You can avoid it by selecting the proper size shade, adjusting the angle of a fixture, or using a low-wattage bulb or one with frosting.

Lighting professionals caution against "glare bombs," fixtures that produce unavoidable, uncomfortable light. A common offender is the bathroom globe or strip light over the vanity; another is the exposed bulb in some ceiling fixtures; a third is an inferior fluorescent fixture that blasts you with bright direct light. In the first case, you might try replacing the bulbs with heavily frosted versions. If you plan to include track lights in your scheme, install baffles over the bulbs. They are

minimum and maximum levels they have established. Some people favor more light; others prefer less. Good lighting begins with taking the recommended levels of light into account and tempering them with your preferences and those of people with whom you live. In common spaces, such as the family room, living room, and kitchen, it is better to err on the side of brightness. Adapt lighting in private areas, such as a study, bedroom, or workshop, to individual needs. Consult the Smart Tip "Recommended Ranges of Light Levels," opposite, as a starting point in establishing your own levels. Once you've determined the level of light you require for each task or activity, relate this light to the surroundings. You can avoid eyestrain by including plenty of ambient light, thereby reducing its contrast to task lighting. Task lighting, the general lighting immediately nearby, and the lowest lighting in the area (as in a room's corners) should not contrast sharply. The light you use to read by, for example, should only be two to three times as bright as the surrounding light in the room.

Recommended Ranges of Light Levels

You can avoid eyestrain by having plenty of ambient light, thereby reducing the contrast to task lighting. Start by determining the level of light needed for the activity or task, and then relate it to the surroundings. (See "Determining Your Lighting Needs," on page 63 of this chapter.) Task lighting, lighting immediately nearby, and then the lowest lighting in the area (as in a room's cor-

ners) should range from no more than a ratio of four to one, preferably three to one near task lighting. You can compare watts and foot-candles cast by various light sources to determine the ratios or approximate them with your naked eye. The following table provides the recommended ranges of light levels for seeing activities in the home. The more intense the activity, the greater the light level should be.

Activity	Easy or Short Duration	Critical or Prolonged
Dining	low	low
Entertaining	low to high	low to high
Grooming	moderate	high
Craftwork *	moderate	high
Kitchen/laundry chores	low to moderate	high
Reading	low to moderate	high
Studying	moderate	high
TV viewing	low to moderate	low to moderate
Computer work	moderate	high
Workbench *	moderate	high
Tabletop games	low to moderate	moderate to high
Writing	low to moderate	high

* Benefits from supplementary directional light.

devices that are designed to reduce spill light and glare. When you visit a lighting showroom, ask specifically to see bulbs and fixtures designed to reduce glare.

When you create a layout for your furniture arrangement, it's always wise to assess it for glare. For instance, if you situate the new family room sofa to face a game table, every time you flick on the suspended pendant light over the tabletop, you're creating glare for anyone seated on the sofa. Always check the field of vision from each seated, as well as each standing, position.

Indirect Glare. Any flat reflective surface can be the source of indirect glare. That includes shiny desktops, countertops, tables, mirrors and any other glass or metal surfaces, and TV and computer screens.

To determine reflected glare, simply place a mirror in front of or on top of any surface you suspect will reflect glare. The mirror will isolate reflected light glare. Place a temporary light where you plan to install a permanent source, and then do the glare check before making your final installation.

Plan #321031

Dimensions: 79'4" W x 59'6' D
Levels: 1
Square Footage: 3,200
Bedrooms: 3
Bathrooms: 2½
Foundation: Daylight basement
Materials List Available: Yes
Price Category: G

The stone exterior and the multiple roof peaks give this home an elegant look.

Features:

- **Great Room:** This large gathering area features a vaulted ceiling and a beautiful fireplace. The area is open to the dining room, allowing convenient flow between the two spaces.

- **Kitchen:** This grand-scale kitchen features bay-shaped cabinetry built over an atrium that overlooks the two-story window wall. The walk-in pantry will hold all items needed for the family.

- **Master Suite:** A second atrium dominates this master suite, which boasts a sitting area with bay window as well as a luxurious master bath, which has a whirlpool tub open to the garden atrium and lower-level study.

- **Secondary Bedrooms:** Two large bedrooms with walk-in closets share the second full bathroom. Each room has access to its own covered porch.

Images provided by designer/architect.

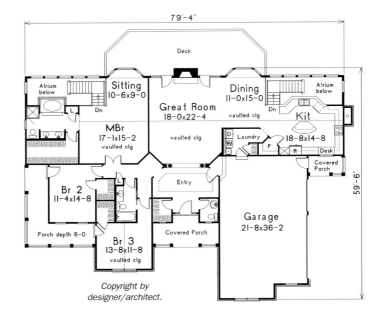

Copyright by designer/architect.

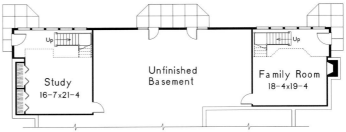

Optional Basement Level Floor Plan

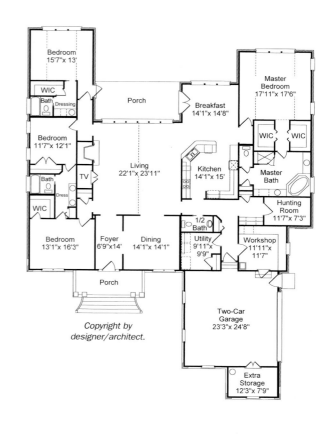

Images provided by designer/architect.

Copyright by designer/architect.

Plan #111007

Dimensions: 72' W x 91' D

Levels: 1

Square Footage: 3,668

Bedrooms: 4

Bathrooms: 3½

Foundation: Crawl space

Materials List Available: No

Price Category: H

Images provided by designer/architect.

Copyright by designer/architect.

Plan #321034

Dimensions: 75'8" W x 52'6" D

Levels: 1

Square Footage: 3,508

Bedrooms: 4

Bathrooms: 3

Foundation: Basement, walkout

Material List Available: Yes

Price Category: H

Optional Basement Level Floor Plan

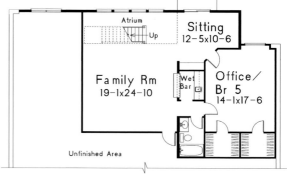

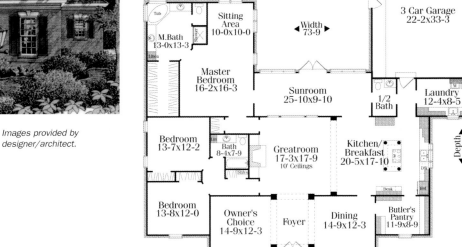

Plan #311040

Dimensions: 73'9" W x 79'3" D
Levels: 1
Square Footage: 3,084
Bedrooms: 3
Bathrooms: 2½
Foundation: Crawl space or slab
Material List Available: No
Price Category: G

Images provided by designer/architect.

Copyright by designer/architect.

Plan #271354

Dimensions: 64'4" W x 55'4" D
Levels: 1
Square Footage: 3,148
Main Level Sq. Ft.: 1,922
Lower Level Sq. Ft.: 1,226
Bedrooms: 2
Bathrooms: 2
Foundation: Walkout basement
Material List Available: No
Price Category: G

Images provided by designer/architect.

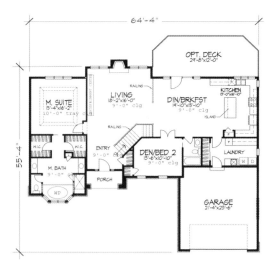

Basement Level Floor Plan

Copyright by designer/architect.

Plan #481024

Dimensions: 87'2" W x 59'8" D
Levels: 1
Square Footage: 3,458
Main Level Sq. Ft.: 2,016
Lower Level Sq. Ft.: 1,442
Bedrooms: 4
Bathrooms: 3
Foundation: Walkout basement
Material List Available: No
Price Category: G

Images provided by designer/architect.

Basement Level Floor Plan

Copyright by designer/architect.

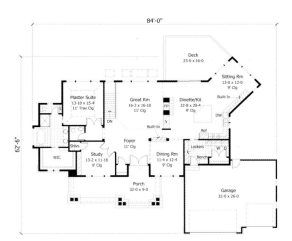

Plan #481025

Dimensions: 82' W x 62'6" D
Levels: 1
Square Footage: 3,772
Main Level Sq. Ft.: 2,227
Lower Level Sq. Ft.: 1,545
Bedrooms: 3
Bathrooms: 2½
Foundation: Walkout basement
Material List Available: No
Price Category: H

Images provided by designer/architect.

Basement Level Floor Plan

Copyright by designer/architect.

Plan #161056

Dimensions: 86'2" W x 63'8" D
Levels: 1
Square Footage: 5,068
Main Level Sq. Ft.: 3,171
Basement Level Sq. Ft.: 1,897
Bedrooms: 4
Bathrooms: 3½
Foundation: Basement or walkout
Material List Available: Yes
Price Category: J

This home is dedicated to comfort and high lifestyle and sets the standard for excellence.

Features:

- **Open Plan:** A wraparound island with seating is adorned with pillars and arched openings, and it separates the kitchen from the great room and breakfast room. This design element allows the rooms to remain visually open and, paired with a 9-ft. ceiling height, creates a spacious area.

- **Great Room:** A gas fireplace warms this gathering area, and the wall of windows across the rear brings the outdoors in. The built-in entertainment center will be a hit with the entire family.

- **Master Suite:** Delighting you with its size and luxury, this retreat enjoys a stepped ceiling in the sleeping area. The master bath features a garden bathtub and an oversized walk-in closet.

- **Lower Level:** Open stairs introduce this lower level, which mimics the size of the first floor, and, with a 9-ft. ceiling height, offers the same elegant feel of the first floor. Additional bedrooms, a game room, an exercise area, and storage are available options.

Images provided by designer/architect.

Rear Elevation

Great Room

Rear View

Dining Room

Outdoor Grill Area

Kitchen

Living Room

Copyright by designer/architect.

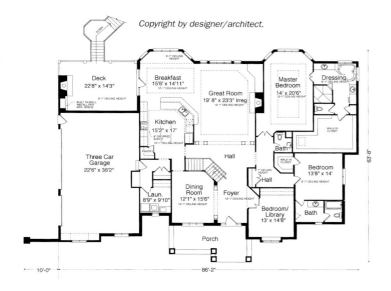

Optional Basement Level Floor Plan

Master Bath

Master Bedroom

Plan #341172

Dimensions: 83'4" W x 54'8" D
Levels: 1
Square Footage: 3,150
Bedrooms: 4
Bathrooms: 3½
Foundation: Crawl space, slab, basement, or walkout
Material List Available: No
Price Category: G

The beautifully proportioned front gables, graceful arched windows, and other design elements combine to make this a stunning home.

Features:

- **Entry:** This covered front entry with a transom window welcomes you into a dramatic main living area, with its spacious open layout. Columns and a bookcase visually divide the main living areas.

- **Family Room:** This gathering area features a fireplace flanked by French doors to the backyard deck. A pass-through counter and open floor plan join the family room to the kitchen/breakfast area, which brings plenty of light indoors from three windows.

- **Master Suite:** This secluded retreat includes a dressing area and a large sleeping area. The private master bath features a shower, whirlpool tub, and two walk-in closets.

- **Secondary Bedrooms:** The second bedroom also has its own private bathroom and dressing area, and bedrooms 3 and 4 share another full bathroom.

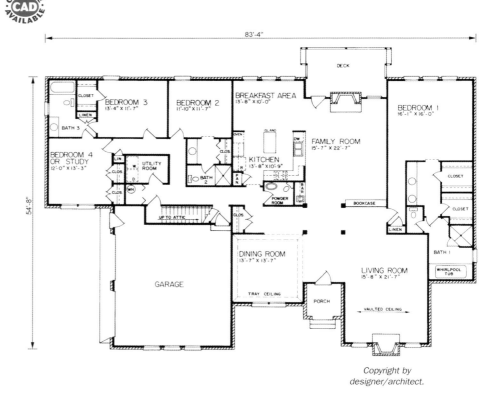

Plan #221085

Dimensions: 113'4" W x 88' D
Levels: 1
Square Footage: 4,190
Bedrooms: 3
Bathrooms: 3 full, 2 half
Foundation: Basement
Material List Available: No
Price Category: I

This sprawling ranch features a stone-and-stucco mix that's all its own.

Features:

- **Great Room:** You'll love the exposed beams and the 18-ft.-high ceilings in this gathering area. The area features a built-in area for the television and a magnificent fireplace.

- **Kitchen:** This unique kitchen features an eat-in island that flows into the nook and hearth room. All three of these areas boast vaulted ceilings.

- **Master Suite:** The cathedral ceiling and double doors to the patio make this sleeping area dramatic. You'll love the large master bath, with its spacious walk-in closet with island and Jacuzzi tub.

- **Bedrooms:** On the opposite side of the home you'll find two additional bedrooms, each with its own walk-in closet and private bathroom.

Images provided by designer/architect.

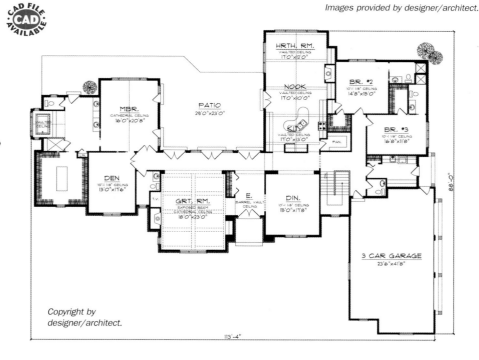

Copyright by designer/architect.

Rear Elevation

Plan #161102

Dimensions: 99'6" W x 84'2" D
Levels: 1
Square Footage: 6,659
Main Level Sq. Ft.: 3,990
Lower Level Sq. Ft: 2,669
Bedrooms: 4
Bathrooms: 4 full, 2 half
Foundation: Walkout; basement for fee
Material List Available: Yes
Price Category: K

A brick-and-stone exterior with lime-stone trim and arches decorates the exterior, while the interior explodes with design elements and large spaces to dazzle all who enter.

Features:

- Great Room: The 14-ft. ceiling height in this room is defined with columns and a fireplace wall. Triple French doors with an arched transom create the rear wall, and built-in shelving adds the perfect spot to house your big-screen TV.

- Kitchen: This spacious gourmet kitchen opens generously to the great room and allows everyone to enjoy the daily activities. A two-level island with cooktop provides casual seating and additional storage.

- Breakfast Room: This room is surrounded by windows, creating a bright and cheery place to start your day. Sliding glass doors to the covered porch in the rear add a rich look for outdoor entertaining, and the built-in fireplace provides a cozy, warm atmosphere.

- Master Suite: This master bedroom suite is fit for royalty, with its stepped ceiling treatment, spacious dressing room, and private exercise room.

- Lower Level: This lower level is dedicated to fun and entertaining. A large media area, billiards room, and wet bar are central to sharing this spectacular home with your friends.

Foyer/Dining Room

Rear Elevation

Basement Level Floor Plan

Plan #171013

Dimensions: 74' W x 72' D
Levels: 1
Square Footage: 3,084
Bedrooms: 4
Bathrooms: 3½
Foundation: Crawl space or slab
Materials List Available: Yes
Price Category: G

Impressive porch columns add to the country charm of this amenity-filled family home.

Features:

- Ceiling Height: 10 ft.

- Foyer: The sense of style continues from the front porch into this foyer, which opens to the formal dining room and the living room.

- Dining Room: Two handsome support columns accentuate the elegance of this dining room.

- Living Room: This living room features a cozy corner fireplace and plenty of room for the entire family to gather and relax.

- Kitchen: You'll be inspired to new culinary heights in this kitchen, which offers plenty of counter space, a snack bar, a built-in pantry, and a china closet.

- Master Suite: The bedroom of this master suite has a fireplace and overlooks a rear courtyard. The bath has two vanities a large walk-in closet, a deluxe tub, a walk-in shower, and a skylight.

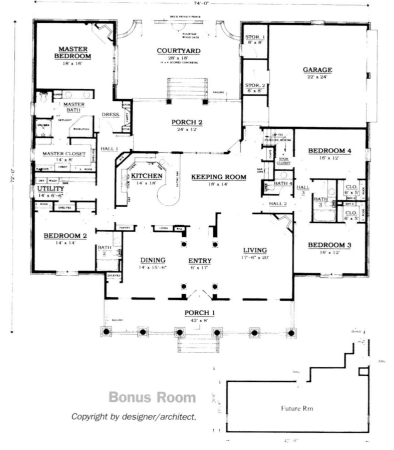

Bonus Room

Copyright by designer/architect.

Plan #161093

Dimensions: 56' W x 53' D
Levels: 1
Square Footage: 4,328
Main Level Sq. Ft.: 2,582
Basement Sq. Ft.: 1,746
Bedrooms: 3
Bathrooms: 3½
Foundation: Walkout
Materials List Available: No
Price Category: I

Detailed stucco and stone accents impart warmth and character to the exterior of this one level home.

Images provided by designer/architect.

Features:

- **Great Room:** This gathering room, which features a fireplace and a decorative ceiling, offers an extensive view of the rear yard.

- **Kitchen:** Spacious and up-to-date, this extra-large combination gourmet kitchen and breakfast room is an ideal area for doing chores and hosting family gatherings.

- **Main Level:** The extravagant master suite, with its private bathroom and dressing area, the library with built-in shelves, and the formal dining room round out the

main floor. Accented by a wood rail, the extra-wide main stairway leads to the lavish lower level.

- **Lower Level:** The two additional bedrooms, adjoining bathroom, media room, billiard room, and exercise room comprise this fantastic finished lower level.

Great Room

Basement Level Floor Plan

Main Level Floor Plan

Copyright by designer/architect.

Dining Room

Master Bedroom

Great Room

Foyer

Plan #151055

Dimensions: 82'4" W x 81'6" D
Levels: 1
Square Footage: 3,183
Bedrooms: 4
Bathrooms: 2½
Foundation: Crawl space or slab; basement or walkout available for fee
CompleteCost List Available: Yes
Price Category: E

CAD FILE AVAILABLE

This stunning large ranch home has a well-designed floor plan that is perfect for today's family.

Features:

• Living Room: This large gathering area features a beautiful fireplace and a vaulted ceiling. On nice days, exit through the atrium doors and relax on the grilling porch.

• Kitchen: The raised bar in this island kitchen provides additional seating for informal meals. The family will enjoy lazy weekend mornings in the adjoining breakfast room and intimate hearth room.

• Master Suite: This retreat, with its built-in media center and romantic fireplace in the sleeping area, features a boxed ceiling. The master bath boasts a whirlpool tub, his and her vanities and lavatories, and a glass shower.

• Bedrooms: These three family bedrooms are located on the opposite side of the home from the master suite for privacy and share a common bathroom.

Front View

Plan #151001

Dimensions: 70' W x 88' D
Levels: 1
Square Footage: 3,124
Bedrooms: 4
Bathrooms: 3½
Foundation: Crawl space, slab
CompleteCost List Available: Yes
Price Category: G

From the double front doors to sleek arches, columns, and a gallery with arched openings to the bedrooms, you'll love this elegant home.

Features:

- **Grand Room:** With a 13-ft. pan ceiling and column entry, this room opens to the rear covered porch as well as through French doors to the bay-windowed morning room that, in turn, leads to the gathering room.

- **Gathering Room:** A majestic fireplace, built-in entertainment center, and book shelves give comfort and ease.

- **Kitchen:** A double oven, built-in desk, and a work island add up to a design for efficiency.

- **Master Suite:** Enjoy the practicality of walk-in closets, the comfort of a private sitting area, and the convenience of an adjacent study or nursery. The bath features a step-up whirlpool tub and separate shower.

Images provided by designer/architect.

Copyright by designer/architect.

Plan #161028

Dimensions: 84'6" W x 69'4" D
Levels: 1
Square Footage: 3,570
**Optional Finished Basement
Sq. Ft.:** 2,367
Bedrooms: 3
Bathrooms: 3½
Foundation: Basement
Materials List Available: Yes
Price Category: H

From the gabled stone-and-brick exterior to the wide-open view from the foyer, this home will meet your greatest expectations.

Images provided by designer/architect.

Features:

- **Great Room/Dining Room:** Columns and 13-ft. ceilings add exquisite detailing to the dining room and great room.
- **Kitchen:** The gourmet-equipped kitchen with an island and a snack bar merges with the cozy breakfast and hearth rooms.
- **Master Bedroom:** The luxurious master bed room pampers with a separate sitting room with a fireplace and a dressing room boasting a whirlpool tub and two vanities.

- **Additional:** Two bedrooms upstairs include a private bath and walk-in closet. The optional finished basement solves all your recreational needs: bar, media room, billiards room, exercise room, game room, as well as an office and fourth bedroom.

Rear Elevation

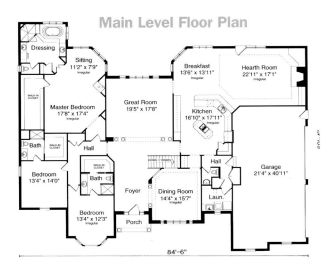

Copyright by designer/architect.

Let Us Help You
Plan Your
Dream Home

Whether you've always dreamed of building your own home or you can't find the right house from among the dozens you've toured, our collection of two-story plans can help you achieve the home of your dreams. You could have an architect create a one-of-a-kind home for you, but the design services alone could end up costing up to 15 percent of the cost of construction—a hefty premium for any building project. Isn't it a better idea to select from among the hundreds of unique designs shown in our collection for a fraction of the cost?

What does Creative Homeowner Offer?

In this book, Creative Homeowner provides hundreds of home plans from the country's best architects and designers. Our designs are among the most popular available. Whether your taste runs from traditional to contemporary, Victorian to early American, you are sure to find the best house design for you and your family. Our plans packages include detailed drawings to help you or your builder construct your dream house. **(See page 374.)**

Can I Make Changes to the Plans?

Creative Homeowner offers three ways to help you achieve a truly unique home design. Our customizing service allows for extensive changes to our designs. **(See page 375.)** We also provide reverse images of our plans, or we can give you and your builder the tools for making minor changes on your own. **(See page 378.)**

Can You Help Me Stay on Budget?

Building a house is a large financial investment. To help you stay within your budget, Creative Homeowner can provide you with general construction costs based on your zip code. **(See page 378.)** Also, many of our plans come with the option of buying detailed materials lists to help you price out construction costs.

How Can I Get Started with the Building Process?

We've teamed up with the leading estimating company to provide one of the most accurate, complete, and reliable building material take-offs in the industry. **(See page 376.)** If you plan on doing all or part of the work yourself, or want to keep tabs on your builder, we offer best-selling building and design books at attractive prices. See our Web site at www.creativehomeowner.com.

Our Plans Packages Offer:

All of our home plans are the result of many hours of work by leading architects and professional designers. Most of our home plans include each of the following.

Frontal Sheet
This artist's rendering of the front of the house gives you an idea of how the house will look once it is completed and the property landscaped.

Detailed Floor Plans
These plans show the size and layout of the rooms. They also provide the locations of doors, windows, fireplaces, closets, stairs, and electrical outlets and switches.

Foundation Plan
A foundation plan gives the dimensions of basements, walk-out basements, crawl spaces, pier foundations, and slab construction. Each house design lists the type of foundation included. If the plan you choose does not have the foundation type you require, our customer service department can help you customize the plan to meet your needs.

Roof Plan
In addition to providing the pitch of the roof, these plans also show the locations of dormers, skylights, and other elements.

Exterior Elevations
These drawings show the front, rear, and sides of the house as if you were looking at it head on. Elevations also provide information about architectural features and finish materials.

Interior Elevations and Details
Interior elevations show specific details of such elements as fireplaces, kitchen and bathroom cabinets, built-ins, and other unique features of the design.

Cross Sections
These show the structure as if it were sliced to reveal construction requirements, such as insulation, flooring, and roofing details.

Frontal Sheet

Floor Plan

Foundation Plan

Roof Plan

Cross Sections

Stair Details

Elevation

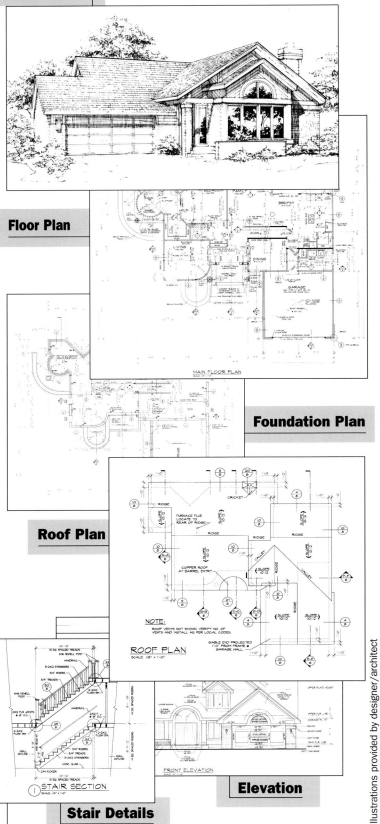

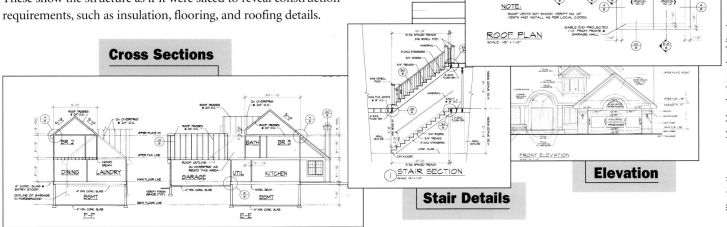

Illustrations provided by designer/architect

Customize Your Plans in 4 Easy Steps

1 **Select the home plan** that most closely meets your needs. Purchase of a reproducible master is necessary in order to make changes to a plan.

2 **Call 1-800-523-6789 to place your order.** Tell our sales representative you are interested in customizing your plan. To receive your customization cost estimate, we will send you a checklist (via fax or email) for you to complete indicating the changes you would like to make to your plan. There is a $50 nonrefundable consultation fee for this service. If you decide to continue with the custom changes, the $50 fee is credited to the total amount charged.

3 **Fax the completed checklist** to 1-201-760-2431 or email it to us at customize@creativehomeowner.com. Within three business days of receipt of your checklist, a detailed cost estimate will be provided to you.

4 **Once you approve the estimate,** a 75% retainer fee is collected and customization work begins. Preliminary drawings typically take 10 to 15 business days. After approval, we will collect the balance of your customization order cost before shipping the completed plans. You will receive five sets of blueprints or a reproducible master, plus a customized materials list if desired.

Modification Pricing Guide

Categories	Average Cost For Modification
Add or remove living space	Quote required
Bathroom layout redesign	Starting at $120
Kitchen layout redesign	Starting at $120
Garage: add or remove	Starting at $400
Garage: front entry to side load or vice versa	Starting at $300
Foundation changes	Starting at $220
Exterior building materials change	Starting at $200
Exterior openings: add, move, or remove	$65 per opening
Roof line changes	Starting at $360
Ceiling height adjustments	Starting at $280
Fireplace: add or remove	Starting at $90
Screened porch: add	Starting at $280
Wall framing change from 2x4 to 2x6	Starting at $200
Bearing and/or exterior walls changes	Quote required
Non-bearing wall or room changes	$65 per room
Metric conversion of home plan	Starting at $400
Adjust plan for handicapped accessibility	Quote required
Adapt plans for local building code requirements	Quote required
Engineering stamping only	Quote required
Any other engineering services	Quote required
Interactive illustrations (choices of exterior materials)	Quote required

Note: *Any home plan can be customized to accommodate your desired changes. The average prices above are provided only as examples of the most commonly requested changes, and are subject to change without notice. Prices for changes will vary according to the number of modifications requested, plan size, style, and method of design used by the original designer. To obtain a detailed cost estimate, please contact us.*

Terms & Copyright

These home plans are protected under the terms of United States Copyright Law and may not be copied or reproduced in any way, by any means, unless you have purchased reproducible masters, which clearly indicate your right to copy or reproduce. We authorize the use of your chosen home plan as an aid in the construction of one single-family home only. You may not use this home plan to build a second or multiple dwellings without purchasing another blueprint or blueprints, or paying additional home plan fees.

Architectural Seals

Because of differences in building codes, some cities and states now require an architect or engineer licensed in that state to review and "seal" a blueprint, or officially approve it, prior to construction. Delaware, Nevada, New Jersey, and New York require that all plans for houses built in those states be redrawn by an architect licensed in the state in which the home will be built. We strongly advise you to consult with your local building official for information regarding architectural seals.

Before Customization

After

Turn your dream home into reality with

an UltimateEstimate

When purchasing a home plan with Creative Homeowner, we recommend you order one of the most complete materials lists in the industry.

1 What comes with an Ultimate Estimate?

Quote

- Basis of the entire estimate.

- Detailed list of all the framing materials needed to build your project, listed from the bottom up, in the order that each one will actually be used.

Comments

- Details pertinent information beyond the cost of materials.

- Includes any notes from our estimator.

Express List

- A version of the Quote with space for SKU numbers listed for purchasing the items at your local lumberyard.

- Your local lumberyard can then price out the materials list.

Construction-Ready Framing Diagrams

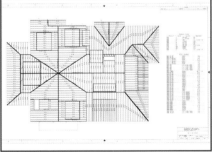

- Your "map" to exact roof and floor framing.

Millwork Report

- A complete count of the windows, doors, molding, and trim.

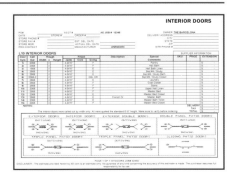

Man-Hour Report

- Calculates labor on a line-by-line basis for all items quoted and presented in man-hours.

HOMEOWNER®

2 Why an Ultimate Estimate?

Accurate. Professional estimators break down each individual item from the blueprints using advanced software, techniques, and equipment.

Timely. You will be able to start your home-building project quickly—knowing the exact framing materials you need to order from your local lumberyard.

Detailed. Work with your local lumberyard associate to complete your quote with the remaining products needed for your new home.

3 So how much does it cost?

Pricing is determined by the total square feet of the home plan—including living area, garages, decks, porches, finished basements, and finished attics.

Square Feet Range	UE Tier*	Price
Up to 2,000 total square feet	XA	$249.00
2,001 to 5,000 total square feet	XB	$339.00
5,001 to 10,000 total square feet	XC	$499.00

* Please see the Plan Index to determine your plan's Material Take-off Tier (MT Tier).

Call our toll-free number (800-523-6789), or visit ultimateplans.com to order your Material Take-off.

4 What else do I need to know?

Call our toll-free number (800-523-6789), or visit **ultimateplans.com** to order your Ultimate Estimate.

Turn your dream home into reality.

www.ultimateplans.com   377

Decide What Type of Plan Package You Need

How many Plans Should You Order?

Standard 8-Set Package. We've found that our 8-set package is the best value for someone who is ready to start building. Once the process begins, a number of people will require their own set of blueprints. The 8-set package provides plans for you, your builder, the subcontractors, mortgage lender, and the building department.

Minimum 5-Set Package. If you are in the bidding process, you may want to order only five sets for the bidding round and reorder additional sets as needed.

1-Set Study Package. The 1-set package allows you to review your home plan in detail. The plan will be marked as a study print, and it is illegal to build a house from a study print alone. It is a violation of copyright law to reproduce a blueprint without permission.

Buying Additional Sets

If you require additional copies of blueprints for your home construction, you can order additional sets within 60 days of the original order date at a reduced price. The cost is $45.00 for each additional set. For more information, contact customer service.

Reproducible Masters

If you plan to make minor changes to one of our home plans, you can purchase reproducible masters. Printed on vellum paper, an erasable paper that you can reproduce in a copying machine, reproducible masters allow an architect, designer, or builder to alter our plans to give you a customized home design. This package also allows you to print as many copies of the modified plans as you need for construction.

CAD Files

CAD files are the complete set of home plans in an electronic file format. Choose this option if there are multiple changes you wish made to the home plans and you have a local design professional able to make the changes. Not available for all plans. Please contact our order department or visit our website to check the availability of CAD files for your plan.

Mirror-Reverse Sets/Right-Reading Reverse

Plans can be printed in mirror-reverse—we can "flip" plans to create a mirror image of the design. This is useful when the house would fit your site or personal preferences if all the rooms were on the opposite side than shown. As the image is reversed, the lettering and dimensions will also be reversed, meaning they will read backwards. Therefore, when ordering mirror-reverse drawings, you must order at least one set of right-reading plans. A $50.00 fee per plan order will be charged for mirror-reverse (regardless of the number of mirror-reverse sets ordered). Some plans are available in right-reading reverse, this feature will show the plan in reverse, but the writing on the plan will be readable. A $150.00 fee per plan order will be charged for right-reading reverse (regardless of the number of right-reading reverse sets ordered). Please contact our order department or visit our website to check the availibility of this feature for your chosen plan.

EZ Quote: Home Cost Estimator

EZ Quote is our response to one of the most frequently asked questions we hear from customers: "How much will the house cost me to build?" EZ Quote: Home Cost Estimator will enable you to obtain a calculated building cost to construct your home, based on labor rates and building material costs within your zip code area. This summary is useful for those who want to get an idea of the total construction costs before purchasing sets of home plans. It will also provide a level of comfort when you begin soliciting bids. The cost is $29.95 for the first EZ Quote and $14.95 for each additional one. Available only in the U.S. and Canada.

Materials List

Available for most of our plans, the Materials List provides you an invaluable resource in planning and estimating the cost of your home. Each Materials List outlines the quantity, dimensions, and type of materials needed to build your home (with the exception of mechanical systems). You will get faster, more-accurate bids from your contractors and building suppliers. A Materials List may only be ordered with the purchase of at least five sets of home plans.

CompleteCost Estimator

CompleteCost Estimator is a valuable tool for use in planning and constructing your new home. It provides more detail than a materials list and will act as a checklist for all items you will need to select or coordinate during your building process. CompleteCost Estimator is only available for certain plans (please see Plan Index) and may only be ordered with the purchase of at least five sets of home plans. The cost is $125.00 for CompleteCost Estimator.

Order Toll Free by Phone
1-800-523-6789
By Fax: 201-760-2431

Regular office hours are
8:30AM–7:30PM ET, Mon–Fri
Orders received 3PM ET, will be processed and
shipped within two business days.

Order Online
www.ultimateplans.com

Mail Your Order
Creative Homeowner
Attn: Home Plans
24 Park Way
Upper Saddle River, NJ 07458

Canadian Customers
Order Toll Free 1-800-393-1883

Mail Your Order (Canada)
Creative Homeowner Canada
Attn: Home Plans
113-437 Martin St., Ste. 215
Penticton, BC V2A 5L1

Before You Order

Our Exchange Policy

Blueprints are nonrefundable. However, should you find that the plan you have purchased does not fit your needs, you may exchange that plan for another plan in our collection within 60 days from the date of your original order. The entire content of your original order must be returned before an exchange will be processed. You will be charged a processing fee of 20% of the amount of the original order, the cost difference between the new plan set and the original plan set (if applicable), and all related shipping costs for the new plans. Contact our order department for more information. Please note: reproducible masters may only be exchanged if the package is unopened and CAD files cannot be exchanged and are nonrefundable.

Building Codes and Requirements

At the time of creation, our plans meet the bulding code requirements published by the Building Officials and Code Administrators International, the Southern Building Code Congress International, the International Conference of Building Officials, or the Council of American Building Officials. Because building codes vary from area to area, some drawing modifications and/or the assistance of a professional designer or architect may be necessary to comply with your local codes or to accommodate specific building site conditions. We strongly advise you to consult with your local building official for information regarding codes governing your area.

Blueprint Price Schedule

Price Code	1 Set	5 Sets	8 Sets	Reproducible Masters	CAD	Materials List
A	$300	$345	$395	$530	$950	$85
B	$375	$435	$480	$600	$1,100	$85
C	$435	$500	$550	$650	$1,200	$85
D	$490	$560	$610	$710	$1,300	$95
E	$550	$620	$660	$770	$1,400	$95
F	$610	$680	$720	$830	$1,500	$95
G	$670	$740	$780	$890	$1,600	$95
H	$760	$830	$870	$980	$1,700	$95
I	$860	$930	$970	$1,080	$1,800	$105
J	$960	$1,030	$1,070	$1,190	$1,900	$105
K	$1,070	$1,150	$1,190	$1,320	$2,030	$105
L	$1,180	$1,270	$1,310	$1,460	$2,170	$105

Note: All prices subject to change

Ultimate Estimate Tier (UE Tier)

MT Tier*	Price
XA	$249
XB	$339
XC	$499

* Please see the Plan Index to determine your plan's Ultimate Estimate Tier (UE Tier).

Shipping & Handling

	1-4 Sets	5-7 Sets	8+ Sets or Reproducibles	CAD
US Regular (7–10 business days)	$18	$20	$25	$25
US Priority (3–5 business days)	$25	$30	$35	$35
US Express (1–2 business days)	$40	$45	$50	$50
Canada Express (1–2 business days)	$60	$70	$80	$80
Worldwide Express (3–5 business days)	$80	$80	$80	$80

Note: All delivery times are from date the blueprint package is shipped (typically within 1-2 days of placing order).

Order Form Please send me the following:

Plan Number: _____ **Price Code:** _____ (See Plan Index.)

Indicate Foundation Type: (Select ONE. See plan page for availability.)

❑ Slab ❑ Crawl space ❑ Basement ❑ Walk-out basement

❑ Optional Foundation for Fee _____ $_____
(Please enter foundation here)

Please call all our order department or visit our website for optional foundation fee

Basic Blueprint Package | Cost

❑ Reproducible Masters $_____
❑ 8-Set Plan Package $_____
❑ 5-Set Plan Package $_____
❑ 1-Set Study Package $_____
❑ Additional plan sets:
___ sets at $45.00 per set $_____
❑ Print in mirror-reverse: $50.00 per order $_____
  Please call all our order department or visit our website for availibility
❑ Print in right-reading reverse: $150.00 per order $_____
  Please call all our order department or visit our website for availibility

Important Extras

❑ Materials List $_____
❑ CompleteCost Materials Report at $125.00 $_____
  Zip Code of Home/Building Site _____
❑ EZ Quote for Plan #_____ at $29.95 $_____
❑ Additional EZ Quotes for Plan #s_____ $_____
  at $14.95 each
❑ Ultimate Estimate (See Price Tier above.) $_____
Shipping (see chart above) $_____
SUBTOTAL $_____
Sales Tax (NJ residents only, add 6%) $_____
TOTAL $_____

Order Toll Free: 1-800-523-6789 By Fax: 201-760-2431
Creative Homeowner
24 Park Way
Upper Saddle River, NJ 07458

Name _____
(Please print or type)

Street _____
(Please do not use a P.O. Box)

City _____ State _____

Country _____ Zip _____

Daytime telephone (_____)_____

Fax (_____)_____
(Required for reproducible orders)

E-Mail _____

Payment ❑ Check/money order *Make checks payable to Creative Homeowner*

❑ VISA ❑ MasterCard ❑ American Express Cards ❑ DISCOVER

Credit card number _____

Expiration date (mm/yy) _____

Signature _____

Please check the appropriate box:
❑ Licensed builder/contractor ❑ Homeowner ❑ Renter

SOURCE CODE CA351 www.ultimateplans.com

Copyright Notice

Index
For pricing, see page 379.

Plan #	Price Code	Page	Total Finished Area Square Feet	Materials List Available	Complete Cost	UE Tier
101004	C	82	1,787	Y	N	XA
101004	C	83	1,787	Y	N	XA
101005	D	178	1,992	Y	N	XA
101005	D	179	1,992	Y	N	XA
101006	D	192	1,982	Y	N	XA
101008	D	235	2,088	Y	N	XB
101009	D	273	2,097	Y	N	XB
101010	D	247	2,187	Y	N	XB
101011	D	277	2,184	Y	N	XB
101012	E	271	2,288	N	N	XB
101013	E	303	2,564	Y	N	XB
101022	D	196	1,992	Y	N	XA
101022	D	197	1,992	Y	N	XA
101035	E	339	2,461	Y	N	XB
101061	C	99	1,681	N	N	XA
101067	C	163	1,770	N	N	XA
111001	F	335	2,832	N	N	XB
111004	F	310	2,968	Y	N	XB
111004	F	311	2,968	Y	N	XB
111006	E	255	2,241	N	N	XB
111007	H	359	3,668	N	N	XB
111013	C	98	1,606	N	N	XA
111014	D	175	1,865	N	N	XA
111015	E	248	2,208	N	N	XB
111016	E	250	2,240	N	N	XB
111017	E	279	2,323	N	N	XB
111018	F	337	2,745	N	N	XB
111019	D	216	1,936	N	N	XA
111020	F	336	2,987	N	N	XB
111030	F	316	2,905	N	N	XB
111051	E	299	2,471	N	N	XB
121001	D	186	1,911	Y	N	XA
121002	B	45	1,347	Y	N	XA
121003	E	290	2,498	Y	N	XB
121004	C	151	1,666	Y	N	XA
121005	B	63	1,496	Y	N	XA
121006	C	86	1,762	Y	N	XA
121007	E	286	2,512	Y	N	XB
121008	C	140	1,651	Y	N	XA
121009	B	20	1,422	Y	N	XA
121010	D	180	1,902	Y	N	XA
121011	C	111	1,724	Y	N	XA
121012	B	23	1,195	Y	N	XA
121013	B	50	1,375	Y	N	XA
121034	E	253	2,223	Y	N	XB
121050	D	218	1,996	Y	N	XA
121051	D	169	1,808	Y	N	XA
121052	D	237	2,093	Y	N	XB
121053	E	284	2,456	Y	N	XB
121055	C	137	1,622	Y	N	XA
121056	B	71	1,479	Y	N	XA
121057	E	280	2,311	Y	N	XB
121058	C	94	1,554	Y	N	XA
121059	C	142	1,782	Y	N	XA
121092	D	204	1,887	Y	N	XA
121105	B	11	1,125	Y	N	XA
121106	D	238	2,133	Y	N	XB
121107	C	147	1,604	Y	N	XA
121109	C	110	1,735	Y	N	XA
121117	D	241	2,172	Y	N	XB
121118	C	103	1,636	Y	N	XA
121119	D	171	1,850	Y	N	XA
121121	C	85	1,793	Y	N	XA
121124	D	168	1,806	Y	N	XA
121125	D	216	1,978	Y	N	XA
121137	B	44	1,392	Y	N	XA
121144	B	54	1,195	Y	N	XA
121163	F	308	2,679	Y	N	XB
121165	C	115	1,678	Y	N	XA
121176	D	239	2,144	Y	N	XA
121208	E	339	2,598	Y	N	XB
121216	B	55	1,205	Y	N	XA
131001	D	113	1,615	Y	N	XA
131002	C	101	1,709	Y	N	XA
131003	C	10	1,466	Y	N	XA
131004	B	35	1,097	Y	N	XA
131005	C	104	1,595	Y	N	XA
131005	C	105	1,595	Y	N	XA
131006	E	248	2,193	Y	N	XB
131007	D	126	1,595	Y	N	XA
131007	D	127	1,595	Y	N	XA
131009	E	232	2,018	Y	N	XB
131011	E	199	1,897	Y	N	XA
131013	B	58	1,489	Y	N	XA
131014	C	8	1,380	Y	N	XA
131014	C	9	1,380	Y	N	XA
131015	D	183	1,860	Y	N	XA
131016	E	214	1,902	Y	N	XA
131019	F	250	2,243	Y	N	XB
131034	C	17	1,040	Y	N	XA
131035	D	227	1,892	Y	N	XA
131036	E	301	2,585	Y	N	XB
131045	E	269	2,347	Y	N	XB
131047	C	118	1,793	Y	N	XA
131054	F	340	2,753	Y	N	XB
131057	D	221	1,843	Y	N	XA
131059	E	267	2,315	Y	N	XB
131064	C	138	1,783	Y	N	XA
131068	C	95	1,554	Y	N	XA
131072	D	233	2,053	Y	N	XB
141004	C	130	1,514	Y	N	XA
141005	B	50	1,532	Y	N	XA
141006	C	164	1,787	N	N	XA
141007	D	215	1,854	N	N	XA
141011	D	214	1,869	Y	N	XA
141021	F	328	2,614	Y	N	XB
141022	F	316	2,911	N	N	XB
151001	G	371	3,124	Y	Y	XB
151002	E	296	2,444	Y	Y	XB
151003	C	135	1,680	Y	Y	XA
151004	D	241	2,107	Y	Y	XB
151005	D	200	1,940	N	Y	XA
151006	C	115	1,758	N	Y	XA
151007	C	123	1,787	Y	Y	XA
151008	D	184	1,892	N	Y	XA
151009	C	133	1,601	Y	Y	XA
151010	B	51	1,379	Y	Y	XA
151015	F	324	2,789	N	Y	XB
151034	D	242	2,133	Y	Y	XB
151037	C	92	1,538	Y	Y	XA
151040	E	315	2,444	N	Y	XB
151050	D	246	2,096	Y	Y	XB
151055	G	370	3,183	N	Y	XB
151057	F	322	2,951	Y	Y	XB
151063	E	295	2,554	N	Y	XB
151069	D	219	1,811	N	Y	XA
151089	D	201	1,921	Y	Y	XA
151104	D	228	1,860	N	Y	XA
151117	D	205	1,957	N	Y	XA
151168	E	276	2,261	N	Y	XB
151173	C	116	1,722	Y	Y	XA
151336	B	43	1,480	N	Y	XA
151383	E	293	2,534	N	Y	XB
151490	D	191	1,869	N	Y	XA
151528	C	107	1,747	N	Y	XA
151529	B	48	1,474	N	Y	XA
151536	D	182	1,933	N	Y	XA
151711	E	288	2,554	N	Y	XB
161001	C	121	1,782	Y	N	XA
161002	D	222	1,860	Y	N	XA
161002	D	223	1,860	Y	N	XA
161005	C	146	1,593	Y	N	XA
161007	C	144	1,611	Y	N	XA
161026	D	274	2,041	N	N	XB
161026	D	275	2,041	N	N	XB
161028	H	372	3,570	Y	N	XB
161037	E	312	2,469	Y	N	XB
161056	J	362	5,068	Y	N	XC
161056	J	363	5,068	Y	N	XC
161093	I	368	4,328	N	N	XB
161093	I	369	4,328	N	N	XB
161095	H	341	3,620	N	N	XB
161098	E	265	2,283	N	N	XB
161100	J	343	5,377	N	N	XC

Index

Index

Plan #	Price Code	Page	Total Finished Area Square Feet	Materials List Available	Complete Cost	UE Tier
341290	B	46	1,472	Y	N	XA
341292	B	65	1,266	Y	N	XA
341297	B	65	1,291	Y	N	XA
341299	B	66	1,115	Y	N	XA
341300	B	33	1,334	Y	N	XA
341302	B	66	1,317	Y	N	XA
341304	B	68	1,248	Y	N	XA
341307	B	68	1,358	Y	N	XA
351001	D	220	1,855	Y	N	XA
351002	D	89	1,751	Y	N	XA
351003	D	89	1,751	Y	N	XA
351007	D	244	2,251	Y	N	XB
351008	E	231	2,002	Y	N	XB
351013	B	52	800	Y	N	XA
351018	C	32	1,251	Y	N	XA
351067	F	263	2,200	Y	N	XB
351077	C	59	1,426	Y	N	XA
351078	D	91	1,508	Y	N	XA
351080	D	109	1,625	Y	N	XA
351083	D	189	1,896	Y	N	XA
351086	E	252	2,201	Y	N	XB
351088	F	304	2,500	Y	N	XB
351089	F	289	2,505	Y	N	XB
361376	F	333	2,692	N	N	XB
361465	C	124	1,688	N	N	XA
361469	E	278	2,261	N	N	XB
361470	E	276	2,313	N	N	XB
361483	E	300	2,507	N	N	XB
361490	B	33	1,356	N	N	XA
361493	E	279	2,350	N	N	XB
361497	C	88	1,774	N	N	XA
361498	F	335	2,778	N	N	XB
361505	D	234	2,066	N	N	XB
361512	D	173	1,802	N	N	XA
361513	E	262	2,260	N	N	XB
361516	B	72	1,237	N	N	XA
361517	B	69	1,321	N	N	XA
361537	E	306	2,551	N	N	XB
361538	D	229	2,011	N	N	XB
361545	E	278	2,270	N	N	XB
371073	C	139	1,783	N	N	XA
371075	D	217	1,904	N	N	XA
371087	F	332	2,643	N	N	XB
371093	B	38	1,300	N	N	XA
371095	F	323	2,725	N	N	XB
371104	C	120	1,795	N	N	XA
371107	D	176	1,825	N	N	XA
371108	D	181	1,829	N	N	XA
371109	D	218	1,839	N	N	XA
371110	D	202	1,844	N	N	XA
371111	D	175	1,901	N	N	XA
371122	F	327	2,774	N	N	XB
371124	C	132	1,746	N	N	XA
381010	E	249	2,225	Y	N	XB
381016	A	34	910	Y	N	XA
381045	B	49	1,015	Y	N	XA
381048	A	22	895	Y	N	XA
381061	C	135	1,575	Y	N	XA
391004	C	119	1,750	Y	N	XA
391006	B	53	1,456	Y	N	XA
391008	B	25	1,312	Y	N	XA
391019	C	164	1,792	Y	N	XA
391025	C	128	1,625	Y	N	XA
391028	C	87	1,771	Y	N	XA
391034	C	88	1,737	Y	N	XA
391038	C	150	1,642	Y	N	XA
391042	B	39	1,307	Y	N	XA
391049	I	346	4,064	Y	N	XB
391059	C	236	2,020	Y	N	XB
391060	B	15	1,359	Y	N	XA
391064	B	67	1,492	Y	N	XA
391069	B	42	1,492	Y	N	XA
401008	C	93	1,541	Y	N	XA
401020	B	14	1,230	Y	N	XA
401023	F	321	2,806	Y	N	XB
401024	B	24	1,298	Y	N	XA
401026	C	97	1,578	Y	N	XA
401041	B	12	1,108	Y	N	XA
401043	A	28	988	Y	N	XA
401045	C	137	1,652	Y	N	XA
401047	B	36	1,064	Y	N	XA
421001	B	29	1,433	Y	N	XA
421003	C	112	1,698	Y	N	XA
421004	C	113	1,698	Y	N	XA
421008	D	174	1,954	Y	N	XA
421009	F	307	2,649	Y	N	XB
421021	F	318	2,836	Y	N	XB
421022	F	340	2,836	Y	N	XB
441001	D	195	1,850	N	N	XA
441002	D	190	1,873	N	N	XA
441003	C	100	1,580	N	N	XA
441005	D	172	1,800	N	N	XA
441006	D	187	1,891	N	N	XA
441007	D	251	2,197	N	N	XB
441008	D	230	2,001	N	N	XB
441009	F	314	2,650	N	N	XB
441010	F	334	2,973	N	N	XB
441011	F	282	2,898	N	N	XB
441012	H	342	3,682	N	N	XB
451194	F	301	2,618	N	N	XB
451210	F	299	2,646	N	N	XB
451230	F	294	2,685	N	N	XB
451263	F	285	2,709	N	N	XB
461009	C	132	1,758	N	N	XA
461032	C	141	1,799	N	N	XA
461035	D	182	1,831	N	N	XA
461037	D	173	1,819	N	N	XA
461045	F	285	2,889	N	N	XB
461046	D	194	1,839	N	N	XA
461048	D	194	1,846	N	N	XA
461063	C	98	1,569	N	N	XA
461064	C	141	1,677	N	N	XA
461081	E	283	2,464	N	N	XB
461090	D	191	1,922	N	N	XA
461093	B	70	1,371	N	N	XA
461097	B	71	1,123	Y	N	XA
461113	B	73	1,474	N	N	XA
461132	D	180	1,958	N	N	XA
461147	C	124	1,693	N	N	XA
471002	A	22	835	N	N	XA
471003	A	26	920	Y	N	XA
471014	A	27	950	N	N	XA
471021	B	73	1,006	N	N	XA
481011	F	312	2,758	N	N	XB
481014	F	305	2,706	N	N	XB
481020	G	344	3,141	N	N	XB
481024	G	361	3,458	N	N	XB
481025	H	361	3,772	N	N	XB
481026	H	345	3,837	N	N	XB
481028	H	345	3,980	N	N	XB
481029	I	346	4,048	N	N	XB
481031	I	347	4,707	N	N	XB
481033	J	344	5,667	N	N	XC
511012	C	160	1,573	N	N	XA
511016	B	60	1,294	N	N	XA
511018	C	161	1,643	N	N	XA
511019	C	165	1,712	N	N	XA
511020	D	225	1,801	N	N	XA
511021	D	224	1,821	N	N	XA
511022	D	185	1,880	N	N	XA
521002	F	295	2,793	N	N	XB
521005	F	318	2,932	N	N	XB
521006	F	313	2,818	N	N	XB
521007	F	284	2,810	N	N	XB
521015	E	283	2,425	N	N	XB
521017	E	268	2,359	N	N	XB
521033	C	160	1,603	N	N	XA
521038	C	142	1,567	N	N	XA
521039	C	161	1,567	N	N	XA
521040	C	96	1,555	N	N	XA
521041	C	145	1,553	N	N	XA
521044	C	165	1,515	N	N	XA
521045	C	148	1,507	N	N	XA
521046	C	90	1,500	N	N	XA

Ultimate**Estimate**

The **fastest** way to get started **building** your **dream home**